H. Beam Piper

CRITICAL EXPLORATIONS IN SCIENCE FICTION AND FANTASY
(a series edited by Donald E. Palumbo and C.W. Sullivan III)

H. Beam Piper

A Biography

JOHN F. CARR

CRITICAL EXPLORATIONS IN
SCIENCE FICTION AND FANTASY, 8
Donald E. Palumbo *and* C.W. Sullivan III, *series editors*

McFarland & Company, Inc., Publishers
Jefferson, North Carolina, and London

John F. Carr has also edited collections of Piper stories—*Federation, Empire, Paratime, The Worlds of H. Beam Piper, and The Complete Paratime*—and has written the Piper-related novels *Great Kings' War* (with Roland Green), *Kalvan Kingmaker, Siege of Tarr-Hostigos,* and *The Fireseed Wars* (forthcoming).

LIBRARY OF CONGRESS CATALOGUING-IN-PUBLICATION DATA

Carr, John F.
H. Beam Piper : a biography / John F. Carr.
p.   cm. — (Critical explorations in science fiction and fantasy ; 8)
Includes bibliographical references and index.

ISBN 978-0-7864-3375-9
illustrated case binding : 50# alkaline paper ∞

1. Piper, H. Beam.   2. Authors, American — 20th century — Biography.
I. Palumbo, Donald, 1949–   II. Sullivan, Charles Wm. (Charles William), 1944–
III. Title.
PS3566.I58Z63   2008   813'.54 — dc22   2008009400

British Library cataloguing data are available

On the cover: Alan Gutierrez, *H. Beam Piper Portrait,*
gouache on masonite, 2007 (www.alangutierrez.com)

Manufactured in the United States of America

*McFarland & Company, Inc., Publishers
Box 611, Jefferson, North Carolina 28640
www.mcfarlandpub.com*

To Beam's Kids — Don Coleman,
Sally Schubert ("The Big Noise"),
Sylvia Coleman, John J. McGuire, Jr.,
Diane Coleman, Mike Knerr, Budd Coleman
and all the rest

Acknowledgments

I am indebted to Don Coleman, whose valiant efforts in collecting together "The Early Letters" have illuminated the heretofore unknown first half of H. Beam Piper's life, for his generosity in sharing them and his unique collection of H. Beam Piper photographs with the world.

I am beholden to Mike Knerr, whose valuable insight into H. Beam Piper's final years have allowed us to learn about the man behind the black cape, and to Daniel Knerr for being so gracious about sharing his father's legacy.

I am also indebted to Terry McGuire for all her help and information on the "lost years" of the early 1950s covering H. Beam Piper's collaboration with her father, John J. McGuire; to John J. McGuire, Jr., for sharing his memories of his father and the "Unholy Four"; and to Anne McGuire for answering all my many questions about H. Beam Piper in such loving detail in a wonderful recording.

I wish to acknowledge David Johnson (piperfan@zarathani.net) for all his help in assembling the H. Beam Piper bibliography, especially the foreign editions of H. Beam Piper's works. I'd also like to thank the following people for their reminiscences and contributions: Jerry E. Pournelle, Bill McMorris, William Flayhart III, Paul Schuchart, Frederick Pohl and Charles Brown.

I am most appreciative of the efforts of Perry A. Chapdelaine, Sr., and Randolph L. Chapdelaine, RLS, president of A.C. Projects, Inc., for allowing me permission to use the John W. Campbell–H. Beam Piper letters.

Thanks go to Sandra Stelts, curator of rare books and manuscripts at the Special Collections Library, The Pennsylvania State University Libraries, in State College for her help in obtaining a copy of the H. Beam Piper diary for 1955.

I am indebted to Peter Weston for sending me copies of Piper's History of the Future and the photographs from the 1957 London World Science Fiction Convention.

Thanks to Dwight Decker, Dennis Frank and Fred Ramsey for their encouragement and for proofing the final manuscript.

A big thanks to Piper researcher Tom Rogers for sharing his many H. Beam Piper finds (the *Pennsy* newsletter, among many others) with me over the years, as well as his encouragement in regards to writing and publishing this book.

A short excerpt from this book was first published in the January 1988 issue of *Analog Science Fiction and Fact Magazine* under the title "The Last Cavalier: H. Beam Piper."

Finally, special thanks go to copyeditor Victoria Alexander, for all her help in shepherding this book through its various drafts for the past ten years.

Contents

PART III: OFF TO BILLTOWN

Preface

For all his knowledge, Beam was no dry intellectual. He was a storyteller; a man who could keep you up all night with his books and his tales. He had respect for the intellect and for intellectuals, but he was never one of the breed. He was a cavalier.[1]

— Jerry Pournelle,
Introduction to *Federation*

On the weekend of November 6, 1964, H. Beam Piper shut off the utilities in his apartment at 330 East Third Street in Williamsport, Pennsylvania, placed painter's drop cloths over the walls and floor and shot himself with a .38-caliber pistol. Marvin N. Katz, a reporter for Grit Publishing, wrote in the *Analog Science Fiction* letter column that there was a suicide note, but it did not give any reasons for the fatal decision. In a typically Piperesque comment, he did state: "I don't like to leave messes when I go away, but if I could have cleaned up any of this mess, I wouldn't be going away. H. Beam Piper."[2]

H. Beam Piper's needless death is one of the true tragedies of science fiction. Not that the field has been immune to tragedy: Stanley G. Weinbaum, who died at age thirty-six after a sudden and meteoric rise, and Cyril Kornbluth, whose prodigious talents were brought to an end by a heart attack at age thirty-five, are two that come instantly to mind. But tragic as these unexpected deaths were, they lack the tragic irony of Piper's suicide, brought about by his mistaken belief that his career as a writer was over, only a few years before the SF boom of the 1960s and 1970s would transform science fiction into a cultural icon and in another decade make millionaires out of its top practitioners.

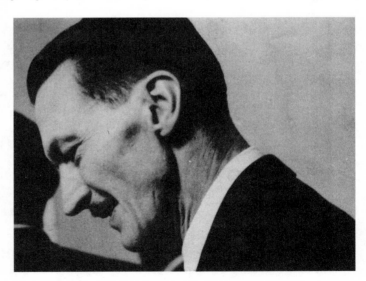

H. Beam Piper (not H. B. Fyfe). Photograph taken in the mid–1950s. According to Peter Weston, this photograph first appeared in the Report on the London Convention (1957) and was taken from a screened print in a convention report published by Seattle fan Wally Weber.

1

H. Beam Piper was a neo-romantic in his approach to his science fiction novels and wrote with the narrative power of Robert Lewis Stevenson, Mark Twain and Rudyard Kipling. He was also a great admirer of Rafael Sabatini and his historical romances. As a lifelong student of history Piper drew much from his study of history, and at the time of his death was working on a historical novel on The Great Captain, Gonsalo de Cordoba.

Where Piper differed from many of his contemporaries in the science fiction field was his impressive knowledge of history and his ability to weave it into his narrative. Piper's understanding of history and his cynical view of human nature kept him from the worst excess of romanticism and provided him with a sense of the grand sweep of history not often found in science fiction.

H. Beam Piper is also one of the most enigmatic writers in the field of science fiction. He appeared suddenly and from out-of-nowhere in 1946 at the top of his form and went on to write a number of memorable short stories in the premier science fiction magazine of the time, Astounding Science Fiction, under legendary editor John W. Campbell. Piper quickly became friends with many of the top writers of the day, Lester del Rey, Fletcher Pratt, Robert Heinlein and L. Sprague de Camp. Jerry Pournelle believes that had Piper lived another decade he would have soon been ranked among the top echelon of SF writers, along with Heinlein, Clarke, Asimov and Bradbury, as well as sharing their financial success along with their growing literary reputations.[3]

Yet, almost all who met him came away with a strong impression of his character. Professor William H. Flayhart III, who met Piper as a fourteen-year-old page at the James V. Brown Library, has this to say: "H. Beam Piper will always stand out in my mind as the absolute personification of a gentleman. He was in fact a shy "David Niven" with a slightly thinner moustache, but with an air of English country elegance even in Northern Pennsylvania."[4]

Even those who counted Piper among their friends knew little about the man and his life as a railroad guard for the Pennsylvania Railroad in Altoona, Pennsylvania. Author Mike Knerr put Piper into perspective with this comment in his unpublished biography, "Piper:" "Part of the reason for the mystery of Piper lies in his origins. His life was common, his formal education almost non-existent and his knowledge of writing gleaned primarily through a voracious appetite for reading that could never be sated. When he died he was reading, ironically, Captain Blood Returns. I took it back to the library for him. Early in his life he knew his way around a library and grew up reading the various pulp magazines of the time."[5]

H. Beam Piper was a fascinating character with a wry wit and irreverent view of science fiction, his own foibles, the politics of his time and the human species. His letters were written with an eye toward posterity and they truly reward and fascinate even the most casual reader. Piper's humanity and informed intelligence grace every page. Beam was an original, even for his own time.

I first encountered H. Beam Piper's work in the 1960s when an actor friend introduced me to his favorite novel, Lord Kalvan of Otherwhen, a tale of a Pennsylvania State Policeman who was picked up by a cross-time craft and accidentally dropped off on an alternate world with sixteenth century technology. Lord Kalvan of Otherwhen was a fascinating story and I wanted to read more of his work. I quickly searched out and bought most of Piper's out-of-print novels, Space Viking, Cosmic Computer and Little Fuzzy, from used bookstores. I found Piper's penchant for inserting historical and cultural data into his stories masterful and incorporated some of his narrative styling into my own early novels.

It wasn't until I went to work with author Jerry Pournelle, as his Editorial Associate, in

1977, that I began my lifelong study of H. Beam Piper. At that time, Jerry was under contract to write the sequel to Piper's novel, *Space Viking*, which was part of Piper's Terro-Human Future History. My job was to research the novel and take notes as preparation for the new book. My research into Piper's future history resulted in a hunt for all of Piper's published short stories and novels to complete Piper's history of the future.

In the late 1970s, all of H. Beam Piper's work was long out-of-print and there was some confusion about who owned his literary estate. It took me over a year to uncover all the rare pulp magazines where Piper had published his early works during the 1940s and 1950s. In 1979 Ace Books Editor Jim Baen (at Jerry Pournelle's urging) purchased the Piper Literary Estate from Piper's cousin, Charles Piper. Due to the lack of interest in the Estate after Piper's death, most of the unpublished works were lost and only a few manuscripts and tear sheets from the published works survived.

The first Ace Books reprints of Piper's out-of-print novels, *Little Fuzzy*, *Fuzzy Sapiens*, *Space Viking* and *Lord Kalvan of Otherwhen* were very successful and Ace decided to collect his short stories into collections. Learning from Pournelle that I had copies of almost all of Piper's works, Jim Baen approached me and asked me to provide him photocopies of Piper's short stories. Shortly thereafter in 1980 Jim Baen left Ace Books to head the new SF line for Tor Books under publisher Tom Doherty and the project languished for a time.

Beth Meacham, the new Ace Editor in charge of reprinting the Piper works, contacted me because of my knowledge of Piper's works and asked me to edit, write introductions as well as collect all of the Piper short stories into coherent volumes. I provided story introductions to Piper's Terran Federation stories for *Federation* and put the later Galactic Empire stories in *Empire*. Piper's Paratime (cross-time travel series) stories were collected together as *Paratime*, while all the non-series stories were put into a volume titled *The Worlds of H. Beam Piper*.

Back then, as now, very little was known about H. Beam Piper the man, or his life as a guard at the Pennsylvania Railroad car shops in Altoona. Piper was very protective over his personal privacy and had a Victorian view of publicity and self-promotion. Most of his science fiction friends and fans believed he was an engineer, of the slide rule variety, working for the Pennsylvania Railroad.[6] Not even his closest friends knew that he began writing as a teenager and received rejection after rejection for close to thirty years before he made his first sale to *Astounding Science Fiction* in 1946 with "Time and Time Again."

As Mike Knerr, author of the unpublished H. Beam Piper biography "Piper," notes: "His life, and the various myths that swirled around him, is as difficult to bring into focus as the character of the man himself. Swathed in secrecy and a verbal smoke screen of self-produced fiction, he lived out his final years in a lonely, frustrated existence that few people, if any, understood. Except when it suited his purposes, he refused to discuss his past and his origins and, when he did, he frequently lied. He generally summed up everything with a favorite expression: 'Man is born, he suffers, he dies; so far, I've done two thirds of this.'"[7]

With the wealth of information I have unearthed over the past thirty years, I intend to lift this veil of secrecy from Piper's life and show my readers the real H. Beam Piper beneath his carefully created facade. More than 90 percent of the information that appears in the present work has never been published or made available on the Internet or any other source. This is the first H. Beam Piper biography. It will reveal "the man" inside the black cape; the animal lover, the friend of children everywhere, the lonely man who was imprisoned by his own solitude and unaware of the high regard he was held in by his peers and the science fiction readership — all of whom were stunned by his unexpected suicide.

There are skeptics who believed that Piper's suicide was a cover-up for murder; a murder that echoed Piper's own locked-room mystery, *Murder in the Gunroom*, so closely it was said to be more than mere coincidence. In *Murder in the Gunroom* Lane Fleming, a noted collector of early pistols and revolvers (much like Piper's friend and mentor Colonel Henry W. Shoemaker, who had a valuable gun collection Piper had catalogued in 1927, and to whom his mystery was dedicated) was found dead on the floor of his locked gunroom with a Confederate-made .36-caliber revolver in his hand. Fleming's suicide was made to look like "death by accident" until Piper's detective, Jefferson Davis Rand, proved otherwise.

Just who was H. Beam Piper? How did he become a writer? When did he first begin to write? What were the events and conditions leading to Piper's death? Was it really a suicide?

I fully intend to answer these questions and further illuminate Piper's life and career with information I obtained from a number of primary sources: Don Coleman, who has graciously allowed me to use the over twenty years of correspondence between his father, Ferd Coleman, and H. Beam Piper he collected into a manuscript; "The Early Letters": the only extant copy of "Piper," a biography written by Mike Knerr, one of Piper's Williamsport friends and Beam's protégé; letters describing Piper as he knew him from Paul M. Schuchart, Piper's schoolmate and lifelong friend; and the H. Beam Piper/John Campbell correspondence which Perry Chapdelaine has so graciously allowed me to review and reprint. I have extensive interviews with Terry and John McGuire, Jr. regarding their memories of their father (John J. McGuire, Piper's only collaborator). Finally, I have an hour long tape of information provided by Anne McGuire, his wife, who answered a list of my questions regarding the Piper/McGuire collaboration during Piper's days in Altoona, Pennsylvania.

In addition to these unique manuscripts, I have in my possession several rare Piper penned articles: a detailed letter to Peter Weston on his Future History, his story log, his own June 12, 1956 record of his weapons collection loaned to the Lycoming Historical Museum and several articles on his writing, as well as Piper's correspondence with a number of important writers including, Jerry E. Pournelle, *Locus* publisher Charles Brown, as well as the surviving H. Beam Piper/John W. Campbell correspondence.

Due to H. Beam Piper's penchant for privacy and misinformation, there is very little biographical information available on his life and work. Other than a few sentences, in the L. Sprague de Camp's biography *Time and Chance: An Autobiography*, and my own article, "H. Beam Piper: The Last Cavalier," in the January 1988 issue of *Analog Science Fiction — Science Fact*, there is very little published biographical data on Piper. Most of what is available on-line or elsewhere are rehashes of my Ace story introductions and *Analog* article.

I am uniquely qualified to write this book, having been the primary authority on H. Beam Piper for the past twenty-seven years since the publication of *Federation*. Until 2006, Ace Books was the copyright holder of record for all of Piper's published works; now, all but Piper's last three novels are in the Public Domain and are available for downloading from the online Gutenberg Project. A number of small publishers and print-on-demand firms have recently re-released Piper's out-of-print novels and stories.

There is very little original or published material on H. Beam Piper in any library or university collection. The Special Collections Library at Penn State does have a small collection of Piper items, including Piper's appointment and calendar diary from 1955 and several original manuscripts of his published works, including "Fuzzies and Other People" and "Full Cycle." Sandra Stelts, Associate Curator, was very helpful in providing me with copies of the diary and Piper manuscripts.

Finally, I have deposited a number of items relating to H. Beam Piper with the John F. Carr Collection at St. Bonaventure University in the Friedsam Memorial Library Archives under the administration of Archivist Dennis Frank. At some future date, all of the H. Beam Piper items in my possession will be donated to the John F. Carr Collection and be made available for study.

Anyone in possession of new information regarding H. Beam Piper can reach the author at *Otherwhen@aol.com* or at P.O. Box 80, Boalsburg, PA 16827. For more information about H. Beam Piper and his books visit the author's website at *www.Hostigos.com*

H. Beam Piper Memorial Fund

The Memorial Fund was founded by Dennis Frank and John F. Carr to collect contributions from fans and readers to purchase a proper granite memorial headstone for Piper's grave in Fairview Cemetery, Altoona, Pennsylvania, and to pay tribute to the memory of H. Beam Piper. Donations can be made via PayPal, or by sending a check or money order to The Piper Memorial Fund, P.O. Box 96, Boalsburg, PA 16827.

PART I

The Early Years

CHAPTER 1

A Prince Is Born

Beam's mother treated him like a prince. He could do no wrong in that household. She made all his meals and did all the housekeeping.[1]

— Anne McGuire

Henry Beam Piper was born March 23, 1904, the only issue of Harriet L. (Mauer) Piper
and Herbert Orr Piper. Both of his parents were middle aged, and Beam Piper was a late
arrival. As Piper researcher David Hines points out, "The Piper-Maurer union was, for the
time, an unusually late marriage for both; Harriet was three days shy of forty when she gave
birth to their first and only child."[2] At the beginning of the twentieth century, childbirth was
hazardous at the best of times. For a woman of advanced age, such as Harriet Piper, there was
always a good chance of birth defects or giving birth to a child with Down syndrome.

Fortunately, H. Beam Piper was a healthy baby. As an only child born late in Harriet
Piper's life, he was feted and spoiled by his mother. Anne McGuire, the wife of John J.
McGuire, Piper's only collaborator, says in a 2001 taped interview: "Beam's mother treated
him like a prince. He could do no wrong in that household. She made all his meals and did
all the housekeeping."[3] He lived with his mother in her small apartment until her death at
ninety-one in 1955.

Don Coleman has this to say about H. Beam Piper's parents: "They had always been a
part of his existence and remained clearly 'near the window.' ... [He] always addressed them
as 'mother' and 'father' rather than *mom* and *pop*. 'Mother' was always there, so the saying
goes, being able to relate so much knowledge of the war between the states— she having been
born shortly before its ending."[4] Her tales led to Beam's fascination with the Civil War, and
his expertise with its chronological history.

Even during his lifetime there were many questions about the elusive Mr. Piper, such as
what the "H." in "H. Beam Piper" stood for. He gave a number of curious answers: Mike
Knerr reports,

Beam mentioned that his first name was Henry, for an uncle, and the Beam was for Molly Beam, an
Indian woman who married his grandfather while he was an Indian agent in Oklahoma. At the time,
I had no reason to doubt his word, but when I began to research his life, various falsehoods started to
fill my notes and my suspicious nature became active. He had lied, of course. Perhaps he felt that the
Indian story was more colorful than the truth, but he should have also known that as an ex-reporter I
would check it out — in this instance with his cousin, Charles O. Piper of Camp Hill.
"He told you what?" Charles asked, chuckling over his phone. "Oh my! The Henry in his name
was for an uncle, but the Beam was for a doctor who perished in the Johnstown Flood on May 31st,
1889." Charles wasn't sure of his full name, but a research of historical records lists a Dr. Lemon T.
Beam, 55, of Market Street, who drowned with his four year old son, Charles C. Beam. There was
also a Dr. W.C. Beam, 35, of Locust Street, who died with his wife, Clara, age 32, and all are buried

in Grand View cemetery, Johnstown.... Bodies from this disaster were found for years after the flood. Both Locust and Market Streets were directly in the path of the huge wall of water and debris that tore the town apart when the South Fork dam gave way in the heavy rains.

Altoona is only about thirty-odd miles from Johnstown and undoubtedly one of the Doctor Beams was important to the Piper family. Fifteen years later Harriet and Herbert named their only child after him.[5]

This is all very interesting speculation on Mike Knerr's part, but, once again, not the real story since H. Beam Piper had a grandfather named Henry Beam Piper who fought in the Civil War! It's this kind of inconsistency — even coming from the family, in this case Charles Piper — that has had Piper researchers tearing their hair out ever since H. Beam Piper's death.

When Piper was asked about his unusual name and why he used a first initial, he was hard to pin down, telling different stories to different people. When asked about the use of a first initial and his middle name, he replied, usually as though in strict confidence, that his first name was Horace, which he couldn't stand — and who could? — and, thus, he preferred to be called Beam Piper. This was the story he told Jerry Pournelle, who was very surprised to learn that the "H." really stood for "Henry" — "not Horace."[6]

In the introduction to "The Early Letters," Don Coleman writes in answer to my report in *Federation* (the first published collection of Piper short stories) that Piper's first name was "Horace": "Without shooting barbs, however, I must square away the record; the forever-utilized initial 'H' preceding Beam Piper was that of Herbert, not Horace, as written on page xii of the Introduction."[7] If Don Coleman, the son of Piper's best friend, is confused about his first name, it provides us with an insight into just how difficult a subject of study Mr. H. Beam Piper has proved to be. As it turns out, "Herbert" was Beam's father's name; interestingly enough, some of Piper's early stories and novels were submitted for publication using his father's name as a pseudonym.

Hines provides the best explanation of his name: "Evidently, he was named in honor of his grandfather, Dr. Henry Beam Piper, a Civil War veteran (E Company, 11th Pennsylvania Volunteers) who died sometime prior to the September 10th, 1902, wedding of Herbert and Harriet — considerably prior [June 22, 1895], as Herbert's mother Mary E. Piper is listed as widowed as early as 1896. About Mary Piper, I know little. About Dr. Piper, I know only that a plaque on the Union Veteran's Legion building (Legion #17, in Altoona) lists him among the deceased members who volunteered for the Union army prior to July 1, 1863.

"The Legion is on 13th Avenue in Altoona, just across 12th Street from the Penn Alto Hotel, where H. Beam Piper liked to get an occasional drink; I imagine him giving a friendly nod to his namesake as he passed by the plaque on the wall."[8]

About Herbert Orr Piper, very little is known. Herbert Piper was born March 7, 1870, and had a number of different jobs. The wedding announcement in the *Altoona Mirror* noted that the groom was "an employee of the Juniata shops (Pennsylvania Railroad)."[9] According to Hines: "During Beam's youth, Herbert [Piper] worked as a driver's assistant and then as a driver for a wholesale grocer before landing employment at the Penn Central Light and Power Company, where he worked variously as a meter reader, an inspector and a clerk. (On his son's birth records, curiously, Herbert Piper's occupation is listed as 'blacksmith.')"[10]

Knerr tells us the following about H. Beam Piper's father:

Herbert Piper was a meter man ... and prior to that occupation had been a teamster driving freight for a local wholesale grocer. Beam seldom talked about his father, except in relation to the older Piper's firearms, but he once showed me a picture of him. It was taken in 1922, at an area hunting camp, showing him holding his new .32 Winchester Special at a kind of port arms. The photo displays a small-boned, thin-faced man with the stern look of the "frontier" in his eyes and a walrus mustache dripping from his upper lip.

His father taught young Beam about firearms early in life and the love of them stayed with him. In later years he mentioned that he half believed that he had cut his first tooth on the barrel of his dad's old 32/20 Colt revolver. Herbert gave him a smoothbore caplock and taught him how to hunt. Armed with his "fowling piece," together with shot and a flask of powder, Beam tramped the woods of Blair County and brought his kills back to the family larder. He once mentioned shooting blackbirds which his mother would cook.

"Jesus, Beam," I told him, "that's a lot of plucking on a damned tiny bird."

His dark eyes flashed and he gave me a typical "Piper's surprised look."

"Oh, no, you don't pluck them. You skin them with this." He held up a small, pearl handled penknife. "The little good knife. The little good knife really holds an edge." The "little good knife," as he always called it, was German and made of Solingen steel; it lived in his mother's sewing basket until she died.

Beam was fourteen when the United States entered the war in France and he may have been younger when he hunted blackbirds with his old muzzle-loading shotgun. His statement could have hinted at the poverty of his parents, or it could have simply been a notation on a lack of game. On the other hand, it could well have been a doting mother preparing what her young son brought home from the woods.[11]

While Piper was too young for the armed services in World War I, he was too old to join up for World War II. In a telephone conversation, John McGuire, Jr., told me: "Most of Beam's friends had seen service in World War II, and it was obvious that having missed two World Wars Beam felt he'd missed out on a rite of passage."[12] Knerr tells us: "Beam joined the local 'home guard' unit after Pearl Harbor and served for the duration. 'We did a damned good job, too,' Piper said laughing, 'There wasn't a single German soldier in all of Blair County!'"

"'Beam's father,' Charles Piper reported, 'never really had a good job.'"[13] Paul Schuchart, who attended high school with Beam, has this to say about Herbert Piper: "His father was a Presbyterian, but worked for the electric company. It was Beam's father who engineered my application to join the Masons in Altoona, Logan Lodge 490. Not only did he get me in, but he also arranged for some sort of special dispensation so that I got all three degrees at one time, rather than one degree each month. My father was the Methodist minister at Llyswen, a suburb of Altoona, and we lived about half a block from where Beam, his mother and father lived. I assume they've both gone to their REEward."[14]

There is even less information on Harriet M. Piper. It is recorded that she was born on March 26, 1864, at Juniata Gap and was six years older than her husband. Both her parents were members of the First Presbyterian Church in Altoona. Hines adds: "According to her obituary, she was survived by 'a number of nieces and nephews,' but I do not know whether she came by them through siblings of her own or through her marriage to Herbert."[15]

The *Altoona Mirror* published this short wedding announcement on Wednesday, September 10, 1902: "Mr. Herbert Orr Piper, son of the late Dr. H.B. Piper, of Tyrone, and Miss Harriet L. Maurer, daughter of Mr. And Mrs. Henry Maurer, were married at 9 o'clock this morning at the home of the bride's parents, 311 Howard Avenue, by Rev. John W. Bain, of the First Presbyterian Church. A wedding breakfast was served and the happy couple left on the day express for a trip to Philadelphia, Wilmington, Baltimore and Washington. The groom is an employee of the Juniata shops."[16]

Knerr quotes Donald A. Wollheim, Piper's editor at Ace Books, who had this to say about him: "'H. Beam Piper is rather enigmatic about his personal life.' Perhaps, to a great many people, that simple statement sums up the whole of the science-fiction writer's life."[17]

The following genealogical information, from J. Simpson Africa's *The History of Hunt-ington and Blair Counties*, traces the Piper family tree back to Colonial times:

Among the old families of the Ligioner Valley in Westmoreland County, Pa, are the Pipers. The first of the name who came to America from Germany some time previous to the war for independence of the colonies, settled in Lancaster County, Pa. But little is known of him, only that he served in the patriotic army, and after the war continued to live in Lancaster County. His family moved into Franklin County, and settled at a place called Piper's Run, where a good number of his descendants still live. He reared a family of children, of whom Peter Piper was one.

Peter was born in Lancaster County in 1756, and remained there until he was eighteen years of age, when he turned his steps westward. He found his way into what was then Indian country, crossing the mountains following Indian paths or trails, and at Fort Ligioner joining a party of Indian scouts. Their operations extended from the above-named fort to Fort Proctor. When Hannastown, the county seat of Westmoreland county, was burned, Peter was in Ligioner Valley, and at once joined the party who pursued the Indians who had been engaged in the destruction of the town and the murder and capture of some of its people. He afterwards became involved in the hazardous business of packing supplies across the mountains to the early settlers of Western Pennsylvania. After the worst of the Indian troubles were over, and his occupation as a scout was gone, he went to work for a Mr. Baldridge (who built the first mills in that part of the State), and learned the millwright's trade. In carrying on their trade in building small mills, where mountain streams made the necessary power, they were compelled to carry their arms with them to defend themselves against Indians and wild animals.

Peter Piper married Miss Catherine Carnes, daughter of Nicholas Carnes, whose family was among the first in the valley. After his marriage he settled on a tract of wild land on Four Mile Run, in what was then Donegal, now Cook township, which he cleared and improved when not working at his trade. On this farm all of their children were born. There were eight sons and three daughters.

Of the sons we will only speak of William. He also became a millwright, and followed the business more or less during his lifetime. After the death of his father, which occurred in 1853, he bought the home farm, which became the birthplace of his five sons and two daughters.

William's second child, H. B. Piper, was born Oct. 15th, 1831. He also learned his father's trade, which he followed when not teaching for a number of years, in fact nearly to the time of the Rebel-lion. Up to eighteen years of age his educational advantages had been confined to the district schools. He then attended the Somerset Academy two sessions, after which he taught school winters, and worked at his trade summers, until he reached his majority, when he attended the Sewickley Academy for two years. While attending the Somerset Academy he boarded with Dr. Fundenburg, under whose direction he studied medicine during his leisure hours and continued to do so until the spring of 1858, when he went to the office of Dr. L.T. Beam, of Ligioner, and commenced the study of medicine in earnest.

H.B. Piper's studies and plans, like those of a great many young men of his age, were rudely bro-ken in upon by the breaking out of the Rebellion in 1861. When the first call was made for troops, he volunteered as a private, April 21st, 1861, in Company K, Eleventh Regiment, Pennsylvania Volunteer Infantry. At the expiration of the three months the regiment was mustered out of service, and at once reorganized, Dr. Piper going out this time as second lieutenant. On the 30th day of August, 1862, he was promoted to a first lieutenancy, which on the 3rd day of June, 1863, was followed by a captaincy.

Capt. Piper participated in the following battles: Falling Waters, Cedar Mountain, Rappahannock Station, Thoroughfare Gap, Second Bull Run, Chantilly, South Mountain, Antietam (where he received a severe wound in the right shoulder), Wilderness, Spottsylvania, North Anna River, Cold Harbor, Bethesda Church, in front of Petersburg, and the battles incident thereto. The regiment, which was commanded by "fighting Dick Coulter" and was one of the best, re-enlisted in the winter of 1864, but owing to his wounds and disease contracted in the Virginia swamps, Capt. Piper was discharged on account of disability, Nov. 23, 1864.

On his return home Captain Piper again entered Dr. Beam's office, and continued his studies therein when not attending the Philadelphia University of Medicine and Surgery, from which he graduated in the spring of 1866. After graduating he opened an office in Harrison City, Westmoreland County, where he remained until 1873, then for three years practiced in Greensburg, the county seat of his native county. He then came to Tyrone, where he has acquired a good practice, and is very pleasantly situated. In politics the doctor is a Democrat, and while in Westmoreland was elected to represent the county in the lower branch of the State legislature, and served during the sessions of 1874–76. He served as chairman of the committee on education, was also a member of the committee on railroads, geological surveys, et al.

On the 29th day of April, 1869, Dr. Piper was married to Mrs. Mollie E. Gay, daughter of Joseph K. Gibson, of Philadelphia. She was born in — —, Chester Co., Pa., on June 27th, 1842.

To them have been born six children, viz:

Herbert O., born March 7, 1870
Charles A., born Feb 12, 1871
James E., born July 15, 1872
Kate E., born Sept 17, 1874
Harry A., born Feb. 18, 1878
William W., June 27, 1881[18]

The Spaceflight Web site adds: "Dr. Piper died on June 22, 1895."[19] The odd note here is that Piper's namesake and grandfather was a figure of more than a little interest, a decorated Civil War veteran. In his day, Dr. Piper was an influential and important man in rural Pennsylvania politics and society. So, why all the deception, obfuscation and misdirection about his name? We will see this pattern repeat itself throughout this study of this flawed but fascinating man.

It was almost as if, to Piper, mundane reality — no matter how odd and fascinating — was no match for his fertile and dramatic imagination. Some of the best examples of Piper's inventiveness at work are the tall tales he told about his marriage. The basic "cover story" was reported by John H. Costello in *Renaissance*, a science-fiction fanzine: "Nearing sixty [actually Piper was fifty-one], he embarked on a disastrous marriage. An expensive European honeymoon, and subsequent divorce proceedings, wiped out his life's savings and left him, in the words of Lester Del Rey, 'with hardly enough money to put bread on the table.'"[20] Jerry Pournelle reported, "Beam told me that his wife married him for an expensive French vacation!"[21]

Mike Knerr was incensed when I reported this in my introduction to *Federation*, the first Piper short story collection, and went out of his way, through the offices of Ace Books, to enlighten me: "Just more Piper bullshit!," he told me over the phone. "Beam loved Betty till his dying day."[22] Still he reports in "Piper": "Many are of the opinion that Beam married a French woman, and, according to him, 'she only married me for an expensive Paris vacation.' He told this to several people, including me, and he lied, as usual. Betty simply spoke French, as well as read it to some extent, and she definitely did *not* marry Beam on any such notion. Hirst is scarcely a French name and anyone whose home is in Carmel (a rather well-to-do area) doesn't need a thousand dollar a year writer to use for a vacation."[23]

On the other hand, Piper had zero tolerance for lies and less than honorable behavior from his friends and acquaintances — and, as we shall see, was intolerant of their misbehavior to an extreme degree. The protagonists of his stories and novels, however, did not suffer from this contradiction; they were straightforward and said what they meant, and meant what they said.

In another attempt to shade the truth, Piper was reported as saying that his father was a minister, which was what John H. Costello reported in "An Infinity of Worlds": "This was given verisimilitude (since Beam was the kind of author who put a lot of himself and his life in his stories) by the fact that the father of the protagonist in his first short story, 'Time and Time Again,' was a minister."[24] I reported that information in my introduction to *Federation* and Paul Schuchart, a lifelong friend of Piper's, wrote me this correction: "Beam's father was NOT a Presbyterian minister, but worked for the electric company." Knerr adds: "Beam's tall tales about himself crop up all the time, even the one that states his father was a minister. Unfortunately, this is more *Piper-fostered* fiction."[25]

Little is known about Piper's childhood and school years. Knerr writes: "He came from a relatively poor family and was raised in a small town whose population probably never had a writer in their midst. He worked at a menial job, struggling for everything he owned and everything he knew. College was totally out of the question and his help was needed at home. To cover up his inability to continue school, he often said he hadn't entered college because he wanted to spare himself 'the ridiculous misery of four years in the uncomfortable confines of a raccoon coat.' He went to work for the Pennsylvania Railroad at age eighteen, after getting kicked out of high school."

Schuchart adds in his letter: "I agree with you when you said Beam never had a formal education, but probably read more books than most professors. I graduated from Washington and Lee in Lexington. My recollection was that Beam was thrown out of Altoona High School, because he shot the bottoms out of several test tubes in the chemical lab."

Hines adds: "Very little information from Beam Piper's youth survives; the earliest photograph of him I know of is circa 1953. I hoped to find a picture of him in the high school yearbook, but to no avail. Piper left high school (as you know, he was reportedly thrown out) before graduating, and in those days only the Seniors' photos were included in the yearbook. He must have made an impression, though: on page 57 of the 1921 *Annual for Altoona High School*, the feature 'Who's Who in the Sophomore Class' contains this line: 'We feel sure Beam Piper will be President of our class when we are Seniors.' It is the sole record of H. Beam Piper's scholastic career. Altoona High School officials could find no record of an H.B. Piper ever attending high school there."[26]

Piper wrote his letters with a view to posterity, and was not above "editing" them to see that it was the ideal past that survived; fortunately, Ferd Coleman thought they all were important. Unfortunately, almost all of Piper's unpublished works were torn up and burned, either in gleeful pyromania with J.J. McGuire, or in his fireplace in melancholy solitude.

CHAPTER 2

Soul Mates of the Quill

The letters found herein are the expressions between friends over a period of six years. Calm, fast, idle, tempestuous, mild, aggressive, they represent many moods, as missives of good friends should.... For, although intended for my diversion through the years as a choice reminder of my early manhood, falling into the hands of others, the thoughts generally of the letters herein may cause the reader to ask, Is not this the record of two minds bent on truth-seeking, though risqué, and objective of interest to all?[1]

— Ferd Coleman, January 26, 1932
Preface to the compilation of letters between
H. Beam Piper and Ferd Coleman

H. Beam Piper was well loved by the science fiction and mystery community, but not well-known. At science fiction conventions and writers' gatherings, Piper loved to drink and talk late into the night about politics, history and writing. He was a gifted storyteller, and a damn good mimic. His sharp eye for detail often captured the foibles, quirks and idiosyncrasies of his fellow *homo sapiens*, which he related with great gusto and style. However, he told his writer friends and fans very little about his "other life," working as a night watchman at the Juniata Yards, or about his camping and hiking expeditions. He told them nothing about his childhood or young adulthood or, most importantly, his personal life.

Piper was quite theatrical and aware of his unconventional appearance, oftentimes reveling in it. He worked the graveyard shift at the Juniata Yards and often haunted the streets of Altoona late at night, wearing his slouch cap and black cape — according to Terry McGuire, daughter of his only collaborator, John J. McGuire — leading to local speculation among the children of Altoona that he was really a vampire.[2]

Don Coleman shares his memories of H. Beam Piper, shortly after he moved to Williamsport in 1957, during a visit to the Coleman home

So, as party times arose — regardless of those included in the gala — Beam was invited automatically and became much more than a standard fixture among the gatherings. He truly loved these parties, and prepared and drank his Piper-made Katinkas at the den bar. Although wearing a fixed face and attitude of supposedly complete apathy, he was on top of the entire curriculum....

Although never reluctant in conversing with whomever would approach, he rarely burst forth ... unless someone else began the chat. Nor did Beam Piper talk into the air unless be it to himself (which was quite common), or directly to somebody who had fired the first shot. However, he talked at will among "genuine" friends. He would puff on his pipe with contentment and ponder his thoughts—generally about his current writing. Because his mind was so vast and deep a reservoir in so many subjects, he weighed his words before he spoke.

Ferd Coleman's top stenographer Eleanor Border recalls: "...when Beam spoke, he spoke very slowly and deliberately — as if like an author he was polishing each sentence before uttering it."

This particular evening wore on, pretty much following the almost identical path of those before. After standing for some time at the bar, and spotting a favorite armchair vacant, Beam would slither across the room as inconspicuously as possible.... Once Beam seated himself and deposited his Katinka on the end table beside the right arm, he would slyly swing both legs over the left arm of the big chair, leaving his booted-feet dangling. He would then gather his pouch from a jacket pocket and load up a fresh pipe and proceed to light up.

Resting his right elbow, he would grab the cocktail with his free left hand — crossing himself in a peculiar manner — and continue uninterrupted with the oratory at hand. Beam would converse about worlds beyond worlds, his writings-to-be, and whatever was coming up in the following issues of this pulp and that one. Those who retained Piper's interest had "The Thin Man's" attention throughout the evening.

Not only did Beam Piper display skill in story writing, but was similarly exceptional in his manner of storytelling... And like anyone else, he had his favorites— one of which actually was a true-to-fact circumstance — occurring sometime during the early Depression. At these parties, it required little effort to grasp the attention of the guests in response to his gripping voice.

The story he was to repeat countless times, involved the likeness of the red-suited, white-bearded jolly red-nosed fat fellow who become the prime time subject of those listening to a local radio station each Christmastide. He would read the demands of "millions of little devils" residing throughout the (Blair County and beyond) broadcast area.

Some months prior to this annual occasion, there occurred a most controversial and unanswered homicide, at least as far as the layman public was concerned. Although the alleged murderer was known to the City Fathers, every effort was made to cut off public knowledge; thus preventing any controversy from leaking out — a matter of politics. But the unequivocal evidence of this action was known to many listeners, including our guy Piper. However, time passed and what was once front-page news, was now deeply hidden within the daily papers ... if it be there at all.

After a short synopsis of background, Beam would take a sip of his Katinka and get on with his story: "So here we find ourselves at Christmas time, listening to Santa Claus reading the many letters from anxious little brats throughout the locale, asking Saint Nick for anything from balls and jacks to little red wagons. One evening, shortly before the Yule, an obviously tipsy and counterfeit-voiced 'Santa' dipped deep into his bloated 'bag' and pulled out another letter from just another brat. 'Ho-Ho-Ho!' he said, as he tore open the letter. 'What have we here — a letter to Santy from little ... ho hum; no name to this little fellow. Well, he'll know who he is when I read off his toys...

Dear Santa,

I hope you get my letter before Christmas because
My mommy said the North Pole is far away. I want a pair of
Roller skates, a scooter, tiddlywinks, a balsa model airplane, a
Sling-shot, and finally most of all, I want a beautiful pearl-
Handled, snub-nose .38 caliber police revolver...
JUST LIKE THE ONE YOU BUMPED MIKEY MACLAUGHLIN
OFF WITH ON HIS OWN BACK PORCH!!!"

The character who represented "Santa Claus," needless to say, was the killer, and was so engrossed in reading countless letters from countless youngsters, that he never hesitated in reciting this particular kid's final request to "a real big" portion of the Commonwealth![3]

It was in 1991 that Don Coleman first wrote me about a manuscript, "The Early Letters," he'd assembled, containing the collected correspondence between H. Beam Piper and his best friend, Ferdinand W. Coleman. It was a tremendous find, as up until that time nothing was known about Piper's life before his first published short story, "Time and Time Again," appeared in *Astounding Science Fiction* in 1947.

Coleman wrote

Beam was an "integral" part of our family for nearly forty years.... Reading your kind words regarding Beam in *Federation*, caused me to recollect and reminisce. As a result, I enthusiastically corralled my lifelong thoughts of H. Beam Piper, including his habits and trivial tidbits that have most probably never heretofore been divulged. In conclusion, the 400-page account includes a compilation of

"Early Letters" followed by "Retrospect," my scribing of H. Beam Piper's experiences among we mortals.[4]

The first meeting of Piper and Coleman came about during a gathering of the Pennsylvania Alpine Club at the mountain home of Colonel Henry W. Shoemaker, the prominent (Pennsylvanian) folklorist and historian, and a staunch supporter of this extraordinary group. Shoemaker's retreat, affectionately named "Restless Oaks," is nestled in the mountainous environs of McElhattan, (located some twenty miles up the river from Williamsport) where he authored numerous folk tales of early Pennsylvania, and was actively involved with issues of conservation of wildlife and forest lands within the Commonwealth. The Colonel loved the woods and wilds, and thrived upon the historical values of the surrounding beauty—just as did the youngsters Coleman and Piper. Although the Colonel was a mutual friend of both, this particular occasion brought the two together for the first time, and needless to say, they became thoroughly absorbed in discourse.[5]

Colonel Shoemaker was a local character of some political and social note. Piper's first published work, in 1927, was a catalogue of Colonel Shoemaker's gun collection published as "compiled by H. Beam Piper: *A Catalogue of Henry Wharton Shoemaker Weapons at Restless Oaks in McElhattan Pennsylvania*, publisher *Times Tribune Co.*, Altoona, Pennsylvania."[6] Piper dedicated his mystery novel, *Murder in the Gunroom*, to Colonel Shoemaker.

There is no question that Shoemaker was a friend and role model to Piper; however, in the years since Piper's death there have been numerous questions raised about Shoemaker's veracity as a folklorist. As Fred Ramsey, author of the introduction to the reprint of the sole Piper mystery novel, *Murder in the Gunroom*, writes:

Henry Shoemaker was a newspaperman in Altoona and a notorious inventor of "local mountain legend and lore." There are real questions regarding anything he ever said in print in his books and articles.

He "invented" out of whole cloth the Princess Nit AhNee myth that gives a bogus explanation for the name of the Nittany Valley, Nittany Lions and Nittany Mountain, here in the heart of Downtown Hostigos (State College). Quite an amusing character. Several books have been written about his creative use of legend to drive commerce and tourism in Central Pennsylvania. His books remain in print today, spreading his sentimental rubbish to new victims.

Beam seems to have regarded Shoemaker as a mentor of sorts. A wealthy man, self-made, also without formal education, I think Beam saw a hopeful precedent for himself in Shoemaker's success and aspired for something similar. They met and worked together because of their interest in history, writing and weapons.

There is no evidence that Beam knew Shoemaker was a con artist. During his lifetime, Shoemaker was highly esteemed for his "discoveries." He made much money from his paper and was a LARGE presence in the community.

Restless Oaks is gone now. But it was in McElhattan, near the West branch of the Susquehanna, east of Lock Haven. This location on the northern boundary of the future Hostigos must have been paradise to the industrial city dwelling Piper.

Woods full of game. Second growth forest, maybe seventy-five years in from the first harvest. The house was located near a small stream at the northern end of a narrow gap that led into Sugar Valley. A site that to someone lost in the love of medieval warfare would have been seen as a wonderful place for a castle.[7]

Don Coleman gives us this background on his father:

Ferdinand W. Coleman was born in 1904. He attended a Catholic school and of course, back then, eleven years enveloped the complete curriculum. He loved to write, and poetry seemed to be his wont, but he knew one couldn't live on poetry alone. He never attended college. He would challenge the world with his own self-learned wisdom.

Ferd was a very smart man; an intellectual. His vocabulary was extraordinary. I also considered Beam an intellectual, but visibly eccentric. Dad was an avid reader; he wore prescription glasses at eight (or younger) and had a profound interest in poetry.

He established the *Shoppers' Guide* in 1922 at age eighteen. He wanted to do something entirely different from the ordinary. He wanted a paper solely dedicated to advertising — not a newspaper. He believed in giving the patron a more personal communication between the tradesman and the house-wife. He concluded the paper would pay for itself, and that not a select few, but everyone, would receive it.

His initial publications measured half a newspaper page (sliced down the middle) — both sides, originally giving him a net revenue of some eight to ten bucks! He started in a small area called New-berry, which actually is within the west side of Williamsport. I don't know who printed the paper originally, but when it eventually became more than just a single sheet, blossoming to a full page and finally into six and eight-page editions. Dad hired out to the *Sunbury Daily Item* (thirty miles down river) to print the publication. After some time with the Item, he began running syndicated colum-nists such as Walter Winchell, et. al.

Ferd rarely ever missed a hunting trip with Beam and Ted (Ranck) in those early days. The amaz-ing point to be made here is he never was a hunter per se. He never shot an animal of any kind, nor was he a fisherman. He handled all kinds of weaponry, but never ever aimed same at a living thing. He loved the outdoors and the eternal camaraderie of his two best friends.

And as Beam and Ted would let the world know — no hunting trip was complete without the pres-ence of Ferd W. Coleman. He was too young for World War I, but advised all the recruiters in town after Pearl Harbor, he would do whatever they required for the war effort, as long as it did not require killing![8]

At the time they met at Restless Oaks, both Beam and Ferd saw themselves as Bohemi-ans (the pre–World War II equivalent of beatniks), and often mocked conventional views of religion, bourgeois morality and politics. One of Piper's 1927 letter closings was "Yours for Free Love and Atheism, Beam."

The same was true with Piper's dress. He typically wore formal attire, even when alone writing. Piper believed in an unconventional lifestyle and got joy out of offending those who considered themselves the pillars of conventional morality and society. It's not surprising that he fit in well with both the mystery and science fiction crowds.

Don Coleman paints a good picture about the beginnings of the Piper-Coleman friend-ship:

We have here two outdoorsmen — one a publisher of a budding shopping newsletter; the other a night watchman and part-time writer, employed by the Pennsylvania Railroad system — what seem-ingly appears a most unlikely compatible pair until they entered into a dialogue. The challenge was actually facing him; standing tall, lank and erect with hands on hips, dressed in jodhpurs and was returning fire to all that the knickerbockered Coleman could muster. After a lengthened conversa-tion, Coleman was confronted with the fact that he'd finally met a man who was as ingenious as him-self. Could this be true?

He quickly learned that Beam Piper was spontaneous in response to solving and resolving the queries and qualms of the day, whatever they be. They each found that neither could tolerate idle conversation. And neither would admit to egoism. So on this day in December, 1925, a matchless friendship was born.

... Aside from the great outdoors, each possessed another and greater common amour ... that of writing. Coleman was editor and publisher of the Williamsport *Shoppers' Guide*. Beam was continu-ally writing both day and night. Whenever his ideas surfaced — even while performing his railroad responsibilities— they were immediately put to paper. Murder investigation and history were his pri-mary literary goals at this time. And sleep was secondary, of course.[9]

CHAPTER 3

The Would-Be Writer

By the way, I've decided to change the name from "Tiadaghton" to something else, as I'm afraid a title so difficult of pronunciation would be hard to sell, not to publishers, but by publishers to the public. What do you think? And can you make any suggestions as to the new title? ... You see, *Hoi Polloi* would have a hard time twisting their tongues around "Tiadaghton," would be apt to forget it after they heard it and would be afraid to discuss it for fear of mispronouncing it and being thereby ridiculed, and that doesn't sell books. In passing, it will probably cost me $1,800 to live while I'm writing the damned thing, and after it's finished it'll be a good break if I get a grand out of it. Stick to journalism, Fernando! The Muse is a hell of a paymistress.[1]

— H. Beam Piper

According to the *Pennsy* newsletter's September 1953 article "Typewriter 'Killer,'" we learn that H. Beam Piper "began working for the Pennsylvania Railroad in 1922 as a laborer; at the age of eighteen, he already was an author of two years standing. He was using all his pocket money for postage, regularly sending out stories to the magazines and just as regularly getting them back." The Pennsylvania Railroad (PRR) was founded in 1845 and was commonly referred to as the Pennsy. The company was headquartered in Philadelphia and was the largest railroad by traffic and revenue in the United States throughout the twentieth century.[2]

Coleman writes: "Piper spent his nights as a watchman amid the Pennsylvania Railroad shops and yards in Altoona, a community that was quite prominent in railroad repair, and a bustling hub of the (rail) systems. The nature of his job required cognizance of the system's security about the vast railroad yards, and his riding the line as a railroad dick brought him within or about the confines of Williamsport numerous times...."[3]

The Steamlocomotive.com Web site has this history of the Juniata Locomotive Shops where Piper worked as a guard for almost thirty years:

As the Pennsylvania Railroad pushed west in 1850, it established an engine house at the base of the Allegheny Mountains where trains could be broken up or additional locomotives added to climb the heavy grades westward. This location now in the City of Altoona, Pennsylvania and the engine house with its small shop buildings grew into the largest complex of railroad shops in the world.

In 1866, locomotives were being built new in the Altoona Works in a shop known as the Altoona Machine Shop. The PRR built a total of 2,289 steam locomotives in this shop before it was converted into a locomotive repair shop in January, 1904. At its high point, the Altoona Works consisted of four units: the 12th Street Car Shop, the Altoona Car Shop, the Juniata Shops and the South Altoona Foundries. These four units were comprised of 122 buildings containing 37 acres of floor space, 4,500 machine tools, and 94 overhead cranes. The complex employed 13,000 people and the rail yard alone covered 218 acres.[4]

In his posthumously published piece in the fanzine *Double-Bill Symposium*, Piper expanded on his early interest in writing:

> In my teens, which would be in the early 1920s, I decided that what I really wanted to do was write; I wasn't sure what, but I was going to write something. About the same time, I became aware of science fiction, such as it was then, mostly H.G. Wells, and fantasy, Bram Stoker, H. Rider Haggard, and then I began reading the newer science (more or less) fiction — Burroughs, Merritt, Ralph Milne Farley, Ray Cummings, et al. This was the Neolithic, or Hugo Gernsback, period of science fiction, and by this time I was a real 200-proof fan.
>
> This first enthusiasm waned slightly after a while. I got interested in history and historical fiction, and for some time read little else in the way of fiction, and every historical novel I read started me reading up on the history of the period involved. I wanted to know just who this guy Richelieu was and why D'Aartagnan & Co. had such a down on him. Then the Prohibition period was in full swing, and I became interested in Chicago gangsters for a while. All the time, I was scribbling stories, few of which ever got finished, thank God![5]

The "Typewriter 'Killer'" article goes on to state: "Mr. Piper, a tall, slim man with sharply chiseled features, and a sinister black mustache, could pass for a villain in his own mystery novel. He spends the somber midnight hours patrolling through the Altoona shops, watching out for trespassers and possible fires."[6] While circumstances dictated that he work as a night watchman to support himself and his writing habit, Piper used those "circumstances" to his best advantage, working the graveyard shift and working on story ideas as he made his rounds of the car shops or, when he had the opportunity, penning rough drafts at work.

It doesn't take much imagination to see Piper — with slouch cap and black overcoat — wandering the deserted car shops, where they built and stored the boxcars, locomotives and railroad flatcars, late at night in a light drizzle like some wraith, talking out the story complications of his latest yarn. Woe to the bum or wrongdoer who ran into Mr. Piper, for — if needed — he could dispense billy club justice with neither sentimentality nor rancor — just the firm application of *force majeure*.

All writers put something of themselves in their work; Piper probably more than most. Many of his stories are set in rural settings not unlike that of the Appalachian Mountains, where he spent most of his life. In *Little Fuzzy* we see the protagonist, Jack Holloway, a grizzled, self-sufficient old prospector on the frontier world of Zarathustra, describe Piper's idea of justice, in answer to the question: "Haven't had any trouble lately, have you?" Holloway replies: "Not since the last time." Piper continues, "The last time had been a couple of woods tramps, some out-of-work veldbeest herders from the south, who had heard about the little bag he carried around his neck. All the Constabulary had needed to do was to remove their bodies and write up a report."[7]

Piper's lack of sentimentality and penchant for writing real characters probably did not help him make story sales in the 1920s and 1930s, a period when outlaws and gangsters were glorified in movies and fiction. As in most things, he was out of step with the times; this never changed. It took him another twenty years of unsuccessful writing before he found a field where "being out in left field" was a compliment, not a put-down.

While he had little faith in the afterlife, it's quite obvious he was interested in this life and wanted to make his mark as a serious author. Probably the major cement of the Ferd Coleman–H. Beam Piper friendship was their love of words, literature, wordplay and writing. Don Coleman provides his father's view of Beam's writing: "Ferd W. Coleman, as a writer himself, surely was capable of tossing barbs of criticism at H. Beam Piper, as well as Joseph Conrad or Ernest Hemingway or any other author of the day, if need be — but in the early going he acknowledged Piper as potentially a good contributor. The force to which Piper put his thoughts to paper (letter writing)—his philosophies and beliefs and the simple advising of his own doing—were extremely welcomed by Coleman."[8]

Ferd himself wrote:

I am sincere, Beam, when I write I enjoyed your letter so much. I think it should not be difficult for you to know why, since nuts or pioneers souls, as you will, like yourself and me, are difficult to discover, with the alternative that such associates as I tolerate are quite commonplace, and, as to letters I receive few, and those of no consequence....

Further, Beam, your letter was well written and convinces me without more ado on that score, that you can write. Your only drawback, as I fathom you, is that which I told you last Christmas at "Restless Oaks"—you haven't lived. ... However the extent of your background, Beam, I wish you would forward me some of the dope you have written. I know I should be keenly interested in it....[9]

Piper fired back: "As for myself, I have been doing little or nothing except writing, and at that only at another unspeakably cheap pot-boiler. I had a little trouble in developing that story I told you about—the one in which a soldier of fortune has the love affair with the married woman and gets bumped off in a duel—and I laid it by until the Muse would get into working order again."[10]

This desultory way of working was typical of Piper until the day he died. He would get an idea, try to work it into a story, then write draft after draft trying to make the story work. He would work and work at a story, often abandoning it at the eleventh hour, because of some suspected flaw. Then he would pine over it, as he waited for inspiration—or desperation—to help him finish the story. Unfortunately, none of Piper's unpublished works from this era survived his death, so it's impossible to do an objective analysis. It is clear from both his diaries and his letters that Piper was rarely satisfied with his stories, even those that later were published, and rewrote them over and over.

Don Coleman writes: "As for Piper, only after drafting his thoughts in longhand, scratching out and adding and re-penning an idea, would he eventually turn to tapping the keys of his anchored Underwood with the final veneer—and never without at least one carbon copy. Invariably a Piper miscarriage would wind up making a conventional return trip to 400 Wordsworth Avenue, it being slammed down aside the typewriter unopened, as meticulously as immediate frustration would allow. And after experiencing the existing disappointment, he would never let the presence of a publisher's rejection impede the continuity of thought he carried.... He would return to the draft he was penning until the segment ... was complete. Then, after feeling content with what he had written, he would grasp and scrutinize the package of denial."[11]

In a letter to Ferd, Piper wrote:

I've been up to the ears for the last week with one thing or another, chiefly re-writing that story, so you haven't heard from me sooner. I think that I have the thing fixed about as I want it and Monday I start finishing it up; smoothing out the rough spots, making the sentences a little better and typing it off.... I toned down the religious argument quite a good bit, as I thought that some of the "intellectual" readers of the magazine might object. Disgusting, but I think that it had to be done. Likewise, I reduced the conversation between the man and girl to the proper level of imbecility.

Well, enough of this. It's always tiresome to talk shop, particularly when it comes to recounting the devices by which stories are rendered comprehensible to the "booboise," so I will shift to more amusing topics.[12]

Even in his twenties, Piper knew what he was aiming for. He took his career seriously, realizing that he would have to put in a long apprenticeship and that he couldn't start out at the top. He needed to develop his technique in an era when literary fiction was largely done by those with a Yale or Harvard credential. One needed a certain pedigree or the right friends to become published in *The New Yorker* or *American Mercury*. Piper had foregone a formal education and so served his apprenticeship in the pulp magazines, rude and colorful magazines that were pitched to readers of Westerns, romances, crime stories, mysteries and tales of other worlds.

Piper wrote:

> I did another potboiler, fifteen thousand words of eyewash about the Rum Row whisky-trade. In it I succeeded in killing off almost the entire cast of characters and introduced several pitched battles in the manner of Herrin, Ill. If those buggers want a "clean story of swift-moving action," they shall have it, so help me, Allah! I hope it sells. If it does, I'll be able to take a few months and write something decent — that novel I was telling you about, for instance.
>
> I was very careful to stipulate that it be published under an assumed name. I don't want that sort of thing thrown in my teeth when I'm writing good stuff. I regard a piece of poor work in the same light as a bastard offspring — it is wise not to acknowledge it publicly. When, twenty years hence, I am known as an author, I don't want to have people say, "Oh, hell, he wrote for *Black Mask* and *Brief Stories*. Their money is just as good as the *American Mercury*'s, but damnit, their reputation isn't.[13]

This statement provides further evidence that he was taking a long view of his career as a writer: of course, in 1926 he had no way of knowing that his first story would not be published for another twenty years! By the 1940s, he was no longer worried about being published in the pulps, nor about his future literary reputation. Thus, Piper used his real name on his first published story, "Time and Time Again" for *Astounding Stories*.

Ferd Coleman, who was a frustrated writer himself, was very supportive of Piper's career. "I sincerely hope you cash in on the manuscript, Beam. You not only deserve to because of your persistence but frankly I believe there is excellent material and tolerable technique behind your work. I forgot whether you told me you subscribed to the *Author and Journalist* when I asked you at McElhattan. If you do not, let me know and I shall send you a batch."[14]

As with hunting, antique firearms, the outdoors and politics, Piper had strong views regarding writing manuals and magazines that catered to would-be writers, like himself:

> You ask if I have subscribed to the *Author and Journalist*. I have not. Saving your presence and asking your pardon, I solemnly hold that trade journals, while excellent for carpenters, undertakers, real-estate dealers, cheesemongers, etc., are not for artists, particularly for authors.
>
> The same thing, by the way, applies also to the numerous Author's Leagues and Writer's Associations.... As for the ten thousand Schools of Story-Writing, words cannot help me express my opinions.
>
> However, I retain a partially open mind. If you have any copies of the magazine, I accept your offer. Mail them on, informing me whether or not you want them returned, and I will give them the once-over, as a true agnostic should, to see if there is any wheat in what I think is a Gargantuan chaff-heap. This is, however, only a personal opinion, subject, like Bannerman's prices on ammunition, to change....
>
> Also, I would be glad to glance over any of the stories you have written, the stories, I mean, that you were telling me about, if any of them are finished.
>
> With sincere hopes that you are well and out of jail, I am, as ever, Your fellow ballock of the devil — Beam.[15]

Piper's condescending air towards self-help journals didn't stop him from accepting them — even if they were bunk, in his words. As with most unpublished authors, he was still searching for the key — either within himself or outside — that would open the gates of the New York publishing establishment. It's a formidable structure, and Piper had already spent several years beating his head against it in frustration.

Just a while later in 1927, he was working hard to learn what was wrong with his technique or style, a question that often frustrates unsuccessful beginning writers. My suspicion is that Piper's voice was too strong for the slick markets and too slick for the pulps:

By the way, that story that I was working on at Brookside has gone forth and returned three times. (*Argosy-Allstory*, *Black Mask*, and the Street and Smith gang) Now, you read it. What in hell's amiss with it? Or have I been sending it to the wrong place? I am not unmindful of my promise to buy a keg of moonshine and go off somewhere with you if it sells. I hope it does. Cold sober, we have had a hell of a good time. Gloriously tanked, we could hold revel as the gods and heroes do in Valhalla.

...do you know anything about this course in fiction writing that Columbia University runs? Anything good, that is? I see rather plainly that there is something wrong with my stuff— these damn blood-and-thunder potboilers, I mean — but the thing is to find out what it is. And how to remedy it. I don't mean the correspondence course, but the course conducted at the University. Let me know your opinion on this.[16]

Here, in this undated letter, we find the young H. Beam Piper attempting to analyze why he's not selling his work:

In this very rare photograph Piper, attired in jodhpurs, shares a flask with friend Stan Moon sometime during the 1920s (courtesy Coleman Family).

I received the book, along with a letter from the Colonel, just as I was starting on a hunting trip, and this is the first opportunity that I have had to answer either. I found it interesting simply no end and for one thing, it showed me just what was wrong with that fool murder mystery story I wrote about a year ago. As I see it, there wasn't a damned thing right about it.

I am convinced that that rum-running story, "Drink and the Devil," is a total loss. Maybe I can sell it after Al Smith gets elected (President), but with all this prohibition sentiment it won't go. I think I'll rewrite it, changing the characters from Twentieth Century bootleggers to Seventeenth Century buccaneers. The W.C.T.U won't object to murdering Spaniards and stealing pieces of eight as they do to selling whisky. Yours, for Rum, Royalism and Rebellion, Beam.[17]

In a letter of January 23, 1928, he discusses his projected trilogy based on local Pennsylvania history for the first time:

I received the *Otzinachson* on the same afternoon that I mailed you my letter regarding the meeting, and I am delighted with it. I'd say, off hand, that it is worth all I am going to pay for it ($15), both as a history of the valley in which I spent some of the happiest days of my life and as a source of information and material for my projected series of three novels dealing with the Fair Play Men. As to the latter, I think it will serve as the foundation, to which I will build up my other research into old records, oral traditions and such.... I find, however, that the author is most damned infernally disorderly and digressive, but I will arrange some kind of an index by which I can put it in proper chronological

Piper with pipe, Coleman donning knickers of the era, and Major Cooper wearing military-issue footwear in the early 1930s (courtesy Coleman Family).

order, and also prepare a bibliography, which it sadly wants. Then, with such notes as I may see fit to append, I will have a first class tool for the work I have in mind.[18]

On January 26, 1928, Ferd replied:

Anent your manuscripts, please go damned slow. Take your own counsel of two months back, derived from Sabatini, read, read, read, the lives, the histories, the very guts of locality, over many a night's midnight oil or gas, in home, not in auto and street, before attempting to write a line of historical romance. My novels of Nippenose, crude as they are, must have been pioneer works because there is so little of the particular valley, and less of that distinct people; I, in fact, had to adopt with them the welcome which all Berks County Dutch accord strangers, I had practically to sleep with them in order to learn about them. The condition, by good fortune, is different with you, not that you may not want to sleep with whomever you may find — but you have splendid research facilities. Let me tell you, boy, you said on your previous visit to me that you didn't want so much the possession of *Otzinanchson*, as you did the information it contained.[19]

Piper wrote back:

I fear you are laboring under a trifling misconception regarding the manuscript that I said I'd send you. I don't mean the manuscript of "Tiadaghton," the first of my trilogy on the Fair Play Men, I mean the manuscript of that short story which I outlined to you while drunk, and which I am calling "Moment of Greatness." Great Thor, I don't even have any ideas as to what the story of "Tiadaghton" will be. I'll have to wait until I've finished my research, first, as there will be absolutely no liberties taken with history and it will be necessary to discover what actually happened on the West Branch in the ten years' time about which I write before I can say what *fictitiously* happened.

As to how I will gather that material, I mean to put in almost or possibly more than, a month on the West Branch, both in the library and doing field work among the Oldest Inhabitants, Local Historians, and Hill-Billies, not to forget the various historical societies, D.A.R. chapters, etc. I look to the last-named organization in its various ramifications, together with the Lycoming and Clinton County Historical Societies for some valuable data, as a historical novel accurately portraying a period in their own locality's history would be all cream for them, particularly with a note of acknowledgement in the book. But don't spring this on your own society until the arrangements are completed for my trip next summer.[20]

According to Don Coleman:

The Otzinachson referred to in the letters relates to the Delaware Indian derivation given the West Branch (and immediate valley areas) of the Susquehanna River which, of course, is most prominent with the Clinton and Lycoming county regions of the Commonwealth.... At this time in their lives, the *Otzinachson* (history book) was the most informative source of Eighteenth Century regional history, to which Piper especially, intended to research and portray in his yet-to-be-started novel.

The letters also bring up reference to "Tiadaghton," another name given by the Delawares. There may also be questions as to how the name came about, but Pine Creek, (a tributary running north of the Susquehanna just west of Jersey Shore) is represented as the "Tiadaghton," and apparently its banks were happy hunting grounds for these two correspondents....

Piper's mention of "Fair Play Men" centers around the early boundary given the western borders of Lycoming County. There was a question as to whether Lycoming Creek, which flows just west of Williamsport to be the bonafide boundary, or the "Tiadaghton" (Pine Creek), which lay further west. If anyone trod west of Lycoming Creek, they would risk being hunted down by the Indians. Many settlers, feeling a strong sense of deception by the Indians in the treaty of 1768, believed the Tiadaghton to be the true western boundary and thus would move on across the line. In order that protection be given these wandering pioneers— within this-all-of-a-sudden no man's land, the Fair Play system was implemented. Beam would tie this in with his proposed "trilogy!"[21]

Piper was equally as interested in writing historical fact as he was fiction, especially in his youth, since it combined his two great passions. Other than the Mosley piece, "Rebel Raider," that was published in *True* magazine, there are no surviving examples of his nonfiction, most of which was published in local low-circulation newspapers, such as Coleman's *Shoppers' Guide.*

It's hard to determine Piper's schedule at the car shops, although we know he did work nights. He wrote: "However, I think I can keep myself at the typewriter and as I don't need to work overtime now I can come home less tired than before and do more efficient work."[22] Piper worked his night guard job around his real work — writing. Unfortunately, later in life, when the Pennsy went into bankruptcy, Beam had no alternative way of making a living, but — in 1928 — those days were far off and Beam was still full of piss and vinegar — or gunpowder.

On October 13, 1929, he wrote about a new novelette that he had just finished, "Racket-Town": "I will be down, Allah willing, about that time. Maybe sooner, if I hear favorably from a novelette of about 30,000 words that I've just sent off. It's gang-war stuff, with murders, and men put on the spot and taken for a ride, and police raids, and 'pineapples' [grenades], and Thompson guns, and bootlegging, and white-slavers, and crooked officials, and a special police officer hero who wades up to his ears in gangster gore and cleans up the town and marries the girl. The girl, by the way, runs a sort of an antique shop. As Louie Bardo says, 'Get it?'"[23]

On May 25, 1930, Piper told Ferd, "'Racket-Town' now has the magnificent record of five rejections. At present it is out for the sixth time, and should I receive a check for it prior to Friday, I promise you that Williamsport will be painted a deep crimson and the City Fathers will be out at the pocket for a considerable repair-bill as a result of the celebration."[24]

In a July 7, 1930, letter, we learn more: "I arrived home in good condition.... On my arrival I found 'Racket-Town' home again, for the seventh (7th) time. This time it was from Street & Smith, and, instead of the usual printed slip I got a personal letter with it. They complain (*mirabile dictu*) of insufficient action. Well, I'll let them have one that won't have that drawback. The entire plot will be as follows: Bang! Bang! Bang! Some of these days I'll arrive, if I keep on like this."[25]

In response to a chain letter from Colonel Shoemaker, which was supposed to pay off magically in three wishes, he told Ferd what his wish would be. "My first choice from the gods' bargain-counter would be, of course, a good break up the river from Williamsport and below Lock Haven, and my second, a million dollars. My third would be the ability to make some impression on the flinty hearts of a lot of these 'lousey' (sic) publishers. I leave that third because I think that I have that ability to do it in time, but I wish to Jesus I could hurry the process up a little."[26]

The above is a rare look into Piper's view of his fledgling writing career, still going nowhere after ten years of hard work. It was only his own belief in himself, and that of a few trusted friends like Ferd, that kept this dream alive. Yet, in the end, all is grist for the writer's mill.

CHAPTER 4

Prohibition — Phooey!

By God, Ferd, if you don't give that son of a bitch, Ames, hell in your editorial columns for that sort of high-handed, insolent tyranny, blazoning him for the "lousy," bigoted, snot-nosed cur he is— God's wounds, does the fellow think he's Torquemada? I never heard tell of such a thing![1]

— H. Beam Piper

H. Beam Piper had a lifelong love affair with liquor that started early in life. At writers' get-togethers and science fiction cons he usually drank Jim Beam, as a "signature" drink. But privately, he was most enamored of Myers's Rum. Terry McGuire has fond memories of Beam and her father, John J. McGuire, sneaking her into bars and giving her sips of their Manhattans.[2] Piper enjoyed drinking the hard stuff, and during Prohibition often said, "I will not cower to such docile means as to sipping my booze from a teacup!"[3]

He was quite hostile about the mayor of Williamsport, an eighty-four-year-old codger who was the black horse in the 1927 mayoral race. As Don Coleman writes: "In spite of [Ferd] Coleman's commitments, Beam railed on in to Williamsport a few days earlier than planned, meeting and partying with Ferd and friends preceding the final eve of 1927.... The hot issue at hand was the terrible Mr. Ames, mayor-elect, and while together with the Billtown [Williamsport] bunch, Beam could not talk rationally about a figure who would force abstinence on such a wonderful commodity as hardcore whiskey. If one did not choose to imbibe, then why should that one put a damper on those who did so. It should be left up to the individual whether he *do* or *don't*!"[4]

On January 12, 1928, Ferd wrote this postscript: "P.S. Haven't had a drop since! [New Year's] Ames, thru his alderman, when apprehending inebriates, is even forcing them to tell where they obtained the stuff, or they go to jail for contempt."[5]

January 14, 1928, Piper answered: "The meeting [the Darlington Folklore meeting] will be on the nineteenth.... Your postscript simply infuriates me. By God, Ferd, if you don't give that son of a bitch, Ames, hell in your editorial columns for that sort of high-handed, insolent tyranny, blazoning him for the lousey, bigoted, snot-nosed cur he is— God's wounds, does the fellow think he's Torquemada? I never heard tell of such a thing! Yours for a lynching in Williamsport[,] Beam."[6]

On January 26, 1928, Ferd wrote back, "Let's hold final sentence on Ames. He's not much, understand; but he must be better than our former Gilmore, for four weeks of his administration have passed, and I have found no occasion to kick him once in my revered publication. Have a large report of another speech of his, and, damn him, if he'd forget this prohibition issue, he'd be about square, in spite of his 84 years."[7]

Piper shot back the next day, "I say that Ames is a skunk. I advocated a rope for him. I hereby withdraw that proposition and substitute faggots and stake, with the rack, hoist, boot and thumbscrews as preliminaries.... His practice of compelling persons arrested in liquor to divulge their source of supply ... there is no punishment quite adequate for him. You say that you've found no occasion to kick against him? What the hell do you call that? An occasion to laud him?"[8]

Paul Schuchart, an old school friend, remembers Piper fondly. "As I recall it, Beam used to like to drink rum and couldn't understand why I preferred 'corn squeezing,' even though I graduated from Washington & Lee University, Lexington, Virginia. I still like bourbon, although, Dr.'s orders, I'm still on the Water Wagon, and I assure you there's no future in that."[9]

Don Coleman summarizes the temper of the times:

The fangs of prohibition had been gnawing into the crust of the nation, including our own beloved West Branch Valley. The terrible Mr. Ames who now presided as mayor of Williamsport, would continue to do exactly what he had set out to do—banish whatever illegal liquor movement and marketing he could track down.... As a newspaperman, Coleman would remain congenial with the mayor but would continue to publish whatever truths may occur, including opinions surrounding laws, whether pro or con....

And of course, Beam finds himself "sorely athirst," turning to his friend Ferd as a source of procurement. ... while half a dozen gangsters were fighting for control of Chicago, to which all had a leg in the booze business—but were killing each other for it—here in quiet North Central Pennsylvania there arose a real prince of a guy from the dregs who would become renowned immediately. His name was Prince David Farington who would be referred to all as the Prince. He had migrated from a North Carolina penitentiary (on recommendation of a fellow inmate) where he served time for bootlegging, and would eventually set up operations of the same caliber—illegally, if you will—in the wooded confines of Clinton County.... Ultimately, Farrington moved up into the Jersey Shore area [Lycoming County] where he would settle and become a friend of and to the populace.

The Prince was not a violent man. He had never "taken to the sword" and there was no reason to do so as long as he could enjoy seclusion from the law.... Not only did the Prince provide for those who could afford such need of "Florida Farm rye" and "Sugar Valley corn," but he administered to those in the relative depths of poverty.... In time all would know the Prince. He was likened to "Robin Hood," or a truly real live bootleggin' tooth fairy! And why? Pennsylvania composed itself of many a wonderful Deutschman, and according to legendary standards, these folks were pretty dog-goned close-mouthed. It would be complete idiocy for any to squeal on a man who was doing good for others while not committing to violence in his present occupation.

And so, H. Beam Piper, among thousands who also found themselves "sorely athirst," had no distinct problem obtaining whatever he might ask of Coleman. Neither he nor Ferd were bad guys; only one found himself closer to the source! Farrington's finest was considerably accessible.[10]

On June 6, 1928, Piper wrote, "It is now 10:15, on Wednesday night. You and Ed are in all probability splendidly drunk, while I am ignobly sober. Jesus Christ, I envy you two! After nine hours in the goddam slave-pen a drink would be a welcome relief, but I am pledged to a policy of economy that would make the average McTavish look like Coal-Oil Johnny, so no can do."[11]

The amount of time Piper devoted to alcohol and partying was significant. He typically coined a name for his current drinking companions; in this case Ed L., Louie, Ted Ranck and—of course—Ferd Coleman were called the Moral Lepers' Club. "As to my recent [October 21, 1928] sojourn in Williamsport, I am convinced that I got all out of it that I could, and if I spent more time there than was needed, the enjoyment of being with you and Ed and Louie and Ted was worth something. God a'mighty, I wish I could spend a Saturday night's heavy drinking with the Moral Lepers again!"[12]

On December 9, 1928, Piper noted: "Will Rogers says that the reason the country went Republican was that the people thought that it was better to have the Prohibition Law ignored by a party that had some experience at it. Not bad, eh?"[13]

On March 3, 1929, Piper wrote: "I will be in Williamsport on the 12th, as planned. I don't know how I'll spend the afternoon, but I will be with you for the meeting of the Story-Tellers' Club that evening. I would suggest that the reunion of the Moral Lepers' Club be held the same evening, either at your office or at Ted Ranck's apartment, as I may be extremely busy the next evening....

"And tomorrow, that unspeakable [Herbert Hoover] that you helped to elect will climb up into the chair hallowed by Washington, Jefferson, Adams, Jackson and Lincoln! Merde! I damn near hope the Federal boys get your bootlegger and shut the liquor off on you!"[14]

On July 23, 1929, Piper wrote about one of his blackouts: "I arrived home safely and soberly, albeit I had something of a hangover from Saturday night. This cleared up for the most part before noon, however. Strange thing; I had only one drink of whiskey and one of beer, a beverage that I had heretofore condemned as being of no account, yet I had a first-class souse and, I am informed, I was under the impression that I was the devil and was laughing at the rest of the crowd because they were all damned. A good time was had by all."[15]

On October 15, 1931, Piper wrote:

Last weekend I caught a devil of a heavy cold which turned to grippe, and I am just beginning to wade out of it. Went out Saturday night on a binge to a shanty some thirty miles from town, rode home in the dawn's early light in an accursed rumble-seat, caught an hour's sleep on the library coach and then went out again to our hunting camp along with my father and several other chaps at eight Sunday morning. I worked like a horse handling saw-logs and big rocks—the latter in a modern version of the ancient Nippenose Valley pastime of building a stone fence — got myself sweated up and then chilled off. Result, a hell of a cold in the chest. God's vengeance on drinking, fornicating and Sabbath-breaking, I suppose.

... Drop in some time, when you feel yourself able. I have a ten-gallon keg of grape wine on the make in the cellar now, and expect later on to stew a raisin-mash and augment it with a keg of raisin-jack, so that we will be in a position to dispense the real old time hospitality.[16]

By the late 1920s, the Moral Lepers metamorphosed into the Unholy Trinity. The first mention of the Unholy Trinity in "The Early Letters" (H. Beam Piper, Ferd Coleman and Ted Ranck) occurs on May 10, 1930, and refers to a photograph probably taken at Piper's birthday on the March 22 in Altoona: "I received the pictures, which I thought were very good, particularly the one of the 'Unholy Trinity.' When I get the ones in my camera developed, I'll send them on."[17]

Piper was a lifelong hard drinker and alcohol aficionado. Whether or not he was an alcoholic is a matter of conjecture; although, if he hadn't crossed the line, he was certainly straddling it. Interestingly enough, there is no mention of his alcohol consumption in the diaries he kept in the later years when his money problems went from serious to catastrophic. However, in a telephone conversation, Mike Knerr told me that when he "cleaned out" Beam's apartment, he found an entire hall closet full of empty Myers's Rum bottles.[18] Alcohol was as much a part of Piper's life as gunpowder, pipe tobacco and typewriter ribbons.

Don Coleman has this to say about his expertise with alcoholic beverages:

Actually, when it came down to the subject of booze, Beam was a real judge of the stuff, as affirmed in "The Early Letters." No one around today seems to know or recall his "rookie" year or whether he really started with Square Number One! Truly in the 1950s, he could be considered a connoisseur; he would orate the origin of, as well as savor any type or classification of whiskey known to man ... black rum continued to be his working-at-the-desk favorite. He also improved a concoction that proved to be a standout with the imbibing bunch, when relaxing with "family" and friends. He called it the "Katinka."

When I asked for the ingredients, Beam pulled out his multi-colored ink pen and a small scratch

The "Unholy Trinity" is portrayed in this framed picture that hung on the knotty pine wall of Ferd Coleman's den and portrays the inseparable trio, Ferd Coleman, Ted Ranck and H. Beam Piper, among the trees of McElhattan in autumn. This particular 1930 photograph of Piper is unique in that he is sans mustache (courtesy Coleman Family).

pad from his inside coat pocket. (As anyone knows who is familiar with the late H. Beam Piper, he was never without paper. And this particular pen he possessed, regardless of its worth, was one of his most valued treasures — less the antiques.) In giving me the recipe, he printed four lines of instructions, each with a different color ... black, blue, red and green:

    3 parts Vodka
    2 parts Apricot Brandy
    1 part Grenadine
    STIR over ice ... DO NOT SHAKE!

This conglomeration would then be strained into a brandy snifter. For years, this "Technicolor" recipe was a part of my wallet. I have gone through many billfolds, just as new automobiles, and somewhere along the way, this folded up little slip of paper has passed into oblivion. But the memory of the recipe lives on.

On one occasion, I dropped into the City Hotel lounge with Beam in downtown Williamsport, and becoming comfortable at the recently renovated bar — with the fork of his cane hanging over his forearm — he would ask for a "Katinka." I remember turning to him dubiously and remarking, "This guy wouldn't know a 'Katinka' anymore than he'd know what he had for supper last Tuesday!"

"Oh HELL!" Beam burst. "Tommy's been mixin' 'em for some time now!"

The year was 1957 and Beam would properly appraise the going rate of his creation "in the vicinity of seventy-five cents."[19]

In a few cases, Piper's binges got completely out of hand; for example, John McGuire Jr. tells a story of when his father was called by the Altoona police and told that his help was

This 1952 photograph finds the "Unholy Trinity" seated at the Republican Club in Williamsport, imbibing at will in their personal pleasures. This is their last group photo (courtesy Coleman Family).

needed at the Piper residence. Since Anne was not at home, Jack elected to take the boy with him. They rode over and found a small crowd.

Piper had barricaded the first floor of the apartment stairway with chairs, furniture and boxes. His small brass cannon was mounted on top of the barricade. A group of policemen were trying to keep a growing crowd back and out of range of the cannon. One of the policemen who knew Beam and Jack told him that Beam claimed he was a Confederate officer making a last stand.

Jack arrived with little John Jr. in tow; Beam asked, "What are you doing here, Johnny?"

"Tryin' to talk you down, Cap'n."

"What for?"

"The War's over, Cap'n. Time to go home."

"It was a good fight. Damn Lee and Roundtree!"

Eventually, Jack was able to talk him down and took Beam and his small cannon back to the apartment. They had a few drinks and left when Beam passed out in the writing room.[20]

Alcoholism is an obsession of the mind and an allergy of the body, and once in its grip an alcoholic will do damn near anything to get their next drink. Piper was aware of the pitfalls of drinking as evidenced by these comments by the protagonist, Jack Holloway — who comes closest to mirroring Piper of any of his characters — in *Little Fuzzy* after Little Fuzzy (a small furry alien) leaves Jack to find his family:

Maybe the little fellow ran into something too big for him, even with his fine new weapon — a hobthrush, or a bush-goblin, or another harpy. Or maybe he'd just gotten tired staying in one place, and had moved on.

He'd liked it here. He'd had fun, and been happy. He shook his head sadly. Once he, too, had lived in a pleasant place, where he'd had fun, and could have been happy if he hadn't thought there was something he'd had to do. So he had gone away, leaving grieved people behind him....

He started for the kitchen to get a drink, and checked himself. Take a drink because you pity yourself, and then the drink pities you and has a drink, and then two good drinks get together and that calls for drinks all around. No; he'd have one drink, maybe a little bigger than usual, before he went to bed.[21]

Like a lot of the writing crowd in the 1950s, including most of the science fiction crew, Piper was a hard drinker. In his early years, Ernest Hemingway was a role model for many. A number of those hard drinkers later died of alcoholism; Randall Garrett and Bill Tuning come to mind, both acquaintances of Beam's. We know Piper suffered from depression — or the "blue devils," his code word — and loved to imbibe. There is no doubt that it added to his depression and possibly contributed to his suicide.

CHAPTER 5

The Deer Stalkers

I do enjoy hunting and, as you know, I am rarely without a firearm of some sort or other in the woods. Yet that does not put me in the same class as these men who can see nothing in the woods but game to be killed, any more than my fondness for good liquor puts me in the same class with a town drunkard or my fondness for biological recreation puts me in the same class with a man whose whole life centers about his genito-urinary system.[1]

— H. Beam Piper

H. Beam Piper had a love affair with guns that started in school and never ended. He had an extensive knowledge of antiquarian arms. In the *Pennsy* "Typewriter 'Killer'" article, he explains the origin of his interest: "'I was fourteen, and the Fourth of July was coming up, I wanted to make as much noise as I could for my money, and I decided that percussion caps and powder were better than ordinary blanks, so I got the catalogue of a New York gun dealer and bought a .44 caliber Civil War percussion revolver for $4.85.' This not only made a satisfying noise, but started him reading about old weapons, buying them, trading them."[2]

Piper quickly became an expert on firearms, especially antiques. He used this knowledge to amass a wonderful collection of antique guns, daggers and swords for rather modest prices. In this May 20, 1928, letter to Ferd Coleman, he displayed his growing passion for collecting antique firearms:

My last letter to you was, I fear, somewhat sketchy, due to the fact that I was in a goddam hurry to get into town and out again to see a yokel who had — had, not has — an old gun and powder-horn. The said gun and powder-horn are on the wall, where I may feast my eyes upon them as I write this. The gun is an extremely good lady's Kentucky rifle, the only one of the sort I ever saw. It is to be identified as a lady's rifle by the fact that the stock is so short and narrow as to make it difficult for a full-grown man to use it, as well as by its extreme lightness.

It weighs barely five and three-quarter pounds and the butt is only fourteen inches in length, from butt-plate to trigger, and three-and-a-half inches wide at its widest part. The rifle is absolutely plain, without even a patchbox, stocked in curley maple (a mighty nice piece of wood, too, finely grained and polished and without any very noticeable defects) and, sad to relate, it has no maker's stamp. I suppose, however, that it is of Pennsylvania origin. Condition, damned fine, almost as new except for a little pitting on the outside of the barrel at the breech. The powder-horn is apparently original with the gun, nicely age-colored and scraped so thin as to be almost transparent — you can see the powder in it when you hold it up to a strong light. All this for $3.50. I wonder what fair lady owned it once.[3]

As with most avid collectors, Piper also enjoyed the hunt: "By the way, I'm on the trail of a rifle made by George Harder, though not one of the rare Harder's Patent Breech-Loaders. More in a day or so."[4]

One of the issues that vitally concerned H. Beam Piper was the "right to bear arms," as noted in this June 2, 1927, letter to Ferd Coleman. "I have been backward about writing, but I must plead to being busy as hell. The State Legislature is trying to pass a damned rotten law restricting the 'sale, use, ownership and possession of firearms and other deadly weapons' and I've been rather busy stirring up sentiment against it, writing to Representatives, etc. The bill — it's know as the Salus Bill, File of the Senate No. 7 — is one of the most grotesque pieces of legislature idiocy ever produced, even in the United States, and that gang of half-wits down there at Harrisburg are loco enough to pass it, if something's not done."

He went on to outline the bill that would have prohibited the sale of blackjacks, daggers, dirks— even camper's knives— no firearm without a license. "This law, if the fools make a law of it, will be a hell of a thing. The crooks will get all the pistols they want by the bootleg process and the honest man won't have any means of protection. It will increase crime 75 percent if it is passed. And such a damned injustice!

"Well, you give this thing hell in your great organ of public opinion and I'll bless you the longest day you live."[5]

Ferd Coleman was a pacifist, unlike his friend H. Beam Piper. This only pushed Piper harder in his attempts to "convert" Ferd into a fellow gun enthusiast. After Ferd was assaulted by a hitchhiker in May of 1927, Piper went into high gear: "You were talking about getting yourself a gat. I recommend a .32 or .38 Colt 'Police Positive,' on a 4-inch barrel. The cost is $27.50. This may seem like a hell of a price, but if you get anything cheaper, it will be liable to shoot at both ends and the middle, and even if it won't blow up, you will not be able to hit the broad side of a freight train with it."[6]

Piper's determined assault finally paid off, and Ferd began collecting antique firearms. Don Coleman writes: "Numerous telephone conversations transpired between he [Ferd] and Piper, sometimes on a daily basis and normally originating from the *Shoppers' Guide* office."[7]

In response to Coleman's request for a historical portrait of the famed Kentucky Rifle, Piper replied:

> I'm afraid it will take a damsite more than a "line" to inform you as to the characteristics of the Kentucky rifle, but I'll try to do it without writing a book about it.
>
> The Kentucky rifle came into use about 1710 or '15, and was evolved from the heavy German rifle. The first of these latter were probably introduced by Germans who came to Pennsylvania shortly after Penn's first colonization, but they were found to be unsuited to conditions here, and a new type was developed.
>
> From the first, the Kentucky rifle —few if any of which were ever made in Kentucky, by the way — had certain marked differences from any other type of arm. They were extremely long, being for the most part over fifty inches in length and often over five feet. As they were loaded with an undersized ball on a greased patch most of them were fitted with a box in the stock, to contain grease, usually tallow, and patches of home spun linen or, sometimes, buckskin. The stock was almost always the full length of the gun, and they were usually stocked with curley maple, although other woods such as beech, black walnut, chestnut, or black oak or cherry were used. All my own Kentuckies are stocked in curley maple, and most of Col. Shoemakers.' Before 1800, the ornamentation ran mostly to life designs, but after, conventional designs were frequently used. Of course, the ornamentation depended on the individual gunsmith. Some were works of art, like my long Tryon rifle, which you saw when you were here, and others were the crudest weapons imaginable.
>
> As to their possibilities, they were capable of very deadly work. Up to a hundred yards they would, in competent hands, shoot true within a few inches, and had an exceptional high velocity, considering the ammunition used (between 1,500 and 2,000 foot-seconds). I've done some really good shooting with my own Kentucky rifles.
>
> At the Battle of New Orleans, Jackson had about 4,000 men, half of whom were armed with these rifles, against Packenham's 10,000, armed with smooth-bore Army muskets. When the battle was over, Jackson reported losing six killed and seven wounded. As the Ouija-board had not been invented then, Packenham was unable to make any report, but his successor reported a loss of over

2,000, killed and wounded. The reason for this almost unbelievable disparity was that the British were mowed down by rifle fire before they could come within musket range of Jackson's forces. The Kentucky rifle was, as you can see, about two hundred years in advance of any other firearm in use at the time.

As to the accessories that went with the rifle, they consisted of a powder horn, a bullet pouch, a bullet mould and, with flintlock rifles, a smaller horn for priming powder. The horn was usually an ordinary cow's horn, drilled at the tip and furnished with a plug at either end.[8]

This is followed by a discussion of current prices for Kentucky rifles at amounts that would make today's gun collectors drool.

Coleman got the collecting bug, as his next letter indicates: "Purchased several more artillery pieces or whatever you call them. Wish to hell, however, you would get here to appraise this stuff, because if it chances to be junk I am financially out of luck. One of the pieces I bought is a gun, not a flintlock, but the other style. I haven't had time to study your technical appendage to your letter. This gun holds two shots like the double-shot rare one you showed me in your collection last Saturday. Wonder what they're worth and also wonder whether I should buy a flintlock which is offered me for $10.00. The chief doubt I have as to the intrinsic value of my gun collection arises in the fact that all my stuff is dirty and I remember your admonitions thereto."[9]

Piper replied: "As to the ten-dollar flintlock, I must be excused from pronouncing judgment. It is difficult, even for 'Altoona's local antiquarian' to appraise a gun on such meager description and at such a distance. As you are not fully interested in having your arms in perfect condition, I would say, buy it if it is still in one piece."[10]

Gun collecting was one of Piper's passions, and in this letter we learn about his own gun collection: "My own collection has been at a standstill since I acquired that combination rifle-and-shotgun (by underhanded means, to be confessed) of which I told you in my last letter. How is your own progressing? I will certainly give it the once-over when I arrive at Williamsport and appraise the arms. The other objects I am no authority whatever. I rejoice to hear that you have seen the light about the condition of your plunder.

As I have always maintained, it must be in as near as practicable to the condition it was when in actual use. Besides, I'll want to show you some of my new prizes, the ones I told you about in my last letter, a little powder-flask I just obtained day before yesterday and a flintlock musket which I am ordering tonight."[11]

As with most hobbies, Piper's collecting interests grew over time: "I recently — as recently as Friday night — came into possession of a Smith & Wesson .44 Schofield model revolver, now quite rare. Like my long Jersey Shore shotgun musket, its front sight has been sawed out of a coin by one of its earlier owners and it is said to have a blood-chilling history, having been used in Texas and New Mexico in the Indian and cattle-war days. That is, I'll admit, a deviation from my purpose of maintaining an exclusively Pennsylvanian collection, but I got it for nothing."[12]

As this June 24, 1929, letter illustrates, Piper was a very savvy collector: "I recently made another trade with young Reinheimer, giving him that old ivory handled dagger, which was in rather poor order and had a cracked handle, for a very nice old English percussion shotgun, in fine order. After I got it, I found on it the name of an old man who had, long ago, been a photographer in Altoona and whom my father had known. The knife was quite old and of considerable artistic merit, but you know how my notions about condition almost amount to fanaticism, and it was in *poor* shape. Yours for Atheism, Anarchy and Adultery, Beam."[13]

Piper also enjoyed the company of other weapons enthusiasts, as this letter of August

19, 1929, shows: "While my gun collection will be an old story to you and the major, Ted has only seen the relatively few pistols that I have carried at one time or another when I've been down to Williamsport, and he, not sharing your pacifist delusion, will be keenly interested in them and will want to spend some time looking them over. In that way, Ted and I can have a gun-cranks' orgy in my gunroom without cutting in on the time we will all want to spend together."[14]

On October 15, 1930, Piper wrote to Ferd, regarding a piece he'd written for him:

Enclosed is the article for the Historical Edition [*Shoppers' Guide*]. I happened to remember that Dillin illustrates and describes the Covenhoven rifles in his Kentucky Rifle and, knowing the limited circulation of that book, I doubt if there is a copy in Lycoming County. I have the only copy in Blair County, for example, as I know all the historians and arms collectors here and none of the others have it. Therefore, such a minute description of the arm would be fresh stuff about a man whom the West Branch Valley has neglected shamefully, considering all he did for it. God damn it, he saved the whole valley, and you haven't even named an alley in the cat-house district after him!

And, as I say, he was around Jaysburg some of the time, so he'd fit in all right with your edition. His arms, with the exception of the stiletto were typical. And I wonder that nobody who's seen the dagger has tumbled to the trade-mark idea. I think I'll do a short story with that as a basis. I'll tell you when I get it down.[15]

Piper also had a strong passion for the outdoors and spent much of his free time, when not writing, camping, hiking and hunting. He learned much of his woodlore and hunting skills from his father, Herbert, an avid outdoorsman. It's also quite likely that he was introduced to Colonel Shoemaker, the well-known folklorist and outdoors man, by his father.

Their shared love of the outdoors and the Pennsylvania countryside was one of the bonds that cemented the friendship of Piper and Ferd Coleman. As Don Coleman puts it in his preface to "The Early Letters,"

Both men loved the mountains where rambling forests and gentle streams were real, and where wild game flourished with grandeur. Nearly 100 miles of mountainous beauty lies between these two communities [Altoona and Williamsport] to which both would generally rendezvous in little-known locales to the world, such as the likes of Jersey Shore, Mount Union, McElhattan, or Loyalsock Creek....

You have to imagine a lush foliage of mountainous grace extending to the right and left, and north and south of every footpath these antiquarians trod. If one can visualize a cabin on the hillside, smoking at the chimney, with two or three cords of firewood stacked in back; a two-holer outhouse located back yonder the trees; a trickling run or stream that would eventually pour its little self into somewhere along the West Branch of the Susquehanna River; and an old clay-topped road winding down the hill from the cabin and ultimately connecting with macadam ... in this setting, any human male likely seen, would invariably be attired in knickers and knee-socks.[16]

Young Piper had many friends. Primary among them — other than Ferd and the colonel — were Major Cooper, another avid outdoorsman, Phil Krause and Eddie Schock. Many times they would go hunting together or on hikes and outings.

Much of the correspondence between the two friends was taken up by itineraries and camping plans, as well as other mundane subjects. But in a November 17, 1926, letter, Piper was making a determined effort to cultivate his new friendship with Ferd and revealed his inner self in a way that he would never do later in life:

In your letter today, you complain that I have charged the owners of the cabin with being interested only in the woods as a place for the massacre of game and, in the same letter, I have stated that I was about to take up my more or less trusty fowling piece and set out in search of the highly elusive cottontail. In this, you appear to detect a trifling inconsistency. Permit me, then, to point out to you that you are in logical error.

I said, and still say, that the said cabin-owners are interested only in the woods from the first of

November to the fifteenth of December and then only in the pursuit and assassination of our little friends in fur and feathers, as the sentimentalists have it. I am not. I go into the woods in closed season and with no intention of hunting whatsoever. When I do hunt, I am keenly alive to the beauties of nature as you are. In fact, I have more than once lost game because I was too busy gaping at some distant mountain. I do enjoy hunting and, as you know, I am rarely without a firearm of some sort or other in the woods. Yet that does not put me in the same class as these men who can see nothing in the woods but game to be killed, any more than my fondness for good liquor puts me in the same class with a town drunkard or my fondness for biological recreation puts me in the same class with a man whose whole life centers about his genito-urinary system.

I think your idea about going into camp some time in early January is a good one. We will, to be sure, want to celebrate the anniversary of our Lord and Savior's unbegotten birth in the immemorial manner, with turkey, little-pig-roast-whole-with-an-apple-in-its-mouth, stewed oysters, plum pudding, etc., etc. This cannot be done properly in a cabin in the mountains....

Write again soon and, if you find any flaws in my arguments, present your rebuttal. You entertain certain views, at variance with my own, about hunting. Let's hear why you are so averse to shooting and eating a squirrel or a deer that would die a natural death anyhow and so go to waste. If we cannot conduct a gentlemanly argument by word of mouth, let us do it on paper.[17]

Despite his fascination with guns, Piper was more an outdoorsman than hunter. In this December 1927 letter, he admits to not having killed his first deer. "As to that deer-hunt which we were to make — but did not — I did not know from one day to another whether I could make it or not. I had hopes that I could and until those hopes were definitely dispelled, I didn't write. I was sorry, for I feel sure that I could have bagged a deer — it would have been my first — in such good hunting ground as the South slope of White Deer Mountain is. Krause and I counted some forty there last March. However, that's ancient history now. Maybe next season."[18]

Still, Piper didn't mind pointing out Ferd's inconsistency about killing animals. "We can, I think, go to a cabin in the woods. I know your attitude on the killing of game — it does not, I recall, extend to the killing of kine and swine in a slaughter-house — but Stan, I do not think, would object to shooting a squirrel or rabbit. Advise him, therefore, to procure a license. If he does not have a .22 or a shotgun, I think I might be able to furnish one for him, though my modern small-game arms are not many and he may be compelled to use a muzzle-loader. In this way, we may be able to vary the monotony of our fare with fresh game."[19]

Piper was quite the hiker and on more than one occasion was enlisted for surveying duty. "I'll be in Williamsport on Tuesday afternoon, as I have finished with my work surveying the Skyline Trail and am on my way home. I don't know whether or not you got my letter from two weeks ago, as I wrote one for you and then tore off leaving it on my desk at home. Since, I have been in the wilds and the few letters that I managed to send out were all either to my parents or to the men backing me. In the meantime, I'll be busy here, but I will stop off to see the dear brothers, yourself included, on the way back home, and tell you about my adventures in the mountains."[20]

Paul M. Schuchart, an old friend, tells us more about this survey:

One time, before I got married in 1929, Beam was asked by Dr. Darlington (I'm not sure), the Episcopal Bishop of the Harrisburg Diocese to mark the Appalachian Trail from the western side of the Susquehanna River to the Maryland State line, sleeping on the Trail and making like a real "outdoor man." Wanting to help Beam and in the event he might run into some snakes, I got him a bottle of Good Bourbon.

Those were the days when I had a bachelor apartment on the North 3rd Street in Harrisburg, consisting of a living room a bedroom and a bath, with a long bathtub, not a shower. When Beam got back, with about half of the bottle left, he was soaking in the tub. What he had left just about filled up a water glass. About that time, the colored girl, who kept the place "clean," came. Beam didn't like the idea of being "inspected" lying in the tub by a girl. The girl told Beam "not to worry" about that and to Beam's disgust, after carrying that bourbon miles and miles, the girl drank all that whiskey. He never forgave that girl and waited until I got married and lived in a house before he showed up again.[21]

One thing Ferd and Beam did not share in common was the love of motorized vehicles. Piper never owned a car, while Ferd owned several. In this July 10, 1929, letter, Ferd wrote: "The 20th is the raftsmen's reunion and also the date for our mammoth Montoursville airport dedication at which many, many air-minded celebrities of this mighty nation will be in attendance. The reunion comes once a year, this ceremony never again; therefore, a lover of spectacle, I think I shall attend the air maneuvers, in which army planes will race, stunts will be done, and what have you."[22]

Piper's reply on July 15, 1929, fairly bristled: "Sorry no end you don't find it convenient to be up to Shoemaker's for the reunion. Of course, you're twenty-one and in your right mind, so you know whether you want to take in the airport celebration or the reunion, but you're making the wrong argument when you say that you can see the reunion any year and the airport celebration only when it happens. Those raftsmen aren't going to live very damn long, while aviation spectacles will continue and get bigger and more spectacular every year."[23]

CHAPTER 6

The Unholy Duo

To get down upon one's shinbones and ask this force, which may not even exist, to lend aid in selling a horse or winning a war — the one is about as paltry as the other — has always seemed to me to be the most idiotic thing that a putatively reasoning animal is capable of. And to stand behind a pulpit and proclaim that this force — familiarly nicknamed God Almighty — is in favor of this silly thing and opposed violently to that —! I wonder if a mud turtle could be guilty of such a thing. I doubt it. Is it a wonder that the rev. clergy are invariably such pathetic dumm-kopfs?[1]

— H. Beam Piper

Both Ferd Coleman and H. Beam Piper, in the free-thinking spirit of the Twenties, questioned not only politics but social conventions. On August 2, 1928, Piper wrote: "I have definitely made up my mind to come down to Williamsport on the 25th, at the very latest, and, of course, I will want a room of some sort, the cheapest the best, though I *must* have two things— privacy and a place wherein I may shit and bathe after some fashion. Although I prefer a room on a second floor over a store or some similar place where I can 'royster' and carouse on Saturday nights, I will be willing to forego that and take quarters with a private family, provided they be able to mind their own goddamn business and do not object to the late and irregular hours which my studious and Bohemian life will make necessary."[2]

In the earliest letter of the Piper-Coleman correspondence, written August 26, 1926, Piper (at age 22) explained his view on God to his new friend and intellectual fellow traveler, Ferd Coleman:

To my Fellow Agnostic,

... The belief in the existence of a supreme being — a God, in other words — is really unnecessary. This supreme being, in fact cannot exist, for there are certain things which are absolutely impossible. The creation of matter, the making of something out of nothing, is one of them. The fact that there are impossibilities absolutely proves there cannot be a supreme being, for a supreme being knows no impossibility. All things are possible to him, or, rather, to it.

Now, this God — I use the word to designate this quasi-supreme being because it is short and easy to write, not because I mean the familiar Christian Deity — this God, being unable to create, can do nothing more than arrange matter from one form to another. What I would ask is: is this necessary? And what proof, if any, is there that any such arranging has been or is being done? It is my contention that the universe has existed, from infinite time past, in the same form as it exists now and that it will so continue to exist for infinite time in the future, if there is such a thing as time.

In other words, all matter is eternal. As planets and suns grow old and waste away and turn to dust, that dust becomes the nebular basis of other suns and planets. Nowhere in the world proceedings is there a real need for a creative, or, rather, arranging agent. There might be one for all I know, but if there is, it is no more worthy of worship than the Law of Gravitation or the Law of Evolution. It is simply part of the cosmos, even as we are.[3]

Coleman, who welcomed the passion of Piper's thoughts and ideas, was warming to Piper as a kindred spirit:

... I am sincere, Beam, when I write I enjoyed your letter so much. I think it should not be difficult for you to know why, since nuts or pioneer souls, as you will, like yourself and me, are difficult to discover, with the alternative that such associates as I tolerate are quite commonplace, and, as to letters I receive few, and those of no consequence. One brave friend I have learned since spring, however (now for God's sake be quiet) and that's a woman — of Brooklyn, N.Y. Circumstances have thrown her into Williamsport, but, by all the oaths of Thor, she has been a marvelous stimulant to me. Though emotion plays an indirect yet definite part, her chief charm is total debunkation, avoidance of morons, excessive intelligence, a feeling for Literature and associate arts, and (now it's your turn) a grim agnostic bordering on atheism. She is devoid of convention, and — she is engaged in marriage to a Brooklyn cartoonist. So you see, Beam, I know I have not violated the faith that I shall maintain your friendship.

And, though I am intensely interested in her, she is largely a mental joy and I suppose shall pass as others have gone. Since your letter was practically impersonal I allowed her to read it, and she fairly gloats over your theistic reasoning.[4]

Appalachia in the 1920s and '30s was considered part of the Bible Belt, and there was a lot of social pressure to be a church fearin' man. Beam and Ferd, to a lesser extent, reveled in their war against mindless Christianity. Nothing incensed Piper more than a Bible thumper taking his platform into the public arena of politics. In a September 19, 1926, letter, he wrote:

Have you had any more tilts with those holy orders lately? If so, let me hear the latest news from the battlefront. I devoutly wish that you were here in Altoona, to take a fall out of some of our pulpit thumpers. God wot, they need it. They have just succeeded in a long and bitter jihad against the local filles de joi and our bordello district is now given over to the bat and owl, a circumstance causing deep and widespread regret. Crucifixion is too mild, by far, a fate for such fiends incarnate.

This despicable victory has made the men of God hereabout big-bellied and stiff-necked. They are quite puffed up about it. Weekly they rant to the gaping throngs of morons, telling them all about the New Jerusalem and the Lake of Fire and Brimstone, while the poor whores are hard put to it to get three square meals and a flop. A hell of a note!

At the risk of being mistaken for a high-toned English butler I subscribe myself,

Your brother in Christ, H. Beam Piper
Long Live the Royalist Party![5]

Ferd was having some problems with the local Newberry ministry and received Piper's wholehearted support in this letter: "I was considerably amused at the account of your war with the local Jesus-brokers, who seem to be a rather swinish lot."[6] On November 13, he added, "I'm glad to hear that you have enlarged your great organ of public opinion. Evidently the local Jesus-brokers and salvation-smiths didn't fulfill their threat of putting the curse on you after all. Keep up the good fight and double-charge your guns with grapeshot. I sincerely wish you were here to engage our Altoona prelates in battle. They are a rotten bunch, all in all. As bad or worse than that gang in Williamsport."[7]

On November 30, 1928, Piper wrote: "I certainly wish I could have been with you and Ted and Fred and, the ladies, and even more do I wish I could have accompanied you ... to the Elks' auditorium to hear [Clarence] Darrow, for whom I have a sincere if not wholly undiluted admiration. I daresay the local Gantries (or is it Gantrys), including Sassaman and the bellicose and armigerous Daugherty, were none too well pleased at this invasion of Williamsport by the Antichrist, and I suppose that sermons on the text of 'the fool saith in his heart, there is not God' will be flying thick and fast in a vain effort to re-take lost ground."[8]

Over the years, Piper grew increasingly intolerant of the local "Jesus brokers," as he called them. "I was a pall-bearer for an atheist friend Thursday last, and fell heir to a nice 1822 model musket. Some goddam Gantry crashed the funeral and engaged in a long-winded prayer and sermon, and rather than cause an unpleasant disturbance, this sonofabitch was permitted to rant unchecked. Hijo de puta!"[9]

Piper was even involved with trying to remove a pastor from the Llyswen church. "Here's more on the attempt on ex-cathedraling the local pastor: The drive to get rid of the pastor at our local church goes on apace. The preacher is beginning to see the writing on the wall, I think, and he is talking about expelling some of the malcontents, my father among them, from the church. Excommunication, anathema and all that sort of thing. If he does, he won't be able to make it stick and will only make the south end of a north-bound horse out of himself, so let him, say we."[10]

In this March 29, 1927, letter to Ferd, Piper re-evaluated his religious stand: "I begin to doubt that 'agnostic' is my proper designation instead of 'atheist.' Not that my opinions are changing, but that I am beginning to understand the two terms better. An atheist, as I see it is a man who denies the existence of a personal and personified God. This I do deny, and with all vigor. Whether or not there is a central creative force, I cannot say. If that be agnosticism, then I am an agnostic, but I don't think it is. An agnostic, again my idea of it, is a man who neither denies nor affirms the existence of a personified God. What's your idea on it?"[11]

This letter got an immediate reply from Ferd:

My Dear Agnostic,

I have received your missive (I was going to say missile because they are generally so well-placed and meaningful) just an hour ago, 6:00 P.M. eastern standard, relatively speaking, cock-eyed as all things in turn are cock-eyed in this relative world — because man's perspective is wholly relative; and I have decided to answer same as best I can at once, first because there's nothing to write about, making all the stronger reason for wanting the abstract obligation off my shoulders, and secondly because my damnable commercial life demands as a rule prompt replies in order to avoid too much accumulation of correspondence.

I have received a delightful note from the Major wherein he told me of your belated return to Altoona, but he neglected to inform me, likely because he did not fully know, of the travail and tribulations which beset your return journey.

In the circumstances I do not blame the motorist one God damned bit for not offering you a lift or even acceding to your request. You will find my reasons for this attitude by easy inference if you will take the time to read an account of myself after I left you and the Major that bright Sunday afternoon of early Spring, as the budding poets might sing.... Jesus Christ the thought of that experience still invades my usual temperamental calm.... Said account will be round in the Mar. 24th (already sent you) and Mar. 31 issues of the *Shoppers' Guide*; therein you will learn of the dime-novel I lived in sixty minutes' human time.

When you have read same I want you to write me telling me what your reactions are to the same and also to my new theory on the issue. The one point to remember is that I picked up a youth whom next day, after all the fracas, I learned had escaped but four hours earlier from the Huntingdon Reformatory. After I had driven him for three hours, a mean distance of some eighty miles, he contrived to get me to stop the car, socked me over the head with a large stone, and, succeeding in getting me out of the car, was going to make away with the machine when fortunately I overtook him again, following which there was melodrama, etc....

Within a half hour of the possibly-fatal tragedy, later recorded in Williamsport, Bellefonte, Philadelphia and Harrisburg papers, through Associated Press dispatches, my reaction was something like this: "That poor son of a cuckold is ignorant, he knows not the Golden Rule (not the Christian) but of the broadminded man, and, unfortunate, blinded being that he is, if he so earnestly requires assistance from his fellow humans, were he to solicit me again this minute, would I find him, I would give him a ride."

Some minutes after this, the culprit by great, good fortune, was apprehended and — to proceed, various findings have contributed to my fund in indicating to me how aggravating and dangerous the incident really was, I then suffered a direct turn of temperament, madly believing that no form of punishment was too severe for him. But it was here that reason left me and the primeval brute asserted itself for a brief span.

Because, a day or two later, with most of the nervousness and attendant anxiety gone, I considered this final statement: "That bum is truly unfortunate, but that, I think, is no fault of his, since he is apparently incapable of caring for himself. Society is the greatest factor in his life. In incarcerating him, society did not properly care for him and develop him into a useful citizen. Had other tactics been used, and I admit an inability to find a solution to this problem, it is likely his entire outlook on life and the living of it have been different, but soured against all, as is natural in his circumstances, it is to be supposed that he would be controlled by any influences his distorted mind might suggest." And so on.

I think I have told you before, regarding the status of atheism and agnosticism, wherein I stated that atheism is in truth a certain, definite adherence to the meager theory that there is no personal God. To my mind, this idea is a little one since it is so confined in the sense that it recognizes no supreme power functioning in the form of a glorified human being, containing brain, nose, ass and other members; no person with a sense of cosmic values could dare to set aside this truth. But this is all atheism concerns. Agnosticism, on the other hand, is damned nearly poetically beautiful, if it wouldn't be so concrete in its major theory that man in his essence is incapable of solving the universal riddle.

Indirectly, agnosticism embraces a principle of an Oriental religion wherein it is stated that no philosophy is greater than the philosopher, no building is greater than the contractor who conceived it, no *Shoppers' Guide* is greater than its editor, and similar disproportions; and, emanating from a great religion this principle smacks of the humanities containing in its entirety conclusions arrived at through human reasoning. In other words, though far from an intelligent despair-er, the agnostic fundamentally acknowledges incompetence to entirely arrive at definite conclusions anent the puzzle. Therefore, old scout, I would not meanly name you a narrow atheist, who, though not as bad as a blind deist, is frequently an unthinking fellow; but I shall greet you always as agnostic, a great word, literally translated as "unknowing."[12]

Piper replied:

I read with considerable interest the first installment of your parlous adventure on the highway, and I am postponing suicide only because I have not as yet read the second. I gather that the passenger that you took on mutinied, slogged you over the head, and tried to seize the ship, but that you vanquished him — by violence, perhaps? — and recaptured the gas-chariot.

I can fully understand your momentary bile against said mutinous passenger. A lump on the head is not, I have found, conductive to calm and dispassionate thought. I also can sympathize with your later reflections. For my part, I have always thought that the reform-school system was an abuse and that the State would be better off if all the so-called reformatories were blown-up with dynamite. I would gladly aid anyone who had escaped from one of them, but I rather draw the line at being sandbagged. I trust, by the way, that this adventure will show you the advisability of getting a good six-shooter, say, about .38 caliber, learning to use it effectively and carrying it with you on trips of this sort.

I've toted a gat for quite awhile and, though I only had actual need for it once, there's no telling when I may get into a bad jam somewhere, just as you did. True, you extricated yourself without a firearm, but from your account of the affair I should call it a piece of phenomenal luck.

I think you are right in your distinction between atheism and agnosticism. In my general outlook on life, I am an agnostic, but I am an out-and-out atheist when it comes to the question of God. I concede the possibility of an after-life of some sort or another, but there I am an agnostic, "unknowing."

I can't agree that the creator must always be greater than the creature. I ask you, was that half-baked Serbian fanatic who shot off a pistol at Sarajevo in 1914 greater than the war he brought about?[13]

In this letter on February 22, 1928, Ferd replied: "I regret that I cannot pray for you [Beam] in the form of Litanies to the Blessed Virgin, or candle-burning to St. Anthony. You are certainly aware that I no longer have faith. You remember you admire these practices only as beautiful ritual, and despite further learning on my part in future years, because it is a part of the Human Comedy, indulged in by the populace of centuries, I know I shall always esthetically flutter in witness of Catholic ritual, both the mob as well as the stolid priest scenes."[14]

Later in the letter, Ferd added, "I enclose the second annual report of the American Association for the Advancement of Atheism. While of course you know I do not subscribe to all the views expressed therein, it is on the whole as good-provoking as the escape of hot piss. You may wish to send on for a free copy yourself; in any event I should like this one returned."[15]

Piper replied on February 28, 1928:

> Don't burn candles for me to St. Anthony. That canonized cad is as little to my liking as the young man in Shoemaker's story about the rafts that were never floated, and for the same reason. And whilst we speak of matters theologic, I was not greatly impressed by the 4A dope-sheet. I do not belong to any church, and I am not even going to make an exception of the Atheist Church. That appears to be all that this association amounts to. It has foreign missionaries, traveling evangelists, revivals, martyrs, gospel-tracts and an itching palm.
>
> Can't some folks discover that atheism is a state of the mind, like pragmatism, romanticism, hedonism or a preference for blondes, and not a sect or party, like Catholicism, Socialism, Presbyterianism, Royalism, Communism or Republicanism? But, at that, for a man of violence, the post of missionary to the wilds of Arkansas or Texas for this Fling Dung Tong appeals to me. Those lads, skipping through the backwoods, fighting Fundamentalist mobs, passing from town to town between suns and just ahead of the Ku Klux Klan, being fired upon and showered with garbage by the godly, must have an interesting time of it.[16]

By the late 1920s their lives were going in different directions; Ferd was becoming the young Rotarian, while Piper was more and more the rebel and Bohemian. This growing divergence has begun to test the strength of their friendship. In this April 6, 1928, letter, Piper tried to convert the pacifist Coleman:

> I received your letter and if brevity really were the soul of wit, then by my codpiece, your epistle was truly witty. This, however, I do not hold against you, knowing as I do that you are bowed 'neath the Atlas burned of your weekly (not monthly) rag. So I will, from time to time, favor you with such pearls of wisdom as I have to let drop, what time I am not engaged in wrestling with the Muse.
>
> Some ideas concerning violence have occurred to me, and I will set them down, hoping to tempt you into an attempt at refutation.
>
> Violence, know you, is the foundation of civilized society. When a man enters a house to steal, by stealth and in the absence of its tenants, that is not violence. But, should the policeman on the beat observe him in the act and, by clubbing him over the head, subdue him and drag him to the calabozo [sic], that decidedly is violence. It is only be violence and by armed force that civilization is possible.
>
> In the beginning, certain tribes of savages became more proficient in the application of violence, that is, in the art of war, than others. In this way, they were able to gain surcease from the molestation of wild beasts and of other savages, and they were able to capture prisoners, who they put to useful work. Thus began chattel-slavery, the forerunner of capitalism. These tribes, having leisure, due to the fact that they were no longer molested by wild beasts or by other savages, and likewise to the fact that the "dirty work" was done by slaves, were thus able to cultivate the arts and sciences, such as they then were; in other words, were able to develop a more perfect civilization.
>
> All great civilizations of antiquity owed their superiority to armed force, and decayed only when they ceased to be warlike. Egypt succumbed to the more warlike Persians. Persia went under only after the simple and soldierly virtues of her people were destroyed by luxury. Greece went by the same path, and Rome only ceased to resist the barbarians after she had fallen victim to Christianity, then a purely pacifist religion — "and if any smite you on the right cheek, turn him also the left."
>
> Now, after owing its origin to violence, Civilization likewise owes its continued existence to force of arms. By force of arms alone are its rulers secure on their thrones and its unruly element held in check. Force is the sole arbiter of every question, saving only purely academic ones. That is, force will not prove the truth or falsity of the Doctrine of the Transubstantiation, or the Nebular Hypothesis or — the Tennessee Legislature to the contrary notwithstanding — the Darwinian Theory of Evolution.

It will, however, determine whether Alsace and Lorraine belong to France or Germany, or whether Senor Hijo de Puta will be dictator of Honduras or not, or, for that matter, whether or not Slim Clancey will rescue the girl.

I mention this last because of some objections I thought I heard somebody down around Williamsport make. These are decisions of more practical worth, to the disputants, at least, than whether a priest can turn blood into wine, I mean wine into blood, or whether an ape can turn into a man. Violence, I think, once decided who should own a Pontiac car, if I remember rightly. But then, in the words of Eve, why bring that up?

Now, having proved, to my own satisfaction if not yours, that violence is a benign thing — you will certainly agree with me that war is better than religion — I will pass to other and more pertinent matters.[17]

CHAPTER 7

The Old Brick House Beside the River

Well, at any rate, this shipwreck of my dreams admits of some slight salvage. I
gained the inspiration for a novel out of this wretched one-sided love affair and
I picked up some rather good antiques at an extremely moderate figure.[1]
— H. Beam Piper

Among the big surprises of "The Early Letters" are its revelations about Piper's views on the matter of sex and romance. In his later life, Piper was very reticent on the subject and, until his surprise marriage in 1955, was considered by those who knew him to be an archetypical bachelor. As these letters reveal, the Victorian gentleman of the 1950s and '60s was both more earthy and more romantic than anyone ever suspected.

On May 4, 1927, Ferd wrote, "Due to the terrible ejaculations of Major and yourself I have secured that damnably-difficult-titled-3-book series of Francis Rabelais. Will report at this juncture that I enjoy it somewhat better than the Boccaccio's [*Decameron*] but have failed to take extreme delight in either on the grounds that frequently there is too little cause for the dirt. I grovel happily in lust when it is necessitated by a severe pressure of dramatic values, but when employed purely for entertainment purposes about a thousand words at a sitting is enough for me with the sittings far apart. Rabelais, however, has more cause, to my mind, for his stinking assertions than the *Decameron,* consequently I revel in his exploits. I guess I'm at the bottom of the philosophically inclined rather than romantically so."[2]

Piper replies: "So you bought a copy of old Francis, then? I trust that you will find it no worse than the conversation of Major Cooper or myself. But when you say that you do not care for the treatment of sex in Boccaccio because you are more philosophically than romantically inclined, all I have to say is, 'Don't shit the troops!' If you were really philosophically inclined, you would revel in that sort of thing. You are romantic, hence sex is more of a serious matter to you than the huge joke it is to me."[3]

Piper's mentions of sex, much less any writings about said subject, are quite limited, which makes this comment in the midst of a scalding review of *Big Runaway* all the more interesting: "Lastly and worst of all," Beam wrote, "the author seems to take an old-maidish attitude toward sex matters—which he imparts to his characters—that is wholly out of place in the 18th century and is more reminiscent of the Victorian epoch."[4]

Nor were his observations of the fairer sex always complimentary, as this August 25, 1930, letter shows: "That damned split who made all the commotion at the McElhattan bridge about whose lap she would honor with her aristocratic arse in your car gave me a heap big pain, but she's the dumb sort of bitch and nothing better could be expected of her."[5]

In November of 1927, Piper suddenly took interest in a new young lady:

By the way, I have a favor to ask you. As I no doubt told you, I am, to put it mildly, somewhat interested in a certain young lady [Lillian Sheffer] but lately come to Jersey Shore. Now I understand your printing establishment is located in the same town, and you no doubt go there frequently. Would it be too much to ask you to get a line on her for me? You must remember that outside of a few bare facts, I know little about her, and what I do know would be of more value for poetic than other purposes. In time, learn all you can about her, and transmit the facts to me, bringing them up to date from time to time.

Above all, tell me whether or not she has formed any entangling alliances. Anything that you tell me will not only be confidential but sacred, and in turn I must ask you not to let it be known that you are making inquiries on my behalf. If you have conversation with her, you don't even know me unless she mentions me first, which is far from likely. Your friend Glosser knows her, I think, and he may help you out. Do this and I will bless your name forever, for you will have conferred a great favor upon — That wicked and bloody man of violence, BEAM.[6]

Ferd answered: "Regarding the female (in a general sense, of course, damn them.), please be advised that she definitely moved into her place on November 1st, that she carries only a small line, makes no specialty of anything, and moved to J.S. because her parents did so."[7]

From the tone of Piper's reply, it's obvious he was very interested: "I deeply appreciate the information you furnished me anent the former Belle of Bellefonte, although I really fail to see your reason for consigning the (more or less) fair sex to perdition. You never heard *me* talk that way, I'm sure. True, I did say once that I would be perfectly willing to trade any woman in Christendom for a cask of hundred-year port, an Andrea Ferrara rapier or a Kabarda stallion, but since then I've changed my mind. I hereby make formal recantation of that heresy. Or, perhaps, Jersey Shore is to be considered outside of the bounds of Christendom. If so, I am still safe. However, let me exhort you not to confine your reports to her business as I — but perhaps I had best haul up. Suffice it to say that I am not entirely interested in antiques."[8]

In this letter of January 4, 1928, Piper was still fishing for more information on the former Belle of Bellefonte, Miss Sheffer, the proprietress of an antique store. "All of which, by association of ideas, brings up this thought, that perhaps if you were to stop at Miss Sheffer's place of business in Jersey Shore, you might be able to pick up something really good in the line of early Pennsylvania household goods or trinkets. She does not seem to have any specialty, as Glosser does, and the chances are that she might have something that you would want."[9]

Ferd did his best to help his old compadre in his quest, but it appears from this letter of January 29, 1928, that Piper was having little success. "So you, too, oh my comrade, have known the bitter pangs of disappointment by the Tiadaghton. That fatal stream is cursed for us — at least where the ladies are concerned. Howbeit, I will come again at a more propitious time and you can visit Jersey Shore on any night when there is no blizzard."[10]

Come June 6, 1928, Piper was still doing reconnaissance: "Of course, you realize that this trip to Jersey Shore is simply a sort of Cossack raid, several of which I must make for the purpose of reconnaissance and minor harassing before I bring up the heavy guns and settle down to regular siege tactics. Although I cannot hold my ground, I may perhaps damage the outworks of the defense. I trust this military jargon, a la Decimus Saxton, is intelligible."[11]

When Piper didn't receive an answer to his letter, he fired off: "I have as yet received no answer to my last letter.... Let me know very damn pronto if I can see you in Jersey Shore when I arrive, and if so, where. I will, as I say reach Antis Fort at a little after 11:30, and I will not care to go to see her until after 1:30, so we'll have about two hours in which to fraternize."[12]

Once again Piper returned to the Belle of Bellefonte in his October 21, 1928, letter. Reading between the lines, it appears the "lovely lady" had another amour and he was out in the cold. Like a reformed sinner, Piper was as romantic and moonstruck as a teenager with his first crush:

> As to that old brick house within range of Henry Antes' four-pounder that I mentioned in my last letter and the lovely lady who lives there — ah, here's another of those letters that will have to be torn up and burned, alas for posterity — don't think, Fernando, that I've given up hope.
>
> I know, you will say "The fool! He won't be advised by me. Look what heartache he's laying up for himself!" but damnit, I can't ever forget how beautiful she is. As I see it, there's a millionth chance for me — about the chance of a man going out in a canoe to take a frigate of the line — but while that chance remains, I absolutely won't forgo it. I think, just now, of ways and means on what I described once to you as "a good recipe for making an Act of God" and I will yet make something turn up. In the meantime, I'm not overlooking anything in the line of casual dalliance that comes my way at Altoona — no use of turning anchorite over it, y'know.[13]

On January 14, 1929, Piper reminisced:

> And, Ferd... Once you wrote me a letter, which you thought would be a big shock to me, telling of your intention to marry. Will it be a surprise to you to learn that I have given up all hope of ever marrying, and that now all that I desire is to forget? Yes, I've decided that it's no use, no use whatever, and if I ever go to Jersey Shore again, it will not be to the old brick house beside the river.... Not that I do not love her now as much as ever; more than ever, perhaps, since I can see she is so utterly out of my reach, but I have simply ceased to hope. Well, it's only one of many fine things that I have looked forward to and then realized that I could not have. The fable says that Lucifer, Prince of Hell, is granted, as a special boon, to stand at the gate of Paradise for an hour each time a mortal soul resists his temptations. I think, myself, that this is surely the worst of his torments, to be so close to the happiness that cannot ever be his, and, like him, I've been close to Heaven and could not enter. So, as I cannot, I fail to see any good reason why I should continue to plague myself over it.
>
> I don't know when this sudden change of heart came about. When I came to Williamsport, I was determined to spare no great effort to win my cause, and when I got off the train at Altoona on Tuesday, I saw quite clearly that I had no cause to win. My own theory is this. On Sunday night, I was most beastly drunk, and on Monday night, I was almost as badly off. Is it possible that these thoughts that I have just expressed had been for a long time brewing in my subconscious mind and were released into my conscious mind while in a state of intoxication?
>
> I was soused almost all the time from Sunday night to Tuesday morning, and it must surely have been in that time that I changed my mind. Then, Beam drunk is wiser than Beam sober, and the moral is quite obvious.
>
> Well, at any rate, this shipwreck of my dreams admits of some slight salvage. I gained the inspiration for a novel out of this wretched one-sided love affair and I picked up some rather good antiques at an extremely moderate figure.
>
> But, Ferd, if you ever learn that she is in any sort of trouble, let me know at once, and if I can help her in any way, though it cost me my life, I will.[14]

In this letter, Ferd, the voice of experience, played Dutch uncle:

> About the amour. As you were not overly surprised at my marital announcement, neither am I surprised that you have truly reached the age of reason. You were too sincere, that was your fault, and so sincere that you placed love and a willing attitude of sacrifice above logic. I don't want to seem harsh, comrade, but if, as you say, you desire to forget the incidents, you betimes will forget the girl. This as I see it is for the better.
>
> Conceitedly I think that you and I are quite different from ordinary mortals, but the same intuitions control us that others are invested with. I have written from the ages of eighteen to twenty-three, three books of alleged poetry, and each of them has a dedication in effect "to the woman I love," yet there were three women in this course of time, and yet further each of the three I was certain at the time I could not do without. Now I have found Fritz, and I write small poetry now, not that Fritz is not inspirational and not that she is domestic, but somehow my vision is just a bit better and I don't need to imagine things as of old. And don't for God's sake tell me you've given up all hope of marrying, you thereby further involve yourself.

Just take what the gods send, and don't think for a moment you're running your own show. I predict for you a still more rapid mental development. While you have learned many lessons and gleaned many observations in this brief experience with the fleeting lady, don't think that equips you for a novel. You are in something of a heat just now, and I would advise at least a half year's wait, and then consider the matter. You have lost a good deal of time on worthless manuscripts, you know.[15]

Whew! Sometimes Ferd just heaped the truth on Piper's head with a trowel. Piper fired back:

Now, as to the comments on the other matter. Battery — Forward! Action front! Unlimber, load and fire at will!

In the first place, you counsel me to forget the lady. In time, you counsel me to do nothing that I had not already made up my mind to do. However, there must be a coroner's inquest over every corpse, even the corpse of a love and by a logical examination of the factors of it, I can more easily persuade myself that, after all, there may be nothing to forget. To be sure I was sincere. I wanted it more than anything else in the world. However, I couldn't get it, so I'd better pick up my rifle and sling my pack and light my pipe and walk on. What the hell, what the hell?

And I am amused at your rather naïve assumption that your poems were written to three different women, when, as is easily seen, they were all written to one and the same woman. You know, we never love more than one woman. We love, at different times, different manifestations of her — this time dark, this time fair, but she is always the same woman. And, the joke of it is— she doesn't exist. We only think she does. Yet, if we see this woman of our dreams clearly in human flesh, of course we recognize her and we say, quite rightly, "I am in love."

Well, and I suppose that somewhere in the world there are other women quite like Lillian in that they also mirror this woman who never lived and whom I love. Without doubt, there are. So, after all, my earlier statement that I would never marry may be a slight exaggeration. However, there is more to be said on this score than I have time to tap off here, so, hasta luego!

I quite agree that I'm not running my own show. The executive end of the business is in the hands of the three sisters who are clad in gray and whose names are Lachesis, Atropos and Clotho.

As far as taking what the gods, or their agents named above, send — why, I can take nothing else, but it's usually scurvy fare.[16]

Over a year and a half later, Piper still carried a torch for the girl in the Old Brick House Beside the River, as this letter September 9, 1930, illustrates: "My guess, now, is that my desire for her will be with me always, like a pistol-ball in some inaccessible portion of my anatomy, to give me rest at times and then, at other times, to ache like the very hell.... Maybe I'll do a story on that theme, some time. Properly used, there's as much drama in inaction as in action."[17]

In love, Piper was like a bulldog worrying a bone; he didn't give up, as this post-script to his letter of October 15, 1930, demonstrates:

P.S. And Ferd... If a copy of that Historical Edition, with my article under my by-line, should stray up the river to a little lady in an old brick house along the bank, it might remind her of me and now, perhaps, she might be a little kinder in her thoughts of me. As Mrs. Staib, of the Chat-A-While, is a friend of mine and knows that I know her, a copy given to her might do the work. You would have a good excuse in showing her what I have written.

As for the paragraph above, try and do it, Ferd. You'll think I'm crazy as hell, but do it anyhow. Humor the mad. But, of course, don't let anybody know you're getting it to her on purpose.

Don't laugh, God damn you, don't laugh! B.[18]

Poor Piper, he just didn't know when to stop beating a dead horse; however, Ferd did send out a copy of the Historical Edition ("I have followed out your instructions otherwise in sending copies to three certain persons"),[19] but no longer mentioned the Lady in the Old Brick House Beside the River to Beam — not even to chastise him. Obviously, this failed romance had stuck in Beam's craw like a fishhook.

Piper's final comment regarding Lillian Sheffer was on May 24, 1931: "I received an invitation to join the Penn's Forestry Association, in which it was mentioned you had proposed my name.... I am most anxious to join it, hoping that I will be given the opportunity this year similar to the one I missed out on last summer.... There's a chance that the association may hold another banquet and motor trip this summer and that *some of the same people will be there*. As our brave Governor-General of the Bastille says, You get it? If you'll recall, I first met Her on an excursion of the sort, and perhaps ... not that I'm superstitious, or anything like that, you know."[20]

CHAPTER 8

Never a Debtor Be

I regret writing you on such cursed short notice, just as I regret my delay in writing you anent my coming down in deer season, but my affairs, financial and otherwise, are in such a damnable tangle at present that I never know, more than a few days in advance, just what I am going to be able to do, and as it is not my custom to make promises and then turn again and break them, I can't help it.[1]
— H. Beam Piper

Throughout his life, H. Beam Piper had problems managing money. For the most part, he lived a modest life, so it is not large sums of cash we're talking about. Still, he had a reckless attitude towards money that would bring him no end of grief in his later years. He spent beyond his means for weapons and clothes. In addition, he usually spent anything that came in almost as soon as he received it; Piper operated on the basis of "more will come when I most need it." Unfortunately, sometimes it didn't come when he needed it; but that never deterred him from spending any windfall as soon as it arrived.

Mike Knerr notes: "Somewhere along the way, Beam developed a taste for 'the finer things' in life and his pursuit of such items was often just plain crazy. A man who constantly wore suits and ties, with a rather paltry income, he spared no expense. Little, if any, of his attire came from Sears & Roebuck or J.C. Penney and his suits were always custom made. His shirts came from the better stores of Williamsport and he usually bought his shoes in New York City.

"All of this *could* have stemmed from his early home life. A lack of money in the household, perhaps a heckling by his young friends about it, could well have given him a taste for good things later in life. One thing is certain. He never learned the value of a dollar."[2]

Don Coleman in a July 20, 2001, letter, wrote: "Sister Syl repeated the same words to me that I had written you some time ago, about the fact that our mother always felt that if she would have remained in Williamsport, this tragedy could have been avoided. The financial aid was there, but Beam was just too proud to ask or accept from family (us). And Ma, if she had been there, would have insisted upon covering his overhead. I know this for a fact, because I am her son! But that was yesterday and today we can only 'guess' how things may have turned out."[3]

In his twenties, the young Piper was much more flexible about borrowing money; at least, in regards to his close friend Ferd Coleman. When it appears that Beam would be unable to attend one of their camping conclaves, Ferd offers him a $5 loan with a ninety-day grace period. As Don Coleman puts it, "A hefty sum, considering it was quite capable of filling a week's grocery bill."[4]

Piper wrote: "I got your letter. Damnably sorry, but conditions are no better and will not be until the end of the month, so I can't by any means go camping now. Thanks awfully for the offered loan, but it won't be any help, aside from the fact that it is against my principles to borrow money from a friend."[5]

By August of 1927, that attitude of his had changed: "I'm evacuating the cabin tomorrow on the 7:56 train, for Altoona. As you will not be down before then, I will take the knives, forks and spoons, the canned-heat stove and your map with me to Altoona, and mail them back to you. I will also mail you the dollar bill that you loaned me (When I get one. Damned near broke again.), and which I am damned glad I accepted."[6]

This is a notable departure from Piper's unwillingness to accept help from anyone, especially friends, and to my mind shows that his relationship with Ferd Coleman was unique and "above" his other friendships. In "The Early Letters," Piper appears just as pig-headed as he did in his later letters, so we can't ascribe this deviation to youth. Nor was this the last time he would borrow money from Coleman.

Throughout his letters, early and late, Piper would make plans, then have to back out for lack of necessary cash. "I find, after consulting my department of exchequer, that I will be able to pay you a visit during the week following Christmas (Christ's Mass, as it was originally spelled), that is to say, the week between the aforementioned fiesta and New Year's Day. If this will suit you, let me know, and tell me what day would be most convenient to you for my advent into your midst. I want, of course, to have a good wind-session with you, and I also want to stop at McElhattan and see the Colonel if he will be there and see the erstwhile Belle of Bellefonte at the Jersey Shore.... I regret writing you on such cursed short notice, just as I regret my delay in writing you anent my coming down in deer season, but my affairs, financial and otherwise, are in such a damnable tangle at present that I never know, more than a few days in advance, just what I am going to be able to do, and as it is not my custom to make promises and then turn again and break them, I can't help it."[7]

Ferd responded: "Next week, fortunately, will be a dull one, and I shall anticipate your visit with pleasure. I don't give a damn when you come, nor do I care how long you stay. Arrangements will be made at my domicile to bunk you."[8]

On January 12, 1928, Ferd wrote: "Am sending under separate cover today your copy of *Otzinachson*. As to balance of $15.00, though I am concerned in obtaining it, please don't let its purchase demoralize your purse. A payment of $5.00 each payday will suffice to keep my hunger-wolf away."[9]

From this January 23, 1928, letter we learn that Piper was paid bi-monthly by the Pennsylvania Railroad: "As to the money; I enclose a postal order for $5.00, which, to my sorrow, is all that I can spare at present. Two weeks hence, however, I will do 'front and center' with nine more, and cancel the debt."[10]

This October 21, 1928, letter shows that Piper had flexible work hours and worked at the Juniata Yards when he wanted, or needed to: "I find that I will have to go back to the galleys for a while. I need a few things, clothes, notably, that will cost more money than I could feel justified borrowing from Father. I don't like to do it, but needs must when the devil drives."[11] Herbert Piper appeared to be okay with his son's desultory work habits and would advance him money on occasion. Despite his financial headaches, Beam had a good support system going while living under his parents' roof.

"The Early Letters" and his diaries show that Piper's financial problems were perennial. His letters to Ferd are sprinkled with comments like the following: "Now tomorrow I'll send you a postal money order for $5.00. Three of them, of course, are yours, and the other two you are to use in paying this repair-bill, 'and whatever thou spendeth more, I will repay when I come again.' So you settle up with George and get the rifle, holding it until you either come to Altoona or I come to Williamsport. I enclose an order on Harder for the rifle. (The only reason I don't send the money now, too, is because I won't have it until tomorrow.)"[12]

As Don Coleman points out: "Three dollars in pre–Depression America could have bought twenty hamburgers at the ballpark. A nickel could handle a loaf of bread, or a double-scooped ice cream cone, or a bottomless sack of popcorn, or a ride on the streetcar, or a couple of newspapers.... And the three dollar I.O.U. could put one hell of a fine pair of boots on Beam! He would frivolously boast of how quickly this hefty sum (and healthy portion of a railroad paycheck) could be annihilated in just thirty minutes duration! 'So be it!'"[13]

Piper wrote on February 8, 1929: "I regret to say that it will be impossible for me to come to Williamsport on the 21st, as I am on the verge of a total eclipse of the billfold that will only be relieved on the morning of the 23rd.... And, with reference to the financial constipation hereinbefore alluded to. Would it be too much to ask you to wait until Saturday morning (the 23rd) for the 'upstairs bill' in payment of my dues for the (Lycoming) Historical Society? (And what in particular hell do you mean, I want to join the society as a matter of record? I want to join because I'm interested in Lycoming County history)."[14]

By 1930 the Great Depression had set in, and the hardships it brought washed across all class and income levels, except for the truly wealthy. Piper wrote: "Altoona is having a double dose of Hoover Prosperity, just now. All the railroad shops will be closed the 23rd to the 5th next month, and the lousy hole I work in shut down yesterday. In a way, it's a nice thing for me, as I'm busy as the devil on my writing."[15]

In this February 13, 1931, letter the Depression had hit the Coleman household, as well:

> Appreciated your commendable comments on my journalistic comments. Alas, however, the *Shoppers' Guide* is indeed become a financial dud. I know not what to do with it, and I love it; yet it is weekly now a bitter loss. You will note in the current issue my lament. It may interest you to know that a good lady phoned at 7:45 this morning and asked that the paper be discontinued to her residence because I "knock too much," specifying Mr. Ames and the ministers, anent my tribute to the Law Enforcement Committee. Ah, yes, the old fight still is in me, but I question whether I can continue to display it?
>
> ... Glosser tells me he believes he has a sale for my guns, if I care to dispose of them. If I can get an agreeable price I probably would. But I don't know what is agreeable for such as I have. Can you give an opinion as to whether I should sell, and, if aye, what price I ought ask?[16]

The next day, Piper replied:

> I'm sorry as hell—almost as sorry as you are—about the financial troubles of the *Shoppers' Guide*. I've known your paper for as long as I've known you, and if you have to give it over now, it will almost seem as though some of Ferd Coleman is gone. And it was such a tough little sheet; always getting into some kind of scrap and usually for an unpopular cause. I hate to hear "Taps" blown over a brave fighter. So I hope to God you'll be able to pull it through.
>
> Sorry you have to let Stan out, too. He was a good sort, and I liked him no end. Well, that's this God-damned Hoover Prosperity. I hope it blows over soon.
>
> As to your guns, I don't know what would be a good price for them. You know, antiques are entirely in a class by themselves when it comes to values. They are [worth] exactly what someone is willing to pay for them and no more. I don't know much what local antique-ing conditions are, except the local dealers don't seem to handle many guns and there doesn't seem to be much interest in them. Arms like those you have are not the sort that arms collectors—that is, specialists in arms, having a good knowledge of the subject—buy (on account of poor condition).[17]

From this March 15, 1931, Piper letter, it appears Ferd may have been premature with his *Shoppers' Guide* obituary. "I noted with interest your 'Herb Ames' article, complete with bean story. Inasmuch as you say the old fool is thinking about running for re-election, I liked the remark that we only have ten months to endure him, and I got a big laugh out of the request that people spare your tender feelings by not requesting their free subscriptions to be stopped."[18]

Not even Don Coleman knows how Ferd resuscitated the *Shoppers' Guide*. In an October 19, 2003, letter, he wrote: "I have never heard of Dad having hard times; even during the Depression our family lived comfortably."[19] A few years later Ferd Coleman purchased his own printing plant and moved the family into a new house. The one thing that would never change: the perennial welcome mat for H. Beam Piper.

I suspect his success may have been due to Ferd's father, who helped him with collections. Getting paid advertisements from cash-strapped merchants during the Depression had to have been an ordeal. However, Ferd had a potent ally. Don Coleman writes: "My grandfather, after retiring from the Williamsport Police Dept., as originally a cop and then becoming the town's first City Detective, went into what he referred to as 'The Private Business.' So, even as a PI, he worked for Dad as a 'collector.' I can still remember making the collecting rounds with him in the summertime and always exchanging pleasantries over a shot and a beer while I settled for orange pop!"[20]

"Annually-beginning about 1940, he traveled to Havana as a starting point, and from there go to either Haiti or Yucatan, and would write of his experiences, publishing them as installments in the *Guide*. Every Williamsporter knew Dad because he was a civil leader—involved in so many functions—yet always had time for bowling, gold and concerts."[21] Just the opposite of his best friend, H. Beam Piper, whose life grew increasingly insular as he sweated over his typewriter, eschewing family and friends, attempting to break into the writing game.

CHAPTER 9

Three's Company

If you honestly wanted to blow your brains out I'd consider it a friendly act to loan you a pistol, although I would greatly deprecate your decision, and if you intend to enter the alleged holy state of orthodox wedded bliss (also alleged), why, I'll attend your obsequies and throw rice with the best of them.[1]

—H. Beam Piper

If there is one universal truth, it is that "things change." Ferd and Beam had a wonderful friendship of equals, but out of the blue, so to speak, Ferd made a momentous leap — he was going to get married. Ferd's letter or postcard announcing his upcoming nuptials is missing from Coleman's "Early Letters," nor is there any mention of his romancing his new fiancée prior to this bombshell. By the strength of Piper's reactions to the upcoming nuptials in the following letters, I suspect that Ferd, who knew of Beam's contempt for the "marriage game," held off telling him anything until he had stepped into the breach, i.e., asked his prospective fiancée for her hand in marriage.

As expected, Piper replied strongly to this new development in his letter of April 10, 1928:

Strange as it may seem, your announcement does not greatly horrify or dismay me, although you are a trifle vague. When you say marriage, do you mean a Church Marriage, a Trial Marriage, a Companionate Marriage or what have you? If either of the last two, I have not a word of blame or censure to utter, and if it is the first, why, goddam it, that's your business.

Another thing; I don't know your fair intended from Adam's off ox, but if she's a pious Christian I'd advise you to chuck it. However, I haven't heard the evidence for the defense yet, and until then I will not be able to return a verdict. Of this be assured, however, your step over among the benedicts will not make a damn's worth of difference to me, Beam.[2]

In Ferd's next missive, after some chat about meeting Piper at his parent's house on Friday, it's quite apparent that his gruff reply ruffled some feathers. Ferd had this to say in his postscript: "Rather than 'your step over among the benedicts will not make a damn's worth of difference to me,' I should prefer that you had said, 'your step over among the benedicts will not make a damn's worth of difference in the warmth of our friendship.' Your attitude, expressed in your phrase, indicated indifference, and I would not have this, for it is my very intention deliberately to seek your counsel, though of course I shall not abide by it!"[3]

Since there's no further mention of this rift between the two good friends, I suspect peace of one sort or another was arrived at; most likely over a bowl of tobacco and a pot of the Prince's best potable.

On May 6, 1928, Piper wrote:

Cooper will join us in Williamsport on Friday, the 11th ... where we will have a binge with the good Edward. So much for that. I saw him (Cooper) yesterday night, and he was heartily in favor of the whole "programme." Thus, the Three Musketeers will be together again.

"By the way, you forgot to confess your impending fall from single cussedness to him when you were up here the last time. I therefore council you to take your courage (Dutch or otherwise) in hand and do so now, if he ever sees in the paper that "Mr. Ferdinand W. Coleman, of this city, one of our most prominent young journalists and booze-fighters, was united in marriage to—" and so forth. Gr-r-r-eat Chr-r-r-ist!!! You know, his view of the holy state of connubial bliss is somewhat bilious, as, I must confess, is my own, to a less degree. To an increasingly lessening degree, perhaps I'd better put it.[4]

On June 6, 1928, he made further inquiries: "By the way, slip me a note letting me know when the more or less happy event comes off, and when you start on the honeymoon. I want to have one more rendezvous with you as a free man. Likewise, tip me off as to the date and other dope about that Great Runaway celebration at Fort Brady. I *must* be there."[5]

At last, the big day approaching, Ferd wrote:

I surely have been something of a cad in delaying this greeting, but god what a truly fascinating experience this acclimation to domestication is; and what sundry details in other endeavors have arisen the past ten days to engage my time, which seems briefly accorded me, indeed.

I marry at 10:00 A.M. on Saturday, June 23rd, 1928 in the rectory of St. Boniface church. My best man is our own beloved Edward, who, when approached by me with the assignment registered a rather sickly smile, and consented to be present at the obsequies.

As to entertainment of friends, acquaintances, near-friends, etc. the minds of myself and wife have been in something of a turmoil, but we have decided point-blank to observe naught else but the marriage ritual, and a wedding breakfast engaged in by the immediate families and the witnesses.

I recognize the fact, of course, that I am necessarily quite mad at this time, what with the possession of a fair lady so close, and yet I believe I am sober and see distinctly that Ferdinand shall be ever at least what he has been.[6]

The remainder of the letter discusses an antique auction at Glosser's and a meeting with Ed Morrell, as well as various stratagems for the two of them to meet — and a final drunk — before Ferd was to leave on his honeymoon. At this point Ferd knew things were changing in his life, would change even more, but wanted desperately to keep his old friendships intact. Piper was standoffish — he'd seen too many others go down the matrimonial path and lose their way. In his reply of June 14, he said, "I have a big bag of talk to open with you, and I want to see you for about an hour before you go away on your honeymoon."[7]

Still, Piper attempted to make the best of what he saw as another comrade falling by the wayside. The following is a transcript (by Don Coleman) of Beam's undated and handwritten note to Ferd via Edward to be delivered after the "ceremony":

"Ferd, I'm sending this by Edward; after the ceremony, he will hand it to you and thus I, while absent in the body, may still be one of the first to congratulate you on what, as I can well understand, will be one of the fullest moments of your life. For I do congratulate you, Ferd, yes, and envy you just a little, for in spite of all my ribald bachelor's scoffing, I think that you are more fortunate than I. (Perhaps that is why I scoffed so heartily, if all truth be known.) But, at any rate, I scarcely believe it necessary to tell you that this slip of paper carries with it my best wishes for happiness to you and to your lady, nor do I need to assure you, as I do, that I remain,

Your friend
Beam."[8]

Don Coleman, who knew Piper from his first steps, wrote: "And so it was; H. Beam Piper's pal-confidant ... became espoused to a fair maiden from the woods and farmlands of Cogan House Township. The marriage of Coleman to a country girl named Freida Baumgartner was surely a gain, not just for the obvious compatibility of each, but for the eventual unselfish (and unique) acknowledgment of H. Beam Piper — who welcomed another hiker to the mountaineer group, 'even though she be female!'"[9]

In Coleman's *Shoppers' Guide* the event was noted by this statement: "Our dear editor Ferd W. Coleman has now passed into the great beyond ... to become a Leap Year victim. The ceremony was sweet and simple, the bride being sweet and the groom simple."[10]

Piper, obviously still upset about his best friend's nuptials, had this rare apology to make after one of their camping trips some two months after Ferd's wedding, on August 16, 1928: "Another thing. I want to beg your pardon for the rather boorish way in which I acted that Wednesday evening at the camp. I don't know what in hell was the matter with me, I'll swear I don't. Nerves all shot, for one thing. I was wishing all evening that I could find somebody to pick a fight on and so relieve myself. As might be expected, I was myself again in the morning, but great God, I did feel like the devil that night."[11]

Letters between the two friends drop off from this point on, as Don Coleman points out: "For nearly two months, written communication ceased between Piper and Coleman, due to the growing addiction to telephones and the prevalence of actual meetings along the Susquehanna."[12]

In his letter of November 24, 1928, Beam again uncharacteristically apologized: "I don't know whether or not my last letter might have sounded like giving you the cold shoulder, but if I did, be assured that it was certainly not so intended. You and Fritz [Beam never wrote Freida's name correctly; he either used her nickname, Fritz, or misspelled her name as Frieda] are always welcome at my home, but under the present circumstances [Harriet Piper fell into an unmarked road-side hazard and injured herself], it simply can't be. However, sometime toward the middle of next month or, better, the early part of January would do very nicely." He ended the letter thusly: "With best wishes to the sir brothers Ranck, Coleman, Lenhard and Bardo, Beam."[13]

Piper during this period of his life had an active social life with lots of friends who shared his many interests, Pennsylvania history, guns, antiques, books, writing, and alcohol.

Freida Coleman was an exceedingly tolerant wife, as is shown by this December 7, 1928, letter from Ferd Coleman: "Regarding your probability of coming around the new year: I like your indifference, like hell I do! You must come. (Incidentally, whenever I use the word 'must' to Fritz, her retort is 'I do not!') Edward and I are planning on you for New Year's Eve, as of yore. While our insobriety activities may not be conducted in my rather clean home, Fritz already has her instructions to go to her mother's or almost any damn place for many hours, or the entire night, leastways to expect little attention from me. While I say you must, I must know shortly whether 'tis so, for a high-class somewhat exclusive set to which we (Fritz and I) belong, also plans raising hell New Year's eve, at one heluva fee, and I should tell them very soon whether or not we are coming. Needless to say, I prefer Edward and you to this."[14]

Piper answered the next day: "Be ye of good cheer. Zarathustra will come unto his disciples to celebrate the feast of the New Year, and he hopes to get so damned good and tight he won't know his arse from four dollars a week. Spread the glad tidings of hope to [Ted] Ranck and Lenhard, the two best friends, bar you and the Major, that I have in this deplorable world. I don't know how much of the inferno the 'high-class, somewhat exclusive set' alluded to plans to raise, but the four of us can, without paying anybody except Prince Farrington or Ted's man from Halifax any fee at all, raise all that Ames-ridden Williamsport can stand. 'All for one and one for all!'"[15]

From the exultation on this January 2, 1929, letter, it's obvious that Piper got along with the entire Coleman clan: "Give my best to your father and tell him I'm sorry he was out when I called at his office. Also to your mother and to Aunt Emma."[16]

However, their close friendship was beginning to fray. In response to Piper's request that he pick up a jug of brandy for his visit, Ferd wrote: "Please desist in ordering the alcohol. It may be because of the sinister and foreboding information my father has volunteered to me from time to time connected with transportation of that commodity: I don't know, but at any rate I have no desire to place my 'finger' before my nose before the law."[17] Ferd Coleman's father was a detective with the Williamsport Police, and he had developed a "learned" caution that Piper didn't really respect — being a contrarian and a self-professed Bohemian.

This note put Piper's nose out of joint and he responded: "Of course, I don't blame you for your refusal to turn rum-runner, Fernando. We are all of us children of our environment, and yours has not been of a sort conducive to illegal acts. From earliest infancy, I fancy, you have been witness to or heard about the capture of those who overstep the law, and I observed long ago that you are a subscriber to that popular superstition to the effect that the criminal is always detected. I should have born this fact in mind when I thought of having you bring a jug up for me. To be sure, I bear you no ill will about it. There is a possibility that something untoward *might* happen, you know. I remember I stuck to that traveling-box of mine coming back to Altoona on the 1st as a Methodist sticks to his Jesus."[18]

Marriage often results in the death of close male friendship, although not in this case. Freida was most accommodating about their friendship, and by all accounts (in the letters and from Don's remembrances) Freida and Beam were good friends, too. She knew when to leave the men alone and enjoyed Piper's companionship, too. Unfortunately, Ferd's marriage wasn't the only attack on their friendship: Ferd's small *Shoppers' Guide* was growing bigger and beginning to be recognized. His editorship of the paper was giving him status and stature within the community of Williamsport, while Piper was still going along his Bohemian pathway. Still, there was a part of Ferd who wished he had the courage (or recklessness) to do as his friend was doing, and he always admired Beam for taking the road less traveled.

In this letter of February 25, 1929, Ferd appeared to be backsliding a bit toward his old habits after a weekend with his friend Beam and his parents, Freida and his brother George:

> I wish to take this prompt opportunity to extend our gratitude to your mother, your father and yourself for the excellent hospitality bestowed upon the members of the Coleman clan who visited with you over last weekend. Really I consider it perhaps the finest "all-around" journeys I have ever made to your hamlet, which I insist is a fair, and an impressive one. Please reassure your mother that whereas I commenced a year or more ago bringing myself and have now attained a company of three, I promise never to exceed this figure and rarely to equal it, but I simply couldn't refrain from taking what chance the circumstances offered toward making my presence with you last week possible.
> While married and loving Freida as no other man does, I hope, yet I delight in her saying, "My sister's coming out tonight to hear the radio," for it means I may vacate the premises without the last censure, if I so desire to. I do. As a consequence thereto Edward and I will likely embark upon a moderate binge.[19]

Don Coleman further amplifies the visit: "Whereas Ferd (a baptized Catholic) and Beam pondered over agnosticism and atheism and other forms of belief, George [Ferd's brother] remained totally devout to his faith — as attested by a commanding note to Mother Piper from son Beam:

> Mother: —
> You are to get George up at eight
> without failure, as he wishes to go to Mass.
> This means get him up, *not* leave him sleep.
> Beam

"One might surmise from the imperious tones Beam Piper put to paper within his own 'hamlet,' at twenty-five, he was surely the czar of 400 Wordsworth Avenue."[20]

The friendship survived Ferd's marriage, but there were other fractures to come in the future as Ferd faced adult responsibility with a growing family and trying to shepherd his small business through the worst of the Depression. Piper, habitually broke, continued to work as a watchman at the Pennsylvania Railroad by night and as struggling author by day.

CHAPTER 10

Moment of Greatness

My third [wish] would be the ability to make some impression on the flinty hearts of a lot of these "lousey" [sic] publishers. I leave that third because I think that I have that ability to do it in time, but I wish to Jesus I could hurry the process up a little.[1]

— H. Beam Piper

It is rare for an editor to take the time to provide feedback or analysis to an unknown author on an unwanted story; therefore, most beginning writers work in a vacuum. This is as true today as it was in Piper's time. In the late 1920s the young H. Beam Piper was still working his way through the maze of the writing game; therefore, it was only natural that he would ask his best friend for a critical appraisal of his latest work.

The first mention of Piper's new story, "Moment of Greatness," is contained in a December 28, 1927, letter: "By the way, I am on a story now, and I got my inspiration from a passage in Nietzsche. 'When he judgeth himself — that was his supreme moment; let not the exalted one relapse again into his low estate! / There is no salvation for him who hath thus suffered from himself, unless it be speedy death.' How does that sound? Promising? Or crappy? But I'll read the first draft of it to you when I see you. Then you can judge.... Your brother in Christ, Beam."[2]

On January 4, 1928, Piper wrote about his difficulties in finding the right title. "I am getting along with that short story about the gangster who gives his life for the girl. I am somewhat at a loss for a fitting title, however. To date I have thought of the following; Paid in Full, Judgment, Atonement and The Flame Burns Bright — flame of courage and honor and all that, y'know. I am not exactly satisfied with any of them, and as I intend to send a carbon copy of it to you, perhaps you may be able to suggest something more fitting."[3]

On February 21, 1928, Beam wrote that he had completed "Moment of Glory":

Now as to the story which I was writing. I have finished and this day it goes ... three guesses whither. To *Black Mask*? Wrong! To the Street & Smith gang? Wronger! "To ... can it be ... *The Saturday Evening Post*? Key-rect as hell! I have decided that I will no longer debase my brilliant ... nay, by the spear of Odin, resplendent ... genius to the penny-dreadfuls. I'm out for big game this time. One does not strain his gun-barrel more by aiming at eagles than at "shitepokes." Fear not. Your copy will reach you as soon as I can sort out the earlier drafts to accompany it. I want you to read the finished product first, to get the full effect, and then check up with the three tentative versions. Then, I prithee, spare time enow (sic) from pandering to the base-born rabble to let me have your opinion on it.

Does the story sell — and you can judge what the *Post* will, if at all, pay for it — my summer on the West Branch is a dead cert. You, best of all, perhaps, understand fully what that will mean to me. Not that I'll not be on the spot anyhow, if I have to turn cut-throat or, worse, evangelist, to get the money. Pray, then, for me, perform novenas and burn candles, not forgetting to kill a horse for Odin and a goat for Thor, so as to be on the safe side with the Old Gods. And leave not Aphrodite out of it, for on her aid I reckon much. (Don't know why all the mythology, tonight. A Cabell hangover, like as not.)[4]

On February 22, 1928, Ferd replied: "I marvel — at your unseemly — unchristly nerve. *The Saturday Evening Post.* Not that they are above you in your literary efforts. Quite the contrary — in justice to the true merit of your creative art; and, in a sense that's why I marvel. The *Post*, of course, is often the standard of your loathful penny-dreadfuls. But be this as it may, your nerve to my understanding arises from the fact that the *Post* is practically a closed market, about as tight, for real functional purposes as the erring *filles-de-joie* after the fourth month.... This particular brain-child you have befriended as excessively and frequently within my notice that I tell you truthfully I anticipate the perusal of the ms, with keen interest. Please send it along, and I promise to devote adequate time to the stuff, both from critical, friendly, and literary angles."[5]

It is apparent throughout "The Early Letters" that Coleman admired Piper, not only for his literary gifts and fearless toil, but for the bravery which allowed him to suffer for his art in the face of constant rejection. "I have flattered you before with the equivalent of, 'By the gods, I envy you, would that my standards, practices and habits were such that I might struggle as economic' as yourself."[6]

On January 23, 1928, Piper wrote: "I am not unmindful of my promise to send you a carbon copy of the story. I will do more. Do you remember how, when you were last in Altoona, we stopped in front of a window display of products made in the P.R.R. [Pennsylvania Rail Road] shops, a display that interested you as much as it pained me? Well, do you recall an exhibit showing various articles in all the stages of their manufacture? That's the sort of thing I'm going to send you, two versions of the story in pencil and the third and final one in type, showing how I actually wrote it. Then, perhaps, observing my method, you will see why I use the typewriter only to put my stuff in presentable form."[7]

In those halcyon days, at least as far as the Post Office was concerned, mail was delivered twice a day, and it was not unusual to send off a letter in the morning mail and receive your reply that afternoon. Three days after sending "Moment of Greatness" to *The Saturday Evening Post*, Piper wrote: "When you marveled at my ungodly nerve, you marveled well. The story is back, together with a politely insincere but personally written note of rejection. I shot at the eagle and missed, but beyond the waste of two rounds of postage stamps nothing has been lost by it, and if I plague these sons of priests enough, they may buy to be quit of me. I will hold the story until I hear from you, so mention such magazines as you think may lend an ear to it.

"The story is under separate cover. Owing to the bulk of all four drafts, I am sending only the final one at present, but as I will be in the West Branch Valley before this time next month, I will give you the others. Beam."[8]

Here is Ferd's analysis, mailed on February 29, in whole:

Dear Beam:

I am enclosing herewith your ms, "Moment of Greatness," and out of my intense love for a comrade I purloin herewith a full hour from business in which to declare the following criticism of it.

I consider the work from three angles: (a) As the work of a friend; (b) As a product of literature; (c) From a general critical view.

(a) As usual, and frequently have I so informed you — your diction is very good, and lends the quality of easy reading to the story. If ever (and this is a foreboding of what is to follow under "c") you do strike the splendid combination of writing a story which best aligns itself to your nature and truest thought, it is going to be excellently done indeed.

(b) As literature, I can only pass sentence, Beam: it isn't. It has in some measure the ingredients of deep human motives, but they are so shallowly presented that one could not entrust himself to the fair belief that the story could live.

(c) And, now, from the technical viewpoint: well, I'm sorry, Beam, and a bottle of Florida Farm to prove the maintenance of my friendship to you, but the story can scarcely sell. In spite of many fair qualities, it is in my opinion not commensurate to the established standards that a popular short story should have. I cannot, and there is no need, in this short space, to enumerate faults or merits in the order of their appearance in the story, but here are some of the things I have thought of for the past two days.

Somebody, perhaps you yourself many years later, could make a most excellent Psychological portrait of the reaction of a hardened criminal toward a woman who had once befriended him — similar to the legend of the terrible lion who in a moment of desired vengeance did not fall upon his prey when remembering that in infant years the prey had removed a large splinter from his paw. But to involve your thought into a story of your dimensions, and treat it in the crude manner that you have done (crude, as to thematic treatment) leaves the story flat. I have not given considerable thought to recommendations, but I believe if in some manner the story (if not entirely psychologically portrayed as above suggested) were more physical, more moving, more active in its plot, with scarce any mental opinionating whatever by Clancey, just blind instinct brought into play because of the girl's early act, the tone of the story would ring truer.

Certainly by an orthodox editor, or reader, a story headed with a passage from the infamous (to many) Nietzsche, would at once stamp it with the atmosphere of "Scrutinize most carefully what this author has to write, in order that the conventions be not violated." I would recommend its removal. A competent author need not resort to the presentation of another's thought, and then incorporate it as a theme for his own story.

In a 7,000-word story, you consume 1,000 before you have Clancey speak to the girl, and they are the two "exhibitory" characters in the story. This is too large a proportion. The problem is eventually to portray Clancey's mode of action when destiny calls upon him to "be himself" in his conduct toward the girl in her dilemma; and since this is the problem, and a short story technically should have but one major problem, everything should be hastened to this climax.

Your language is excellent, Beam, and thus it is at fault. This is a hard story, and while of course you are good enough not to force your personal scholarship before the reader, you are not good enough deliberately to refrain from high-minded wordings when common expressions in this above-dubbed "hard" story should be the ruling. I have told you this before.

Akin to this complaint, is the tone of dialogue. I simply don't always like it, Beam. (In this respect, of dialogue, I am anticipating keenly how well you shall translate the German hill-hawk dialect in your forthcoming Tiadaghton novels.)

Par. 2, p. 5, far-fetched. A hardened, strong criminal if he could get into a chest at all, no matter how tight, would not be in agony "soon."

Pages 11–17, inclusive, well done as a whole.

The meeting with the girl, p. 18, too abrupt.

P. 20, "Oh, God," paragraph — too soft, for Clancey, even in this moment of emotional greatness.

Now, then damnit, it isn't, I assure you, because I frown upon violence, but for purely technical grounds: in god's name, need there be all that gore which followed. Why must all be killed. Is death to others the logical manner in working out one's moment of greatness?

Surely even the editor of a magazine, entitled Blood and Thunder would shudder at the swift, repeated murders Clancey commits. I don't see how the story can sell with this modus operandi in it, Beam. Though as to all the other details I do not insist on revisions (after all they are merely opinions) on this latter suggestion I insist on a change. I know if I were the writer I should not change a damned thing. I'm that beautifully temperamental, and you know it; but as a sober would-be commercial project, one must face the facts embodied in short story technique as is.

I like your last hundred words beautifully, Beam. Splendidly done, but of course a "Stickful" of art doesn't redeem the quality of the whole. I like your use of the word, gallant, Beam. And somehow that's how I think of you, in real life — a gallant gentleman; and, having the temperament of a gallant gentleman, one cannot live the lives of crooks, for one must fully know his characters. I think some of your story projects are coarser than your thoughts really are, and since this is the cheerful circumstance, it follows that you cannot best express yourself in this type of writing. In this connection of gallantry I well can understand your predilection to violence in its relation to knighthood and the adventures thereto, and precisely as a result of this feeling of mine toward you, am I confident that your historical novels narrating the days that were in the Susquehanna Valley will be beautiful, indeed, and actual literature.

I regret that in this department c, Beam, I cannot give a more favorable report, but so it is. However, you know I wish you all dame fortune has to offer in your future work. Even were this story very good, I have so fallen from the literary market-ways, what with my grossly material business, that I am afraid I could not competently suggest a selling point.

May I ask your purpose in visiting the West Branch the latter part of March? I trust to hear from you soon.

Coleman[9]

Unfortunately, even as rich as "The Early Letters" correspondence is, it is limited by the fact that a lot of the communication between the two friends occurred during telephone conversations and in face-to-face meetings. Piper's first reaction to Ferd's critique was contained in his reply of March 1, 1928: "I received the manuscript and your appended commentary. While there are some things in it from which I dissent, I value it highly. One has few friends who will be so honest. As to the criticism, I make no answer. That must hold until we meet."[10]

This meeting was aborted when Piper became ill. From the following letter written on March 16, 1928, by Herbert Piper, it's obvious that Beam was completely himself at home and his unusual mannerisms were accepted — if not enjoyed — by his parents!

Dear Ferd:

Beam's "slight indisposition" yesterday developed into a case of acute Appendicitis.

Mrs. Piper called his doctor who arrived at seven o' clock last night and ordered him rushed to the Hospital. At 9:45 he had been through the operation and was back to his room resting well and in good shape.

I saw him this morning and found him complaining very much about the shortage of cigarettes, but I think his grounds for complaint have been removed before this as his mother is with him now and she said she'd take him a supply along with a book or two.

He asked me to tell you that all dates being cancelled temporarily does not mean that other arrangements are off. To use his language he says hold all arrangements especially the SUGAR-VALLEY DEW until he can lick the man who KNIFED him in the SOLAR-PLEXUS.

No doubt he will write to you in a few days when the doctors will permit him that much exercize (sic).

With best wishes I am

Most Sincerely
Herbert O. Piper

P.S. Should you come in contact with Col. Shoemaker acquaint him with the circumstances.[11]

Ferd replied to Piper on March 16, "Your honorable sire has advised me of your rather dishonorable condition. I trust you will not be bed-ridden for any unfortunate length of time. Your suggestion of transferring the meeting-time to Wednesday, March 12th, is agreeable to me.... May I suggest that to alleviate your ailment you read Mary Baker Eddy's *Key to the Scriptures* and *Science of Health*.[12]

Ferd took this "opportunity" to jab his poor laid-up friend in the ribs, since Mary Baker Eddy was the founder of Christian Science, and one of its beliefs is that you can mentally cure yourself of your ills. I'm sure Beam had a painful laugh over that jibe.

A few days later, we get Piper's version of the appendicitis attack.

This is the first day I got out of the hospital.... On Monday, the 12th, I was taken ill with what I took to be a painful but unimportant belly-ache. It persisted on the next day and the day after, when I became somewhat worried. I had my father write you the first of his two letters, I being too ill to run the Underwood, and called the doctor. He arrived the next day (Thursday) and to my horror and dismay he informed me that I had appendicitis and that I had my choice of the surgeon or the mortician. I chose the latter and was taken to the hospital that same evening....

Two hours after my arrival there, the appendix was as dead as Nero and I was coming out of the ether. There I remained, flat on my back, until late yesterday evening, when I came home. I can inform you, I am glad to be back among my guns and other antiques and to eat the unscientific but palatable products of my mother's kitchen again.... I will be with you anon, when I am well and hale again, and we may once more drain the flowing bowl and smoke the pipe of peace.[13]

After his stay in the hospital, Piper was confined to bed for several weeks; this was typical of the medical practices of the 1920s, where long stays in bed were *de rigueur*. With all this time hanging over him, he had lots of time to stew over Ferd's critique of "Moment of Greatness." His appendectomy was a fortunate accident in a historical sense, since otherwise he would have discussed Ferd's critique in person at their proposed get-together and we would not have this look into how he approached the craft of writing.

On March 28, Piper presented his initial response to Coleman's critique:

I am going to take your advice on the story, in part. I will re-write it changing the first part of it so as to speed up the meeting of Slim Clancey and the Girl. I think I will start the story with Clancey entering the room where the Girl is writing — by-the-bye, did the description of that room and of the Girl herself cause you to think of something? — and I will let the things that have gone before, the robbery and the pursuit, be brought out in conversation. I will also adopt a more skillful method of bringing out Clancey's past life and his service in the Army, together with his regrets for his present mode of life.

As to the dialogue — it was on purpose that I had the Girl talk in the high-toned manner in which she did. There is a small touch of symbolism to the business, and I wished to make clear that she was everything that Clancey was not, that she was something far above him. Hence, I had Clancey speak in thieves' argot and she in the purest poetic English, by way of striking as sharp a contrast as possible.

As to Nietzsche, I may let him go by the board. You will recall, when someone brought Napoleon the sword of Fredrick the Great and suggested that he wear it, the Little Corporal replied, "Oh, as to that, I have a sword of my own."

As to the massacre, that was, in the first place, even more necessary to Slim Clancey, the gunman, than it was to Beam Piper, the author. How in blue hell could he get that Girl out otherwise — by holding a gospel meeting and converting the others to Jesus? He had to kill all of them. Besides, in killing all he wiped out the outward symbols of his old life. There is another phase to it, too. While I was writing that, I was killing those men, myself. Subjectively — in my imagination — of course, but I was killing them none the less. Slim became himself. The Girl became — well, another Girl you know of.

Those men menaced her. And, as I would shoot down or dirk her enemies and glory in it, so Slim Clancey dirked and shot and took no small delight in his shooting and dirking, for I was, briefly, Slim Clancey, and I tell you, Fernando, it gave me great joy to see those men go down to the floor writhing in pain or collapse like lengths of chain that may have been held up and dropped or simply sag and fall like toy balloons with the air let out of them.

I regret, somewhat, that it was only in my imagination. Even Slim's death was such a death as I greatly hope the Old Gods send me, when I am ready for Valhalla. And, as to Valkyries — but perhaps I'd best haul up. I've wasted enough ribbon and paper on this already, and you, I recall, are a busy business man, not a carefree convalescent.[14]

Piper could not leave it alone, and he had more to say in this letter of April 18, 1928: "I have finished the re-writing of the short story, 'Moment of Greatness,' and, as I have omitted the quotation at the beginning and the old title is hence without point, I have re-christened it 'Exit, A Gentleman.' Other changes that have been made are: some toning down of the dialogue, particularly the alleged 'highfalutin' talk of the Girl, a hastening of the meeting of Clancey and the Girl, and — this will please you, 'passivest' — I have made the killing of Nick the Greek a little less atrocious. No changes, however, were made in the casualty list. At the end of the story, the Girl alone was left alive to tell the tale."[15]

He then went on to tell about another yarn he was working on, and that's the last mention of "Moment of Greatness" by any of its titles in the collected letters. However, Ferd's criticism of this yarn stuck in Beam's craw like a fishbone and, it's obvious from the remaining letters, that things were never the same; true, they remained friends, but their special camaraderie was gone for good. More and more often Piper made excuses for not writing, such as this one sent on February 9, 1931: "I had meant to write you much earlier, but every time I sat down to my desk I was confronted by a pile of manuscript of my present attempt at potboiling, and the number at the head of the last page was always too low to suit me, so my prostitute Muse is to blame rather than myself."[16]

From 1931 on the correspondence between the friends dwindled to a small trickle and we learn little about Beam's writing throughout the rest of the 1930s and 1940s. Ferd's harsh criticism of "A Moment of Greatness"—even more than Ferd's marriage and children—distanced the two men and left their relationship less than it had been before.

CHAPTER 11

Changing Fortunes

Well, anyhow, congratulations— or commiserations, however you prefer. This, I suppose, means another rattle. My honorary nephews and nieces are increasing in number.[1]

— H. Beam Piper

Until the birth of Sylvia there was nothing in Ferd's letters, other than the mention of Freida's "illness," that suggested she was pregnant. Don, who while writing the prefaces and afterward to "The Early Letters" had his mother's help in reading between the lines, writes: "As for absence among friends, Freida had been maintaining a low profile as of late, due to a coming addition — or as Ferd would prefer, 'the first edition!'— to the Coleman clan. As noted throughout recent Piper letters, before signing off he invariably give his 'reguards' [sic] to Fritz; not that he wouldn't employ such respect as standard process, but more so to the automatic concern of the present circumstances."[2]

In this letter of September 25, 1929, the proud papa made his announcement:

Dear Comrade:

Lest my guilt be greater through further postponement, I hasten to advise that a daughter shares our household. The happy event occurred Sunday at 4:30 A.M. Others received conventional greetings of the arrival, but I purposed letting you know by personal letter.... Infant and mother are well, indeed.

Yea ... but by God I've got a gallon of the Prince's "hisself." And may I tell you what a treat the familiar but hitherto absent stuff really is. I hurt you by saying, wish you were here.

Edward breezed around last night and we made merrie (sic). He and I wished sorely you had been here. King Edward knowing much of humankind lost no time in advising me wisely in the care of the young.

Sylvia May is the name, Sylvia mind you for the woodlands I love too well and May for Freida's deceased sister, to her mind, for the spirit of youth and Spring to my mind. Some wag, however, recognized the term Sylvia, joshed and guessed the forthcoming male might be named Forrest Glen.[3]

"Eventually, a letter would come from Piper, acknowledging the arrival of Fritz's spanking-new she-born," Don Coleman writes. Unfortunately, Ferd was so busy showing the letter to friends and family that, as Don put it, the letter "never reached his [Ferd's] bound volume of 'Thoughts of Friends' ... from which these writings are captured."[4]

Here is Ferd's October 10 reply to that missing letter:

I speak frankly that your brief communication of a week ago is one of the finest bits of good literature, to my way of thinking, that you have ever issued to me. Its contents were of such a general and withal impersonal nature that I had no hesitancy and much pride in exhibiting it to the immediate family, to father and to Edward.

You state the possibility of coming to this fair clime next week. I wish you would do so, because, while you may be neglected by me at times, you know it is possible to bunk you at the house by putting the maid with Freida and you and I together, though I remember your reactions to sleeping with one another.[5]

Piper wrote back on the 13th of October: "I regret to say the chances of my coming to Williamsport much before the beginning of November are gone 'napoo,' but I will be down, Allah willing, about that time.... But if I come, depend on it, I will not infringe on your hospitality except for a meal, perhaps. The notion of putting Frieda [sic] to any sort of inconvenience, under the circumstances! ... I am of course, anxious to see little Sylvia May, and equally anxious to congratulate the parents."[6]

While the letters from here on out grew less and less frequent, there was always a light in the window for H. Beam Piper. As Don writes: "Beam would be punctual with his annual 'pilgrimage' to Coleman's Williamsport, thoroughly delighting in the festivities of New Year's eve. Although each and all about the land were in a depressing state of Prohibition, the miraculous availability of bootleg bliss would persevere in these parts."[7]

However, the relationship was changing — and not for the better — and Piper's pot shots at a roadside sign sparked off a "shoot-off" between the two friends. On January 14, 1929, Piper wrote: "Have you examined the sign-board on the road above Williamsport yet? I'm curious to know how many of the six .45's and two .22's scored on it. It's a damn shame we didn't think to bring a big can of oily waste along too and complete the work. And I'm sorry you and Edward didn't come along. You'd have gotten a kick out of it, as you a newspaper man in particular, as it was a good simulation of a Chicago gang killing from a car."[8]

Ferd's reply on January 16, 1929, sounds positively parental:

About the Moorish and moronic sign-board shooting. Think not that I am in the least in sympathy with the group that sponsored it. It reeks of a more odiferous brand of Intolerance than that practiced by stupid Christians, because it was perpetrated by friends of otherwise staid and sober mien. I remember about a year ago I wrote you advising about the existence of the society American Association for the Advancement of Atheism, or something like that, the 4 "A's," telling you I would send you some of their tracts. You wrote me that you were scarcely dogmatic as Christian doctrine, and that you therefore wished not to subscribe to the beliefs of any sect, no matter how closely they might teach in accord with your private philosophy.

I thought that strange of you. Yet it is actually funny to observe that now you would spend your time demolishing the false monuments of other faiths, rather than going to the source, the Christian himself, and through him eradicating the pestilence bred by his actions. Once his teaching is out the immediate end is obtained by him. When an editor says something that grates someone, rarely indeed is the paper in which the remarks occur burned, or shot at — the editor himself is approached and given either fisticuffs or words.

Indeed, I would sooner see you kill a Christian than destroy a meaningless sign-board. Enough of this. It takes time, but some day I hope in your presence my oral attributes are well-lubricated, Until then knowing you are a man of reason, I conditionally absolve you. One parting word as to the above, I understand from authority that I cannot question that the county detective has got the scent of this thing. I can only say, with credit to him, he's a fair tracker, but I seriously hope nothing leaks out about the prank.[9]

Coming from "compadre" Ferd, this was a scathing letter, and a volley like this demanded a return salvo. Piper fired back on January 18, 1929:

About the comments on the bombardment. I am somewhat amazed that you are not in sympathy with our deed. Fear that you are becoming domesticated, and if this is the case, I will offer sacrifice to Thor and Odin for my own escape. You say that the shots were aimed in intolerance. I most assuredly admit it!

I can't see how in the hell anybody with more than a twenty-grain intellect could be anything but intolerant of those S's of B's. You say that you would sooner shoot a Christian than shoot that sign-board. Jesus Christ, who wouldn't? You make some mention of my attitude toward the "4A's." I said that I was not joining any church, not even the atheist church. They can be dogmatic as they damn please for all I care. I don't mind dogmatism in another; what I object to is interference with my own brand of dogmatism. You talk about going to the source, the Christian himself. I would, but I don't have enough money, enough men and enough guns to shoot all the Christians in the country.

Will you rob me of the poor satisfaction of shooting them in effigy, then? You know, the only way you can — "eradicate," I think, is the word you so glibly used — this pestilence of "religeon," [sic] is by eradicating the "religeous" [sic]. They are incapable, by reason of the auto-hypnotic state that they are in, of being educated. The only thing to do with them is to either eliminate them, preferably with insect spray, or to segregate them, as one does lepers.[10]

The letters following this screed, certainly from Piper's end, were less personal and more formal. True, the friendship survived for another twenty-odd years, but its "transcendent" quality was lost. This letter was also symbolic of the change in their relationship: Beam, the irresponsible child-man, and Ferd, the responsible family man.

Ferd noticed the change himself in this letter of August 19, 1930, "Now, I feel better, that you have written. For not in recent years have you cast me aside so lengthily, and I pray of you never, never do it again. I am busy as you know with the commercial ills of this world, and must betimes needs be excused, but though you have wrought a piece of undying literature, I consider you have meditated upon and lived with it solidly for six weeks, the period since I last heard from you, to the exclusion of all else."[11]

What had changed in Piper's world, I suspect, was not the amount of time he was spending writing "undying literature," but the amount of time thought about his busy friend Ferd Coleman. By 1932, this new order had become accepted, even by Ferd, who gathered together their letters and bound them up.

There were more changes ahead at the Coleman household. On October 15, 1931, Piper wrote: "Sorry to have delayed so long in felicitating you on your male heir, but I've been a bit under the weather.... You know, the friend with whom I mentioned playing chess between trains in Harrisburg was expecting an heir at any moment when I was down there, and he became a father of a daughter about six hours before your son arrived. I had been waiting for reports from both of you with some interest.

"Well, anyhow, congratulations — or commiserations, however your prefer. This, I suppose, means another rattle. My honorary nephews and nieces are increasing in number."[12]

This December 13, 1931, letter, as Don Coleman writes: "closes out the written correspondence for the year 1931, and also brings to an end some six years of near-consistent exchanges of outlooks, opinions and personal happenstance of life among friends. We must recognize the sharp deceleration occurring over the past year in the flow of missives between comrades."[13]

In Beam's final missive of 1931, he wrote: "Give my best 'reguards' [sic] to all brethren, to Frieda [sic], to Sylvia May and to the infant." As Don says, "The man from Altoona knew not the moniker [Don] given to the male newborn, and this newborn had yet to realize the existence of a man named H. Beam Piper."[14]

Ferd survived the worst of the Depression and his *Shoppers' Guide* continued to prosper. In 1936 the family moved to "a brand-spanking-new-house" in an expensive suburb in the north of Williamsport, an area called Vallamont.[15]

Don Coleman writes: "The most revered space within this house was the den located on the basement floor with a wall-to-wall and floor-to-ceiling bookcase. The remaining three walls were blessed with natural knotty-pine wood paneling. Opposite the bookshelves, a variety of mounted antique weaponry....

"This lair became Piper's living quarters whenever he visited Williamsport.... In 1939, the conservative Coleman purchased a 'Guest Log,' to be inscribed by one and all.... Beam auspiciously holds the timely honor of being the second individual to autograph said log.

DATE: 4/13/'39
NAME: H. Beam Piper
ADDRESS: 407 Wordsworth Ave. Altoona, PA
REMARKS: "In the past five months I have written some 100,000 words, and I cannot think of a goddam thing to say except: this man, Ferd Coleman, is my friend."[16]

Time appears to have healed the wounds of the past, but due to family responsibilities there were few visits. Don Coleman writes: "The majority of Beam's visits were generally but a single night, depending upon his security instructions aboard the railroad. Whenever the schedule permitted him two or three days—which was unusual but not rare—he serviced Coleman's flintlocks and affiliated paraphernalia, always accompanied by a can of fine machine oil, gun blue, and a good bottle of whiskey. When he made it in, the meeting between himself, Coleman, and Ted Ranck [the silent member of the "Unholy Trinity," as they called themselves] would continue through the night with their muffled voices reverberating through the maze of air vents within the walls until just before dawn.

"There were many gatherings inside this den among the trio of intoxicated humanity, which could be monitored by the muddled conversation through the vents."[17]

Because of his graveyard shift at the Juniata Yards in Altoona, Piper had picked up some strange sleeping habits. Don Coleman recounts Piper's stay in the Coleman den: "This lair became Piper's living quarters whenever he visited Williamsport. A magnificent antique cherry wood table, completely nailed with wooden pegs, acted as his desk and workbench. And nestled against the main wall of flintlocks and pistols, powder horns and powder flask, bullet molds and rapier—there be a cushioned and elongated couch for rest. Although never an admitted insomniac, Piper's assessed time of slumber would be minimal—not enough for this humble piece of furniture to get warm. As a bona-fide outdoorsman, Beam traveled as if the night were to be dealt in the woods.... Even though the comforts of warmth and shelter were afforded him whenever dropping into the neighborhood, he habitually carried his sleeping bag, whether he used it or not."[18]

"Coleman, in the meantime, had found that a great deal of legwork is required in obtaining local advertising quotas and maintaining enough column inches of area babble and syndicated news—in order to keep the weekly *Shoppers' Guide* kicking. For a time—a very short time—he would wonder if such a profession was worth a lifetime's endurance. Of course! He was as Piper ... devoted to his calling."[19]

In 1951, Ferd Coleman wrote the following penciled addendum to the preface of the collected letters: "And now, Sept. 1951 at 47, almost twenty years after, the friendship has endured thru these two screaming decades. The relentless requirements of living have limited our time and frequency in letter writing, but several times annually Piper and I (and Ted Ranck) meet. Piper now has of the past four years finally arrived on the professional author's pedestal while for me participation in active literature remains a wistful hope."[20]

Don Coleman adds:

Less then six months after writing this addendum, Ferd W. Coleman met with such an untimely death, that the shocking news could not be digested by his friends and associates, many of whom he had just seen him at a Miami convention two weeks earlier. He had been vacationing as well as writing of his experiences in the Yucatan for publication in his beloved Williamsport *Shoppers' Guide*, and while en route from the Isle of Cozumel to the capital of Merida where he would then return home—the plane's engines began malfunctioning and the aircraft literally "fell apart" at an altitude of about 6,000 feet. One American and nine Mexican citizens perished near Hoctun, Yucatan, just forty miles east of their destination. The date was Saturday, March 15th, 1952.

The Piper-Coleman friendship did not dissolve at this point. Both Piper and Ted Ranck were two of the six pall-bearers participating at the funeral rites over two weeks later. Actually, this friendship would never dissolve. Later on, down the footpaths of time, H. Beam Piper would move lock, stock and barrel (how ironically true, this cliché) to Williamsport."[21]

PART TWO

The Writer

CHAPTER TWELVE

Success at Last!

"GREAT CLAPS OF THUNDER!" Beam roared. The day had come. "I cannot determine whether Great Thor, son of Odin, is the true benefactor of my pleadings, but whosoever it be, 'Jeff Rand' is about to meet the masses!"[1]

— H. Beam Piper
1953

It took over twenty-five years of hard work and perseverance before H. Beam Piper made his first story sale, "Time and Time Again," on September 25, 1946, to John W. Campbell, the legendary editor of *Astounding Science Fiction*. Piper had spent his whole life trying to be a writer and when he arrived, he made the most of it. He went to writers' workshops, conclaves, conventions, and meetings. He became a member of both the Mystery Writers of America and the Hydra Club, the science fiction writers' organization of the time and the precursor to the Science Fiction Writers of America.

Piper was a character, even before his first story sold, but afterwards he "worked" at being distinctive — even fabricating a life that was fascinating in and of itself. And succeeded, I suspect, beyond his wildest expectations. It's unfortunate that he wasn't around for the Piper revival of the late 1970s and 1980s. He would have loved the attention — a lot more than Robert Heinlein, who appeared embarrassed by his fame.

"Time and Time Again" made its appearance in the April 1947 issue of *Astounding Science Fiction*. The editor of *Astounding*, John W. Campbell, was a well-established author before he turned his hand to editing; he is widely considered the originator of modern science fiction and was almost single-handedly responsible for pulling the genre up by the bootstraps and out of the pulp quagmire where it had originated, beginning with Hugo Gernsback's *Amazing Stories*.

It might appear incongruous that H. Beam Piper, who grew up in rural Pennsylvania working as a railroad night watchman, would end up writing science fiction stories. However, by his own admission, he was an early science fiction fan, although he didn't start writing in the field until the 1940s. In addition, he was already writing pulp adventure stories in the 1920s and was a fan of historical adventure romances, such as those penned by Rafael Sabatini and Lawrence Schoonover.

Science fiction only really came into its own in the late 1920s with the first of Gernsback's pulps, *Amazing Stories*. Within a few years, science fiction magazines were multiplying like rabbits and Piper got his introduction at the local newsstand and drug store.

In "Piper," Mike Knerr writes: "It is obvious the 'pulps' nourished him mentally and taught him much of how writing was accomplished. The so-called pulps, for those too young to remember, were the pulp paper magazines that were largely the training ground for aspiring writers."

Black Mask, Weird Tales, etc., were the markets that Piper had been pitching stories to back in the 1920s and 1930s. The pulps cost twenty or twenty-five cents and were a modern version of the 1880s dime novels. By the end of the 1950s they were all gone, victims of rising paper costs and declining sales — mostly due to television and changing tastes.[2]

Unfortunately, the letter in which Piper notified the Coleman clan that he had made his first sale is among several missing letters. However, it doesn't take much imagination to guess that Piper was floating on air — he was finally a published author, by Odin and by Thor! And, he did it all by himself. I can't recall any other prominent science fiction writer who labored and toiled as long as H. Beam Piper did before his first sale and publication. I dare say it was the happiest day of his life.

Piper was good friends with Fletcher Pratt, an interesting writer, who had success both in the science fiction and historical romance fields, as well as with military books and nonfiction. He's also considered one of the fathers of modern war gaming. Pratt's *Great Battlefields of History* is still considered by many to be one of the great military history works, and one Piper was quite familiar with. Fletcher Pratt, writer and editor, wrote the introduction to one of the first science fiction anthologies, *World of Wonder*, published by Twayne in 1951. This anthology contains two Piper stories, "He Walked Around the Horses" and "Operation R.S.V.P."

In his introduction to "He Walked Around the Horses," Pratt gives us insight as to what the science fiction fraternity of the mid–1940s thought about this *new* author:

> When the name of H. Beam Piper appeared for the first time on the contents page of *Astounding*, there was considerable speculation as to which of the well-known writers of science fiction was using this pseudonym. It seemed all too obviously the sort of disguise that would be employed to cover ventures into fiction by some scientist or engineer whose primary concern was with electronics. Also, there was the fact that the writing had the indescribable professional atmosphere which is the result of long experience with exactly how many words are needed to give the illusion of reality to an imagined emotion or scene.
>
> Of course the speculators did not know that the Beams and the Pipers are two of the oldest families in that curious little enclave of northeastern Pennsylvania which lives so much by itself. Neither were they aware that this particular scion of the stems had cut his literary teeth on solid and rather learned works in history. Born in 1903, Mr. Piper is an engineer on the Pennsylvania Railroad — not the train driving kind, but the type who stays in a shop and operates a slide rule. It is worth noting that the singular disappearance of Mr. Benjamin Bathurst is a recorded historical incident.[3]

Pratt's story introduction shows that Piper's first story appearance made a good-sized splash in the small puddle of science fiction.

In L. Sprague de Camp's 1996 autobiography, *Time and Chance*, he records his impressions of Piper after a meeting circa 1950. "In Altoona we got in touch with a science-fictional colleague, H. Beam Piper. He came to our hotel and later showed me his collection of weapons. Piper had a defect of speech like that of the hard of hearing, giving his voice a loud, harsh timbre. Moreover, while he seemed glad to see me, women made him so ill at ease that he almost ignored Catherine [Mrs. de Camp] while she was in the room."[4]

Piper was rarely at ease with women until he was familiar with them. While almost twenty years older, he did make quite an impression on Ferd Coleman's "Gal Friday," Eleanor Border. In a letter to Miss Border, he writes: "There is another Piper masterpiece on the newsstands at present ['Flight from Tomorrow'] ... and my story, 'Last Enemy,' will possibly appear in the next issue of *Astounding Science Fiction* with color illustration. There are three other pieces coming up in different magazines, but I have no dates for any of them at present."[5] According to the entries in his Story Log, things would never again look as rosy as they did in July of 1950.

The period from 1947 to 1955 was the most fulfilling and rewarding period of H. Beam Piper's life — a time when all things were possible and new surprises were on the horizon, as Don Coleman recounts:

> Without doubt, Beam was quite capable of having several irons in the fire simultaneously. The following month ... a nonfiction chronicle emerged. Maintaining a vast knowledge of the Civil War era, it was incredible what weapons of those battles he could sketch from the smallest insignificant fitting, to the enormity of a complete cannon.
>
> However, when it came to drawing, small arms was his forte. And he could run off the chronology of a complete battle. One would merely mention a specific date between 1861 and 1865 and Beam would muse for a moment, then quite narrowly pinpoint the action that was taking place on that date. His expertise in telling the stories of history was superb and his verbal illustration of the situation at hand was visually transmitted to within the listener's mind with ease; much more readily than the complexities involved with science fiction.
>
> So, when a short [piece] entitled "Rebel Raider" sold to *True Magazine* ... Beam's reaction was exhilaration that he had become one of the proud contributors to such a reputable publication.[6]

In actuality, it was his agent, science fiction editor and author Frederik Pohl, who would make the sale to *True Magazine*. "That man," Piper exclaimed in a letter, "could sell snow to Eskimos!"[7]

Coleman continues:

> The article portrayed the Confederate Army Colonel John Mosby and his behind-the-lines exploits with the Union armies. In most cases, this colorful cavalry unit, known as Mosby's Rangers, was successful.... H. Beam Piper was fascinated by Mosby, one who would gamble and take the consequences of high risk and peril; a perfect subject to write upon. Anxiously, he had decided to present just a small episode of a very costly and bloody war and as a result of this factual adventure, the author's credibility continued to rise among his peers.
>
> With the telling of this story, another facet of Beam's character surfaced in his delight over a fan letter he _had_ received after the article's publication. It was from a reader in Virginia who insisted that Beam had to be a southerner. He cackled happily every time he told the story. He truly loved that kind of feedback and personally felt that the people of the Shenandoah Valley, after July 1876, should have built a monument to Crazy Horse and the Sioux Nation for having knocked off George Armstrong Custer at the Little Big Horn.
>
> Soon after publication, Ferd Coleman received an elated telegram from Piper, advising that Walt Disney Productions had offered a price for movie rights to the article. Beam, of course, agreed to the negotiations at hand. However, some years passed without any indication of this particular story coming to the silver screen.[8]

In "Typewriter Killer," Beam says: "Why Walt Disney bought the movie rights to that article, I've never figured out. Will Colonel Mosby be played by Mickey Mouse and General Phil Sheridan by Donald Duck? It's baffling. However, I was glad to get the check."[9]

Almost twenty years later, in 1967, the "Rebel Raider" story appeared as a Disney movie, as *Mosby's Marauders (aka Willie and the Yank)*. There's been some question about the 1957–1958 television series called *The Gray Ghost*, which ran for thirty-nine episodes, being inspired by "Rebel Raider": however, it was produced by CBS and based on Virgil Carrington Jones' 1956 novel, *Grey Ghosts and Rebel Raiders*. No earlier commitments had been instituted regarding television rights or royalties — so Beam received nothing other than the original dispensation from Disney ($1,800.00 + $200.00 for the agent's fee) on June 6, 1951 (appendix A).

Don Coleman writes: "The following year brought more Piper tales to the newsstands, including 'Dearest,' 'Temple Trouble,' 'Genesis' and 'Day of the Moron.' And in 1952, his short novel, *Uller Uprising*, would by-pass the pulps and wind up as part of a trilogy under hard cover...."

"The Thin Man was on his way."[10]

Piper's unfinished literary trilogy "Tiadaghton" was lost in the mists of time, but not forgotten. He alludes to it in the Colonel Shoemaker dedication in *Murder in the Gunroom*. Beam refers to "an old and valued friend, who was promised this dedication, with an entirely different novel in mind, twenty-two years ago."

Beam was overjoyed by the sale of his first mystery novel in 1952: "GREAT CLAPS OF THUNDER!" he roared. The day had come. "I cannot determine whether Great Thor, son of Odin, is the true benefactor of my pleadings, but whosoever it be, 'Jeff Rand' is about to meet the masses!"[11]

According to Don Coleman, Piper presented Ferd Coleman with "a hard-bound double-spaced 339-page carbon edition of the original manuscript in 1941." It was entitled "Murder Bereaves Hattie." At that time, he used the pseudonym of Herbert Orr — his father's name. Piper penned in the following entry on February 12, 1941: "To Ferd Coleman, who read this in two weeks, which is, for Ferd, a feat comparable to reading the *Bible*, Shakespeare and the *Encyclopedia Britannica* in forty eight hours. H. Beam Piper, alias HERBERT ORR 2/12/41."[12]

As with so many other Piper works, both before and after, he wrote and rewrote endlessly, although not to editorial prescription, but to his own — sometimes flawed — view of the marketplace. Once he got a good idea, he hated to drop it. If the story didn't sell, it wasn't poor editorial taste or his idea. In his mind it was his execution of the story that was at fault; thus, he would rewrite the entire work, often before the story or book was rejected — or even finished. *Murder in the Gunroom* is a good example, as we know of at least three different versions. The Piper process was long and laborious, short story or novel, it made no difference; both got the full "Piper Treatment."

Of Heinlein's Five Rules for Writing, the one that is probably the most misunderstood is "Rule Three: You Must Refrain from Rewriting, Except to Editorial Order."[13] A lot of lazy writers have used this as an excuse for turning out sloppy first drafts and calling them finished works. What Heinlein meant was, once the story or novel is finished — which may entail considerable rewriting — don't keep going back and rewriting every time it comes back from a publisher or agent, unless someone offers to buy it if certain changes are made. Piper's output would have gone through the roof had he listened to this simple advice; on the other hand, in his letters and diaries Piper was continually moaning about being bereft of ideas. Obviously, for a writer, it's better to endlessly rewrite than to write nothing at all.

Don Coleman remembers: "In 1946, after rewriting and renaming this mystery novel and chipping it down to 250 double-spaced pages, he presented a new-bound carbon edition to Coleman, bearing its new title, "No Cash Drawers in Coffins." Again, in a matter of weeks, the manuscript was renounced and thus set aside for more important things as probing into the worlds of the unknown; the stampede of sci-fi competition. Then, in 1952, when Beam had eventually proved that this many-times-worked-over manuscript dating back over ten years, was worth reading — it was long-last convincingly sold."[14]

The sale of *Murder in the Gunroom* also brought Piper some fame at work. The *Pennsy* "Typewriter 'Killer'" article provides the best word picture we have of Piper's daily routine in the early 1950s.

At 7:00 A.M. he goes home to the third-floor apartment he shares with his aged mother, and gets into his pajamas and drinks a glass of black Jamaican rum — "not Puerto Rican — I'm very bigoted on the subject of rum," he says.

"Then I light up my pipe with Serane tobacco — been smoking that brand the last thirty years — and either go over what I wrote the previous day or plan out what I'll write that afternoon. I usually go to bed about 8:30 A.M.

"I wake up about 3:30 or 5 P.M., depending on how much sleep I've been doing without the past few days. I have breakfast, which consists of a bottle of 7-Up and a pot of coffee — black, of course. Then I get to the typewriter and work two to four hours, which gives me time to have dinner and report to work at 11 P.M.

"There are times when I'm going well on the typewriter, running hotter than a two-dollar pistol on the Fourth of July, and I'm a little sad about dropping what I'm doing and going to work. On the other hand, sometimes when I'm going through the deserted shops at night, some plot development that has me stumped will suddenly clear up — the whole thing will light up like an electric sign."

Mr. Piper's first mystery novel, published by Alfred A. Knopf last March, was *Murder in the Gunroom*, a story of intrigue and violence among firearms collectors. The book gave him a chance to make use of his extensive knowledge of antique weapons, another interest of his that goes back a long way.[15]

The book advance for *Murder in the Gunroom* was $750.00 (minus a 10 percent agent's cut to Fred Pohl) for a total of $675.00 in Beam's pocket (appendix A). Using an inflation calculator, the $675.00 in 1952 dollars is the equivalent of $5,179.00 in 2007 dollars. There is no further mention of any royalties in Piper's Story Log so it is doubtful the book ever earned out its meager advance, although the amount Piper received was typical of the time for a "new" mystery author. In retrospect, even after fifty-plus years of inflation, $675.00 was a piddling sum for a book involving many years of labor and at least four different rewrites.

Piper's editor at Knopf probably wasn't interested in a sequel, despite a good review from the *New York Times*, because the first volume never earned out its small advance. That, of course, didn't stop him from writing at least two different sequels, "Murder in the Conference Room" and "Murder Frozen Over," with who knows how many rewrites. However, *Murder in the Gunroom* was Beam's first novel sale and as such represented a big step up in the world of professional writing.

In "The Early Letters," Coleman writes: "The next time the author was in Williamsport — unknown to all — he taxied up to the white house at the top of Highland Terrace, waving the cabbie off with adios. With small satchel in hand, he made it up to the front door stoop, entered the unlocked house unannounced and directed himself to the den. Knowing every inch of the late Ferd Coleman's lair, he pulled the '46 bound manuscript of 'No Cash Drawers in Coffins' from the shelf and quickly laid it open on the cherry wood table. He bent down and made an inked entry on the title page:

Final Title

MURDER IN THE GUNROOM

"He then turned to Freida Coleman who had followed the unseen noises to the den and now faced him from the doorway, awestruck. He closed the old bound edition, walked over to Freida and handed her a pre-autographed fresh copy of the new published book, which read:

For Frieda Coleman
with years of friendship
behind us, and, I hope
many ahead.

H. Beam Piper

"Suddenly he performed a rarity. With outstretched arms, he flat and outright hugged her!

"'I miss Ferd, Freida,' he resounded with guttural delivery. 'I must return home tomorrow but would like to spend an evening of nostalgia within this room. These walls know me well and I can speak to them without equivocation. After all, it may be the last time.'"[16]

CHAPTER 13

A Late Bloomer

> Received the invitation to your wedding. I sincerely regret that I won't be on hand, but the only social function I could get away from work to attend on a Saturday would be a funeral, and that my own.[1]
>
> — H. Beam Piper

We know very little about H. Beam Piper's romantic interludes, or their absence, after the 1930s, except for his courtly romance with Ferd's "gal Friday," Miss Eleanor Border in the late 1940s and early '50s. As Don Coleman tells it:

Whenever Beam arrived in Williamsport prior to noon, contingent upon his railroad schedule, he would make his way to the *Shoppers' Guide* office and after greeting the pleasant secretary — generally talk Ferd into lunch....

Through the early 1940s, Piper's favorite friend ran his business from a second floor office overlooking Market Square in the center of downtown Williamsport, where many store owners were domiciled on ground floor locations and doctors, lawyers, realtors and insurance firms occupied the upper part of the buildings surrounding the "square." This intersection split up the north, south, east and west of the city, with a black and white pagoda at the immediate center where a policeman was based, monitoring and directing traffic. Coleman's *Shoppers' Guide* was printed some thirty miles down the Susquehanna at Sunberry, and trucked back up river late each Thursday night for Friday morning distribution.

After so many years of farming-out the printing — for all his efforts and success — he was now able to purchase a speck of city land and build his own printing plant. And about this time, he had also gained a most apt and intelligent secretary who actually could be referred to as the real and genuine "gal Friday."

From time to time, Ferd would have Miss Border join the two whenever his spontaneous thoughts required enumeration. Her shorthand was impeccable and swift.... On these occasions the young secretary became quite fascinated with the studious Mr. Piper and his power of speech. And, although Ferd typed his own personal letters to Beam, separate greetings from his star steno would not be uncommon under the same postage.

Even today, this lovely lady can see Beam most vividly, sitting at lunch and presenting his views of the tale at hand. And all the while, he is completely absorbed in taking his teaspoon; employing same as a spade and digging a neat hollow in his mound of mashed potatoes, after which he would thus plant a healthy sprig of parsley! Spooning up residual around the foothills of the mound, he would then "pack it in" about the little stalk. The planting had been accomplished!

What woman could resist! H. Beam Piper was truly a sophisticate of sorts but definitely one who could care less of what this troubled world thought of him while supping with friends in public. If he wished to pluck a stem of foliage atop a pile of fluffed potatoes, he would do so without pretense ... the man was enjoyed for exactly this type of antic.

Beam invariably would spend his New Year's Eves in Williamsport or in the vicinity if at all physically and financially possible. There had been those times when he could not — no matter what the circumstances — come up with the familiar pot to piss in.

His "Time and Time Again" had been picked up by *Astounding Science Fiction* and published in the

April 1947 issue, really starting the trip, followed by "He Walked Around the Horses" and "Police Operation." Finding himself in a mellow and [financially] eased interval, he decided to ask Miss Border out for New Year's. As a perfect gentleman, he had given the lady plenty of time to consider, and the invitation was accepted without any ado. Beam initially asked the somewhat trite questions, "What are you doing New Year's, Eleanor?"

Eleanor Border was infatuated with [such] a cunning mind as Piper's, it having a legitimate answer for whatever was asked. After reading an article in a reputable monthly periodical, she wrote a question to Beam regarding the great Dr. Watson, ... the highly respected sidekick of Sherlock Holmes. If one such as Beam was to write criminology, he surely must have researched the works of Sir Arthur, even though he had not yet made a sale in this category.[2]

In fact, Piper did do a Holmes pastiche, "The Return," with his only collaborator, John J. McGuire. In this fascinating science fiction tale, which was reprinted in a 1960s science fictional Sherlock Holmes anthology in Britain, the survivors of a worldwide holocaust live in a backwoods environment similar to those of Piper's Pennsylvanian ancestors. Holmesian deduction and references are used as the denouement of this delightful little yarn.

Coleman continues: "Knowing 'The Thin Man,' it took no research to toss Miss Border a written reply." He quotes Piper's message:

Your letter, accompanying the Mawster's, very gladly received. No, I hadn't the dimmest idea that it had been you who'd sent me the clipping on the new method of aiming guided missiles by the stars. I should have thought of you, since you gave me another clipping of a similar character, about some French scientist who claimed to have developed some sort of a "perpetual daylight" system. I read the note ... but instead described it as "...a clipping and note from Ferd Coleman."

I didn't see the hitherto unpublished Sherlock Holmes story, and forgot about it after reading your letter until now, when I am referring to it to see just what you wrote me that I'm supposed to be writing an answer to. I've been hip pockets deep in alligators for the last six or eight weeks on a long novelette, and am just wading out. If I can still find a copy of what it was, at the time of your writing the current issue of *Cosmopolitan*, I'll have to read it....

No, I was not the Holmes fan who mentioned the theory that Dr. Watson was a woman. Inasmuch as his beard and mustache are mentioned in a number of Holmes stories, and inasmuch as it is explicitly stated that he married a young lady who was involved in the celebrated case of the *Sign of the Four*, and inasmuch as there is some mention of his wife's death and his return to 222b Baker Street to resume his bachelor-quarters with Holmes, and inasmuch as he was a medical officer with Lord Roberts in Afghanistan and was shot in the leg (or in the shoulder; Doyle had him wounded in both places, in different stories), I would say, off-hand, that definitely, no woman was Dr. Watson.[3]

Coleman continues: "Subsequently, Beam and Eleanor continued to date on occasion, but on a definite platonic scale.... Beam's perimeter of learning was invisible and as far as the amiable Miss Border was concerned, it would forever show no limits.

"Eventually, she would become attracted to a skilled young printer employed at the *Shoppers' Guide*. Overcome with romantic vivacity, the enamored couple wasted little time in such decision-making as marriage; and the unforgotten Mr. Piper became ... an early recipient of the traditional invitation."[4]

Beam's reply was immediate:

H. BEAM "PIPER"
407 HOWARD AVE.
ALTOONA, PA
7/9/50

Dear Eleanor,
Received the invitation to your wedding. I sincerely regret that I won't be on hand, but the only social function I could get away from work to attend on a Saturday would be a funeral, and that my own. So, in lieu of my presence, you'll have to accept my congratulations and best wishes, as well as a token which will follow this letter in a few days.

You may be sure that the best wishes are of my most sincere top-quality variety; I hope you have every sort of good fortune in your venture into matrimony.

I was sorry that what the radio people call "unavoidable travel schedules" made it impossible for me to see you when I was last in Williamsport. For that, blame the PCA — if they hadn't advanced the time of that flight to the ungodly hour of 9:40 A.M., we could have had lunch, complete with jet-propelled sundaes, on Monday.

There is another Piper masterpiece on the newsstands at present, this time in a thing called *Future*, a standard-sized pulp with a lurid cover. The story is "Immunity," which you may have read in carbon copy, but for some reason known only to himself and, possibly, God, the editor re-titled it "Flight From Tomorrow." It is billed, under that title on the cover. And my story, "Last Enemy," will possibly appear in the next issue of *Astounding Science Fiction*, with cover illustration. There are three other pieces coming up in different magazines, but I have no dates for any of them at present.

Repeating my best wishes for the good fortunes of Mrs. Ardrey, I am, as always,

Cordially,
Beam Piper[5]

H. Beam Piper may have been a romantic when it came to courting, but when it came to taking care of his basic needs, as Mike Knerr writes, Beam had a whole different side:

He enjoyed telling stories about himself, about the odd and funny things that had happened to him over the years — and in some instances, he would drop his carefully cultured Victorian guard and shock his listeners (always men) with the talk of his adventure with a New York call girl. This, of course, would have to come after several Myers's Rum highballs.

At a hotel one evening the urge hit him and he made a phone call. The girl came to his room, took off her clothes and looked at him curiously.

"What do you want?" she asked, not knowing what sort of *party* he was interested in.

"Well," Piper said simply, "lay down on the bed."

She looked surprised. "Oh! You just want a good old-fashioned fuck!"

"Yes," Piper replied in delight, "that's it!"

He didn't like to write about sex and he maintained a kind of aloof attitude about it most of the time. His story of the call girl was the only one I heard him tell. In fact, if we would get into a conversation (among the trio who usually hung around his apartment) about various girlfriends from our past, Piper would simply sit at his desk puffing at his pipe with a slightly amused expression on his face.

After Robert Heinlein's *Stranger in a Strange Land* made such an impact on the country I asked him about using a little sex in his stories, since the American reading trend seemed to be moving in that direction.

"Heinlein," Beam replied with squinch-eyed frankness, "can do what he likes. I prefer to keep my heroine *virgo intacto* until the end."[6]

CHAPTER 14

The Campbell Years

"Space Viking" itself is, I think, one of the classics—a yarn that will be cited, years hence, as one of the science fiction classics.[1]

— John W. Campbell

H. Beam Piper was never a hard science-fiction author, i.e., one whose primary interest was in technology and science. While he was fascinated by scientific progress, he was more interested in human beings and how they related to larger historical forces. Thus it was that he created his Terro-Human Future History, the framework for most of his stories from *Uller Uprising* to *Space Viking*.

In the *Double-Bill Symposium* fanzine, Piper, writing shortly before his death, provides the following answer to these questions: "During your formative writings, what one author influenced you the most? What other factors such as background, education, etc., were important influences?"

Piper's response: "My formative writings go back a long time, and one tends to forget. I am sure, however, that their name is legion. In the early days, as soon as I'd discover a new favorite, I'd decide that I was going to write like him. I was going to write like James Branch Cabell, which would have taken a lot of doing. Before that, I was going to write like Rafael Sabatini, and like Talbot Munday, and like Rider Haggard, and even, God help us, like Edgar Rice Burroughs. I never wanted to write like H.G. Wells, he spent entirely too much of his time on a soapbox. Eventually I decided to write like H. Beam Piper, only a little bit better. I am still trying.

"As my stories all have a political and social slant instead of a physical-science slant, I think the one author who influenced me most was Nicco Machiavelli, with H.L. Mencken placing and Karl von Clausewitz showing."[2]

Probably the best description of Piper's own view of his science fiction (mostly aimed at John W. Campbell's *Astounding*, to which Piper was a frequent contributor during the early 1950s) is contained in this excerpt from *Murder in the Gunroom*. It is made by Pierre Jarret, a science fiction author and confidant to the protagonist, Jeff Rand—in answer to the question: "What are you writing?"

"Science fiction. I do a lot of stories for the pulps ... Space Trails, and Other Worlds and Wonder Stories: mags like that. Most of it's standardized formula-stuff; what's known in the trade as space-operas. My best stuff goes to *Astonishing* [a barely disguised *Astounding*, jfc]. Parenthetically, you mustn't judge any of these magazines by their names. It seems to be a convention to use hyperbolic names for science fiction magazines; a heritage from an earlier and ruder day. What I do for Astonishing is really hard work, and I enjoy it. I'm working now on one of them, based on J.W. Dunne's time-theories [Piper's Paratime series was based on Dunne's time theories, jfc], if you know what they are."[3]

In this excerpt, Piper provides a personal assessment, from his perspective, of early 1950s science fiction magazines and a rare look at his own writing. In editor John W. Campbell, he had found a kindred spirit; plus, an editor who highly admired his writing and wrote him detailed letters on how to improve or strengthen — as determined by Campbell, of course — those stories. And, in a few cases, ideas for more stories in "that future history of yours." Beam, who had wandered in the wilderness of rejection and dismissal for over thirty years, must have felt like Moses finding the burning bush!

Lester del Rey, noted writer, book reviewer and editor and founder of Del Rey Books, had this to say about the legendary John W. Campbell:

> Back in the early days of science fiction, everyone knew it was impossible to make a living in the field. There were only two SF magazines being published each paying somewhere around $200.00 for a long novelette and perhaps $25.00 for an unusually good short story. Even when a story was accepted, a writer might have to wait months after publication before he was finally paid for his work. Furthermore, no science fiction books were being published; so once a story appeared in a magazine, there would be no further income from it.
>
> Writing science fiction was a hobby, not a career and nobody questioned that obvious fact — nobody but John W. Campbell! Against all logic, he not only determined to make science fiction his life's work, but he succeeded, becoming almost single-handedly the creator of modern science fiction. And eventually, others with less genius or less folly found it possible to follow the trail he blazed.
>
> Toward the end of 1937, he was asked to be the editor of *Astounding Stories* (soon to be renamed *Astounding Science Fiction* and later *Analog Science Fact/Fiction*). He continued as its editor until his death in 1971. As a writer under either pen name, Campbell had been one of the best; but as an editor, he quickly became the greatest. If that is a personal judgment, it is one shared by most writers and editors in the field.
>
> When he took over as editor, the magazine had settled into a dull routine; and other magazines were folding or turning to blood-and-thunder stories. Campbell rapidly changed all that. He had a clear vision of what science fiction should become, and he began teaching that vision to all the established writers capable of learning it. He also discovered a host of new writers within the first few years of his editorship. Most of the leading science-fiction writers today are ones he discovered and trained: Asimov, de Camp, Heinlein, Sturgeon, van Vogt, and many others.
>
> Writers were developed, too, not merely discovered. Faulty stories went back with pages of detailed criticism of plot and technique that meant more than any dozen courses on how to write. Ideas for stories poured out from Campbell to his writers, and many of the best-loved stories in the field came from those ideas. He had the marvelous talent of suggesting just the right idea to a writer and putting it into a form that a writer could best handle.[4]

H. Beam Piper's most important writing relationship was the one he had with Campbell, the editor who bought Piper's first and last stories. Campbell's "competent man" was very similar to Beam's own self-reliant man, almost to the point where some readers and critics thought Piper was "pitching" his story ideas to what he thought Campbell would buy, as indicated in his *Astounding* editorials. This was not as far-fetched as it sounds, since several authors, such as Randall Garret, admittedly did just that — and made a good living doing it, too. Campbell, like Piper, was a man who knew what he liked, said what he thought and believed every word. And, he had a stubborn streak that matched Piper's own.

Was Piper just a Campbell puppet, like many other writers, who echoed John's editorials for a quick sale? Or did they share the same ideas and philosophies? While most of the Piper-Campbell correspondence could be described as pleasant and mutually respectful, it's obvious from the tone and words of Piper's letters that he was no "yes man." In this 1951 letter, where Piper is discussing the pros and cons of dealing with agented story submissions, he wrote: "I'm afraid, though, that your suggested solution would do more harm than good, by angering authors; it could easily be reflected in author's instructions to agents: 'Send it to anybody but that s.o.b. at *Astounding*.'

"Another solution, that of refusing to buy from anybody but agents, would result in shutting off the manuscripts from new authors—if you'd had a policy like that in 1946, I'd never have gotten published anywhere. It would leave you with a dwindling staff of old-timers, while the new writers were all going to Sam Merwin or Horace Gold."[5]

This letter demonstrates that while Piper was respectful of Campbell's feelings, he was not afraid to speak the truth—even if it was to the man who made his writing career a reality. Piper, still a night watchman for the Pennsy, made light of his economic dependence upon Campbell and Street & Smith in his letter's closing comments: "Sorry I can't think of an answer that wouldn't cost money, or lay me open to the accusation of scheming to bore a hole in Street & Smith's money-box to my own advantage and enrichment."[6]

In this interesting letter from January 15, 1951, Campbell wrote to Piper's first agent, Frederik Pohl, regarding the short story "Day of the Moron"—a story about nuclear reactors and human error that is prescient of the Three-Mile Island incident.

> Dear Pohl:
>
> Please tell Piper that this one, as set up, is too hot for us to handle. It'll have to be changed slightly. As set up, it's enough to make most union men ready to chaw the handiest publisher's representative; this we consider an unhealthy phenomenon, as we need publisher's representatives.
>
> The thing to do is to make it clear that the union officials <u>have been misled</u> by misinformation from the two discharges, and are equally aware of the necessity, once they get the true picture. In other words, the <u>union</u> isn't to blame, but the individuals are.
>
> ... And it could be done fairly readily by installing a scene in which the union leader confers with the fired shop steward and organizer, and is given deliberately misleading information.
>
> Point is—we got unions too, you know.
>
> Regards.
> John W. Campbell, Jr.
> Editor[7]

Piper made the necessary changes and "Day of the Moron" appeared in the September 1951 issue of *Astounding*. Piper appeared willing to listen to editorial suggestions, especially if it meant a sale; a sound practice for a budding author. What's unusual about this letter is watching the legendary John W. Campbell back away from a fight—although New York unions in the fifties were easy to rile and he was probably right to be wary of putting his hand in that particular lion's cage. Especially since most of the magazine distributors were Teamsters and could have easily refused to ship the magazine. Still, it's a side of Mr. Campbell rarely seen in personal anecdotes or in print.

Piper didn't always have the best luck with agents, one reason Kenneth White—a man he both liked and respected—was to play such a pivotal role in Piper's future. In this 1954 letter, Piper wrote to John Campbell about his recently fired agent, Frederik Pohl.

> Dear John:
>
> I've been having a bit of trouble about some money due me from my former agent, Fred Pohl. In fact, I'm having trouble finding out just how much money he owes me. It occurred to me that you might be able to help me check on one minor item.
>
> I notice that your "Who Goes There?" appears, under the title <u>Wer Da?</u> in the Karl Rauch anthology *ÜBERWINDUNG VON RAUM UND ZEIT*, along with my "Time and Time Again" (Zeit und Wieder Zeit). Did you ever get any money from Karl Rauch for that, and if so, how much? Pohl never paid me a goddamned cent—exchange difficulties he said. I realize that this is a very small item, but I want to check up on everything, no matter how small. If you got paid, that blows the exchange difficulties story.
>
> H. Beam Piper[8]

On July 21, 1951, John Campbell wrote back:

Dear Piper,

My friend, I had trouble with Fred Pohl years before you did. You are indeed having exchange difficulties with him: I know enough of the story of the Pohl Agency to understand that. But in the case of the German translation, I think you're not out much: the German public wasn't as ripe for science fiction as Gotthard Gunther thought they were.

But I can't help you on the <u>Wer Da?</u> problem. I have my difficulties, too, you see — and my difficulty is that Shasta Publishers handled "Who Goes There?" They may be somewhat better than the Fred Pohl's agency, but believe me, not much. I haven't had an accounting from them in nearly two years; Korshak sold pocket book rights to "Who Goes There?" despite the fact that he didn't have a right to, and then neglected to inform me that he had done so — particularly, he neglected to send me any of the $1500 proceeds that he owed me.

You think I know what royalties Karl Rauch paid? Hell, I wasn't even informed that Dell had paid $1500!

Regards, John W. Campbell, Jr.[9]

As his "fame" as a science-fiction author spread, Piper began to tailor his life along those lines, paying more attention to scientific events and their effects on the future.

In 1956 Piper wrote one of the seminal works in his Terro-Human Future History, which he called "The Knife Edge" (it was later re-titled "The Edge of the Knife") in which he tells the story of a history teacher who can "see" into the future — sometimes with disastrous results. He not only sees into the near future but the far future and the First Empire.

During the mid–1950s, Piper was often in New York and while there would have luncheons with various editors, often Campbell. On November 7, 1956, Piper noted in his diary: "Lunch with John W. Campbell — he is not buying 'Knife Edge' because it conflicts with the strategy he has adopted in trying to boost psionics."[10]

That's a very strange reason to bounce a story, but if Campbell hadn't liked the story, he would have let Piper know. And, Piper, who almost always picked up the "Analytical Laboratory Bonus" for most popular story, was certainly one of Campbell's favorites. Of course, Campbell did have several agendas, Dianetics in the late 1940s, psionics in the 1950s and perpetual motion machines, the Dean Drive, in the early 1960s.

In Mike Ashley's analysis of the *Astounding/Analog* Analytical Laboratory (a feature where readers' votes for their favorite stories were *supposedly* tallied and the authors given a monetary bonus), in his *Complete Index to Astounding/Analog*, Piper ranked third in overall cumulative Analytical Laboratory voting, which is amazing considering he didn't publish all that many stories and novels in the magazine — only one behind C.L. Moore (who is now almost forgotten) and the number one vote getter, Robert A. Heinlein.[11]

Parenthetically, Campbell confided to a few associates that very few fans actually sent in Analytical Laboratory votes for their favorite stories, so Campbell picked the winners himself, and used it as a means to raise the word rate for those authors whose work he most valued. This demonstrates that Campbell valued Piper very highly, since many of the *Astounding* regulars published two or three times more fiction in the Street and Smith publication than H. Beam Piper. As John McGuire Jr. told me, Campbell was always asking Piper and his father to write more stories.[12]

It was the early Robert Heinlein and H. Beam Piper, of all the *Astounding* science fiction writers, who most epitomized Campbell's philosophies. In a Piper retrospective "H. Beam Piper: An Infinity of Worlds," in the fanzine *Renaissance*, John H. Costello writes: "Into his stories he put a great deal of philosophy — of the Campbellian sort.... Piper was a 19th Century Liberal, a creature with whom neither conservatives nor libertarians can be completely comfortable; and like their creator, he did not believe that anyone had a right to automatic sustenance. Throughout his career, he remained a 19th Century Liberal and a Citizen in the

Campbellian sense — quite firmly dedicated to the ideal of Civilization and individual self-reliance."[13]

In many ways H. Beam Piper epitomized the Citizen, as described by Campbell: "The fully developed Citizen actually seems to be every bit as hard-headed, ruthless and dangerous a fighter as any barbarian — he just uses his ruthless determination wisely instead of egocentrically."[14] The essence of the Piper hero is best described by himself in "Oomphel in the Sky," as a person who "actually knows what has to be done and how to do it, without holding a dozen conferences and round-table discussions and giving everybody a fair and equal chance to foul things up for him."[15] This is a fair description of Pappy Jack from *Little Fuzzy*, Calvin Morrison of *Lord Kalvan of Otherwhen*, Conn Maxwell of *Cosmic Computer*, Campbell's Citizen and for that matter Piper himself.

As Mike Knerr notes in "Piper": "Shot down on this tack [psionics], Beam did what all writers do — turned it all over to his agent and began scribbling notes 'For a new SF novelette (the poor fisherman who sold the holy relic).' Beam had, of course, long ago learned the most important lesson a writer can learn — pay no attention to rejections. Most scribes can paper their den with those odd little slips of paper that say 'Thank you for your submission, but we regret to return your manuscript as it is just not right for our needs at this time.'"[16]

In regards to their editor-author relationship, it's quite apparent from John Campbell's letters that Campbell had a lot of respect for Piper's work even if he didn't buy everything Piper sent him. In a November 6, 1961, letter to Piper's agent, Kenneth White, Campbell wrote:

Dear Mr. White:
Beam Piper's Slave ["A Slave is a Slave"] yarn is a lovely thing; he's got some lovely lines in it — and some very sound philosophical points."
There is, however, one [philosophical point] that belongs here so solidly that I'd like to have Beam insert it, in his words, where he thinks it fits, if he agrees it fits — and I believe he will!
St. Augustine, nearly 1500 years ago, made a very interesting point. The fabled "innocence of a babe," he pointed out, has nothing whatever to do with innocence of intent, but innocence of opportunity and power. A lamb isn't a sweet, kindly, inoffensive creature — it's just weak. It's actually, a mean-tempered, stupid, and remarkably nasty little batch of protoplasm.
Much of the oh-so-liberal love for the Common Man is based on comparing his "gentleness" with the ruthless, aggressive behavior of the uncommon man. The common man is, in fact, like the lamb and the babe — innocent of deed only because he is incompetent, but anything but innocent of intent.
The massacre at the end simply represents precisely what the common man wanted and intended all along.
St. Augustine's point, I think, belongs. One should not mistake inability to carry out vicious desires for innocent intent.
"The check for the manuscript — $750.00 — will be along shortly."
Regards,
John W. Campbell[17]

H. Beam Piper's reaction was quite positive, as reflected in this November 8, 1961, diary entry: "Called John Campbell, first at his office, and then at his home — he is quite delighted with it ["A Slave Is a Slave"], John is almost as big a fascist sonofabitch as I am — but wants a couple of points hammered home a little harder." He assured Campbell that he would get right on it as soon as he got back to Williamsport. Then he went down to Robert Abels and "bought a sword, late XIV or XV century for $125.00."[18]

There were some things about Piper's writing that Campbell did not like, as shown in this May 13, 1959, *Little Fuzzy* rejection letter:

Dear Piper:

First, I'm drowning in novels, four times more than I can use.

The thesis of this one is one that I'm keenly interested in, but I feel that you've somewhat ducked the central issue which you established. That is, the "talk and build a fire" rule is shown to be no proper test; in the end you have the Fuzzy's speech picked up and understood. Remember Hal Clement's starfish people who had no sonic communication — but wig-wagged with several thousand tendrils over their body surface. "Look, Ma ... no speech!" Also no telepathy.

But the basic problem of "whaddaya mean ... 'human'?" is an enormously important one. You've made it "sapient," which is an excellent idea.

But I feel this novel isn't as strong as it could have been. You, in your detective experience, found that life is-in-fact made up of a most awful confusion of too many people who might be involved. You must have learned how to mentally juggle two dozen relevant characters at once in your work.

The average reader hasn't. Your story would be more effective for John Q. Public if you trimmed the cast of characters to about six individuals, plus assorted off-stage stooges who don't have to be remembered. Detective stories are fun; sure. But this isn't a detective story; it's a philosophical problem story. The problem has some tendency to get lost, strayed, or forgotten under the deluge of characters.

Regards,
John W. Campbell[19]

In retrospect, it's interesting to note that *Little Fuzzy* is Piper's best-selling novel and was his only work nominated by the fans for the Hugo Award. Piper may have juggled more characters than Campbell liked; but Campbell usually overlooked this fault. Today, however, multiple-viewpoint works are much more common in today's fiction, thanks to TV and movies.

CHAPTER 15

The Collaborators

In their own times, ninety-nine percent of all great authors and artists were
always out of fashion!

— H. Beam Piper

John Joseph McGuire, H. Beam Piper's only collaborator, was a very interesting man in
his own right. Jack, as his friends and family called him, was born on August 25, 1917, in
Altoona, Pennsylvania, and was a graduate of Shippensburg State College. Shortly after graduation he joined the army and fought in Germany during World War II; there he won a Silver Star and other decorations. For a while, Jack worked for Wild Bill Donovan in the Office
of Strategic Services (OSS), the fledgling World War II intelligence service which later became
the CIA. Part of Jack's work was going behind enemy lines and robbing German banks in an
attempt to disrupt the Nazi economy and damage enemy morale.[1]

In a May 8, 2001, telephone interview with Jack's daughter, Terry McGuire, she told me,
"Once, I asked my Mom: What was Father like as a young man?"

Her mother, Anne McGuire, answered, "Before the war your father was studying English;
we'd both had dreams of acting and writing. In those days he was quiet and very gentle."

"I was shocked," Terry said, "this didn't sound like my father at all. While of average
height, in most ways he was a larger than life figure: he was good looking, a hard drinker,
had a radio announcer's voice and unpredictable mood swings due to post traumatic stress
disorder — or shell shock as it was called in the post–World War II era."[2]

Jack's oldest son, John McGuire, Jr., further expounded over the phone on May 10, 2001:
"Father was a battle-hardened soldier with flashbacks. He was never able to sleep an entire
night — 'Don't ask, don't tell!' was his motto."

Jack was also an out of control drinker who by the mid–1950s was well on the road to
alcoholism. After the war, the McGuires stayed in Germany, where Jack worked as a criminal prosecutor and investigator with the Adjutant General's Office. When Jack arrived in
Bavaria in November of 1946, he had to shoot and kill a Nazi sympathizer who came to assas-
sinate him. He wore the assassin's jacket home when he returned to the States in the late for-
ties and settled in Altoona.

"But nobody would have guessed his past from looking at him," Jack explained. "My
father could be in a room with fifty people and they all had one thing in common — they all
liked my father! He was outgoing and interested in people. He used to say, 'Everyone has a
story. Even if it isn't true!' He was also a science fiction fan, read *Astounding Science Fiction*
and was an admirer of John W. Campbell."

After Jack left Germany, he worked for the Adjutant's Office on several army bases around
the U.S. before arriving in Altoona, where he got a job teaching English at Keith Junior High

School. According to John Jr., "Dad was one of the first speed reading teachers. As a new teacher at Keith, he was stuck with mostly teaching children with learning disabilities. He didn't like it much there at Keith since his specialty was geared for high achievers. He would teach for nine months out of the year and then gave private lessons as a tutor for children with reading problems during the summer."

John Jr. paints a vivid picture of mid–1950s small town Appalachia: "Altoona was poor and it was dirty. Bishop's Cathedral was based on St. Peter's, but was gray from all the soot in the air, from the car yards. Everyone worked in the mines or the railroad yards and there were lots of lay-offs. It was a lot like Victorian England; the yards ran the whole length of Altoona and even the snow was gray in the daylight — a good place to commit suicide!"[3]

One of Jack McGuire's dreams was to be a writer. Terry reports: "My mother was very naïve, a small town girl and a good prose stylist. She had her own writing and acting dreams. In the family, Jack was the author, while she kept the family together. Jack read all the 'pulp fiction.' He was honing his skills by reading other writers."[4]

John Jr. adds: "Dad had been writing since 1948, but he was a very slow writer, and would agonize over his prose. He was writing poetry, some science fiction and an occasional mystery story; he never sold anything before he met Beam. We could all see he was getting discouraged. He was convinced that working with a successful author such as Beam would be his entry into the world of writing." From all the internal evidence, Jack took working with Piper very seriously. Probably more seriously than Beam did.

As John McGuire, Jr., recollects, "Piper grew up locally and was not known in Altoona as a science fiction author, but as an employee of the Pennsy. His family had deep roots in that part of Appalachia. He knew everybody and their family and they knew him — the small town mentality. One thing about Beam though; he knew the damndest things — look it up, Piper was right! He read a lot, too.

"Beam always addressed my dad as Jack, and in many ways they were like older and younger brothers. Beam was moody, but he always listened very closely to everyone. He asked great questions, and would have made a great defense attorney."[5]

According to Terry, "When Jack found out Beam lived in Altoona, he mentioned to his doctor [Dr. Jack Strassman], who was also a close friend, that he wanted to meet Beam. This doctor was also a friend of Beam's, and arranged a meeting at our house. The three men had a roundtable discussion about science fiction and began to discuss fantasy. Beam had lots of 'is it possible medically?' ideas. The next week they were joined by another friend [Sam Park] who worked in the pharmaceutical business, 'a drummer,' who could answer questions about medications and their effects. The Roundtable began."[6]

In a 2001 taped interview, Anne McGuire says, "They probably met in 1950 or 1951. I remember Jack was about thirty-five and Beam was ten years older, although he didn't look it. Jack was writing from the time he was in college; he wrote before he was drafted into the army, where he was for five years. But when he came home from Germany in 1947 he went back to school teaching, and he had occasions on summers and weekends on which he wrote. He did not sell anything. He wrote many things and sent them out, but they always came back rejected. Sometimes there was a publisher's note, but usually just a small rejection slip."[7]

John Junior has a different view of how Beam and Jack got together:

Dr. Strassman purposely brought the two men together, because he knew Beam was a writer, while Jack was both a dandy and college graduate. Science fiction was not that big in working class Altoona. He thought they'd get along famously — and they did. Neither Father nor Beam had much money and Dr. Strassman offered to pay for the postage costs for sending out their finished manuscripts.

Originally, the game plan was that Beam was there as Father's advisor. He was direct and logical in person and he talked like he wrote. Beam had a very dry, ironic wit, and a slightly ironic way of talking. Beam wouldn't seek out social affairs, but he was having a great time and he soon went from advisor to collaborator. The four of them would sit around the table drinking and pitching ideas—it was a wonderful atmosphere to grow up in. The four of them looked, acted and drank like film stars. Even then, I knew I was very fortunate to witness their collaboration and to be a small part of this great group of men.

Jack and Beam would brainstorm ideas, and bounce them off their friends. Occasionally, outsiders—like Fletcher Pratt or the local music teacher—would join in. Other people would visit, bringing their personal exploits and life experiences. They just soaked it all up. They were all very passionate with their views, whether it be about politics or music. Once you were a part of the gang, such as friends like Fletcher Pratt, you could come and go as you pleased. However, they were like Southern Gentlemen — prickly about points of honor.

Beam became a constant visitor to our household and was soon more than a visitor—almost a family member, eating many meals with us. He lived within walking distance of our house on 214 Willow Avenue and often came over to watch the weekly fights on our television. Mother would make popcorn and the whole family would watch the fights, while Beam and Jack would score each round.[8]

In a sense, H. Beam Piper adopted the McGuire family just as he had adopted the Colemans twenty years earlier. Piper might have never had his *own* family, but was certainly a big part of several families. As John Jr. put it: "Beam had the run of the house. Holidays, Beam celebrated with us— he always made a big deal out of July 4th!"

In regards to their collaboration, John Jr. remembers: "Jack and Beam would sit at the table talking over the story line and characters. Nothing was ever written until everything was verbally explored and they agreed on a basic plot. They would call my mother, Anne, into the room and give her the plot and story line. She would write it down, then Jack would write the first draft, which would sometimes run into a second, third and even fourth draft. Beam would read the original draft, and would then 'polish' it, making sure there were no 'dangling' plot lines, conflicts in events and overall continuity. Then it was back to my mother to retype; both Jack and Beam would read it, making any final corrections."[9]

As Anne McGuire remembers:

Beam had a good agent [Frederik Pohl]. There was little doubt that the story would sell. He allowed us to hang on to his coattails, so to speak. So Jack was able to earn a small reputation as a writer. We were grateful for that. We never saw the manuscript after we turned it over to Beam. He apparently did his own corrections and typing before he sent it to his agent. Jack learned a lot from that method with Beam because when the manuscript was printed, we would compare it with the manuscript we had provided to Beam so Jack could see the areas where the professional touch had been added. It was less awkward and flowed better. Jack learned from that and as they continued to write there was less editing to be done. This was the method of collaboration they followed from their very first story, which I believe was *Null-ABC*, and continued through each succeeding collaboration.

They worked beautifully together; there was never the slightest argument or disagreement about anything. Their minds were as one. It was almost uncanny the way they would finish each others sentences as they worked. It was a lot of fun. When one presented a new idea, the other would grasp it so fast and begin a rush of suggestions. When they first began their sessions and did all this talking, I was there with my trusty little steno book and was asked to take down all their comments, including notes as to what Piper said and what McGuire said—and get it all down.

They would both become so enthusiastic and so loud; it was really difficult. Finally, I protested and said, "I can take shorthand at 120 words a minute, but you guys are going faster than that! There's no way I can transcribe it and make sense out of it, and you'll have to slow down." So they pacified me: "No, no, we don't expect you to get every word. Just takes notes and type it up the next morning. Then when we next meet we'll look over all this. All we need to know is at what point we stopped and we can continue from there." So that's what I did; I really had my hands full. I had a house and three kids, but I dutifully did my typewriting in the morning on a little typewriter. It wasn't really work, it was fun, and we looked forward to when Beam would come the next night, or the following night. He would visit three or four times a week when they were working or developing the creative process.[10]

During this time, Piper was still working evenings as a guard for the Pennsy and writing his own stories. According to Anne McGuire, Beam and Jack wrote a number of stories after they sold *Null-ABC* to John W. Campbell at *Astounding*.[11] According to Piper's Story Log (appendix A), *Null-ABC* was finished on October 17, 1952, and appeared in the March 1953 issue of *Astounding*. It was a sharp satire about the public school system; undoubtedly inspired by Jack's actual experiences as a junior high school English teacher.

Terry tells about their first sale: "Beam and Jack finally did it! They sold their first story. My mother may still have a copy of the first check. Beam lived with his partially blind mother on the second floor of an apartment. She kept house and cooked for him. Beam kept a small cannon there, and had a tradition of firing it when he sold a story. This huge production of Beam loading the gunpowder took place. Mother and I covered our ears, expecting a huge bang. It was a very small bang. But everyone was delighted."[12]

As John Jr. adds,

Beam and Jack loved to talk even more than they loved to write. They would talk their stories out, with inflections and feeling. I always believed the stories were better before they were written down; they lost some of their flair when put to paper. They were both great verbal storytellers. Mom would take shorthand notes and write the dialogue down. Sometimes they would argue over every word of the stories after they were written down, but Beam always had the last say. Their goal was to write simply and concisely. The problem was that some of the best prose was sacrificed for clarity.

A lot of story ideas were germinated at these sessions. I remember them talking about Fuzzies. Sam Parks drew pictures of what the Fuzzies would look like on his yellow pads! It never went anywhere until Beam wrote *Little Fuzzy*.

Both men wanted to be acknowledged as writers, wanted to be known for what they were. The "day job" allowed them to control things. Beam, especially, liked to be in control. They never talked about being full-time writers. Beam used to say, "In their own time, ninety-nine percent of all great authors and artists were always out of fashion!"[13]

This last statement supplies some insight into how Piper was able to keep writing for twenty-five years in the face of constant rejection.

John added,

Story money was not real money to them. They wanted to sell their stores and re-sell them, to anthologies. More to get them into print than for the money. Mother never heard Beam or Jack talk about mundane things, such as bills. When the money arrived—"Oh Goody!" They'd spend it all up.

Beam and Jack both considered John W. Campbell and Anthony Boucher as the best editors in the business. They would talk to Campbell on the phone and he would complain, "You don't write enough!" These guys were very great individualists and wrote what they wanted to.

They were very much into the Elizabethans, especially William Shakespeare. Beam loved how Shakespeare wrote both for the highborn and the pit. They looked for plots in his plays and sometimes their stories would be titled with Shakespearian quotes. They both also loved Sherlock Holmes; I remember them listening to the Holmes' radio shows.

Jack also did some radio work at Station WFHA announcing in Williamsport and local game commentary. He had a wonderful voice. He worked off and on at the local radio station. A lot of the smaller stations during the fifties made use of radio transcripts that they would have read over the air featuring local announcers. Jack did a lot of that and sometimes read from the Teletype and did the news. Occasionally, he would do a special show; once he actually interviewed Beam about his writing. Great fun was had by all!

We'll never know how many stories they wrote together. If a story didn't sell after making the rounds of the science-fiction magazines, Beam and Jack would get drunk and "celebrate" by burning the offending manuscript and rejection letters in a big drum trashcan![14]

Terry adds: "Mother would often hide the carbons so they wouldn't burn everything. They got very drunk and exuberant. It was their 'letting go' ceremony, I guess. Sometimes, when they sobered up the next morning, they'd regret burning their stories—not that they'd ever admit it!"[15]

Beam and Jack together wrote four published works, two short novels, *Null-ABC* and *Lone Star Planet*, and two novelettes, "The Return" and "Hunter Patrol." Unfortunately, only *Null ABC* and "The Return" were sold during the time they were working together. They were so enthused with *Lone Star Planet* that they wrote an outline for a sequel, which they never wrote since their agent had trouble placing the first story.[16] Unfortunately, the *Lone Star Planet* didn't sell until 1957, and only then to a salvage market—*Fantastic Universe Science Fiction*.

The story is kind of a hoot, but I can see why most magazines found it a hard story to buy. It still reads like Piper and McGuire were more interested in entertaining each other with tall tales than writing a "salable yarn." Still, *Lone Star Planet* has done well for itself, appearing as an Ace "double novel," both in 1958 under the title *A Planet for Texans* and later in 1979 when it was published under the original title, *Lone Star Planet*, with *Four-Day Planet*.

"The Return" is their best story, maybe because it draws upon their mutual love of Sherlock Holmes for the denouement. It's a classic Campbellian puzzle story with an intriguing post-holocaust setting. Not surprisingly, a slightly longer version—maybe the original uncut version before Campbell's editorial "suggestions" were taken into account—appeared in the 1960 anthology, *The Science-Fictional Sherlock Holmes*. Piper scholar Tom Rogers generously provided me with a copy of the original manuscript, which is several thousand words longer than the *Astounding* version, with Beam's holographic corrections.

Overall, with only two sales in three years, it could be said the Piper-McGuire collaboration was not a big success. On the other hand, it did provide Piper with a ready-made family and some great times. John McGuire went on to publish four more short science fiction stories, including one in *Astounding Science Fiction*. Most of his later stories draw upon his experiences as an undercover operative in World War II and are much more grim and realistic than anything he wrote with Piper.

CHAPTER 16

Beam's Kids

Well, buying diapers, and pink ones at that, is a hell of an assignment for a bachelor of alleged good repute. Much as I would serve a comrade, but damned if I would, unless I were first made drunk.[1]

— H. Beam Piper

As he grew older, H. Beam Piper turned into a beloved honorary "uncle" to many of his friend's children. One of the first of his close friends to start a family was Ferd Coleman. What's unusual about Beam's Kids is just how much all of these children appreciated Beam's visits and how he touched each and every one of their lives. All of Beam's Kids to this day — when some are in their seventies! — remember Beam Piper as vividly as if he died only last year. All were and still are moved by his tragic death. I know very few people, including those who've lost parents, beloved grandparents or uncles, who hold their departed relatives in as much esteem as Beam's Kids hold him. Obviously, his tragic suicide increased their sense of loss; but, regardless, this phenomenon is a tribute to Beam's humanity and sense of fair play.

Mike Knerr writes: "For all of his brilliant grasp of history and the painstaking craftsmanship of his writing, Beam had a child-like side to him that was amusing. He constantly befriended stray animals and regularly took peanuts to the squirrels in various parks. Once, as a watchman in Altoona, he bought a pint of milk for a stray cat that happened by. His 'armor' would not allow him to admit that he actually liked children, but he did. If asked if he liked children, however, he would usually reply with a W.C. Field's line: 'Yes, if properly cooked.'"[2]

"He might have been hard on the outside, but where kids and animals were concerned he was Nutty Putty."[3]

Part of his success in reaching children — it certainly wasn't from familiarity with children, since he had no siblings or children of his own — was that he treated them like little adults. Furthermore, Piper treated the girls about the same as the boys, i.e., he brought them toys generally thought to be for boys. Nor was he above letting the kids baby-sit his pistol when the need arose!

Little Sylvia was the first of Beam's children. On December 23, 1930, Ferd Coleman wrote: "Both Sylvia and myself are much enthused over our Christmas gifts from you. It constitutes just one more ball to Sylvia's collection, but no girl as small as Sylvia can have too many balls; they are much preferred over dolls."[4]

In a February 1931 letter, Piper commented to Ferd: "And so Stan Moon has mutinied. Well, buying diapers, and pink ones at that, is a hell of an assignment for a bachelor of alleged good repute. Much as I would serve a comrade, but damned if I would, unless I were first made drunk. Get me good and 'shicker,' though, and I'd even purchase Kotex."[5]

90

In an October 15, 1931, letter, Piper wrote: "Sorry to have delayed so long in felicitating you on your male heir, but I've been a bit under the weather.... You know, the friend with whom I mentioned playing chess between trains in Harrisburg was expecting an heir at any moment when I was down there, and he became a father of a daughter about six hours before your son arrived. I had been waiting for reports from both of you with some interest. Well, anyhow, congratulations— or commiserations, however your prefer. This, I suppose, means another rattle. My honorary nephews and nieces are increasing in number."[6]

In the following passage, Don Coleman gives us a personal and up-close look at what it meant to be one of Beam's Kids and what they saw, heard and experienced during one of his treasured visits:

Upon eventual encounter [after Beam's arrival], Piper and Coleman would participate in one or two "hello" drinks before proceeding to the house on the hill. Once there, another cocktail would satisfy Beam as Ferd selected his customary bottle of beer before sitting down to supper. The night was young and so was I at this period of time, but suitably adept to perceive that Piper's favorite of meals around these parts was that of spareribs and sauerkraut, mashed potatoes and apple sauce on the side ... with plenty of black coffee. Somebody obviously flagged the chef each time he called upon this Vallamont residence.

I don't think I was particularly fond of sauerkraut as a youngster, but as I matured, these awful foods of yesteryear seemed to have suddenly become palatable. Piling my kraut over the mashed potatoes and stirring the two vigorously together has become a habit I inherited from Beam, himself. Maybe that's why I savor this item so much today, maintaining an addiction passed on by a fine friend.

I remember Beam always sitting to my left at the dinner table, because ordinarily, I being the only son at this time enjoyed the entire side to myself ... having to face my two sisters across from me. And whatever the subject of conversation, Beam invariably would acknowledge such with a customary and contemplated — though somewhat elongated and resounding —"yeusss." And while feasting, the audible clickety-clacking performance of his dentures can still be heard in my waning mind![7]

Piper, as a young man, had longstanding problems with his teeth. In May of 1931 he wrote: "For one thing, the teeth that have bothered me so much in the past. I'm having them all out, to be replaced by the kind you can take out, and these extractions—four or five at a time — have been making a hell out of my life."[8]

Coleman continues:

At supper's end, he and Ferd would retire to the haven below while Ted Ranck made his typical entry through the garage. As a child at bedtime, it was traditional, but not a requirement, that we kids kiss any visiting folks who were considered family. Beam, without a doubt, was no exception. So, with the appropriate time of fanfare approaching, I was summoned to make an appearance to the den, which at this hour was completely enveloped with tobacco smoke. Ferd Coleman did not enjoy the habit but did accept such practices within his household — especially of his friends. Piper and Ranck were staunch pipe smokers, but generally on these particular occasions, each would address the cigarette.

In spite of the smoke that would cloud the room, I was somewhat reluctant to pucker up to H. Beam Piper; his straight and jutting nose slightly obstructed my line of attack, and I had to contend with the perfectly-scissored mustache. But on command, I managed to perform.

These occasions in the den would generally begin quietly, almost serenely, as each would choose and prepare his own weakness. There was plentiful assortments of liquor and mixings to cover the desires of all.... As the evening wore on, and we were now in our little beds above, the conversation accelerated and the sounds below became that of pandemonium ... laughter was at its height.

The air registers about the rooms of the house would echo ... but it was usually difficult to ascertain their words by the time the sounds reached the upper bedrooms. And then, after many hours, complete silence would envelop the house ... be it ever so shortly. The serenity of the hour was slashed by the raising and then slamming-down of the garage door — the whirring sound of its mighty springs vibrating throughout the residence.

This, of course, was Ted Ranck leaving for home. Being a local Williamsporter, he had not far to reach his own abode a mile or so away. And it was damn good and well he hadn't too far to move ... in his present state!

Even with Ted gone and Ferd tucked away, the heavenly quiet would once more be broken by the mumblings of H. Beam Piper, continuing through the wee hours preceding dawn. He would talk constantly to himself, in all levels of tone. Eventually it became clear to me that Beam — regardless of the extent of inebriation — was talking-out and portraying the specific roles of his players of a proposed book-to-be. Alone with his characters (as far as he knew), he would circle the cherry-wood table puffing, blowing smoke and muttering — completely unaware of the world around him ... including a young eavesdropper positioned on knees at the keyhole!

Invariably Beam would make it to the kitchen by late morning — hung over and drawn, of course — with a pair of eyes whose whites resembled miniature road maps. Locating a kettle, he would proceed to fill it with water and place on the stove to boil. Being completely familiar with Fritz [Freida] Coleman's galley, he would then pull a box of saltine crackers from the cupboard, which he would drop into a large soup bowl. In the meantime, he would mumble although it was impossible to ascertain what wordage was being expelled from his mind.

Finally, the boiling water was withdrawn from the range and poured over the saltines. Beam would then take the large salt and pepper shakers from above the stove and shake briskly over this incredible mess! Next, steaming black coffee would be poured in a mug into which he would submerge an ice cube seated on a shaky spoon.

It was wise to vacate the kitchen at this time, in order to allow The Thin Man to curse Lucifer and all his kin for the muddled condition he presently found himself in. Despite the severity of the moment, and their regularity, these occurrences were actually minutes in duration.

This 1951 photograph shows Piper performing a periodic cleaning of the antique firearms in Ferd Coleman's den, utilizing the antique cherry wood table as a work bench and writing table. The everpresent bottle of whiskey accompanies the necessary cleaning solvents (courtesy Coleman Family).

It would be profound fabrication to proclaim that H. Beam Piper's hangovers, such as this, were not repetitive. He loved his hooch and accepted the aftermath with clear humility. Two hours following the saltine ritual, he was once again himself and able to resume life by tapping the attic of his brain for more discoveries.[9]

Sylvia, Don and Diane Coleman were the first, but there were more of Beam's Kids to follow. As Paul M. Schuchart wrote to me in an April 19, 1981, letter, "I knew Beam Piper, for we lived near his home in Altoona, Pennsylvania. Beam used to spend a lot of time with us. After I got married, Beam was a regular visitor here. Having a kid brother in Williamsport, the last time I saw Beam was on Sunday up there. Beam took me to his apartment.[10]

"For our two daughters, Beam was about the best babysitter we ever had. He'd entertain them by drawing pictures of his gun collection. Whether or not daughter Sally, who lives in Chapel Hill, North Carolina, has any of those drawings remains to be seen. At any rate, if I were you, I wouldn't hold my breath until I get the dope from her."[11]

Piper had nicknames for many of his "Kids," and Sally's was "The Big Noise." Sylvia Coleman was affectionately referred to as "Di-Dee-Lou."

Schuchart adds: "My wife does remember the time Beam came down from Altoona for several days, one evening of which he intended to take my wife to the Inaugural Ball for some governor, shortly after we were married.

"He came down some time later to accompany me to Washington to see the inauguration of Roosevelt as president. Beam came downstairs with a big handgun, telling me he always carried a gun. I told him, regardless of whatever he always did, there would be no gun in his possession for that event. Beam couldn't understand that, but he was willing to trust his gun not to my wife, but rather to the girls, and we went on our way."[12]

Terry and John McGuire, Jr., have fond memories of Piper. In many ways, Beam symbolized the best of times of the McGuire household and their idyllic life in Altoona. Terry writes in a March 26, 2001, e-mail, "First let me explain that I am Jack's [John J. McGuire's] daughter. My older brother is John and my younger one is Mike. We have a sister MariPat. Mike and MariPat are too young to remember Beam, but Mike is a great fan of all my father's and Beam's work.

"My older brother has lots of stories to tell of playing with Beam's cane (which concealed a sword inside). Both my father and Beam felt girls should be good shots, and encouraged me to practice target shooting. Beam and Jack both loved weapons, especially concealed ones."[13] In our telephone conversation on May 8, 2001, Terry added,

People really do carry knives up their sleeves, I learned that from Beam. He used to carry a two-shot derringer.

Beam didn't buy the traditional roles and upbringing for children: "Anyone can be anything," he used to say. "The key is to learn and not allow yourself to be *limited*." Beam used to encourage me to take apart his gun and build things. "Just because you're a girl doesn't mean you can't do it!"

Beam and my Father were unconventional men — not normal men. They worked at being different, Bohemians.

Beam wanted to be Shakespeare. He would have us kids memorize Shakespeare's lines and speak out the various parts. We acted out *Hamlet*, and *King Lear*— Beam's favorite.

Beam used to have a human skull he kept on his desk in his Altoona gunroom. He'd often turn it upside down and use it as an ashtray. When we were "acting" out *Hamlet*, Beam would sometimes give us the skull to talk to. He had us act out *Romeo and Juliet* and we had to know our parts!

Beam had a dark side as well. Because of his penchant for dark clothing, capes and slouch caps and working all evening as a night watchman of the Altoona rail yards, he would come home late at night. Some people, mostly kids, thought he was a vampire; Beam encouraged this kind of speculation. He would laugh in that raspy voice of his; he enjoyed terrifying children.

I had terrible nightmares at one point, and no one could figure out why. Finally, Jack mentioned it to Beam. He asked me what I was dreaming about. I said, "A big monster comes up from the ocean and cuts me open with a long claw and eats me while I'm alive!"

Beam looked around the room they used to write in and asked, "Where is your bedroom?"

My room was directly over the writing room and the radiator pipes went up to my room. Beam found a large opening there, went upstairs and moved my bed to another wall. "I think your nightmares will stop now."

They did. My Mother realized I was directly by the opening and in my sleep, heard plots and scenarios for stories. Beam was very serious with me in calming my fears, but later laughed with Jack, and told him that sometimes, "the obvious is the only answer."

Mother never worried when Johnny or me would go somewhere with Beam. Sometimes it was to a bar, where we ate the cherries out of his Manhattans, pretzels and peanuts. Women talked to him, since there were two children with him. In those days women sat at tables, never at the bar unescorted.[14]

On May 10, 2001, John McGuire, Jr., and I talked for several hours. John is two years older than Terry and was more aware of what was going on in the McGuire household. He also spent a lot of time over at Beam's in the gunroom, where Piper did most of his writing and kept his weapons. It was a fascinating conversation about Beam, his father and the "Unholy Four," as John said they called themselves. A chill ran up and down my spine when John Jr. mentioned the "Unholy Four," as it brought back memories of the "The Unholy Trinity"—Beam, Ferd Coleman and Ted Ranck and their get-togethers in Ferd's den in the 1940s and '50s. The "Unholy Four" consisted of Beam, John McGuire, Sam Park (a friend and medical drug salesman) and Dr. Jack Strassman. Obviously, Piper was the leader of this new pack of "romantics" and would-be-Bohemians.

"These four men were bigger than life," John said.

There was an air of mystery about them — I was in awe of them. They lived large, talked large and kept their word. They detested those who blabbed before Senator Joe McCarthy and the House Committee on Un-American Activities— to a man they supported Dashiell Hammett. They were all very well read and connoisseurs of everything — boxing, vintage weapons, politics, literature. They looked, acted and drank like film stars— I felt privileged as a boy to be in their company. The four of them loved life and didn't try to blend in.

Beam reminded me of Sherlock Holmes, his incisive intelligence, deductive reasoning and decisive mannerisms. He even resembled Basil Rathbone as Sherlock Holmes. Beam was the low-key member of the "Unholy Four," but everyone listened when he spoke; he was like a hero from the 1930s adventure film, very witty, picked and chose his moments carefully — a great showman. I had a lot of great times with Beam; he absolutely molded our character as children.

They all loved boxing, especially Beam. The "Unholy Four" used to come to our house to watch the fights on our TV. There was always lots of drinking, and then talking and autopsies of the fights.

I met Fletcher Pratt, too. My mother used to let me go with father when he went to Beam's apartment; she trusted Beam and saw me as father's chaperone. Once we went to his apartment when Fletcher Pratt visited. His mother was visiting the neighbors and they were all gathered in the gunroom — where Beam did his writing — drinking and telling tall tales, Piper, Fletcher Pratt, my father and Sam Park, who was a big man, taller than Beam, a hulking Viking, but bald.

Beam had a display case, larger than the average windowsill, where he kept some of his weapons. Parks and Pratt were fooling around, taking weapons in and out of the case and inspecting them. Saying, "On guard" and things like that. Suddenly words were said — they both yanked swords out of the case and started swinging. They weren't paying much attention to us bystanders and suddenly steel was clanging. I was transfixed; it was like watching a movie come to life right before your eyes!

Beam grabbed me and pushed me under the table, while my Father picked up the brandy bottle, as Park and Pratt crossed swords right in the gunroom. They went at it with lots of slashing steel and war cries. I can still hear the clink and the rings as their swords clashed. It was a miracle no one got hurt; afterwards everyone was laughing so hard they were teary-eyed.[15]

Mike Knerr remembers a similar occasion: "Once I made the mistake of asking [him] just how they fought with swords, since I only knew about foils and rapiers. Beam jumped up, grabbed two four-hundred-year-old swords from the wall and handed me one. I had some misgivings about subjecting such relics to any kind of hard usage. Piper didn't care and proceeded to show me how to use them. When we had exhausted ourselves the swords were in fine shape but there were a lot of nicks in the desk and other assorted bits of furniture."[16]

"All these men had pasts—hard pasts, dealing with death and destruction," John told me. "Park was a World War II veteran and drug drummer, the doctor dealt with death every day and my father was a highly decorated World War II veteran; he used to work for Wild Bill Donovan. One of his jobs was to rob German banks behind enemy lines—very dangerous and his 'work' left some bad scars. Later he worked as a special prosecutor in Germany after the war.

"I think the only thing Beam regretted was that he didn't have his own dark past.... These men had done the things Beam only wrote about—saving lives, dodging death, shooting guns at real people and taking lives. He loved to draw them out and hear their stories. I got one hell of an education from those gunroom conversations."[17]

CHAPTER 17

Betty

Another of Betty's lovely letters. How I hope things work out for us all right and nothing gets in our way.[1]

— H. Beam Piper

In 1954 H. Beam Piper finally fell in love with a woman who reciprocated those feelings, Elizabeth (Betty) Hirst, formerly of Carmel, California. There's very little known about Betty's background except that she grew up in Carmel; even in the early part of the twentieth century it was an expensive upper-middle-class beachfront area, south of San Francisco. It's a place people usually migrate to, not move away from. Betty was a divorcée, who had money and traveled frequently to Europe, as part of her work for the Council on Student Travel — one of the first of the student foreign exchange programs.

According to the Council on International Education Exchange, Inc., Web site:

The CIEE was formed in May 1947, beginning as the Council on Student Travel (CST). Initially, the Council on Student Travel lacked a permanent office and staff, but it played a significant role in fostering student travel from the start, assigning work to committees and arranging transportation for students who wanted to study abroad. The Council on Student Travel was quick to point out during its first months of existence that it was not a travel agency; travel arrangements were made with travel agent associate members. Instead, it described itself as a nonprofit association interested solely in encouraging and facilitating educational travel abroad, endeavoring to create young "ambassadors" versed in different cultures whose experiences would improve international relations.

The Council on Student Travel's orientation programs became more comprehensive as the 1950s progressed, evolving into a fundamental aspect of the organization's effort to create ambassadors to Western European countries. Thanks largely to the hugely popular orientation programs, the Council on Student Travel established itself as a recognized facilitator of international student travel, and its influence quickly grew despite losing access to military vessels. By the mid–1950s, the Council on Student Travel oversaw the transport of 50,000 U.S. students and 45,000 foreign students annually.[2]

According to L. Sprague de Camp, it was Inga Pratt (Fletcher Pratt's wife) who played matchmaker. "On Inga Pratt's advice, he married an attractive school teacher of about his own middle age."[3]

Mike Knerr writes: "Beam did have other things on his mind than stories— he was in love. His lady, Betty Hirst, lived in New York where she worked for a student travel service called the Council on Student Travel.... Beam used the trains to commute to her on his days off. In the interim, he spent his off hours from work writing, listening to the Sherlock Holmes radio program with Sir John Gielgud in the title role and talking with John McGuire, his collaborator on *Lone Star Planet* and other stories."[4]

Piper not only worked the graveyard shift for the Pennsy, but he worked over the weekends, too. In this January 12, 1953, letter to Allan Howard, of the Eastern Science Fiction Association, he apologizes for not being able to attend a meeting he had been invited to give a talk at. "I'm really sorry that I won't be able, in the foreseeable future, to attend one of your meetings; I am not writing full time, but am also working for the Pennsylvania Railroad Company, in their shops here, and it happens that weekends off are practically an impossibility for me. My equivalent of a weekend is Wednesday and Thursday, and on Sunday I am tightly chained to my galley-oar."[5]

Most of his train visits to Betty and his New York friends took place in the middle of the week. In "Piper," Mike Knerr writes: "Betty had worked in the [Council on Student Travel] office from 1951 to 1954."[6] Therefore, Piper must have met Betty at some point during 1954; however, there's no mention of their meeting in the diaries. In this September 4, 1955, letter to Freida Coleman, announcing his new marriage, Piper filled in some of the blanks:

> When I said that I should have written you long ago, I meant that I should have written last March, when I had the wonderfully good fortune to marry a charming lady I met in New York. Her maiden name was Betty Hirst, but when I met her, she was Betty Engquist, from a previous marriage. She has a position with an organization called the Council on Student Travel, which charters ships and provides low-cost passages to American students going abroad and foreign students coming to America. She is still in New York, and I travel back and forth on my days off; we have a little one-room-bath-and-closet-kitchen apartment in the Roger Williams, on Madison Avenue. I thought I was lucky to find someone like Betty when I married her; now, when mother's death would have otherwise left me utterly alone, I have even more reason to think so. It's bad enough as it is, but without my wife it would have been very bad indeed.[7]

In the novel *Little Fuzzy*, Jack Holloway, the protagonist most reminiscent of H. Beam Piper in all of his books, who keeps a diary just like Piper: "then went to the kitchen, poured himself a drink and brought it in to the big table, where he lit his pipe and began writing up his diary for the day."[8]

I am certain this is exactly how Piper wrote his own diaries, right down to the drink and pipe smoking ritual. Knerr writes: "He burned all of his diaries up to 1955 on June 14, 1956, but as usual gave no reason for it. His entry is mysteriously Piper: 'Burned all my diaries up to 1954 incl.' Why? Why up to that particular year? Because that was the year he began his life with Betty? Or, perhaps because it was the year that his mother died — the year he broke his association with John J. McGuire — the year...?

"It was the year he was finally on his own. The year when H. Beam Piper became an individual, a writer and a husband. The diaries seem to bear this out."[9] It's also likely that Piper burned the pre–1955 diaries to cover his tracks, that is, the other women in his life — mostly bar pick-ups and prostitutes. As Knerr writes:

> The diaries indicate that the answer to this question can be dropped into the lap of his mother. Beam doesn't say so "in so many words" but the hints seem conclusive. Here was a man fifty-one years old, who had never married, who lived with his mother and who courted his best girl in Harrisburg or New York. Mother, I suspect, was a strong willed woman and the 1955 diary will bear this out to a degree.
>
> The typical Piper way of hiding the facts, the almost cloak-and-dagger way in which he covered up his life, can be read in the "Piper Code." "Bought the brass cannon and some other junk for Lkee." The code isn't that complicated ... the key is BLACKHORSE with each letter being assigned a number from one to zero. Lkee translates into twenty-five dollars. Did Beam want to keep expenditures on antiques from his mother? Would she have raised hell with him about that? Probably no one will ever know for sure, but the code *could* serve to keep gun collectors from knowing just how much he bought a piece for.
>
> For whatever reasons, secrecy had become so deeply ingrained in Piper's character by the time he reached fifty that it was a way of life. Like an old Indian scout he was forever covering his back-trail.[10]

Piper's surviving diaries begin on January 1, 1955, when he mentioned writing a letter to Betty. On January 17, he wrote: "A nice long letter from Betty, how she just read 'Last Enemy.' Science fiction seems to be a fascinating new world for her."[11] "Last Enemy" was published in the August 1950 issue of *Astounding Science Fiction*, so it had been out for over four years. If Betty was only now reading Piper's stories and getting introduced to science fiction, I doubt that at this time they had known each other for even a year — probably only a few months. Her reading of his stories was part of the "getting to know you" phase of a relationship. Next she read "Time Crime," which was serialized in the February and March 1955 issues of *Astounding*.

In a January 27 entry, Piper revealed something of his growing romantic feelings for Betty as well as his fear of involvement. "Up 0900. Working on story A.M. Started a letter to Betty, tore it up. I'm beginning to be afraid that we're beginning to become emotionally involved with each other beyond the safety-point."[12] Things were heating up in the romantic department, even more than Beam realized.

On Wednesday, February 2, Piper worked the 3:00 A.M. to 6:50 A.M. shift at the car shops. "Home about 0655.... Had to commit my 'strategic reserve' again. Got #32 [train] for NY and slept all the way. As soon as I got to the Piccadilly, called Betty at Midston and up to join her for MWA Meeting. Business meeting, not very interesting though she gave a good simulation of interest.... Got to bed a little past one." He spent most of the morning shopping, for shirts and targets, then the rest of the afternoon and evening with Betty. "Back to hotel and bed, alone, alas. About 0130."[13]

Only making around $50.00 per week at the Pennsy, Piper was already experiencing financial difficulties with his bi-city romance. His "strategic reserve" was his savings account, which he was beginning to hit fairly regularly. While travel expenses were slight, since he often got free railroad passes at work, they were eating out a lot, often at expensive nightspots like the Stork Club.

On February 7, he wrote: "Up town shopping P.M. Bought a Valentine, an amusing thing with a couple of affectionate cats."[14] This romantic H. Beam Piper, buying "cute" Valentines, is so completely at odds with our cynical young bachelor of "The Early Letters" that it's somewhat disconcerting. He was beginning to act like a teenager in love: The Belle of Bellefonte was Piper's first great love, but it was unrequited and thus never came into the light of day. This infatuation with Betty was turning into a raging romance. Three days later he wrote, "Letter from Betty. Now she's three letters up on me; will have to get one off to her."[15]

Mike Knerr writes, "In early February of 1955, there lurked not a wisp of storm clouds in the blue sky of their romance. Marriage was just around the corner and Beam was as giddy as a schoolboy, his feet usually about six inches off the pavement.... He was wallowing in a romantic mist and his writing, of course, suffered accordingly. 'Another of Betty's lovely letters,' Piper writes in his diary. 'How I hope things work out for us all right and nothing gets in our way!'"[16]

He was wallowing in a romantic mist and his writing, of course, suffered accordingly. In the hours he had free from his job at the car shops, Piper would hammer out a few pages on "The Young Immortals"; the next day he would tear them up and start over. He couldn't sit still. He took walks, ate dinner at the Penn Alto or the Dutch Kitchen, or went over to John and Anne McGuire's house to watch the fights.

Mike Knerr adds: "Even with the prospect of a rosy future before him the Piper's disgust of stupidity rose glowingly to the fore. He drew money from his bank account in preparation for 'the Federal shakedown,' as he called the IRS, and 'Find that I only owed Public Enemy #1 the sum of $16.62.'"[17]

Interestingly, Piper had still not introduced Betty to his mother. On Saturday, February 19, 1955, she came for a visit and he wrote: "It [the train] got in 1725, Betty on board, and we went to the Dutch Kitchen for dinner, stayed there for a while, and to the Penn Alto for a Katinka. *Betty likes Katinkas.* Saw her to the train and then home at 2110. Hydra meeting on 24th ... so we'll see each other again soon."[18]

Betty was in Altoona—for the first time, yet—and yet he never introduced her to his mother, Harriet! True, it might have been a shock to his ninety-year-old mother, but it's surprising that Betty didn't make more of a fuss to meet the reclusive Mrs. Piper. I suspect meeting mother was the reason for Betty's visit. Beam must have spun a fanciful tale to get out of this jam.

Knerr explains it this way:

> Beam's love for Betty is apparent throughout all of his diaries, and it was glaringly obvious to me in our conversations, yet it was scarcely the kind of love most people would opt for. It is, I believe, safe to say that Betty undoubtedly found it less than to her liking. Most things, it would appear, had to go Beam's way or, like the rigid person he was, he would pick up his marbles and go home.
>
> In attempting to understand the relationship between Beam and Betty, and, of course, the eventual breakup, it is necessary to not only use the journals but to read between the lines. It was even more important to watch his eyes and listen to the sound of his voice when he spoke of her. In the end, one gets the strong feeling that Betty was a woman who made the mistake of marrying a man too old, too set in his ways and too uncompromising in his belief.[19]

On February 23, he met up with Betty, visited with friends and then went out to dinner. Then to Brooklyn to visit a friend of Betty's, also named Betty. "Stabbed myself in finger very painfully while cracking ice with a big kitchen-fork."[20]

The next day he had breakfast at the hotel, took a walk up 5 Avenue and had lunch at the Press Box with *Astounding* editor John Campbell. "Got away from him at 1600, had to run like hell to change shirts and shave, to keep date with Betty. Mad rush down town by cab, the driver breaking every law of God, man, and the City of New York, and landing me at 179 Broadway at exactly 1700. A drink with my dearest at Child's place, then up town for dinner at St. Denis and then up 5th Avenue and to Fletcher Pratt's for a Hydra Meeting— very jolly affair, lasted until 2400."[21] The Hydra Club at this time was the author's organization of published science fiction writers. It folded and was later supplanted by the Science Fiction Writers of America, which was chartered in 1965. Piper was a member of both the Hydra Club and the Mystery Writers of America by way of his mystery novel, *Murder in the Gunroom.*

On the 28th of February, he wrote, "A nice long letter from Betty with plans for a trip to Altoona on the 9th."[22]

March 3 was the first time the word "marriage" comes up in the diaries. "Another letter from Betty. She has the same idea I have—let's get married now. The only thing I'm afraid of is that I may fail Wassermann-Test positive."[23] The next day: "To Altoona Hospital to get a Wassermann; couldn't. Have to have a request from a physician—Goddamned bureaucratic stupidity!"[24] For a committed bachelor, who only a few months before was worrying about how fast the relationship was developing with a woman he met less than a year before, it's surprising how fast Piper got in over his head. Obviously, the two lovers had been making plans that weren't reported in the diary.

Behind the scenes Piper's friend and collaborator, John McGuire, and his wife, were trying to talk him out of his marriage plans. In a phone conversation, John Jr. told me: "My parents were skating on thin ice the moment they expressed their concerns about the marriage. They thought Beam was acting out of character and didn't trust Betty's motives. Beam, when it came to relationships, was an innocent. They had no idea of the depth of his feeling for Betty or they would have kept quiet."[25]

Five days later on Tuesday Piper wrote: "Up town. Cashed check, saw about hospitalization through PRR and arranged to shoot at Railroad Police HQ. Did some shopping, and had blood sample taken by Dr. Strassman for Wasserman. Will hear verdict on Monday. On Wednesday, off to see Betty again in Harrisburg. At 1738, we got in on #23 [train]. We punched out a couple of medallions ('Beam Loves Betty,' and 'Betty Loves Beam') on a coin-in-the-slot thing at the station.

"Then to the Harris Ferry Tavern for dinner (a damn poor meal) and walking around and drinking in a bar, where I have a dreadful suspicion that we walked out without paying for our drinks, and kissing goodbye at the station with an audience of laborers."[26] H. Beam Piper was hopelessly, head-over-heels, in love. From the diaries, it's apparent he was as surprised by this torrent of emotion as were his friends, who saw him as a life-long bachelor. Mike Knerr remarks: "Beam was fifty years old, but Betty's love had reduced him to a sophomoric level that was still obvious nine years later."[27]

On March 11, Piper wrote: "Up at noon. Letter from Betty, with enclosure re: New York marriage license procedures. My God, if anybody had told me a year ago, that I would be rushing into wedlock, I'd have told him to get back in his padded cell before the doctors missed him!"[28] This is further evidence that he didn't meet Betty until sometime late in 1954.

He went to a local photography shop to see about getting a picture of himself for Betty. "Started two letters to Betty — Isn't there anything to write about but Betty? *No, there isn't.*"[29] Piper had hit the wall with his fiction writing, with "The Young Immortals" completely stalled — and didn't care.

The next day he wrote, "Am worried like the devil about that Wassermann-Test. Maybe I'm imagining symptoms. I hope so. Monday will tell."[30] His trysts with prostitutes and bar pick-ups were coming back to haunt him. In his defense, in those puritanical times sex without marriage was difficult and prostitution was a quasi-acceptable outlet.

After a letter from Betty on the 17th, he wrote: "Her mother is coming to New York? Without saying when. Must be troubled about the latter."[31] Next day two more letters from Betty. "I still don't know what the trouble is, or when her mother is coming to New York. I wish I dared to telephone her from here."[32] Piper still had not told his mother about his impending marriage or fiancée. On Saturday, "A letter — very short one, this time — from Betty. Nothing about the crisis, which may have been a mare's nest."[33]

What's surprising is how fast this romance unfolded. Betty had been married before, and she had to have been the engine behind this quickly moving matrimonial machine. Piper was cautious and restrained, and a self-professed confirmed bachelor. It must have taken serious prodding on Betty's part to move him from worry about where the relationship was going on January 27 to "let's get married now" less than two months later.

Betty had to have been romantically attracted to Beam the man, since he had no money, although with his custom suits and courtly ways he may have initially given the impression that he was successful. But once Betty learned that he worked as a night watchman at the Pennsy car yards and lived at home with his mother — so much for any fantasies about wealth or family position. It had to have been a love match. Piper was set in his ways and it's hard to imagine him — no matter how romantically involved — rushing into marriage.

On March 21, Piper wrote: "Two more letters, on arrangements for Wednesday and Thursday. I'm going to have to be a lot gentler, and very patient — she isn't quite as tough-minded as I am. Up town in evening. Got proofs of pictures at Schaeffer's, and the blood test certificate at Strassman's. Wrote Betty a hasty letter in the bar at the Legion and mailed it."[34]

Piper had it bad. The next day he wrote: "Napped in evening — nothing much to do, plus; can't get my mind off Betty enough to do any work." The marriage was set and he was getting nervous. "Last minute worries — will my pistol permit be acceptable as 'evidence of age' for marriage license? Shouldn't I have gotten birth certificate? — too late now. Hell of a note if I get over the blood-test hump to be stymied on an idiotic formality like this. (Every time I look in the mirror, I see another 'evidence of age' in my mustache or at my temples.)"[35]

Wednesday the 23rd came, and he was off to New York. "Slept all the way to New York and arrived 1630. Met Betty at Doubleday bookshop in station, where I had bought *The Hydrogen Bomb*, and had a couple of drinks at station bar, talking about tomorrow's plans. By cab to Piccadilly. Spent evening in, reading. Couldn't get to sleep."[36]

Thursday, March 24, 1955, "Up 0750. Met Betty for breakfast, and downtown to municipal building for marriage license. Got through all the bureaucrap, and it didn't hurt a bit. Up town, looked at and decided upon apartment at Roger Williams, got photos at Altman's, bought wedding rings, Betty bought me a tie ... as an additional birthday gift. Napped in the afternoon, and Betty and I to dinner at Xochitl, and about town, watched skating at Radio City rink. To bed 0130."[37]

It's hard to imagine Piper doing such touristy things, but with Betty at his side he was a changed man — for the moment, anyway.

Friday, March 25 — wedding day. "Up 0500. Betty and I breakfasted at Piccadilly and started on foot for the Pratts,' but decided to take the 5th Avenue bus; arrived 1005. Inga with us by cab to be our witness. A ghastly ceremony, performed by a low-county political apparatchik. Then up to the Piccadilly to get our luggage, and to Penn Station for lunch. Inga left us about 1300; at 1400, took #23 home, leaving my lawful bride of three hours behind."[38]

So here it was, the wedding — a low comedy ceremony and a dashing bridegroom — going where, why back home to mother! Betty must have really loved Beam to put up with this kind of nonsense. It's apparent he feels a little sheepish, but clearly not enough to do anything about the situation.

He didn't see Betty the next week and instead spent Tuesday going "to Dr. Cooper's with Mother's lower plate to be fixed."[39] Wrote a couple of letters to Betty and finally got around to telling John McGuire that he was a married man. The next day he was reading a book, *Faithful Are the Wounds*, and watching the fights that evening over at the McGuires.'[40]

On Monday, he wrote: "Two letters from Betty, mostly on details about our new home at the Roger Williams, and plans for next midweek."[41] Obviously, Piper was not happy about the separation from his new bride. The next day he wrote, "Napped in evening after dinner, 1900–2100; still sleepy and feeling like hell. 2300 Juniata II. Back to work at the car yards."[42]

Wednesday: "Caught #32 for New York, slept all the way, getting in late. Went directly on foot to the Roger Williams and was there when Betty arrived. Dinner at the apartment by Betty ... called Betty's mother in California — she seemed to bear up well under the news."[43] More of Beam's understatement. However, I suspect that Betty's mother was told in advance about the wedding, unlike Harriet Piper. Later that evening they went to a Mystery Writers of America meeting at the Press Club with a talk on legal procedures.

"Up 0700, and got breakfast while Betty was dressing (bacon and omelets). Betty off for work 0800; I dressed more leisurely, and out shopping. Bought can-opener, and electric extension cord for kitchen, and a card-table, a horribly expensive ($15.50) thing, but wonderfully well-made, for a dining-table." That afternoon he took Betty to meet his then-agent, Harry Altshuler, and then met Mrs. Altshuler — probably for the first time. "Home at 1830, had dinner, and off to see *Teahouse of the August Moon*. Home early and to bed about midnight."[44]

He mentions several times about dipping into his "strategic reserve." "Had to tap the

"Strategic Reserve" again — only $100 left in it. Don't dare tap it again till I can get some more money in it."[45] By mid–May, he's getting worried about finances: "Worked on 'Young Immortals,' trying to get some first draft out, and got about as much done as last Tuesday, the last time I did anything on the damned thing. I wonder when I'll get sufficiently accustomed to being married to get some work done to support a wife?"[46] On July 19, he wrote: "Having a bad time about all this— no money, can't seem to get anything salable written; don't know how I'm going to get along."[47]

Obviously, the famous Piper pride would not allow him to tell Betty of his predicament and so he would soldier along, drilling holes in his "reserve" until it was completely empty — or a miracle occurred and another check arrived. The next day, once again, the cavalry to the rescue: "Check from Harry Altshuler for *Astounding* bonus on first installment of *Time Crime*, $210.00 less 10%—$189.00. Used with care, this ought to see me through Bread Loaf (a Vermont retreat and writer's conference) and eases my mind a great deal. Worked on revising and repairing story in evening."[48]

Ten days after bemoaning the fact hat he was almost completely tapped out — even the "strategic reserve" was empty — on Friday, July 29, Piper nonchalantly wrote: "Up 0700; get breakfast. Left Roger Williams about 0930. Up town to bank and *got out* $500.00 in a cashier's check for deposit in Altoona" (italics mine). He already had bled his "strategic reserve" dry; where did he all of a sudden get $500.00 to "deposit in Altoona"?[49] Where did this unexpected windfall come from?

The answer is found in a short diary entry on Monday, August 1: "Up town evening to bank the money from joint account, and home by 1930 to work some more."[50] It was Betty's money from their joint New York checking account. He was in such desperate condition that he probably wanted the money in a cashier's check so it could immediately be applied to his own Altoona personal checking account. It appears the Piper pride got into the backseat while he took money from Betty, who certainly had it and *was* after all his wife. I suspect for Piper it was a humiliation and a loss of manliness to accept money from Betty and would create a long term resentment.

Betty's obituary in *The Chicago Times* for March 7, 1990, states that "Elizabeth Hirst Piper had died in a retirement home in Honolulu, bequeathing her estate of $550,000 to the US Government."[51] It's an interesting choice, revealing there were no close relatives and that she stayed single after her marriage to Beam. Piper, on the other hand, needed money desperately all of his life; a real incongruity and certainly a hot issue in their marriage. Which makes Beam's infamous declaration that Betty only married him for a "French vacation" ring with irony.

On August 2, Piper wrote, "Up town shopping. Didn't get everything I wanted — heat affecting me worse than any other time this summer. Sent check off to Middlebury College."[52] The Bread Loaf Writers' Conference money. Plus, knowing Beam, maybe a few new shirts, a pair of shoes and a new suit.

CHAPTER 18

The Case of the Missing Pistol

Packed McGuire's watch for mailing, and wrote a letter to accompany it. Am leaving no room for doubt that he is through as far as I am concerned. I wish I'd done this long ago.[1]

— H. Beam Piper

The split between H. Beam Piper and John J. McGuire clearly began sometime during the previous year, in 1954. It wasn't all about Betty, either. The collaboration was not working out; certainly, they weren't selling stories. The stories they did have out, making the editorial rounds, were collecting rejection slips; two of them would later sell, but not for several years. Nor were they writing together much anymore. On top of that, Piper's own writing was stalled as well — his only solo sale for nineteen fifty-three was for the short novel, *Uller Uprising*. Rich Horton on the Internet at alt.books.isaac-Asimov offers this background on the Twayne Triplets:

Sucker Bait (by Isaac Asimov) was written to be part of one of the first attempts at "shared world" type SF stories, the Twayne Triplets. A scientist would design a "world" and a situation, and three writers would be commissioned to write novellas based on the world/situation.

Only two Twayne Triplets were ever published, and one of them, *Witches Three*, didn't really fit the format. (It collects Fritz Leiber's already written and published novel, *Gather Darkness*, and adds two novellas written to similar themes, "The Blue Star" by Fletcher Pratt, who was the editor, and "There Shall Be No Darkness" by James Blish.)

The other is *The Petrified Planet* which includes *The Long View* by Pratt, *Uller Uprising* by H. Beam Piper, and *Daughter of Earth* by Judith Merril. Twayne went out of business, or at any rate discontinued the Triplet program, before the book with "Sucker Bait" in it could be published.

The only other prospective Twayne Triplet stories I know of for sure are another pair of which the third was not completed: "Get Out of My Sky," again by Blish, and "Second Landing" by Murray Leinster. The prospective third story was *First Cycle* by H. Beam Piper.[2]

Piper was never able to sell the follow-up novel for the next Twayne Triplet, *Full Cycle*, to another book publisher or magazine. In terms of sales, 1954 was just as bad as 1953; the only story of Piper's that sold the entire year was "Time Crime" to *Astounding Science Fiction*.

There's also an interesting anomaly in Piper's Story Log — there is no listing among the 1953 entries for "The Return," the most recent Piper-McGuire story sale, which appeared in the January 1954 issue of *Astounding*. This is not a case where the title was changed by editorial direction, nor was it a minor sale.

So why wasn't there an entry for "The Return" in Piper's Story Log? Piper was very meticulous about listing his sales and money earnings. Was there a dispute between the two men over writing credit or the monies? I doubt it was an oversight, since there's no entry on the 1960 page for the sale of the anthology rights in 1960 to *The Science-Fictional Sherlock Holmes* either. Yet, Piper is credited as co-author on both works. Could this have something to do with his growing animosity towards Jack?

According to John McGuire, Jr., his father's drinking was starting to get out of control during their last couple of years in Altoona. "My father's English classes at Keith Junior High were for children with reading problems and he was under a lot of stress at work to produce results. He was dealing with a lot of problem kids, delinquent trouble-makers and some border-line mentally retarded students. He didn't cope with pressure well, as he was suffering from shell shock, or what they call today Post-Traumatic Stress Disorder."[3]

Piper, who was an intensely private man, was certainly beginning to feel crowded by Jack, who visited at all hours without prior invitation or calling beforehand. On January 8, 1955, Piper wrote: "McGuire hasn't been here, at least to my knowledge, since the lock went on the door. A chance that he came here, tried to get in, couldn't, and went away offended."[4] He doesn't say why the lock went on, but he certainly implies that it had to do with Jack's unannounced visits—possibly because during this time Piper wasn't home much, spending his middle of the week "weekends" off in New York courting Betty and attending writer's meetings.

Four days later, Piper noted: "McGuire dropped in about 1700. Don't know whether he'd been here before—suspect he had. He was griping about the lock on the door. Got a couple of pages typed after dinner. Over to McGuire's in evening to see fight on TV."[5] It's quite apparent Piper was not very happy about their relationship; on January 16, he wrote: "McGuire called in, saying that he and Sam Park were coming over. I believe that I am beginning to make it understood that I have some rights to privacy. They arrived about 2300, and I rode to Juniata [the car shops] with them. McGuire has finally taken the coat he left here around the end of last year."[6]

Still, Piper continued to be a regular visitor to the McGuire household. "Over to John McGuire's. His TV was out of order, so he, Sam Park and I saw the fight at Nick's, and back to his place afterward for a mess of *cuufs a chervil*, cooked by Anne and I."[7]

The next day, "Up to Keith Junior High—John, Sam [Park] and I fired fifty rounds in the basement range, and then over to the Dutch Kitchen for a few drinks."[8] Since John McGuire was an English teacher at Keith Junior High, they had access to the basement firing range any time they wanted.

On February 1, Piper wrote: "Spent late P.M., early evening, trying to get some kind of an idea of how I'm going to bring 'The Young Immortals' to a conclusion. John McGuire in about 2100."[9] The next day, Tuesday: "Had to commit my 'strategic reserve' again. Got #32 for NY all the way. Arrived NY about 1630. Snow had been bad here, too; streets sloppy and slushy. As soon as I got to the Piccadilly, called Betty at the Midston and up to join her for MWA Meeting. Business meeting, not very interesting, though she gave a good simulation of interest."[10]

After Piper's mid-week "weekend" in New York and two evenings with Betty, he returned to Altoona on Friday. "Got in about 1650. Home, and napped after dinner until 2000, when John McGuire put in an appearance, pissed off about some trouble at school—his prize monster, Grecco, again. He stayed till time to go to work, 2300."[11]

February 10, Piper wrote: "Up town 0300. Lunch at Penn Alto; did a little shopping, and to Keith Junior High for pistol practice, all double action, on the ... profile target. Sam Park disgraced both John and me by beating us roundly. Then to Dutch Kitchen for a few drinks. In evening, John and I went to Legion Home. Only five boys—I talked on Colt revolver: showing examples. To McGuire's afterward. Home by midnight."[12] He was still spending considerable time, while in Altoona, with Jack and Sam Park, but there was little talk about their writing projects.

This diary entry from Tuesday, February 15, signals a major turning point in their friendship: "John McGuire showed up, plastered to the walls, insisting that he is going mad, and that I call the Veteran's Hospital to come and get him. I called a cab for him and he left about 2100, presumably for that destination. He has been under considerable mental strain — probably needs hospitalization."[13] According to John Jr., his dad's drinking was steadily growing worse as was his insomnia. He was haunted by flashbacks from his time in Germany and a growing sense of paranoia. Jack would often wander through the house with a pistol late at night.[14]

H. Beam Piper was a hard drinker, so it took something pretty significant for him to suggest hospitalization for a friend. With Beam spending all his free time in New York and having trouble concentrating on his own writing, his focus was no longer on John and their collaboration, or with the McGuire family as it had been for the past several years. His growing love for Betty was unsettling all his relationships, not only with all the McGuires, but with his mother, too.

While Harriet Piper doted on her only son, I doubt that at ninety she was prepared for him to leave the nest, or abandon their life together of some fifty-one years. Beam Piper must have seen it that way, as well, or he would have introduced Betty to his mother — prior to their engagement and marriage. I'm certain he was more worried about Harriet's reaction to Betty than vice versa, since there had been no previous romances to test the waters. He was most likely worried that his mother would take it personally and be hurt; an emotional scene Piper would have had a difficult time dealing with.

Plus, Harriet Piper was growing blind, and she fretted about it. In his September 4, 1955, letter to Freida Coleman, Piper wrote: "her vision had been deteriorating so rapidly that when I would go to the hospital I would have to come within a few inches of her bed before she recognized me, and for a long time she had been worried about the certainty that she wanted to die before that happened. I believe she was most worried about being a burden to me."[15]

The next day he wrote: "Worked P.M. on story, and early evening. Called Anne McGuire and found that John was at home, laid up with a cold and fever. Up to see him, and saw remarkable fight on TV — Bobo Olson vs. Tiger Jones."[16]

Jack began to fade out of Piper's life after the February 15 bender; on the 21st "John McGuire sent his son, John Jr., for some manuscript he'd left here."[17] It sounds as though Jack was too embarrassed to show his face.

There's further no mention of Jack until the 26th, when Piper wrote: "John and Anne McGuire in about 2130, for a short while."[18] He is steadily formalizing Jack's name, evidence of their growing estrangement; later in the diaries he refers to him only as McGuire, and then just by the initials JJ. Piper was freezing Jack out of his life. McGuire was helping him by clinging and acting out.

On March 1, 1955, he wrote: "John McGuire in just at dinner time. Gave him some of my curried rice and chicken, whereupon he was delighted."[19] After a long night at the yards, "home 0655. Stayed up almost 0945, writing a letter to Betty. I took it down and mailed it, and then to bed. Got up around noon, and back to bed — seemed to have forgotten what day it was. Next thing I know it was 1700, and John McGuire was in to see me slightly potted. Pissed off about trouble at school. He went away after a while."[20]

The next day: "Was writing a letter to Betty when John McGuire and Joyce B. showed up — we sat in the middle room and talked and doodled until 1700. John and I stopped for drinks ... and talked over a story idea for a while."[21] They were still working on stories at this point; however, their collaboration had taken a distant second place to his trips to New York to see Betty.

A few days later: "Was going to get to work on story, didn't get around to it before dinner, wrote a letter to Betty, and then John and Anne McGuire in for a long session on a short John and I have cooking (Wait till I have my secretary with me, too!)."[22] Piper was referring to the collaborators' practice of having Anne take dictation for their stories. I suspect that becoming Beam's personal secretary was not going to go over well with Betty.

On March 10, Piper wrote: "Sent Betty a card and over to Dutch Kitchen, where I had lunch (lobster tails, excellent) and to work on the dueling talk I was scheduled to give at the Sons of the Legion this evening. When John and Joyce B. arrived. John informed me that the talk is postponed to next Thursday, at which I am not at all disappointed."[23]

On March 13: "Worked on story; got a couple of pages typed. John McGuire in about 2050. Pulled up the Iron Curtain enough to let him in on my impending marriage. Hope that wasn't a mistake." (At the bottom of the page he wrote: "I suspect that it was.")"[24] There were a few reasons behind this: first, he couldn't count on Jack keeping his mouth shut, especially if he'd been drinking. Secondly, both Jack and Anne had repeatedly attempted to talk him out of his impending nuptials. The third and most compelling reason was that Piper was probably afraid that Jack might accidentally tell his mother. Overall his lack of trust in either Jack's character or his sobriety didn't bode well for the future of their friendship.

Things were not looking up, as this March 17, 1955, diary entry shows: "Had photos taken at Schaeffer's (for Betty) and then over to Dutch Kitchen. McGuire and Joyce arrived a little later: the pistol lecture is again postponed. Up to the Legion for a devilishly boring affair — bargain-basement style show and St. Patrick's Day party. McGuire won the first door prize, a lady's handbag. Drinking with McGuire afterward. Had to get firm with him when he tried to interfere in my personal affairs."[25]

I suspect there's a lot hidden beneath the line "Had to get firm with him." The personal affair was almost certainly about Betty and their upcoming marriage. Jack was on very thin ice and appeared oblivious to Piper's growing distance. No indication of who Joyce, McGuire's new companion, was to Jack. Probably another teacher and/or drinking partner.

The next week was the wedding, not to be shared with the McGuires who opposed it. He didn't see Jack McGuire again until Sunday, the 27th, when John came over to listen to the radio. He didn't tell McGuire about the marriage until Tuesday: "Didn't get a damn thing done, this evening. McGuire in about 2100 — told him about marriage."[26] The following evening: "To McGuire's 2100, saw a hell of a good lightweight fight; some newcomer who won (split decision) over Willie Pep, which took some doing. To Nick's, afterward, for a while. Home 0045."[27]

On Monday the 11th of April, he wrote: "Got a little work done before McGuire put in an appearance at 2100."[28] Thanks to Jack's persistence, they were spending a lot of time together, but were doing very little work on their writing. Mostly, they were drinking at the Dutch Kitchen, listening to Sherlock Holmes on the radio or watching the fights on TV.

On Sunday, May 8, Jack dropped by and Piper wrote, "Told him about the declassification of the marriage subject." Finally, several weeks later, it was safe to mention the marriage. He didn't give Jack's reaction to this announcement, in fact, rarely did, but then dropped a bombshell. "John says he has stopped drinking and joined Alcoholics Anonymous, which seems like an excellent idea for him."[29] For Beam to welcome AA for a fellow drinker is surprising; he must have believed that Jack's drinking was completely out of hand.

Piper's decision to spend more time in New York with his new wife had unexpected ramifications. This one was profound enough to sever his bonds with John McGuire for good:

On Friday, May 13, after spending Thursday and Friday morning in New York, Beam wrote: "On getting home, found that John McGuire had been here on Thursday evening; Mother left him in the gunroom and he took the 9mm Browning pistol and left a wrist-watch on my desk. Tried to call him at 1400, but his wife told me he was out."[30]

He didn't articulate his fury here, but he quickly and completely cut Jack and the McGuire family out of his life. According to John Jr., "Dad was the kind of guy who would give his right arm for a buddy and expected the same in return. I don't believe he really understood — or believed in — Beam's rigid code of honor. Jack was much more flexible; he expected to be forgiven — he'd just 'borrowed Beam's gun.' I don't know whether he pawned it, or just went shooting. He left his watch as a sign of good faith; he meant to return it sometime. Beam wouldn't listen to him; when wronged, he was a hard man.

"They talked on the phone one night and were going to fight a duel over this situation. Sam Park was going to be dad's second. Jack even went target practicing at the range. It was like something out of *High Noon*. The duel fizzled out when Dr. Strassman refused to be Beam's second."[31]

On Saturday, May 14, Piper wrote: "Packed McGuire's watch for mailing, and wrote a letter to accompany it. Am leaving no room for doubt that he is through as far as I am concerned. I wish I'd done this long ago."[32] This note provides conclusive evidence that Piper had been looking for an excuse to terminate his friendship and working relationship with Jack.

The next evening: "Wrote a letter to Betty; after dinner (pork and sauerkraut) took it up and mailed it, also the letter to McGuire and his god damned wrist-watch. Spent rest of evening on 'The Young Immortals' and got out two pages."[33] Piper was having an awful struggle over this new short story, which was never sold. I'm sure that McGuire became a convenient lightning rod for that frustration.

On May 16, Piper wrote: "Up town in evening and withdrew $50.00 from my dwindling bank account, now down to $84.00. On my return home, about 2000, found the stuff I had left on the landing gone." I suspect this "stuff" was some of Jack's possessions: old jackets, clothes, pipes and maybe even unfinished stories. "A few minutes later, McGuire tried to talk to me on the phone, I hung up on him at once. At 2100, the doorbell rang, and I found him sitting on the doorstep, apparently quite drunk. I had to shout at him and curse him to get him away. Finished packing lunch. Hope this is the last I hear of him."[34]

According to Terry and John Jr. the aftermath of this breakup was horrendous for the McGuire family. "We really didn't understand what was going on at the time. Almost right after the incident with the watch we left Altoona, and never saw Beam again."[35] The McGuire children loved Beam and their father just didn't lose a friend — they lost a beloved "uncle." For the older McGuire children this was the beginning of the end of their childhood; for their father, a descent into the dark depths of alcoholism. As John Jr. said about his father, "Jack loved Beam! When he couldn't make a reconciliation — he was never the same."[36]

On Friday, June 3, Piper wrote: "Home and napped after dinner. Sam Park in about 2100. Told him about excommunication of John J. McGuire. Park has also dropped him, for approximately similar reasons."[37] I suspect their reasons had to do with Jack's advancing alcoholism as well as his growing mental instability — long term traumatic stress reactions due to his wet work for the Office of Strategic Services (OSS) behind enemy lines in Germany.

According to Anne, Jack was awfully broken up about Beam shutting him out. "Jack called in the evening; Beam just cut him off."[38] Piper was now watching the fights alone at the Wm. Penn bar — "Archie Moore knocked out Bobo Olsen in 19 seconds of 3rd round."[39] However, things were not going well on the story front: "Spent late afternoon and evening trying to get the story into shape — thought I had it well in hand, but I don't. Got practically nothing done but repetitive notes and tore them up. Seem to be losing all my ability to write anything."[40] June 22, he wrote: "Worked on story, P.M. And early evening. Tore up everything to date and made a new second final start on first draft — finished to page 15."[41]

There's no further mention of Jack in the diary until Saturday, July 30: "Letter from Ivan Washebeugh, wondering what happened to McGuire. Will probably have to give him details."[42] H. Beam Piper's excommunication of John McGuire devastated the McGuire family and cut them off from most of Jack's friends. The "Unholy Four" were disbanded; no more TV fights with Beam in attendance, no more listening to Sherlock Holmes on the radio, no more trips to the hotel bar with Beam, no more writing sessions, no more hope.

John Jr. says, "After the split, father started drinking much more heavily, he almost stopped writing. In 1956 we moved to Red Bank, New Jersey where he taught English. They were going to let him teach speed-reading; he liked that. He'd had a miserable time at Keith Junior High. But after the move he continued drinking and started smoking more — he developed emphysema in the early sixties from too much smoking. He began to get very frail. The years in Altoona with Beam were the best times of our childhood."[43]

On the 9th of August, Piper was still worked up about McGuire: "Met Jim Beaty outside. Find that he has heard from Sam Park, the story of the 9mm Browning. He also says McGuire has teaching job in New Jersey."[44] In an interesting coincidence, the McGuires were moving to Red Hook; the same town where Frederik Pohl — science fiction writer, editor and Beam's former agent — lived. Fred at this time was well known in science fiction circles as a former fan, pulp magazine editor and rising star of the science fiction field. Pohl's *Space Merchants* is still regarded as one of the 1950s classic science fiction stories. In the early sixties. Fred would take over the helm of *Galaxy Science Fiction* and as editor buy "Graveyard of Dreams" from Piper.

When I talked to Fred in 1979 about the whereabouts of John McGuire, he told me, "I know him. He still 'lives' around here. He's the town drunk; once in a while he comes to the back door to beg for money from my wife. We felt sorry for him for a long time and gave him handouts, but had to stop — we weren't helping him. I don't think he's sober long enough to interview these days."[45]

CHAPTER 19

Weekend Marriage

I intend, at the first opportunity, to take your advice and fall in love. A wider experience in that sort of thing wouldn't come amiss. In order to become sapient, I must first become a sap. I'll not be sap enough to get married, though. That's one sort of experience that I can do quite well without. One doesn't need to be sucked in on a three-shell game to understand finance.[1]

— H. Beam Piper

According to H. Beam Piper's diaries, the couple fell into a "weekend marriage"—Betty working in New York and Beam in Altoona. On his off days he grabbed a train into New York and played the role of husband. At the end of his mid-week "weekend" he would take the train back to Altoona and his job as night guard in the car shops.

On Wednesday, April 20, 1955, Piper was back in New York at their apartment at the Roger Williams. "Spent all evening at home — great triumph — we completed the *Times* crossword puzzle together.... Betty gave me a lovely trench-coat, albeit a little large. Will have to get it exchanged for sure tomorrow."[2]

Thursday, Piper became the House Husband: "Got breakfast while Betty was dressing. Put screw hooks in door of kitchenette to hang utensils. Found that the back of the light-globe, hung over door on extension cord, had blistered paint. Up town a little later to exchange coat.... Lunch at St. Denis and saw picture.... Home at 17000. Put hook in kitchenette door for light. Betty and I up town for the MWA Edgar Dinner at the Stork Club. Betty delighted with it. Home early and to bed by midnight."[3] Then on Friday back to Altoona and his other life.

On Monday: "Letter from Betty, full of happiness, and enclosing a sample of the Stork Club lipstick."[4] In the form of a kiss, one would assume. The two newlyweds were still frolicking—in what little time they have together—like teenagers. A week later and Beam back in New York playing husband. "Slept all the way to New York, getting in about 1730. On foot to Roger Williams, buying rum (Myers's, and Bacardi for cocktails) and lemons. Found Betty at home when I arrived. To Waldorf to pick up her mother, and the three of us to St. Denis; after dinner to ... Waldorf and then home, and soon to bed."[5]

For the first time, he referred to Betty as "my wife" in the diary: "Up 0700 and got breakfast while my wife dressed. Betty off to work at 0800." That evening it was back to the Waldorf for Betty's mother, and they went to see *Witness for the Prosecution.* "Enjoyed immensely. Back home after getting rid of Mrs. Hirst, had a couple of drinks."[6]

Finally the big day arrived, Saturday: "After I got back (from market), had a couple of drinks and told mother about Betty. Quite a jolt to her, but she seemed more pleased than otherwise. Sat up talking to her about 1100, and then to bed. A great relief that I can wear my ring, and that I don't need to maintain security — whole business de-classified."[7] I believe Beam really thought Harriet would take the news of his marriage badly. He always had a problem with expressing his emotions, and what more volatile subject to discuss with an aged mother for a bachelor, than a secret marriage? Thus, he hid his feelings for Betty, like a teen-ager, until it was no longer escapable. At ninety-one, I'm sure Harriet was relieved, in the sense that her son would have someone to look after him when she died. And, maybe a lit-tle betrayed.

Later in the day, Piper noted, "Wrote a letter to Betty, telling her the news of my reve-lation of our marriage. Will go to New York Thursday, and more frequently in the future."[8] I suspect Betty's having her mother visit was a gentle nudge in his direction, saying: "Beam, it's time to tell Mother."

He visited Betty again on the 18th of May, writing: "Home 0655; changed, and up town to get #70 for New York, by day — coach to save money. (Forty-five minutes late out of Altoona; into New York about 1500.) ... Arrived home about 1530. ... spent rest of evening working a double-crossword and just being in love."[9]

Beam and Betty were both fans of double acrostics. Crostics, or acrostics, are challeng-ing and popular puzzles. The objective of a crostics puzzle is to build a quotation by answer-ing a series of clues. All the letters in the answers fit into the puzzle in a specific location. It's not surprising that they appeal to literary types and people who enjoy puzzles. Crostics are tough, but really satisfying when you solve them.

On the home front, Piper was still stalled on "The Young Immortals": "Spent most of night working on rearrangement of "The Young Immortals" and have about reached the con-clusion that the story is hopeless and the best I can do with it is put it in closed storage for a while and do something else."[10] However, he was enjoying his new marriage. "After dinner (pork chops, mashed potatoes, gravy, peas; damned good; by Betty), we worked two, repeat TWO, double crostics. And so to bed. DIDN'T HAVE TO SET THE GOD DAMNED ALARM! (For first time in our married life.)"[11]

The next day: "Spent all morning getting up; had breakfast somewhere in the middle of the process. Entire process very pleasant. Betty to get tickets for Victor Borge show, while I stopped at Piccadilly to keep my memory there green ... after a curried rice dinner, to see the show. I was too sleepy to enjoy it, and we left after the first act, or spasm, had a cocktail at the Astor Bar, one of our pilgrimages and shrines, and so to home and bed."[12]

On Friday, as usual, Piper returned home to difficulties. "Mother becoming a bit difficult; however, still balking when asked to consider the question of Betty coming to Altoona."[13] This was just for a visit since Betty was still working full time at the Council on Student Travel and not about to leave New York. After Harriet Piper's accepting the marriage, it's hard to fathom her refusal to meet the bride.

On May 31, he wrote: "The news of my marriage is out at the Penn Alto; congratula-tions from everybody."[14] I'm sure they were all shocked. If anyone was a "born" bachelor, it was H. Beam Piper, even by his own admission.

On his next trip to New York, the Pipers attended the MWA Meeting, but on Thursday they had their first cocktail party. "Betty arrived at 1700. By 1730, guests started arriving. Party lasted till past 2000. By 2200, we went to bed."[15]

He arrived the next week for the Hydra Club meeting. "Ate a little before 2100, and took a cab down to Andy and Deby Crawford's, where the Hydra Club was meeting. Present: Sprague de Camp, Algis Budrys, Ted Sturgeon and wife, Jim Blish ... and others. A very good meeting, broke up about 2400."[16]

By June Piper's weekly visits have become routine. Betty seems to accept this bi-city living arrangement, but there may have been trouble brewing under the surface. Piper rarely committed emotional matters to paper, but when he did, it was only when they had come to a complete boil, as in the McGuire fiasco. For a reputed isolate, Beam with Betty had a very active social life, visiting friends, like Bill and Nancy Boylan. Plus lots of dinners at New York hot spots and various writers' gatherings.

On June 14, he wrote, "Another letter from Betty, written on Sunday—we don't answer each other's letters any more—we just fire them off at each other and let them cross in the mail."[17] Another visit to Betty at the apartment and another cocktail party—very William Powell and Myrna Loy.

On July 5, after getting a card from the Pratts about a Hydra Club meeting on Thursday, he called Betty and told her he would be arriving on Wednesday instead of Thursday.[18] "Slept all the way; arrived 1630. Home about an hour ahead of Betty. Cold dinner with ice cream, and out in evening to Central Park, as far up as the zoo. Met some nice animals, including a friendly eland and a dignified llama, walked about, small rodents (unidentified) among rocks and home by 2230, just ahead of terrific thunderstorm, which we watched from our window."[19] Beam and Betty would "adopt" several of the Central Park Zoo animals and become quite attached to them.

The next week back in New York Beam wrote on Friday: "Picked up a paperback copy of Edward Sapir's *Language: An Introduction to the Study of Speech* at Doubleday's; will be useful in next story."[20] This book sparked the genesis of one of Piper's most praised short stories, "Omnilingual."

In the following July 11, diary entry, the first inkling of their money problems crop up: "Letter from Betty—serious crisis at Council on Student Travel, much money needed; she wanted advice on lending them some money. Called her up and advised her—I hope, rather without much conviction—to do so." Later in the same day another trouble spot popped up: "Up town to bank money and cash check for Mother in evening. Call from Betty while I was out—she and Mother had a little talk."[21] Piper was decidedly uncomfortable about being in the middle of the two women he loved.

He was back in New York on Thursday, July 21, where he was preparing for their trip to Bread Loaf Writers' Conference. "The Bread Loaf Writers' Conference meets at the Bread Loaf Inn, a cluster of wooden summer-resort buildings in the hills near Middlebury, Vermont. This is the oldest of many writers' conferences that now take place every summer."[22] Piper loved going to writers' meetings, conclaves, workshops and conventions. "Got plane tickets, bought scrap-book for the Beam-and-Betty letters, did some miscellaneous shopping, and back to Roger Williams 1130. ... and up to Central Park. Visited our friends at zoo—didn't see the eland, but saw some nice monkeys and chimpanzees and one seal. Dinner at Tavern on the Green (which was Oomph!) and had our pictures taken by camera girl.... We're a hell of a good looking couple."[23]

The next day back in Altoona, Beam learned: "Notification for Bread Loaf arrived. We are in 'Brick' at $125.00 per capita."[24] On the 25th: "Letter from Betty, very happy and full of love."[25] The next day he wrote, "Up town shopping P.M. Bought three pair of colored shorts (Another change in preferences due to marriage—never wore fancy underwear before!)."[26] This is definitely a new H. Beam Piper. The honeymoon stage was still in force.

"Had dinner—mostly a mixture of Heinz potato hash and rice—and then up to Central Park, stopping on the way at New York Public Library, where we looked up some crossword-puzzle words. Home about 2300."[27] Next day: "Put in all A.M. on 'Allergy' and made some progress. Up town on foot—got chair for return tomorrow, bought shirt at Lunine's, lunch at Astor, and on foot downtown—bought tinned foods. Got back to work on plotting, with time out for a nap 1430–1600."[28]

On August 4 there was trouble: "At 1700, Mrs. MacGrew called from Altoona, telling me that Mother had fallen and injured, presumably fractured, knee, and is in hospital. Looks as though Bread Loaf is out the window. Phoned, got non-committal answer.... Park in evening, saw our animal friends at zoo."[29]

The next day, he wrote: "Left hotel about 0930, took #75 to Altoona. Read *Penguin Island* on the way home. Arrived Altoona 1745, and directly to hospital. Found Mother in much better spirits than I had expected. Got her comb and Kleenex at hospital cantina. Home, spent about three-quarter hour resting and enjoying a rum highball, and back to hospital. Mrs. MacGrew [a next door neighbor] took my laundry, yesterday, and paid for it — paid her — Good fences may or may not make good neighbors, but good neighbors are damn useful. Didn't get any sleep."[30]

The following day, August 6, Beam took care of the household chores usually done by his mother. "Up town about 1700, dinner at Penn Alto, and to see Mother 1900–1930."[31] Then off to work and "Home 0700; slept till 1500. Had breakfast, wrote a letter, and up town to mail it. Had a pint of ice cream for dinner — didn't feel up to cooking anything. To see Mother at hospital in evening. Still don't know what's wrong with her or how long she will be there, or anything, and worrying like the devil about whether Betty and I can make it to Bread Loaf. Managed to get three pages of story typed."[32]

Monday, August 8: "Took a short nap to 1100, and up to hospital. Talked to Dr. Hull. Mother's knee-cap is fractured, and she will be in hospital until I return, so Betty and I will not be defrauded of our vacation and honeymoon. Back to the apartment, wrote Betty a letter giving her the news, wrote checks for rent and telephone, and up town to banks. Transferred $200.00 from Mother's account to mine to meet hospital bills. Did some shopping, and then up to hospital to see Mother. Mother has a very pleasant bed-neighbor ... who talks to her and keeps her company."[33] The next evening, "Dinner at Penn Alto. To hospital in evening to see Mother. Met Jim Beaty outside. Find that he has heard from Sam Park, the story of the 9mm Browning. He also says McGuire has teaching job in New Jersey."[34]

He left for New York on Wednesday, August 10. "Dinner at home and up to Park, our friends the animals are feeling the cooler weather ... very playful. Polar bear more comfortable and their yak (incredible) out.... Sat on our bench by the lake — sky was spectacular on account of low ceiling. Light rain as we were leaving about 2100."[35] The Pipers now have their own rituals; out to dinner, usually, a nightcap or off to the Central Park Zoo. In the morning, acrostics or the crossword puzzles. With friends coming over for cocktail parties or just to visit; this was not the H. Beam Piper of Williamsport who lived alone and wandered the streets in his beret and black overcoat at all hours.

On Friday: "Up at 0700. For a change, Betty got breakfast. Don't think much of idea — breakfast was wonderful, but timing unsatisfactory.... In about 1810, home, had a drink and up to hospital to see Mother, who was operated on and has leg in cast. Visited the MacGrews, had a couple of drinks with them, till 2145."[36] Beam woke the next morning to "the edge of Hurricane Connie, which came up as far as Chesapeake Bay, killing at least nineteen and doing $5 million damage. Completely soaked from knees down, boots full of water." Beam had to work all night at the car yards — good weather, bad weather. Very little writing was done during this period. "Up to hospital in evening to see Mother. Spent rest of evening packing lunch, straightening up a little around the apartment."[37]

Piper was still planning his trip to the Bread Loaf conference. On Sunday, he wrote: "Dinner up town at Crist's (everything else closed) which was just barely edible; and to hospital to see Mother. Spent the rest of the evening trying to think of what I have to do before

I leavea."[38] Beam spent most of Monday packing and getting ready for Bread Loaf. "Dinner at Penn Alto, and then up to see Mother; left the little radio and a lot of extra batteries with her. Home again by 2000, and continued packing."[39]

The next day it was off to New York. He read and finished Sir Leonard Woolley's *Digging Up the Past* on the way up. Dinner out at Stoeffer's and off to Central Park to see "our friends the animals." Afterwards, Beam and Betty "walked all the way home, stopping to refuel at the Whaler."[40]

The next day, Wednesday the 17th, they took a flight out of LaGuardia to Burlington, from there a bus to Bread Loaf just in time for the opening session. A lot of time was spent with friends (Fletcher Pratt for one, who lectured on the short story), going to talks on different aspects of writing and lots of dining and drinking — lectures, and short story and novel clinics. Fun was had by all. On Saturday, the 20th: "Robert Frost read poetry and lectured in evening."[41] Even found time for a square dance on the 23rd, "in which Betty and I participate much against our better judgment. Good fun, but rather exhausting."[42] The dapper Mr. Piper square dancing — that must have been a sight!

Leave it to Beam, he found a deserted stone quarry, and on the 24th, "out target shooting at the stone quarry, in the afternoon."[43] On the 25th, a little fracas started by their friend, Fletcher Pratt who gave the evening lecture, "Mass Media." "A stupid Catholic woman indignant about something Pratt said about the Legion of Decency; going around denouncing him as a Communist."[44] Out for drinks afterwards at the local tavern.

Next morning: "Betty slightly provoked at me for waking her when I came home drunk last night." That was a first. "Breakfast at the Inn — Non-Fiction Clinic Magazine article subjects. Short story clinic — a very bad homosexual opus."[45] On the 27th, it appeared Betty was growing restive: "Betty proposed that we leave Conference and go to Canada for the week and the first part of next week. We therefore cut classes for the morning, packed and said our goodbyes, at pre-lunch cocktails at Tremen and elsewhere. By taxi to Middlebury for the bus to Montreal, with an hour for dinner at Burlington."[46]

Piper's mother's medical situation deteriorated while he was in Canada, and she was in very serious condition when he arrived back in Altoona with a bottle of wine. "Found her looking very badly, breathing with difficulty. At about 1940, called a nurse, who became alarmed, called the head nurse and an intern. Some fumbling attempts to take blood pressure.

"Mother was given an injection, and an oxygen tent was called for, but before it could be rigged, she died. Brought home her few effects, but left the wine I had brought." Lying on her back for three weeks probably led to pneumonia and respiratory distress.[47]

At ninety-one, Harriet's death couldn't have been a great shock to Beam. True, she was in good health for a woman her age, but no one lives forever. Nor did he appear to be broken up at the funeral. "I thought it was going to be rough as hell, but it wasn't really bad. Hicky [the mortician] did a fine job on Mother, considering that the goddamned blockheads at the hospital lost her false teeth."[48]

Mike Knerr has this to say about Harriet's death: "The death of Beam's mother upset him, although he never mentioned it in the diaries. One had to read between the lines, and know the man, to understand his true feelings. The truth surfaces in his entries, such as on September 11th: 'At 1700, started to get dinner. Baked pork chops (burned) mashed potatoes (not very good) gravy (frightful). Definitely not one of my better meals.'"[49]

In Piper's September 4, 1955, letter to Freida Coleman, we get some rare insight into Beam's feelings of loss.

I thought I was lucky to find somebody like Betty when I married her; now, when mother's death would have otherwise left me utterly alone, I have even more reason to think so. It's bad enough as it is, but without my wife it would have been very bad indeed.

I can't, however, feel sorrow about Mother's death, except selfishly. She was ninety-one — I didn't realize how old she was until last evening, when I had to hunt up an old family Bible to get her birth-date — and her vision had been deteriorating so rapidly that when I would go to the hospital I would have to come within a few inches of her bed before she recognized me, and for a long time she had been worried about the certainty that she wanted to die before that happened. I believe she was mostly worried about being a burden to me.

Well, there isn't much more to say. I hope to be able to get to Williamsport to see you again, some day, and I hope you and my wife will be able to meet.... I still remember the wonderful fun we all had, when Ferd was with us — the New Year's Eve party at the Republican Club ... the champagne party in honor of my first published story; an awful lot of good memories.[50]

As Knerr writes: "Betty was the bright spot in this time of gloom: 'Letter from Betty, full of plans for a Christmas trip to Bermuda, with which I am most heartily in accord.' While awaiting this sojourn to the world's most northern coral reefs, Piper busied himself with cleaning up finances and his apartment. Through it all he attempted to write, but had little success. On the weekends he, at first, horrified Betty when she discovered the tinned wild boar he had bought at Altman's, and later charmed her with how good it tasted.

"His own vacation from the car shops started on the 12th and, while he waited, Beam busied himself around the apartment at the Roger Williams, in New York, hanging up Christmas cards and playing housefrau. His own cards to friends he usually signed by drawing a '[Scottish] piper on an H-Beam.' This year, of course, there was another piper on the H-beam.

"The weekend the Piper newlyweds spent at the Hamilton [Bermuda] was a bit like a belated honeymoon and they both relaxed in the warm sun of the Gulf Stream. Years later, in Williamsport, Beam looked back fondly at his memories of the island. They returned to New York and he spent the remainder of his vacation being the typical husband until he returned to the car shops on December 30th."

"'This has, in spite of everything bad that happened, been a pretty wonderful year. Betty is what makes the difference. It would have been a horrible year without her.'"[51]

CHAPTER 20

Piper's History of the Future

He had me pegged as a gun-totin' militarist until one night we were having an argument with Bill Stroup, a pacifist. Years later, I mentioned the incident to him and he slammed his palm on the desk. "Yes," he roared, "that was the night you were giving aid and comfort to the enemy!"[1]

— Mike Knerr

"The New Year came in with a whimper in Altoona with 'No whistles blown, and a faint scatter of shots up in Fairview as the years changed guard,'" Michael Knerr writes. "Beam busied himself in cleaning up the aftermath of his mother's death and, naturally, found himself eating sauerkraut and frankfurters for New Year's dinner; pork would probably have been more traditional, but it was still the custom."[2]

It was around New Year's when Betty told Beam that the Council on Student Travel was considering transferring her to the Paris office. Knerr tells us: "Betty's employer was considering sending her to the Paris office since she had been there from 1951 to 1954 and spoke rather fluent French."[3] Obviously, Betty was in a position of some importance (Beam never provides any information on her position or job duties); also, she just had "loaned" them some money. While this first visit appears to have been a vacation, it was really just a shake down cruise prior to their later move.

H. Beam Piper's June 12, 1956, letter to Lycoming Historical Society (regarding putting his weapons collection on display while he was out of the country) provides some insight as to what *he* thought were their future plans: "I have very recently and very suddenly found myself obliged to go abroad indefinitely, and among the possessions which I cannot take with me is a collection of eighty-odd pistols, dating from the early Seventeenth to the early Twentieth Centuries. I cannot bring myself to sell them, and would much rather have them placed on exhibition where others could see them and enjoy them than boxed away in some storage-warehouse."

He goes on to say: "Moreover, I can assure you that any work you do on setting up the display will not be wasted on any over-night exhibition; the collection would remain in the Society's museum for a year at very least, and quite possibly for a number of years. When I return from Europe, I expect to locate in New York, where the Constitutional 'right of the people to keep and bear arms' is non-existent with respect to pistols, even antiques, and I may be staying there a while."[4]

Obviously, there is a lot of confusion in Beam's mind about the length of their stay in Paris, although he does expect to relocate in New York. Therefore, it's safe to assume that Piper did not foresee a permanent move to Paris, France, at this point in time. Certainly part of Beam's hostility towards their stay in Paris and his comment that "she married me for an

115

expensive Paris honeymoon" story was fueled by his resentment over the length of their stay in France. With the railroad industry in big trouble — closings, mergers and outright bankruptcy in some cases, his own job was not secure. And, Piper's writing income for 1955 was pitiful — by any standards.

On February 9, 1956, Piper purchased a map of Paris and picked up passports. That spring he was attempting to learn French. "The dictionary has definite limitations. Am still worried what in hell has become of *Lone Star Planet* and 'Hunter Patrol'; a simply deafening silence about both of them."[5]

These were the last of the un-sold Piper/McGuire collaborations; not only did they represent dearly needed revenue, but an end to an era he would prefer to forget. Mike Knerr adds: "This sort of frustration carried over into his job. He would forget to turn in his keys, then have to take them back to the railroad office. Once he locked himself out of his apartment and had to climb over a neighbor's roof and through a kitchen window to get in. Constantly in trouble with his writing, and now without an agent, Piper struggled to produce stories while spending his nights guarding the railroad property. He still commuted to New York on his days off but his story ideas were mainly a lot of doodling. "Can't seem to get a clear idea on what I want to do."[6]

Even at the apartment things were in a state. A fuel strike had complicated the couple's lifestyle and had "cooled off" the city. "Effects of fuel strike," Piper wrote, "being felt here at Roger Williams — we are running the tub full of hot water to heat the rooms."[7]

Piper's concern about "Hunter Patrol" was solved on February 27, 1956, when it was bounced by *Fantastic Universe*, "With a nice but non-negotiable letter."[8] On March 15, he was working on "the — let us devoutly pray — final first draft of 'Omnilingual.'" Their passports were being processed, although Piper was uncertain as to when the axe would fall at the railroad. He suspected lay-offs were coming, but in the meantime they were making preparations to leave for their vacation to France.

Beam was without an agent. He had become disenchanted with Harry Altshuler back in November, when "Plausible Motive" came back with a note alleging it to be un-salable. According to Knerr: "An admission Fred Pohl, for all his faults, would have never made. 'Have decided to get rid of Altshuler,' Piper wrote and did just that later that day. 'Wrote letter to Altshuler, firing him.'"[9]

He was now selling his own stories without much in the way of better results: "*Lone Star Planet* was rejected on March 30th."[10] Meanwhile, Beam continued to work on his pet project, around which his stories would revolve and from which they would evolve. It was called, in his words, "Piper's History of the Future" and was an outline of what he thought the future would be. "Omnilingual" was to be about the first expedition to Mars which he felt would take place in 1996, or A.E. (Atomic Era) 54.

"The Atomic Era is reckoned as beginning on the 2nd December 1942 Christian Era, with the first self-sustaining nuclear reactor, put into operation by Enrico Fermi at the University of Chicago."[11] Piper often added this addendum to notations on the Atomic Era dating: "The dating of the Atomic Age will be numerically correct, and not based on the life of some upstart Jewish carpenter."[12]

Mike Knerr tells us: "Beam was also fascinated with time travel. It was scarcely a new idea, since it had been dabbled in by nearly everyone — including H.G. Wells. Piper added his own variations by creating parallel time levels and a police force to keep everything under control.

"'Yes,' he once pointed out, 'anyone can write about time travel.'

"'But not about parallel time and a police force?' I asked.

"'No. I own the copyright to that.'"[13]

Time travel was important and a theme central to many of Beam's stories. During a discussion of Piper, Jerry Pournelle told me, "Piper once admitted to me that 'He Walked Around the Horses'—a time travel tale—was a true story."

"'I ought to know, I was born on another timeline.'" Even now Jerry can only say, "Beam looked me right in the eyes when he said it. And if there was a twinkle in his eye, I couldn't find it." Jerry's still not sure whether he believes it, but he's almost certain Beam did.[14]

After reading that incident in my introduction to the Piper short story collection, *Federation*, Mike Knerr wrote:

Piper was an expert at confusing the issues and extremely careful how he did it. He started the same sort of story with me that he had sprung on Jerry but hastily backtracked verbally when I told him that I had read the books of Charles Fort and knew about Benjamin Bathurst. It is no coincidence that his second story "Police Operation" begins with a quote from Fort's book *Lo!*.

The fun, where Piper was concerned was keeping people off balance. It worked nicely on him, too. He had me pegged as a gun-totin' militarist until one night we were having an argument with Bill Stroup, a pacifist. Years later, I mentioned the incident to him and he slammed his palm on the desk. "Yes," he roared, "that was the night you were giving aid and comfort to the enemy!"

To try to dupe me, he shifted to reincarnation rather than the timeline bit. He once asked to read a manuscript I had written based on the so-called Great Runaway of the Susquehanna River in 1778. I was reluctant at first, but I finally relented.

"It's good," he told me after reading it. "You stayed with the history and your hero solved his own problems."

"What about the Runaway? History doesn't mention Indians attacking the flotilla of rafts."

Beam's eyes squinched a little. "I once had a dream in which I was dressed in buckskin on a raft. We were shooting at the shore of a river. Yes, I think you wrote it right."

He was lying of course, but this was how he taught people to write. What he was saying, in effect, was that the scene I had written carried the story and, since history made no mention of attacks, my guess was as good as anyone's.

Beam was a natural writer with very little training in the trade. Most of his creative ability had been picked up by reading. He was always a voracious reader with extremely catholic tastes in books. Although he knew about narrative hooks and plot development, I doubt that his study of writing mechanics taught him about the wave formula or other such tactics.[15]

Mike Knerr knew H. Beam Piper personally, but there was a lot he didn't know. As his letters to Ferd confirm, Piper was very aware of literary conventions, although maybe not in a formal way; he wouldn't have been caught dead taking a *course* in writing at a local university. However, he spent a lot of time at writers' meetings and talked shop with other writers. There were few writers in science fiction with a better command of narrative structure than Piper, or who could do time-place narrative shifts with such finesse and smoothness. Part of this talent was that Piper wrote a lot—and rewrote even more. This is why his stories "feel" so solid; reading a Piper story is like reading a nonfiction account because it's that *real*.

His reply to the *Double-Bill Symposium* question below shows Beam's mastery of the craft of writing: "What suggestions can you offer to the beginning writer concerning the development of 'realistic' characters and writing effective dialogue?"

Know your characters intimately. Plan them just as carefully as you plan the action of the story, and let them develop in your first draft, and by the time you are ready to start on the final draft know their background, past life, education, experience, etc., and understand how they will react to any situation.

This, of course, is most important with the means-of-perception character, the "viewpoint" character as the old technique writers called him, through whom the reader experiences the story, because not only what he experiences but his reactions and attitudes will be a part of the narrative. You don't include the thoughts, as such, of other characters, but you have to make their overt behavior plausible and consistent.

And don't break means of perception. Switch it from one character to another in different scenes if you can't get the story across with a single means of perception, but never change means of perception in a single scene or action-sequence.

Name your means of perception character in the first paragraph, if possible, and don't name him thereafter unless someone addresses him by name, or something like that. You're giving his thoughts along with his experiences and actions. You don't think of yourself by name; not often, anyhow.

In dialogue, know your character, think how he would express himself. Everybody has individualities of speech; make use of that, but don't overdo it. (Don't overdo anything, of course.) Dialogue, of course, is people talking; they talk to convey information (or misinformation) to one another. In a story, dialogue can also be used to convey information to the reader. This, of course, can be overdone, too. I recall a movie, *The Iron Curtain*, I believe, in which two Communist spies in America went into a five minute dialogue about basic Communist doctrine and Soviet policy, a terrible false note, because these were fundamentals to which they both subscribed, and would have no business to discuss with each other.

Just have your characters do and say what you think people of their sort would do and say, under the circumstances.[16]

For all Piper's knowledge of writing and thirty-six years of putting his words to paper, he had always been a part-time writer; the "other job" paid the rent and put food on the table. As Mike Knerr writes, that was all about to change: "On May 23rd, the axe had fallen at the Altoona car shops and Beam drew a small guillotine on the page for that day. 'To police HQ to get my check and learned that the positions and functions of watchmen have been abolished. After Friday I don't have any more job than a jackrabbit unless I bid onto the Stores Department or something like that.' The following day he went back and talked to 'Corporal Yost and Sergeant Gutchell,' then scribbled something in his diary about going on relief, or getting another job.'

"By May 28th, he had made up his mind: 'Went directly to Police Office, where I announced my decision to quit, and turned in my pass and wrote out my resignation. Now I have no more job than a jackrabbit!' He returned to his apartment and hammered out another four pages of 'final first draft' of 'Omnilingual,' with a break for supper."[17]

What doesn't make any sense is that Beam *resigned* from the Pennsylvania Railroad, rather than waiting until they laid him off — at which time he *might* have been eligible for unemployment or some severance pay. Was it the uncertainty of not knowing when the axe would fall that forced him to resign? We'll never know, but it was a self-defeating move, which could well have cost him any chance at a pension or other compensation. In 1956, Piper was thirteen years away from Social Security eligibility or a Pennsylvania Railroad pension, which in those days were not available before age sixty-five. Then there's the question of his eligibility, with his on-again, off-again work history, with the Pennsy, and whether or not it would have been affected by his resignation.

Mike Knerr writes: "The next day Beam wrote a letter to James Blish about getting his agent, Kenneth S. White, to 'handle my end of "The Heavenly Twins." [Probably *Full Cycle*, which was slated for an upcoming Twayne Triplet.] Apparently this was another story that had its seeds sown in barren ground, but it began his association with White, a one time editor of *Adventure* magazine turned author's representative."[18] Ken White and Beam really clicked; Ken could sell Piper's work better than anyone else.

Bill McMorris, Piper's editor at G.P. Putnam's Sons, had this to say in an October 4, 2005, e-mail response to my questions about Kenneth White:

When I knew Ken in 1958, he was small, slender and slightly stooped. He wore a gray-blond moustache tinged with nicotine and I recall him as always squinting through a haze of tobacco smoke. He and I both loved martinis and tobacco and if we could repeat one of our lengthy luncheons today, I believe it would kill me.

I did not know him beyond our business contacts, but he was an amusing luncheon companion and had a pretty good sense of what kind of material I was looking for, a not very common attribute of literary agents at that time. I had known of Ken before I came to Putnam, because he had sold short stories and articles to *Boy's Life* magazine, where I worked as an editor before I entered the book publishing business. We did not have any contact through the magazine, but I was aware of his accurate sense of what was publishable for readers of the magazine.

When I was hired by Walter Minton at Putnam (1958) to take over the juvenile department, Ken White was one of the first agents I contacted, His description of Piper, who Ken claimed was living at the YMCA in Altoona at that time, was delivered with a combination of admiration and puzzlement: "He is a *One*."[19]

Even taking into account inflation, Beam Piper was not making much money writing science fiction—his best year's earnings were only a little over $3,000.00. Nor, at that time, was anyone else in science fiction making a lot of money, other than Robert Heinlein, who was making most of his income from sales to *The Saturday Evening Post* and his juvenile science fiction novels. Paperback sales were few and far between, but a revolution—thanks to television—was going on that would undermine the entire field, starting with the death of the pulps.

As early as the mid–1950s, the pulp magazines were in trouble, many disappearing like mayflies. Most science fiction authors made the bulk of their income from the ½-cent to 4-cent rates paid by the magazines, *Astounding Science Fiction*, *Galaxy Science Fiction* and *The Magazine of Fantasy and Science Fiction* being the major and best paying markets. But, each had its own appeal—a Campbell author could rarely sell more than three or four stories a year to *Astounding*. The other best paying markets were more adventurous: *Galaxy* under Horace Gold, emphasized sociological science fiction versus *Astounding's* more realistic or scientific science fiction, while *The Magazine of Fantasy and Science Fiction* was more interested in "literary" science fiction. Few writers sold to all three. To make a living a writer needed the secondary markets—even though they paid poorly. The young Robert Silverberg made a good living in the mid-fifties pounding out adventure science-fiction tales, sometimes filling entire issues of small circulation pulps with stories and short novels under different pseudonyms.

Anthology sales were few and paid badly; for example, Beam, who was paid $147.00 for "Time and Time Again" in 1946 by John W. Campbell, only received $37.80 for the anthology rights to the same story a year later from *A Treasury of Science Fiction*—one of the most successful early anthologies. Piper made twice that selling a short story, "Immunity," to *Future Stories* in 1950, which was a salvage market. However, there was more prestige in being published in anthologies, and for Piper that was a big plus.

In the same time frame, Philip K. Dick, another writer with no business sense, was starving in Berkeley, eating dog food when times were bad. Theodore Sturgeon, a writer who managed his finances even worse than Piper, was living in hovels and eating over at friends' houses to keep from starving. Everyone else had a day job; many were engineers—or living like grad students. Or like Reginald Bretnor—another unique character—living off his wife's earnings and the occasional story sale.

As Mike Knerr, who published enough men's adventure, crime stories and soft-core porn during the late-fifties and early sixties to support himself, puts it:

If beginning writers, as a rule, do not make large amounts of money, the scribes of the sci-fi genre during that period made even less. To the "Gee, I could write a book" crowd who ... arms themselves with a ream of typing paper and a typewriter, the cold hard facts of the business are enough to make one cry. Yet, as with Piper, the heady wine of that first sale spurs them on to another story, and another, until somewhere in the maze of their lives it is *all* they can do. When that point is reached, the writer becomes a sort of blend of emotions and feelings that has taken over the original entity and the typewriter becomes a hungry maw that insists on swallowing enormous amounts of paper.

Beam Piper, flushed with his early successes, and no different from any artist who lives on hope, was seeing that his craft was beginning to catch on. He attended to each story with the fanatic devotion of a newlywed husband caring for his wife and her first pregnancy.

There are few trades in the world which might require up to ten years of study and finally, when graduation comes, produce less money per year than is made by the average laborer. A rather well known sci-fi writer, at one of Forrest J. Ackerman's parties in Los Angeles, confided that he probably had made 3 cents per hour for his work on the typewriter.

In past years, writing had been something of a hobby and the railroad check came in with a regularity that publishing would never match. The world, however, was changing. Suddenly the booming troop trains of the 1940s were gone and, due to trucking, the freight business of the 1950s was in its death throes. Railroads were merging with one another just to keep their heads above the current of progress. The iron horse was fading into the same murky twilight that had swallowed up the village blacksmith.[20]

The move to France was by now a fact; Beam's last excuse — his job — was no longer part of the equation. There was no way — although he was not at all eager to go abroad — he could refuse. After all, it was a job-related decision by Betty; and he no longer held a *job*. For Beam, after the disaster of 1955 with no new sales or stories, it would have been impossible to mount a counter-offensive to the change in address, especially when a writer can work anywhere that he has a typewriter and paper.

On June 2, Hans Santesson bounced "Plausible Motive," but mentioned that he liked *Lone Star Planet*. He wanted to talk about paring it down, however, Beam wasn't exactly happy. It's not surprising, as Piper would have to do all the work himself since he was no longer talking, or in contact, with John McGuire, who was now teaching and living in Red Hook, New Jersey. Just another delay, and no guarantee that even if he did make the recommended cuts — without gutting the story — the sale would go through. In addition, *Fantastic Universe* was a salvage market, paying about a penny a word.

Piper was busy trying to find a temporary home for his weapons collection, close down the Altoona apartment, settle the last of his mother's affairs and get ready for their preparatory vacation to Paris. Then, on top of all this turmoil, a close friend died on June 10, 1956. "Letter from Betty; news of death of Fletcher Pratt. A great loss to all of us." Mike Knerr notes: "Pratt was only fifty-nine years old when he died of cancer at Monmouth Memorial Hospital, New Jersey, and the news had a profound impact upon Beam, just seven years younger. They had been good friends, both members of the same clubs, and Beam had been an admirer of Pratt's historical works for years. He spent the evening in writing a letter to Betty, with one of condolences to Inga Pratt."[21]

Fletcher Pratt's death was especially devastating to Piper since Pratt was in many ways, according to Knerr, his role model as an author. He sold fiction of almost every stripe, including science fiction, as well as nonfiction and — best of all — both historical novels and military nonfiction. Everything Beam himself wanted to do and more.

In truth, Piper was a better fiction writer than Fletcher Pratt — who by the opening decade of the twenty-first century is almost completely forgotten as a science fiction writer — and if "Rebel Raider," Beam's only published nonfiction historical work, is a good example, he was as good a historical writer, too. Few men on the planet could quote and issue forth on history like Beam Piper, as both Don Coleman and Mike Knerr have attested repeatedly.

Mike Knerr writes: "Amid all the hustle of getting everything ready for the voyage on the *Arosa Star*, Beam 'saw Ken White — think I have a good agent lined up in him.' He continued his writing of 'Omnilingual,' which was beginning to hang together in a way that was suitable to the author's critical eye."[22]

Beam would make a new friend in his new agent, Kenneth White. Ken would be his lifeline for the next ten years. Unfortunately, Piper's fortunes would both rise and fall with those of Ken White.

CHAPTER 21

French Vacation

Franc devaluated again — legal rate now 420 to $1.00, old black market rate. What a goddam country![1]

— H. Beam Piper

In "Piper," Mike Knerr writes: "With the help of Freida Coleman, he managed to get things arranged and packed by June 21st and made it to the Coleman residence that evening, finally having dinner at the Hillside Restaurant. The party also included Ted Ranck, a long time hunting buddy. The next day he took a plane to New York to get ready for the trip to Paris."[2]

Beam and Betty managed a last Hydra Club meeting at Jeff Markell's house and left by plane for Wolfe's Cove and their ship for Paris — not, however, without confusion. For all his courtly, meticulous ways, Piper never seemed to get anything done "by the numbers." He saw Ken White and said, "I think I have a good agent lined up in him."[3] The ninety-five-minute plane flight from New York to Montreal was uneventful, but the flight into Quebec was a snafu. Beam found himself on one flight and Betty on another; confusion reigned in the shipping as well. "After some phoning, and general hell-raising, the typewriter, Betty's suitcase arrived; hat-box still overdue 2345."[4] Eventually even that surfaced and the day ended well.

On July 3, they boarded the *Arosa Star*, and Betty spent most of the day embarking three hundred, sixty-three students. The ship got under way from Wolfe's Cove at 1800 sharp and they headed across the Atlantic. While Betty babysat her students, Piper worked on "Omnilingual." As his diary indicates, he had mixed feelings about this working vacation. He was eager to see some of the historical spots he'd read so much about and looked forward to visiting museums and battlefields. Despite all this, Beam was a homebody, and traveling in Europe would soon prove wearying despite the good company.

The boat trip to France was mostly uneventful, and Piper continued to work on "Omnilingual." After their arrival, Beam and Betty settled into the Hotel Raspail in the heart of Paris' Left Bank. Betty tended to her job with the council while Beam wrote and made friends with numerous French cats.

As Mike Knerr writes:

For the first time, Piper was *on* the soil that he had been studying about for most of his life and he took full advantage of the opportunity, beginning with the Louvre where he inspected the crown jewels and the state swords of monarchy. He added a trip to Napoleon's tomb ... "(tombs of Vauban, Roch thrown in gratis)," but he was also getting a taste for Europe that would eventually rub him the wrong way. "Hot water," he wrote on July 17th, "still not-existent. Non-bathing situation critical."

While he worked on "the final-final draft" of "Omnilingual," he managed to see the palace at Versailles, noting dryly in his diary that the main attraction in the Hall of Mirrors needed cleaning.

121

Naturally, he "did" the *Champs Elysees* and the *Arc de Triomphe* and on the 23rd wrote happily that *eau chaud*, the hot water, was finally running. Of his more practical discoveries in Paris, he was delighted to locate the Gastinne-Renette range on Av. Franklin D. Roosevelt where he kept his shooting eye in firing a dueling pistol.

He and Betty did their usual pastime of visiting the local zoo and Beam's love of animals surfaced when he found a mouse in their apartment in the hotel. Instead of setting a trap for it, he fed it crackers which it ate under the dressing table. In fact, when he laid in a supply of rum that was "getting low" he also bought more cheese crackers for their mouse, who later became two mice and he fed them both.[5]

Piper spent August taking walks, working on "Omnilingual" and shooting pistols. They were scheduled to return to the United States in October, leaving October 3 from London. In Paris, living in the Hotel Raspail, he had nothing to occupy his time but sightseeing and writing. He got right down to work on "Omnilingual" without any of the false starts, stops and rewrites that plagued his writing throughout all of 1955. He finished "Omnilingual" by the first week in August, and, on his strolls, was amused to hear a jukebox playing "Davy Crockett." He mailed the manuscript out to Ken White on the 6th, continued to get lost in Paris and kept up his shooting of dueling pistols. He began the plotting of a story called "The Knife Edge."

Knerr writes:

Ken wrote him on August 31st, 1956 with the good news that his story, "Omnilingual" had been bought by John Campbell of *Astounding Science Fiction* for $630.00. Bolstered by cash, he began to work on the new story and Betty went to work ... "both rejoicing over the news." They were both packing things to be shipped to London, their point of departure for the States on October 3rd.

The trip to London and their embarkation on the *Arosa Sun* from Cowes was not exactly in a straight line. The couple spent the month of September touring a great deal of Europe, their itinerary included Geneva, Montreux, Zermatt, Zurich, Heidelberg, Mainz, Cologne, Brussels, Bruges and London. Beam took in every museum he could manage, and was properly impressed with the Matterhorn and was introduced to old friends and places in Geneva. Betty had been there in 1954 and even located an old acquaintance in a cat named "Lucrezia." On the 19th they took a boat to Dover and a train in to London checking in at the Regent Palace hotel.

Although Beam played tourist at parks, museums and various art galleries, he did manage a side trip that stunned him. "Went to Baker Street, found 221 occupied by a big office building, learned that the Sherlock Holmes Museum *is now in New York*!" To soothe his outraged Holmes-fan-ego he took a train as far as Salisbury to visit Stonehenge. Even at this he was annoyed by English problems. He got a bus to Amesbury, but couldn't find transportation "of any sort" to Stonehenge. He ended up walking the last "two miles each way."[6]

It was the little things of Europe, which the natives shrugged off as normal, that most bothered Beam — not being able to go where he wanted to go, difficulty in finding food and personal items he was accustomed to and trouble with the facilities such as hot water, private restrooms, etc. One quickly gets the feeling that while he enjoyed sightseeing in Europe, he would have been much happier at home in Altoona working on his stories, hiking in the woods and drinking rum with his friends.

Knerr writes: "While they waited for their ship to sail, they saw Windsor Castle, Westminster Abby and the Tower where Anne Boleyn lost her head, then did Stratford-on-Avon, Anne Hathaway's cottage and Shakespeare's tomb. His entries read like a rushed tourist's card and by the time they boarded the *Arosa Sun*, at Cowes, both of them should have been exhausted."[7]

The Atlantic crossing was rough and Betty suffered almost constantly from seasickness. Beam seemed immune and finished up his latest Future History yarn, "The Knife Edge" (published in *Amazing* as "Edge of the Knife") between Labrador and Newfoundland. Betty enjoyed it. "Beam hopes the editor will, too."[8] Ken White appeared pleased with it and even tried to sell it to the top market of the day, *The Saturday Evening Post*; a sale to the *Post* would have been quite a feather in Piper's cap — alas, it was not to be. It was bounced from the *Post* on October 23.

"Getting back to New York wasn't as easy as leaving had been," Knerr writes.

The *Arosa Sun* found a mess with Canadian customs, the passengers being held for two hours on "B" deck, "a horrible experience," Beam wrote. In New York, there were no apartments available at the Roger Williams, but they were given a temporary room until one became vacant. To top off a somewhat lousy trip when they returned to their room they found the key wouldn't work. The next day, Betty left for the office and Beam had lunch with Ken White and Kelly Freas who had just finished the illustrations for "Omnilingual."

In spite of the "mess" of travel, Beam was home and had launched into the nebulous beginnings of the plot of "The Keeper," which would eventually be bought by *Venture Magazine* (a more daring version of *The Magazine of Fantasy and Science Fiction*). His traveling odyssey behind him, Beam settled down to the task of unpacking everything and, on October 16th, talked to Hans Santesson who told him that *Lone Star Planet* had definitely been accepted and would be published in *Fantastic Universe*. In the evening, Beam and Betty attended a Hydra Club meeting at Basil Davenport's and saw Inga Pratt for the first time since Fletcher had died."[9]

"The Knife Edge" was returned by *Astounding Science Fiction* on November 7, and Beam sent it off to his agent, Ken White. Meanwhile he was working on a story about "the poor fisherman who sold the holy relic."[10] Beam picked up tickets for a trip to Williamsport slated for the day after Thanksgiving and continued to punch away at the typewriter. By November 17, he had finished "The Little King of Lagash," but apparently this story was a flop in the publishing world.

Just before Thanksgiving he and Betty flew to Williamsport and were met by Freida Coleman, who took them to the Lycoming Historical Museum. There they unpacked Beam's collection of pistols and set them out to be displayed (appendix D).

After Betty returned to New York, Piper visited Altoona to clean up some details with his mother's estate and purchase a granite plaque for her grave. Altoona, after all his travels, was changed: "This town is dying on its feet," was his judgment.[11] He left to return to New York the next day. Actually, it was Piper who was changing, becoming more cosmopolitan, the result of living in New York and traveling to Europe. The Pennsy was still in business, but things were slow at the car yards. Altoona looked the same as always; it was Piper's point of view that was different.

Knerr writes: "Settled again in the Big City, Beam went to work on 'The Keeper' and Ken White informed him that the 'Little King of Lagash' would need cutting. He was fighting 'The Keeper' by the first week in December, noting that the 'story as now planned is less and less satisfactory; everything seems too pat and contrived, story doesn't grow naturally out of situation.' The next day: 'Scrapped entire story-outline, eliminated one character, revised beginning and end.'"[12]

In mid–December he received a check from Hans Santesson for *Lone Star Planet* and felt "glad to be shut of that thing."[13] It was one of two final collaborations with John McGuire that Beam still had on the market and by far the bigger story, a short novel. It signaled the end of an era. Piper received a "check from Ken White — $360.00 for "The Knife Edge," which would appear under another title in the May 1957 issue of *Amazing Stories*.

Piper finished the year still trying to get "The Keeper" into shape for submission. He picked up a copy of *Astounding* on January 4, 1957, and he liked the *Astounding* version of "Omnilingual," particularly the Kelly Freas illustration with a pun on the "tables."[14] He finished "The Keeper" on January 18 and mailed it out. He received a call from Donald Wollheim, of

Ace Books, who wanted to publish a paperback edition of "Null-ABC." Piper was also engaging a tailor to make him a new suit. By the 25th of January, he was outlining "Graveyard of
Dreams" and commented: "looks as though it's going to develop into a real story."[15]

　　　Knerr writes:

> Beam's cooking, over the past year, duly noted in the diaries, appears to have fallen into a rut. He
> and Betty took turns ... but the days of Beam making such things as wild boar had shifted to an old
> standby—fried pork chops, fried apples and sweet potatoes. The diaries never say, but the description
> of food (cooked by Beam) seems boring.
>
> 　A trip to Betty's hometown was in the offing by the first of February as Beam points out: "After
> dinner, did some packing for the (gulp!) trip to California..." They left for San Francisco on February
> 7th, spending 12 hours and 40 minutes on United Flight #501, landing in San Francisco at 1840 to
> check into the Sir Francis Drake. The next day they took a brief flight to Monterey and were picked
> up by Mrs. Hirst for the drive to Carmel.
>
> 　Beam appears to have liked Carmel, enjoying the company of Mrs. Hirst's friends and neighbors—
> particularly "a nice fat bulldog named Boy." The Pipers stayed a couple of days in Carmel, then
> returned to San Francisco to tour the town, including helping to push a cable car around on the
> turntable. They returned to New York on February 12th. It would appear, although Beam doesn't say
> so in the diaries, that this trip was a kind of farewell to the States and Betty's mother.[16]

It had been less than six months since their vacation to France, so this move abroad was
no surprise. Betty must have worked it out one step at a time, as Beam was still in denial
about the permanency of their upcoming move.

　After the short trip to Carmel, California, to visit Betty's mother, Piper learned
from Ken White that John W. Campbell of *Astounding* had bounced "The Keeper." He went
back to work on "Graveyard of Dreams," a deepening of Piper's panoramic outline of
the future. "Graveyard of Dreams" would lay the groundwork for *The Cosmic Computer*
novel. Prior to "Graveyard of Dreams," Pipers stories were somewhat isolated — even though
some were in his Terro-Human Future History (appendix C). Now Beam was beginning to
get a handle on something that would influence him in the coming years, the Terran Federation.

　Still, at the moment, nothing was to come from the typewriter without a great deal of
literary sweat. Dissatisfied with the way "Graveyard of Dreams" was going, he scrapped it all
on February 8, and started over. Left with just the embryo of a story, he doggedly returned
to the machine to begin again.

　On February 21, 1957, Piper wrote: "Council on Student Travel office a madhouse, getting new shipping schedule out, everybody sick."[17] Knerr notes:

> Betty had been having a time of it during the past year, suffering what appears to have been stomach
> trouble. It would plague her during much of their time together. One little bright spot, in this hectic
> period, was "a lovely little dachshund puppy in a pet shop window."
>
> 　Betty fell in love with the little dog and they learned that the price of ownership was $100.00.
> Beam, with his characteristic caution, was a bit dubious.
>
> 　Mrs. Piper won over whatever protests Mr. Piper might have voiced that night at the Roger
> Williams and the next morning Beam bought the little dog. "On Betty's suggestion, we are calling
> him Verkan Vall...." The pet shop owner agreed to board the new addition to the Piper household
> until they were ready to sail for France. Although Beam might have had some doubts at first, he soon
> found himself captivated by Vall, or "little squiggle," as he often called him.
>
> 　The next few days he and Betty visited the pet shop whenever they could. "Up town to visit Vall at
> the pet shop." They found him in good spirits and very active, chewing on his towel. The puppy was
> quite aware of which pocket of Beam's overcoat the goodies ought to be in. In typical Piper fashion,
> Beam noticed that Vall's ears got in the way of his dinners. To solve the problem, he bought the dog
> a hairnet to keep his ears out of his Alpo, or whatever he was eating. The experiment "was not a suc-
> cess" and Vall went back to eating the way dogs had for centuries.[18]

Paul Schuchart came to visit about this time. "The next to last time I saw Beam was in New York. I was there to attend some kind of meeting and called Beam. It was when he was having problems with his wife; all because he (Beam) had got his wife's dog drunk on 'very dry' martinis, served in a dish. That Beam even married-up surprised me. Beam and I had a few drinks before the evening was over. I do not remember meeting his wife."[19]

CHAPTER 22

The Big Breakup

When I was in Paris, I was miserable because I didn't have a home. Now I have
a home, and I'm miserable because I don't have Betty and Vall![1]
— H. Beam Piper

Early in March the Pipers began packing for both the voyage and move to Paris on March
27, 1957. This move was a major life event; maybe not for Betty, who loved living abroad, but
certainly for H. Beam Piper. This time the journey was a relocation, not a vacation. This could
not have pleased Piper, but without a steady source of income he had no grounds to halt the
proceedings. Knowing Beam, he probably stewed in silence. There are no records in the diaries
about his view of the upcoming venture until the day they left: "Betty finished her packing
while Beam cowered in bed."[2]

Betty continued to live in France until after 1964, so it appears that this was not meant
to be a temporary change of venue. Paris was to be the Pipers' new home. Piper hadn't minded
the visit — or at least, the tourist part, trips to museums and libraries — however, he had not
enjoyed the living conditions. In addition, without his railroad job, he was now completely
dependent upon his writing for money. And, while there had been more story sales, with
fewer stops and starts in 1956, than in 1955, Beam was a long way from having a stable, financially rewarding writing career. Had he still maintained a residence in Altoona and not lost
his job at the car shops, I doubt that he would have permitted this move to happen. Of course,
Betty, who loved her job with the Council on Student Travel, would have had her say, in
which case the breakup would have happened in early 1957.

Knerr writes:

Finally packed, they checked out of the Roger Williams just before noon and boarded the *Queen
Mary*. The sea became rough on the 29th to the point where Beam decided to forego writing and
Betty retired with a case of seasickness. The weather settled itself the next day, however, and Beam
went back to work. The sea became very rough on the 29th to the point where Beam decided to
forego writing and Betty retired with a case of seasickness.

By the first of April they were unpacking at 70 *rue d'Assas*, Paris, and settling in. The hotel they
tried to adopt as home was the *Chambre Dix*. ... It was there that a somewhat significant phrase was
first recorded by Beam who was attempting to finish "Graveyard of Dreams." "The little girl in the
next room has a pet hamster — saw it today. Cute little fuzzy."

While Beam continued working on "Graveyard of Dreams," Betty began her job at the Paris office
of the Council on Student Travel. Betty, while she continued to work, was not feeling very well — her
stomach acting up a good bit of the time. Vall was also having health problems, but being a puppy
and full of energy kept bouncing back. He had developed an infection in his ears which his adopted
parents tried to correct, and he was being taken to a local vet for shots.

Beam was also doodling on a detective novel, namely "Murder Frozen Over," and perhaps the

H. Beam Piper's crossing to Europe aboard the *Queen Mary* was a happy one, as attested here with his canine friend Verkan Vall. The author's words on reverse of photo: "Vall telling Pappy a little secret" (courtesy Coleman Family).

germ of the little fuzzy novel was also starting to take shape in his mind. He was, during this period, filled with ideas for stories, but the never-ending problem of getting them down on paper to suit him was always difficult. For some reason, writing a goodly amount of pages on one day would be followed by a dry period on the next.[3]

On April 16, Piper mentioned that Vall was listless, "showing symptoms of ill health"[4] which he attributed to the shots. This was not the case, and the little dog's sickness was to get worse.

Unable, or unwilling, to express his feelings, Piper's emotions come to the surface over little things, such as the price of cigarettes. After buying a couple of packs for Betty, he complained that the "price was outrageous," and these frustrations would continue to grow.[5] Betty was quite conscious of spending money, but Beam was not.

Piper was more bothered by the restraints of not having money than by its actual value. Piper loved to spend money, and often threw it around like confetti, but the idea of "getting a job to earn money" would enter his mind as a last resort — only then to be rejected. Betty was a frugal child of the Depression, while Piper was at heart still a Bohemian. Maybe his disdain for money was a reaction to growing up poor, or he believed it was ignoble to the soul of the true artist. He certainly regarded foreign currency with contempt: "I never thought of French money as anything but wallpaper," he said, years later to Mike Knerr.[6]

One also has to take into account that this move from Altoona and the change from part-time author to writer had to have had a major affect on Piper's writing. No longer could he sit at the car shops and write first drafts longhand, or walk through the shops mulling over ideas for new story ideas or plot developments. This was a man who was born and bred in the Pennsylvania soil and loved to write its history, and who'd had youthful dreams of writing a literary trilogy on the area. Now he was in a completely foreign environment and all his guns were back in Lycoming Historical Museum in Williamsport, along with his hunting and drinking companions. Beam's long cultivated weapons collecting network was abandoned; no more writers' meetings, editorial lunches, awards dinners at the Stork Club and science fiction conventions.

But the work must go on, and "Graveyard of Dreams" was finally finished on April 19, 1957, after "doing over" several pages. "That's usual," Piper comments, "after a burst of production like yesterday's."[7] The interesting part is that he put almost as much work into an eight-thousand-word short story as he did to a novel and damn near the same amount of time; it took him four months to finish "Graveyard of Dreams." Of course, the late 1950s was the beginning of a radical ground shift in science fiction and genre fiction in general, away from short stories to novels. Piper had more freedom to put the odd scene and extra character in a novel, whereas in a short story everything had to be concise and pertinent to the theme, or at least, plot. However, it would be a few years before Piper took advantage of this development.

Piper mailed "Graveyard of Dreams" off to Ken White on the 23rd and began the plotting of a new story the next day. On the last day of April, he made reservations for the London World Science Fiction Convention, slated for September 6, and began to think about what he and Betty would wear to the masquerade party. In the end, they decided that Beam would go as a fan magazine editor and Betty would be a fan. Piper had all kinds of problems with this bit of costuming, but it was typical of Europe in general.

Knerr writes:

"Betty to office, Beam to work on story." Nearly every page of the 1957 diary begins with this sentence. Piper was a dedicated writer and often worked late into the night trying to get a story line straight in his mind. Although his, or any writer's, workday has no fixed hours, Beam usually spent more than an eight-hour session at the typewriter. This, of course, would be interspersed with breaks— shopping or taking Vall for a walk.

June 17th: "Lots of mail, including letter from Ken White— both Campbell and Mills bounced 'Graveyard of Dreams,' H.L. Gold has it now." Later in July, "Beam went to *Chien Elegant* for Vall's dog food and found that he owed them 2000 francs on the previous purchase. He paid it and went back to the hotel to find ... 'copy of "Null-ABC" re-titled *Crisis in 2140*,' God only knows why— in mail, but no word of check." He wouldn't receive the check, for the second half of the advance from Ace— a whopping $225.00 less 10% commission— until August 19th.

Beam got a letter from an English agent, E.J. Carnell, who wanted 'He Walked Around the Horses' for an anthology. Beam agreed, writing letters to Carnell and Ken White, then worked on notes ... "trying to get story back on track. Still not doing enough work in advance, starting to write with story unclear." With all the weekend trips, from a writing standpoint, "Murder Frozen Over" was into heavy going.

July of 1957 was "infernally hot" in Paris and all the Pipers suffered from it. Having limited cooking space and no refrigeration, food spoiled-milk in particular, and the bathing situation had to be done in various places. Betty took her shampoo to the office to wash her hair. The only plus to the hot weather was that Beam could move their tub out on the balcony and let the sun heat the water. He wasn't exactly bubbling over with joy about this, but then he could generally "make do" in such situations.[8]

While it might have taken a long time in germinating, Beam's anger with Europe was beginning to show through in his normally bland diary notations. Whether or not he and Betty discussed this sort of thing is never mentioned, but I feel certain that the subject had been broached from time to time. After spending several days looking for a mortar and pestle (to be used for breaking up Vall's dog biscuits because of his intestinal illness) he finally managed to locate one. A great deal of shoe leather was wasted in the process.[9]

As the Pipers settled into life on the Continent, Beam's dissatisfaction with living abroad grew. He missed his friends, even though he'd never admit it, and most of all the Good Ol' US of A. Betty, on the other hand, was settling into the life she loved. Knerr writes:

July 10th, 1957, proved to be a red letter day for them with Betty passing her driver's test and happily reported home with the news before going back to the office. Beam's joy came later when he wrote: "The hot water began running at about 1800."

Two days after they went on a trip in Betty's Volkswagen to Mont St. Michel with another couple. They arrived at the Hotel Mere Poulard on Friday and when they went out Saturday visiting the local tourists' sights they arrived back at the hotel to "learn the management are trying to charge us for meals we didn't eat. An inconclusive hassle, the management insists on charging us," with Beam and Jack Kneller insisting that they don't owe him.

To add insult to insult, the Pipers returned to Paris only to learn that Beam had lost his Dunhill pipe at the hotel. The loss of a Dunhill, to Piper, would have been a hell of a loss. They do not come cheap and the only time Beam was without a pipe was when he slept.[10]

Back at their Paris hotel things were not to be normal either. "Water leak developed at our sink," Piper wrote, "much fussing on part of Monsieur the Landlord, and now we have hot water but no cold water." The following day a plumber came to fix it. A day or so later, at a restaurant they encountered a rather unpleasant scene: "Uproar caused by drunken or demented character shouting insults at customers from the sidewalk."[11]

It's obvious from the diary entries that Piper was more and more bothered by everyday annoyances in Paris. He didn't talk about his homesickness for the States, but it comes through in between the lines. Nor was he getting much work done. Piper's inability to speak French made everyday problems almost insurmountable, even getting ready for the London World Science Fiction Convention.

Vall tugs at Piper's moccasin in their hotel room. On the back Piper wrote: "a new plaything" (courtesy Coleman Family).

Piper took this photograph in 1957. On the back it reads: "Vall and Betty in the Luxembourg" (courtesy Coleman Family).

As Knerr writes: "His next set of irritations with Parisian life came when he tried to gather the material for the costumes they were to wear at the up-coming London convention—namely an eyeshade, since he was going as a fanzine editor. He spent most of the day of August 30th looking all over the left bank, but couldn't find one. On September 4th he was still looking: '...over town, still trying to find an eyeshade. Christ!' Just why the French feel compelled to sell such things in a bicycle shop isn't clear and Beam doesn't bother to elaborate. On the following day he picked one up and on September 6th, the Pipers left for London."[12]

"In London, Beam took in the Tower and its arms collection as well as the Convention, but noted that he and Betty had to leave in the middle of John Campbell's talk on psionics to catch their plane back to Paris."[13] I suspect that was not an accident, since Beam had a long memory and a certain luncheon where Campbell rejected 'The Knife Edge' comes to mind."

As demonstrated in this May 13, 1957, letter to Freida Coleman, Piper was trying to make the best of an unhappy and uncomfortable situation. The contrast between the picture Beam painted in his diary, and the one in this letter, is worth noting.

Dear Frieda:

Your letter of 19 April finally caught up with us, after being re-directed a couple of times and following us over by boat. We left New York in March, came over on the *Queen Mary*, and arrived in Paris on 1 April. We have been here ever since, and have been having a splendid time.

Our family has now increased from two to three, the new-comer being a little satin-smooth brown dachshund, a little less than five months old, extremely active and playful, and he is having a wonderful time in Paris, too. I was delighted with the write-up on the collection (Museum Displaying Collection of Antique Arms—*Williamsport Sun-Gazette*, Thursday, April 18, 1957); I've had such stories about my pistols a number of times, but this was the first one I've ever seen that had all the facts

John W. Campbell and H. Beam Piper shaking hands at the 1957 London World Science Fiction Convention. Photograph by Norman Shorrock (courtesy Peter Weston).

H. Beam Piper signs autograph for Barbara Silverberg at the 1957 London World Science Fiction Convention. Photograph by Norman Shorrock (courtesy Peter Weston).

straight. All the facts about the pistols, that is; I noted they had Ferd's middle initial wrong. Betty liked the story so well that she sent the clipping to her mother, in California.

Very glad to hear that the pistols are covered by the general museum insurance. I had been intending to do something about insurance, but never seemed to get around to it. The remark of the man from Watsontown is strictly comedy; I bought most of these pistols from dealers, at least all the more expensive ones, and the most I ever paid for anything was $225.00 for the pair of Manton dueling pistols. I'm very glad to hear of the interest they have aroused. Liked the way Ferd's guns are put up, too— somebody ought to close the bolt of the Arisaka Japanese rifle, though.

I'm writing Ted in this mail; please give my best to Mr. Coryell and the other people in the Historical Society, and to Sylvia and Diane and Don and Buddy and the Colemans.

Best wishes from all three Pipers[14]

Little Vall was sick most of the time, Betty had stomach problems and Beam was homesick, but you'd never know it from the above letter!

There were more difficulties on their next jaunt, with another misunderstanding about breakfast at the hotel — which wasn't served at their room, but available in the main dining area. Little things, but indicative of a groundswell of frustration at living abroad with Betty. He loved Betty, there is no doubt about it, but he was growing very tired of France. Perhaps as an indication of his state of mind at this time, on July 31, he recorded: "Lost a day — Tuesday's entry for today." This is the only time he missed a day in his diaries. His displeasure with France was growing.[15]

Knerr writes: "On Monday, back in Paris, Erich (one of Betty's co-workers) had a run-in with a truck in the new VW resulting in both right side fenders bashed in. Betty took it for repairs, probably at the Pipers' expense.[16]

Things were building to a head and on September 13, Beam scribbled: "Spent evening packing for another weekend trip, this time Deauville." Knerr writes: "His writing, or rather printing, looks a trifle scrawled and probably mirrors his displeasure. The first part of Saturday morning went well enough, but trouble was to develop when they went to dinner at about 7:30 that evening. 'Out for dinner 1930,' he writes. 'We went to a rather expensive (1,200 francs) restaurant. Betty wanted to run as soon as she saw the menu — I insisted on staying.'" As Knerr notes: "At 420 francs to the dollar the meal would have been less than $3.00."[17]

Piper wrote: "She became furious, and as a result, words were exchanged when we left, ending in my getting my things out of the hotel and, after paying the bill, leaving. Found the station closed and no train to Paris before 0645 tomorrow. Put up at a hotel for the night and was given an alarm clock to wake myself at six."[18]

There's little in the diary to explain the breakup. Even their actual "fight" is a non-event; all married couples argue over restaurant prices on occasion — they very rarely split apart over them. Piper hid his deep feelings. He never expressed them publicly, other than in a few letters to Ferd Coleman, and now in private to Betty; certainly never in his own diaries, except between the lines. "The storm clouds began with the previous French 'vacation' or scouting trip, lighting up again in New York before their departure with Beam 'cowering under the bed' while Betty packed."[19]

The real problem was Betty's work with the Council on Student Travel and her desire to live in Paris. I'm sure she had enough clout — after all, she was an "investor"— to remain in New York at the main offices of the Council on Student Travel, but she had lived in Paris for four years, and appeared determined to do so again — despite her husband's wishes to return to New York.

I have no doubt that H. Beam Piper at fifty-three years of age was not an easy man to live with. Charming, gracious, and learned, he was. But he was as stubborn as a jackass, and had been pampered for fifty years by a doting mother. The Prince wanted it all his way, but so did the Princess—and she had the bigger dowry. Beam, however, was as hard as the flint of his Kentucky rifles when it came to sticking to his guns.

Had Piper kept his job at the Pennsy, things might have turned out differently. He would have had more say in their future residence. When he lost that job as watch guard—as unglamorous as it was—Piper lost most of his earning power and the marriage dynamics shifted. Betty was now the wage earner and it's obvious she was no shrinking violet, either. A career woman, at a time when they were still a minority, as well as a divorcee living by herself in New York City, Betty had no problem living in France—with or without Beam.

As Mike Knerr notes: "The restaurant at Deauville, and the incident that followed, appears trivial in the extreme. Piper puts it in a more direct light in his last entry for the day: 'I am going to miss both Betty and the little dog like the devil. I think Vall is going to miss me, too. But, at last, I can go back to my own country! I needn't be an exile anymore.' And, that, is the crux of the breakup: Beam wasn't happy in France; Betty was. Beam didn't like their living quarters; Betty did. Beam wanted to go home: Betty didn't."[20]

Before Piper could leave France, however, Betty located him and attempted to patch things up. He had packed his belongings and caught a morning train back to Paris, checking into the Hotel Unic. Knerr writes: "Betty found him on Tuesday, the 17th, and was waiting for him in his room when he returned from shopping. 'Seems she'd put in a couple of busy days trying to trace me, and put a French private eye on me—he probably located me by some corrupt tie-up with the cops.' They went back to her hotel room, picked up Vall, and had dinner at a Chinese restaurant."[21]

Piper's final entry regarding the breakup: "Betty's idea—I go back to U.S., join her here in November for a trip south. My reaction—negative. I've had it with Europe."[22] She wanted to stay in Paris, he was determined to leave. Neither would give an inch and their marriage, for all intent and purposes, was over.

Mike Knerr sums it up this way:

Beam's love for Betty is apparent throughout all of his diaries, and it was glaringly obvious to me in our conversations, yet it was scarcely the kind of love most people would opt for. He wore their wedding ring until the day he died. It is, I believe, safe to say that Betty undoubtedly found it less than to her liking. Most things, it would appear, had to go Beam's way or, like the rigid person he was, he would pick up his marbles and go home.

In attempting to understand the relationship between Beam and Betty, and, of course, the eventual breakup, it is necessary to not only use the journals but to read between the lines. It was even more important to watch his eyes and listen to the sound of his voice when he spoke of her. In the end, one gets the strong feeling that Betty was a woman who made the mistake of marrying a man too old, too set in his ways and too uncompromising in his beliefs.[23]

CHAPTER 23

Sputnik

DAMN! If only Odin had given me a clue. And Thor himself must have surely known![1]

— H. Beam Piper

On his last day in France, H. Beam Piper tried to sort his feelings out over a cup of coffee, but in the end felt that his decision to leave was the only one he could follow. "It won't do any good for me to go on that trip with Betty in the winter — we'd both be at each other's throats inside a month. Will try to persuade her to come back to the States with me when her vacation starts."[2] He was not happy living abroad and probably felt hornswoggled when Betty maneuvered them into living in France. Betty wouldn't, or couldn't, leave her job. She could have agreed to vacation in the States, but when she didn't it showed her commitment to the marriage was not rock solid. They were both stubborn, and they'd pay dearly for it over the following years.

Here's the letter he wrote to Freida on September 9, 1957, before he left France:

Dear Frieda,

I am returning to the States immediately, sailing on the *Ile de France* from Le Havre tomorrow. I will be in New York for a few days, and then will come to Williamsport. I wonder if it would be too much to ask of you to put me up for a day or so, until I can get an apartment. I am coming back alone, but I have every hope that when I can get established Betty will come to join me. I'll explain all about it when I see you; at the moment it is rather painful for me to go into. The worst of it is that we still love each other; if we had parted spitting curses at one another it would be much easier on both of us.

Even coming home alone, however, will be better than staying here any longer, and it will be very good to be in Williamsport again, and I hope I may be able to remain there for the rest of my life. I always wanted to live in Williamsport, you know.

This seems like a very incomplete sort of letter, under the circumstances, but there is so much that I haven't space or time to write about now, and I can't seem to think of what to select. In less than two weeks, I should be talking to you, and can tell you all about it then.

My very best wishes to you and everybody in Williamsport. I'm writing Ted Ranck also.

Beam[3]

It's obvious that this was not an easy letter to write, and it's hard to believe that even Beam really expected Betty to join him back in the States— in Williamsport! He was asking her to give up her job, leave her friends in New York and Paris to live in the Bible Belt — not likely. I think Beam knew he was just whistling in the dark.

On the other hand, Betty was asking the impossible from Beam, as well. She was demanding that he live in a foreign country, after a World War that had left it impoverished (compared to the United States), where Piper did not know a soul, nor spoke the language. From the beginning, he was not happy in Paris and felt like a second wheel to Betty, who had her work and job-related friends. Plus, Betty spoke French fluently and knew her way around, having already lived there for four years. At this point, Beam had made all the sacrifices: he'd given up his country, his friends, his hobbies all for love.

Knerr writes: "Piper took the *Ile de France* out of Le Havre on September 10th, 1957 and enjoyed a relatively easy voyage across the Atlantic to New York, arriving in New York on the 26th. On the way over he worked on 'Murder Frozen Over' and got Chapter Two finished. Once docked he checked into the Plymouth Hotel and called Ken White who told him that Horace Gold had bought 'Graveyard of Dreams' for $210.00 — the author's share being $189.00. The next day he called Freida Coleman about moving to Pennsylvania.... On the 30th, he arranged to have his gear shipped to Williamsport, then stopped at Michael's Pub on 48th Street where he was surprised: 'In Michael's, saw Ernest Hemingway alive and at large.'"[4]

Don Coleman writes: "With a happy voyage to Europe aboard the *Queen Mary* and after enjoying a life of leisure in Paris, it soon ended with an unhappy return to New York aboard the celebrated liner *Ile de France*. Upon debarking the vessel, Beam's only words regarding his lady were: 'It was a matter of either my leaving Paris and the beautiful *Champs Elysees*, or, winding up killing each other. In spite of the temptation, I chose the former alternative!'"[5] This is not Beam's true feelings, but more Piper armor to keep the pain and humiliation at bay.

It's no surprise that he returned to the States. However, Beam not only lost Betty when he fled France, but his dog, too. Don Coleman writes: "He loved and idolized his dachshund Vall, and leaving the dog was a trying experience — especially for a tough guy like Beam who was so hypnotized with adoration.... Somewhere, some place, is a small black and white photo of Vall tugging at a slipper intact aboard the author's foot, while he sat back in a recliner perusing a manuscript. Why in such a short time, had this photo been so manhandled? Obviously, Beam showed off this jewel to everyone — knowing the critter probably considered itself *this* man's only friend abroad."[6]

Knerr continues:

> The next day he called Freida Coleman about moving to Pennsylvania and bought a red-leather sewing bag for Betty before going back to the hotel to write. The following evening, October 1st, he caught a plane to Williamsport and was met by Don Coleman, Freida's son. He spent the night at the Coleman residence and the next day rented an apartment at 330 East Third Street. The rent wasn't much [$40.00 jfc], but neither was the apartment and it was two floors up. The one hand feature of it was that it was within walking distance of the downtown section, the markets, the bookstores and the James V. Brown library. It suited Beam....
>
> During this period of "settling in," and later on, the two best friends Beam had were Freida and Don Coleman. They put him up at their house, fed him and took him around in their car so he could gather the essentials necessary in making his apartment a home. "— am making a shameful burden of myself, I'm afraid." Typical Piper comment, but I am sure that Freida and Don would have never thought it, any more than the rest of his friends would. He had a great many more friends than he realized.[7]

A few days later the Soviets shot up the equivalent of the first atomic bomb: they put an orbiter in space, accomplished the impossible and the Space Race was on. Like most American science-fiction writers of the time, Piper was chagrined that it wasn't an American craft orbiting the Earth, and at the same time was in awe of this new miracle of science:

> The Russians launched the first artificial satellite from the Baikonur cosmodrome in Kazakhstan which demonstrated the technological superiority of Communism (actually more of a propaganda pain for the US). They equipped the Sputnik with transmitters to broadcast on frequencies at 20 and 40 MHz so everyone will know it's up there.
>
> The United States was shocked. Senator Lyndon Johnson said the Russians have jumped way ahead

of us in the conquest of space. "Soon, they will be dropping bombs on us from space like kids dropping rocks onto cars from freeway overpasses!" [from a movie that dramatized the emotional impact of that day]. Everyone in the United States were constantly reminded that the Russians were well on the way in conquering space and newspaper headlines, "REDS ORBIT ARTIFICIAL MOON" and "SOVIET SATELLITE CIRCLES GLOBE EVERY 90 MINUTES."[8]

As Don Coleman remembers:

In early October 1957, Beam was enjoying a "Katinka" cocktail at Freida Coleman's den bar when a news bulletin broke over TV, announcing the launching of the Russian satellite *Sputnik* that was gloriously circling the earth. It was a severe blow to US technology, learning that the Soviets had fired off an orbiting satellite that would hurl about the globe indefinitely.

"DAMN! Beam growled. "If only Odin had given me a clue. And Thor himself must have surely known!"

Shaking his head in anger, he continued, "They got the jump on us. And the DAMN thing is no bigger around than a boxcar wheel; and only a mere 25 pounds heavier than yours truly!"

He turned to the bar, pulled the ever-existent pad of paper from his breast pocket, and taking his multi-color pen to hand, began to draw "Sputnik." Beam utilized the four colors of ink on the small sheet of paper, telling us all the details of how it worked, how it was built and how it was launched. He was so excited because this was something he excelled in! He would sketch what he termed as a "simple spherical space-oriented vehicular orbiter."

Diane Coleman Simpson, who was in Beam's presence this evening and also occupied the other half of Freida's duplex, continues: "Amazing thing happened the next day; the newspaper had a full account of it, including a staff drawing. It was astoundingly similar to the picture Beam had drawn the night before!"

Far from crude, the likeness by Piper was undeniable in fact, and as sound as his own logic in his conception of space.... In less than two months, it burnt up returning to earth, but another had been launched (with dog) just thirty days after the first launching. This irritated Beam further, not only because the United States of America had yet to get a satellite successfully of the pad — but it "interfered" with his own fictional "space program."[9]

Piper had good reason to be irritated, other than sheer unapologetic American patriotism. This orbiter had just invalidated his own near-time Future History, in which he had invested a good deal of work and a number of recent stories. Never again would he write any story closer in time to the present age than several hundred years.

In a 1964 letter to Peter Weston, a British fan — in answer to a question asked for his fanzine — Piper wrote a short piece titled "The Future History of H. Beam Piper," which includes the following addendum: "Beyond this, with the exception of one story, 'The Keeper,' (*Venture*) about 30,000 years in the future when the Fifth Empire was at the height of its power, and Terra was in the middle of another glacial age, I have not done. Nothing else, with the possible exception of a novelette called 'The Edge of the Knife,' *Amazing*, May 1957, belongs to the History of the Future. This was a story, time 1973 C.E. (Christian Era), about a history professor who got his past and future confused, and had a lot of trouble as a result. It was written and published shortly before Sputnik I invalidated a lot of my near-future stuff, and made me swear off doing anything within a couple of centuries of now."[10]

Don Coleman adds: "I had approached Beam sometime before this break-through, inquiring, 'How in the hell are you ever so far ahead in writing such goings-on in space when, in reality, they are becoming fact every day?'

"'Oh HELL,' he responded quite loudly, waving an arm about. 'I just have to maintain a distance of a few centuries or so, which sometimes, I find difficult to uphold.'"[11]

Piper was true to his word: Most of his pre–*Sputnik* stories take place in the "indefinite future," or near future, while after *Sputnik*, almost all of his stories take place several hundred, to several thousand, years in the future.

Mike Knerr concludes, "In many ways, Beam was an old softie — a romantic — and it crops up in his writing. He was tough and hard, yet it was possible to catch him off-guard. Once, when I had had enough rum poured down my gullet to acquire a certain amount of bravery, I asked him if he thought he and Betty would ever get back together again. He squinted at his ring for a moment and said, with emotion: 'I hope so.' Then he recovered, sidestepped verbally and began a discourse on the battle of Crécy, or the collapse of Swiss pikemen, or some such thing."[12]

PART III

Off to Billtown

CHAPTER 24

Leaving Altoona

No, no ... HELL no! Great Thor, son of Odin, would not approve of such femininity! Drink and THRUST the glass to the wall with spirit![1]

—H. Beam Piper

In his September 9, 1957 letter to Freida, Piper wrote: "I always wanted to live in Williamsport, you know."[2] He had always loved the beauty of the West Branch Valley and had many good memories of his time spent with the Colemans. His old hunting buddy, Ted Ranck, lived there with his wife. In addition, it contained a first-class library, James V. Brown Library, and a good library was a necessity for Piper. He was through with Altoona; on his last visit he had been repulsed by how small and shabby his hometown had become.

After the split with John J. McGuire, his "forced" retirement from the Pennsy, his mother's death and impending divorce from Betty, there were no longer any ties—other than personal memories and a few old friends—to keep him in Altoona. Thus, it was no surprise that Beam decided to move to Williamsport in 1957 and attempt a new beginning.

As Don Coleman tells it, it was a traumatic experience in many ways:

I refer to this extraordinary episode as an exodus.... Other than himself, the remaining Altoona-based antique firearms and paraphernalia were the top concern.

The momentous move began on a day in the fall of 1957 when Freida Coleman and son Budd departed for Williamsport for Altoona in her year-old Chevrolet.... Obeying the implicit instructions laid out by Beam, Fritz and Budd arrived at the Piper establishment well prior to noon.

Beam always greeted guests—in this case *family*—with utmost subtlety.... However, upon entering the apartment—just after all salutations had been rendered—a *battle* was about to begin. His initial move was to pop the cork of a domestic champagne and pour it into several wine vessels lined up on the buffet. There was an array of glasses of various shapes and forms—acting as troops about to enter combat—awaiting the upcoming onslaught. Fritz, anticipating a long and wearisome two hour drive back to Williamsport, acknowledged Beam's offering of the grape with a hesitant nod ... indicating a mere sip would suffice.

"No, no ... HELL no!" Beam resounded. "Great Thor, son of Odin, would not approve of such femininity! Drink and THRUST the glass to the wall with spirit!"

Beam, in all his glory, after pouring a soft drink for Budd, swallowed the contents of his own drink very quickly and shot the glass to the opposite wall before the two visitors had barely raised their beverages to their lips!

SLAM! CRASH!

The expression of H. Beam Piper at that precise moment was a stare of maniacal concentration.... He insisted the two *drink up* and pitch to the Wall!

BANG!

He then proceeded to pour champagne into other awaiting glasses, whether they be goblet or wine glass, liqueur or sherbet glass, or highball or parfait glass. It really made no difference. All were doomed to destruction. Each bottle filled with champagne, wine, vodka, rye, gin and rum flowed into the surrounding glassware.

Freida cut off very quickly due to the responsibility of getting the black and white coach over a hundred miles of possibly dark terrain.... In the meantime, the author drank his liquid hardware while the young one swallowed his cola — then each flung his drinking vessel to the wall.

If perchance a glass did not shatter, which was unmistakably rare, Beam would curse the *gods* for not having the power to do so! He would then retrieve the offending vessel and hurl again without a refill. This continued until Freida made a move to gather the various items meant for this move. Eventually, the glassware was exhausted and the empty liquor bottles were appropriately hurled dispassionately against the defending wall. Finally, the chinaware was removed from the cupboards and welcomed to the *arena*!

Budd Coleman recently reminisced, "Beam's behavior the day of the move was unique — you might say 'flip.' Besides dishes being hurled against walls, I remember them also flying out the window to land somewhere on the lawn below in a pile of broken rubble. It was a wild scene — the comical and the bizarre combined. Looking back on it all, I don't think an apartment in Altoona, Pennsylvania was Beam's idea of how to live. I think there were a lot of personal problems at that point that were the real meat of the story."

Beam chose Williamsport as his new and final residence — something he had considered and concluded many years before. He had implied this town was to be his eventual home throughout his early letters, and later used it as a backdrop for this first published work, "Time and Time Again." He had developed more friends in this part of the Commonwealth than in his own birthplace. His mother and father were gone from this earth, and he hardly spoke of other kin. Apparently, a cousin or two existed but were never revealed in conversation. Surely he knew that the act of removing himself from his Altoona habitat would bring upon him the closeness and camaraderie of his Williamsport family of friends. And vacating Altoona, regardless of any nostalgia that naturally enveloped his mind, was really not a hard thing to do.

Budd Coleman, a veteran member of the Marine Corps and familiar with combatant situations, resumed his recollections of the Piper exodus: "the place was a mess. I've never seen anything like it since; except in the streets of some village in Viet Nam, or at the town dump. A couple pictures of the scene would be all one needed. It was dramatic enough that I'll probably never forget the mess or atmosphere that surrounded — or rather prevailed — throughout the apartment. It was like the Viet Cong had mortared the place; it was pure havoc.

"I think, maybe incorrectly, that Beam had a gentle, non-violent nature about him that would prevent him from ever harming anything alive. But he certainly could show violence to dishes and himself. He enjoyed himself throughout the attack. I dare say he was having fun.

"This was probably the most fun Beam had had in a long time. I guess the landlord wasn't around since I don't remember any police arriving. I don't remember anyone else around at all to complain or inquire what was going on. I found the whole scene entertaining. I'm sure we were laughing, while being surprised at his outlandish behavior. But really, it was more sad than funny because of the reasons behind it. It would take a Freud to figure it all out."

Shortly before leaving this scene of total destruction, Beam pursued one last course of action. As lean as he was in stature, the weight and bulkiness of the kitchen stove was of little concern to his strength. With a minimum of concentration, he grabbed ... and pulled ... and turned over the stove ... with such force, that unseen dust — possibly hiding from view for a *millennium*— immediately mushroomed into a fog about the room. His final blow had been served! The place was totally trashed! And, as a result of all this, there was no claim as to it being a national disaster and there had been no call for the intervention of the National Guard.

And finally at last ... Beam began to mellow.

The time had come to get down to serious moving business. The circus was over. Two hours had passed with only a single item being prepared for shipment — the typewriter. With the initial temblors abated and Beam transformed into meekness, Fritz could go about the room collecting what she surmised to be collectable — without having to concentrate on un-called-for levity cropping up behind her.

Beam sat on the arm of a chair, holding between his hands a one-time jelly jar that now contained a pony of dark rum; all vessels suitable for libation of any sort having already been destroyed! He recited another one of his oracles that thirteen-year-old Budd found incomprehensible ... but amusing. After a while, the lad joined the liberated Mr. Piper in assisting Fritz with the move. However, Beam's earlier energy was now replaced with apathy.

Very few possessions were loaded for transport: the remaining antique firearms and cleaning oil, handguns and boxes of assorted caliber cartridges, manuscripts and published works, a library of crated reference material and a few dining utensils. The guns occupied prime space while all other articles were loaded "according to priority"—squeezing within any visible airspace throughout the car.

Beam's own clothing he considered secondary and, only after items essential for the sustenance of life itself—including remnants of un-drunk whiskey that were safely stowed aboard, would he finally allow for such sundries such as shirts, ties, trousers, hose and underwear. A dilapidated grip and small luggage pieces found their way aboard. Some small articles of furniture were positioned in the trunk with blankets and bedware cushioning the cargo. In conclusion, two elegant Piper heirlooms emerged as the remaining members of the *exodus*. A cut-glass relish tray and floral-embossed serving dish were fortunate enough to elude the *guillotine* ... making their way to freedom.

Once the dust had settled about the battlefield, there remained but one framed picture hanging from the abused wall. This makeup of this item was imperceptible to the naked eye until some weeks later, when one of the fair Coleman ladies rid it of a good thirty years of coal dust. In the span of time Beam lived within Altoona, pictures such as this traveled along without care ... neither *bathed* nor *groomed!* This one turned into a colorful scene of the famous Horseshoe Curve, depicting a famed massive steam locomotive tugging a passenger train of the renowned Pennsylvania Railroad.

Piper, knowing the true interpretation of good-bye—God be with ye—would never wish these words upon this chaotic dwelling, even in spite of his agnostic views toward the existence of an Almighty. He departed the building with barely a sign of intemperance. His eyes shot straight ahead. There was no time to turn around and gaze upon what had transpired. With his beloved beret atop his head and his pipe seated securely between his teeth, he strutted directly (almost) to the vehicle—carrying his typewriter case in one hand while swirling his cane about with the other.

H. Beam Piper became a resident, and no longer would he ever be a visitor to Williamsport. He moved what little he chose to rescue from the Altoona destruction scene into a third-floor apartment on E. Third Street. It was necessary to purchase some items immediately while in the meantime his sleeping bag and other sundry items would suffice....

Then came the day he summoned me for a ride out to Loyalsock [Creek] to a used-furniture establishment where he would thus barter for his office equipment, consisting primarily of desk, chair and file cabinet. Once again, weighing his *priorities*, the matter of a bed to sleep upon would be made available at a later time.

He was quick and not extravagant in choice. The immense wooden desk had registered some miles, but it displayed a smooth and expansive top; the caster chair showed wear but these items were manufactured for use and that's exactly what its predecessor had given it; and with the exception of a nick or two from previous moves-around, the four-drawer wooden file cabinet would serve its purpose well (the second drawer ... would immediately become the Piper liquor storehouse).

The ensemble was chosen in a matter of minutes, and Beam paid but a minimal two hundred dollars for the entire lot, including a "fluffy" easy chair with monstrous arms to sit back and puff on his pipe, and ponder his thoughts. His local bank account was very young, for there were but only a few entries made within his checkbook.

Next was the question of delivery. Fritz's black and white Bel Aire had been utilized as a cargo carrier from Altoona to "Billtown," but the delivery of the furniture bought this day would be left in the hands of a friend with a pickup. Corralling another buddy who joined us at the white building on E. Third Street, we three (less Beam, of course!) began toting the first piece of equipment; the humongous ... wooden desk. One must visualize an enclosed stairway in a structure dating circa 1900, having papered walls that surely could not have been more than three feet apart, and steps that rose almost to the angle of a typical stepladder. The stairs were so narrow that it was impossible for anyone to squeeze in on either side but to handle the monstrosity at the ends. Due to the *gold bar* weight, two of us maintained position at the aft end while the smallest individual of the three guided the load upward and forward.

In the meantime, H. Beam Piper directed the operation with cane in hand.

Trudging and sweating up three flights of stairs in near darkness was truly an ordeal. With the continuous arid wit contributed by Beam as we lugged, the load did not become any lighter; but finally, after considerable grunting and the expulsion of an occasional obscenity, we reached the objective — the area Mr. Piper would thus refer to hereafter as *the writing room*. With the exception of the immense "fluffy chair," which required considerable "direction" up the stairs, the remaining items gave us no problems. After the sweat had been removed, Beam set forth with a rare smile, offering us the gold at the end of the rainbow — alcoholic amendments.

Once Piper was established, it was a matter of sitting down and recouping what continuity he may have lost during the transition. The file cabinet, in reiteration, not only contained the absolute essential of this man's livelihood — various writing supplies pertinent to his vocation, loose manuscripts, penciled thoughts and notes, a drawer dedicated to the NRA housing boxes of ammunition for most all caliber small arms — but not forgetting space for his favorite booze — Myers's dark rum.

Whenever I was present in the "writing room," Beam would grab the rum bottle standing on his desk (it already having been accosted), pour me out a favorable unmeasured amount over ice, followed by a touch or two of 7-Up. He then would return to the rum and add to his own already sweating tall glass seated next to his typewriter. The ice bucket, situated at the northwest corner of the desk, also displayed a ring....

The rum highball was Beam's best writing drink because in as many occasions I appeared within this third-floor retreat, I never spotted anything other than this island *amour* on his desk while typing. However, other whiskeys and dinner wines occupied the special file drawer, second up from the bottom! On Sunday when he would cook up an unprecedented pork roast, we would share a bottle of Tokay or Sauterne with the meal. I have eaten more than a few meals prepared by the unique Mr. Piper, who obviously did well within the confined kitchen, having been a bachelor for so many years.

Normally on Sundays, Freida would, after attending church services, stop by the apartment and bring Beam to the house for dinner. This became a frequent practice, especially [after] she had sold the home at the top of Williamsport; it was now a straight shot out E. Third Street to her new residence on Russell Avenue ... only a matter of minutes.

The author was well-situated in this particular locale. He was only three blocks from the center of town. The James V. Brown library was just over a block and up the street and the City Hotel was but a few blocks further. Accommodating the cleansing of the perpetual white shirts worn by Piper, Gummo Laundry was only a short stroll out E. Third Street. Probably the furthest place to which he would frequent was the Lycoming County Historical Society and Museum on the west side of town, but he was a true hiker of earlier times — so distance never became an issue. Even the state liquor store was well within his radial reach and became a definite *must* on his periodic wanderings. So with cane in hand and beret atop his head, he would set out for any number of destinations.

The cane; the inseparable cane. Piper possessed several walking sticks and always took along a staff when walking about town. Just as his pipe was a staple, so were his canes. Reminding myself of a conversation *way back when* — possibly during *his* Roman period — he related the story of a .22 caliber slug passing through the fleshy part of his calf while cleaning (?) an "unloaded" target pistol. However, he had never shown a sign of limping in the thirty-plus years of our friendship. Nevertheless, what possibly began as a necessity, the use of a cane, became something of an addiction to him....

A good percentage of Piper's thoughts were extracted and placed into audible sounds while strolling. His walks through the streets of Williamsport was where he did his creative thinking, working out story ideas. The only difference between the man wearing the beret and anyone else was the fact that he did his thinking out loud, with his head generally facing the pavement. He gave no thought to physical surroundings, or what others may have wondered in seeing him in this state of mind. In fact, there were times when he would walk himself into vehicular traffic without realizing it until a honking horn would break through his daze.

I would guess that many onlookers and passers-by about the streets had him diagnosed as *out* of his mind, but those folks obviously did not know H. Beam Piper. Those that did know him and greeted him vivaciously on the street, always received a spontaneous and cheerful "HELLO" and a wave of the cane.[3]

And, thus it was that Piper cut himself off from his former home of fifty-three years, his life with Betty and his own past.

CHAPTER 25

Back to Work

I just don't want to do things, any more; all I want to do is write.[1]

— H. Beam Piper

It took Piper a few weeks to get his new apartment in shape. Mike Knerr writes:

A good part of the next month was spent shopping in the various stores for such things as wastebaskets, broom and dustpan, along with the dozens of little things necessary to setting up housekeeping. Through all of this Beam did manage to get a few more pages done on the book: "Finished — very unsatisfactorily Chapter V late P.M. and early morning."

Sunday, October 6th, was Don Coleman's birthday and Beam attended the party. "...an event which makes me feel *tres ancien*. Big celebration, with his favorite dish, leg of lamb, which I loathe for dinner."

The next few days were a bit on the hectic side as Beam tried to get his gas stove hooked up, the phone installed and generally suffered at the hands of workmen who didn't show, or came at awkward times. He arranged to travel to Harrisburg, to his cousin Charles' house to pick up his pistols and wrote: "To bed again, about 0100, mentally fagged out. Hope my subconscious works out something on this damn story."

Then, on a more serious note, after an attack of what he called "the blue devils," he added: "When I was in Paris, I was miserable because I didn't have a home. Now I have a home, and I am miserable because I don't have Betty and Vall."

The next day a letter arrived from France. "Letter from Betty, relayed by Ken White. Vall has been very sick, but is getting better, we hope. I wish I could be with her — or, better still, she and Vall with me. Symptoms sound like some sort of poisoning or infection."

Vall died of whatever problems he had developed. Beam wrote on April 15, 1963: "As I had feared, Vall is dead. He died soon after I left." For some reason Betty never mentioned it, until the divorce was in progress — perhaps thinking that there was no point in making Beam feel bad. The diary doesn't mention anything about why.[2]

Knerr notes: "'Murder Frozen Over' was progressing with the usual Piper blocks and frustrations. He would work all day on it and end up throwing everything away except a couple of pages. The hell of it was that after all that work, he never could sell the novel. His entries are typical: 'Spent evening working on story; like the dinner, not one of my better days. Manufacturing wastepaper at a great rate, ended with two satisfactory pages.'"[3]

Beam would have loved word processors — the ease of rewriting would have saved him endless hours of re-typing the same pages over and over again. On November 5, a letter from Ken White, "enclosing letter from J-n McG-e [John McGuire], re *Lone Star Planet*, which Ace wants for another double-back pocket book." It was eventually released with the title *A Planet for Texans*.[4]

Once again a publisher arbitrarily re-titled one of Piper's books; of course, during this seminal period of science fiction writing, editors were gods — or had godly powers. Writers didn't see them the same way, as Knerr notes:

All the years of rejection and humiliation in trying to sell his stories, left Beam bitter about the publishing business. Although he had many friends in editorial positions, he used to laugh at them as well — on at least one occasion referring to them as the "lowest form of animal life in the universe." He always pointed out that there were not enough desks in the editorial world and "when the music stops, everyone grabs a desk. It's how," he would add, "New York rearranges their editors."[5]

On one of his walks, he found a brass sash weight shaped like a teardrop. He bored it out to .177 caliber and mounted it like a miniature naval gun, and called it the "eensy brass cannon." Its purpose was to celebrate the selling of stories. He would dump a few grains of black-powder down the barrel, followed by a copper BB and lastly ramming a wad of lint down on top of everything. It was touched off with a cigarette and, while it didn't make a lot of noise, it usually drove the BB into the plaster of the far wall. The wallpaper of his apartment was literally pock marked with BB holes.[6]

Piper continued to correspond with Betty, and she would regularly report on Verkan Vall's condition. "On October 24th, Beam wrote asking her to come over during the following month, or for Christmas. His morale seems to have been sagging considerably and was added to by Betty's reply: 'Coming over for Christmas is "unthinkable."'"[7]

Piper continued work through December 1957 on "Murder Frozen Over," which was becoming, in his words, "A horrible thing — just saw how story can be much improved by postponing one of the events in it; will have to re-plan, and scrap the last twenty-five pages, painfully rewritten this week."[8] It's hard to fathom what Beam was thinking during this period. *Murder in the Gunroom* had done tolerably well for Knopf, but not enough that they bought the sequel, "Murder in the Conference Room." Now, here Piper was, five years later working on another Jeff Rand mystery. Who did he think would publish it? As Mike Knerr puts it: "In writing mysteries he was creating errors of judgment that eventually would come home to roost."[9]

Drawing room mysteries were passé, and a new mystery reading public had emerged since the War. This new public, weaned on the carnage and destruction of World War II and Korea, wanted hardboiled detectives and mean streets. Piper's mysteries hearkened back to a kinder, gentler period of Arthur Conan Doyle, Agatha Christie, Dorothy Sayers and John Dickson Carr.

As Mike Knerr sums up: "Beam's mystery novels were as meticulously planned as anything he had ever written, but the publishers and the public were not much interested in them. Perhaps there was too much of the 'Victorian' in them at a time when readers wanted Mickey Spillane, Richard Prather or Fredrick Brown.

"On the other hand, Beam's science fiction stories were always well accepted and he seldom finished out 'of the money' in the *Astounding/Analog* bonuses.... 'He Walked Around the Horses' was anthologized around the world, including a British school reader. *Murder in the Gunroom*, by comparison, fizzled out to the point where ... even Beam didn't have a copy of it, except in carbon."[10]

He went hunting with Ted Ranck, but he had the flu and that took a lot of the fun out of the hunt. "The camp got a buck late in the afternoon of the first and on Tuesday Leo Stroble got a second one. Beam didn't even get any shoot in. 'Flu all gone, but tired — this is just too much for me.'" Piper had planned on going back to town with Ted Ranck, who learned that he was to be a pallbearer for a funeral, but on Friday Beam got lost in the woods and arrived in camp too late to catch a ride.

"That was the end of the hunting expedition in the wilds of Tioga County as well as the last time Beam went afield. They divided the meat on Saturday and Piper went home in Ted's car. Back at the apartment, he shared his meat with the Colemans and took some down to his neighbors on the lower floor — adding that he met their toy terrier. As an afterthought, he wrote: 'They also have a child, not too poisonous a specimen.'"[11]

By the end of the year, Piper was struggling to get the new mystery novel under control. "I hope I am not being optimistic in saying that I think I finally have the story planned the way I want it, but believe I have." The new *Galaxy* magazine hit the stands just before Christmas and he picked up a copy since it had "Graveyard of Dreams" in it. "Was afraid wordage cut would ruin it; it didn't — story reads very well."[12]

Beam's loneliness for Betty and Vall seemed to grow rather than diminish, and his work suffered. Piper began the year with this New Year's resolution: "Never to start a story in manuscript again until I have it *completely* planned."[13] This resolution didn't last through April. "I've done it again; started first drafting a story without proper planning."[14]

Knerr writes: "Still, he doggedly plugged away at 'Murder Frozen Over,' went for walks and fired his pistols at the YMCA range. During one of these walks, on January 21, he slipped on an icy sidewalk and hurt his back. 'Have a devilish pain in my side,' he wrote on the 25th. 'Don't know if I hurt something when I fell on ice Tuesday or not.' Whether or not the fall on the ice was the cause, the back problems returned again in November, concerning him enough to write: 'This is really something serious.'"[15]

This slip-and-fall accident on the sidewalks of Williamsport and the resulting back injury would plague Piper throughout his remaining years. Happening at a time when he could financially afford treatment, he was too stubborn to seek out medical attention. For the rest of his life, he would pay for this neglect with chronic back pain which would rob him of his night-time working hours and peace of mind.

Knerr writes:

While the back pains came and went away, Beam finished the first draft of "Murder Frozen Over" on January 27th, 1958. By now, since the novel had been started in France, he had probably gone through several reams of typing paper in his efforts to get it right. The following day, while he girded himself for the final draft battle, he doodled on a science-fiction short story. "This is going to be an idea John Campbell gave me — the practical Romans and the philosophic Greeks, in terms of a Galactic civilization. Beginning to get some ideas."

He was a little worn out from banging away on the "revised revised first draft" and not quite ready to launch into the final. "...doodling at nothing much, and just feeling like a spent bullet. Will take it easy for a few days, and then get cracking on final draft." While he rested up, Ken White wrote him and informed him that "Ace is publishing *Lone Star Planet* in July or August."

Don Coleman invited him to dinner on February 2nd, "a magnificent feast in honor of Dianne's 22nd birthday." While there, he learned that the Army had launched their own satellite on January 31st, and commented: "Don much chagrinned that the Army succeeded where the Navy failed." Don, as might be guessed, was a Navy man, presently in the reserves.

When Beam began the final draft, a couple of days later, he immediately ran into problems. "After lunch, started on the final, or white-paper draft. A hell of a job, spent hours on the first paragraph of the first page. Style is something that can't be planned, it has to be revised." Quite possibly Ernest Hemingway would agree with him, but not all writers. One can become so obsessed with revision, as Jack Woodford once pointed out, that one couldn't write a note to the milkman without revising it several times.

He made it to page 131 by February 20th, maintaining an average of ten pages a day, but typically ran into problems. "Whole thing sour — typed one page and saw I'd have to re-plan everything. To work on that after dinner, and by 2000 reached decision to scrap the whole thing and rewrite from the beginning: 'This is a dreadful thing and will set me back at least a month, but may make the difference between sale and no sale.'"

It didn't make a difference in the long run, but writers often cannot tell that. The end result was that "Murder Frozen Over" wasn't mailed out until April 7th. On February 28th, he did receive the first check from Ace Books for *Lone Star Planet*, and that helped bolster his sagging finances.[16]

On March 18, Piper wrote: "Did a little doodling on a science fiction idea, to be worked on when I finish 'Murder Frozen Over.'"[17] Mike Knerr writes:

Such was the birth of *Little Fuzzy*, a book destined to be another novel Beam would agonize over until it had gone through the hands of more than a dozen publishers. When it finally found a home with Avon Books, that company had already rejected it three times.

In addition to the gun exhibits and his writing, Beam read constantly, and his opinions on writers were as definite as his opinions on writing. And, for all of his reading, the factors that produce a national bestseller escaped him. In reading Ayn Rand's *Atlas Shrugged*, he wrote: " — heartbreaking to see a good story idea like that mangled to death." Again while reading the same book in early April [1958]: "I certainly wish I'd written that story — it would have been about 75 percent shorter." He couldn't *see* the whole picture but, at times, one would have thought he had tunnel vision. Once, when I mentioned that I liked Robert Heinlein's work, Beam exploded — slammed his tobacco pouch on the desk. "Heinlein wastes plots," he roared, although later he admitted that he too liked the man's writing.

The *Little Fuzzy* idea, still in the womb and kicking for birth, seemed to go into false labor early in April when Beam picked up a copy of John Dewey's *Reconstruction in Philosophy* "and came across an idea ('Ministry of Disturbance') that looks like something useable. Hope I can get a story out of it."

"Ministry of Disturbance," like any other Piper's creation, was not slated to be laid out on paper without a hitch. "I have done the same goddamned thing I always do," he wrote on April 26th, "gotten antsy to start the story before I had it planned. I wonder if I'll ever plan a story properly before I start it." The next day, he confided to his diary that "whole thing is a bloody mess. I'm doing everything wrong the way I always do it." By the last of the month he had decided, "the whole thing needs drastic revision — maybe I'll have a chance to plan this story as it should be planned." He was concerned as well about the title, toying with the idea of calling it "Last Challenge."

By the first week in May, Beam was wallowing in literary confusion, totally sure of what he *wanted* to write, and just as totally unsure of *how* to do it. He solved the problem by shopping for tobacco and rum, and having "peanut parties" for the squirrels in Brandon Park. He had, by now, switched from Dunhill tobacco to Brindley's Mixture. He decided to "change means of perception" on the story and, as usual, he tore it all up to begin again.

Freida and Don Coleman came to his rescue, although they probably didn't know it, and took him for a drive to Cogan Valley (several miles north of Williamsport) which gave him a new perspective on the story — albeit: "Not saying anything rash."[18]

Beam, as usual, was having problems getting his latest story down on paper. There are two basic kinds of writers: unconscious writers, who write by the seat of their pants, and conscious writers who plot everything possible before putting a single word down. Of course, many writers are somewhere in the middle, like Piper: "There seems to be a limit to how closely I can plan a story; I can't allow for what my imagination adds to it while working on it."[19] By June 3, Beam was correcting the final draft of "Ministry of Disturbance," but flew to New York for a Mystery Writers of America meeting and didn't mail it to Ken until the 7th. He noted sourly that *Cosmopolitan* had bounced "Murder Frozen Over" and started "work on preliminary planning for a bastard science fiction short (parallel time)."[20]

After attending a lecture on early Pennsylvania canals, Beam wrote that he "may work up a historical novel out of the canal pirates." Instead he finished the first-first draft of the short story and added that he was planning to call it "Outsider," which eventually was changed to "The Other Road."[21]

"Outsider" fell apart on June 27 when Piper "decided I was going at it the wrong way — surprise ending to be reinforced by putting story on another time line, the stranger to come from our world." He completed the short story on July 3 and, after re-titling it "The Other Road," shipped it off to his agent. While up town he got his pistol permit renewed and noted that there was a "remarkable and laudable absence of chicken-shit about that."[22]

Back at the typewriter, Piper was "thinking of doing a short on the theme of Jack the Ripper killed by an intended victim." The story got "sick and died" before it was more than an idea and Beam began to work on the "negamatter meteor" story which eventually developed into "The Answer."

"Ministry of Disturbance" sold right away to John W. Campbell. The check for "Ministry of Disturbance" arrived on July 8 of 1958 to give his bank balance a transfusion, but the present story was going badly and his morale was low. He finally finished the first draft, "rough as hell," of "The Answer" and promptly put it aside to toy with ideas on the Jack the Ripper story and *Little Fuzzy*.[23] By the middle of July he had decided that the Jack the Ripper story was hopeless and started the final draft of "The Answer," which he mailed on the 24th. He began work on *Little Fuzzy* with a first draft start on August 1.

Knerr writes: "By August 11th, Piper was in another literary jam. 'The Little Fuzzy story seems to have gotten very sick; will put it to bed and let it have a nice long rest and maybe it'll get well again.' Unable to forget mysteries, he started plotting a *new* Jeff Rand story hoping by the time he had worked out the details *Little Fuzzy* may be up and about again.'"[24] If Piper was anything, he was persistent. He never gave up on his orphaned Jeff Rand series and continued to plot and write new ones, even in the face of constant rejection.

He missed Betty and Vall. And, despite the fact that he was actually producing salable copy — instead of "wastepaper" as he did through most of 1954 and '55 — he was angry and frustrated. "I wish it didn't take me so God damned long to get the right slant on a story!"[25] His frustration with writing was beginning to follow a pattern. Added to all this he had periods of not feeling well, yet somehow he managed to get *Little Fuzzy* up to page 51 by August 17. "Soon it will be a year since I left Betty and Vall," he wrote on August 19, 1958, and promptly fell into a depression. "This was about the lowest my morale has been so far, since I came here."[26]

Knerr writes: "In an attempt to beat his depression, he took a train trip to Baltimore and stayed in 'a fleabag' near the train station. The trip wasn't much of a success and he returned to Williamsport to get back at the typewriter. He got very little done on the story and by the first week in September his morale was still drooping even lower."[27]

In typical Piper fashion, he scrapped most of it and started over. "I seem to be working like hell and getting nowhere, and am now wondering if I'm not working on a job that won't amount to anything if I ever get it done."[28] By the end of August he was still sweating out the story line and not doing well at it.

Piper decided that *Little Fuzzy* wasn't going anywhere, and in the first week of October he took a trip to New York for a Mystery Writers of America meeting and a talk with Ken White. He usually flew to New York from Williamsport, as he was no longer getting free passes on the Pennsy. These trips to visit Ken and to meet with other writers recharged him, and he had recovered enough of his sense of humor by the 9th to write beneath his diary entry, "Pope died," and on the next day's page: "Great consternation in Heaven; Pope long overdue and still unreported."[29]

Back in his Williamsport apartment, the story wasn't going any better. "Can't seem to get anything accomplished; just running around in circles."[30] Piper's health was deteriorating, whether from his back injury or from his older knee injury. He was having pains in his legs, as well as a stomachache. To add to the general run of problems Ken wrote and told him that both "The Answer" and "The Other Road" had been rejected.

Knerr writes: "On October 21st, he learned that his New York, and his local bank accounts together were below $1,000.00 so he cancelled plans to go to a Hydra Club meeting in the city. Toward the end of the month, as a change of pace, Beam helped John Hunsinger, a teacher at Lycoming College, put a cannon into shape to be fired at football games. He went along to several games and helped with the firing, but his morale didn't get much of a boost. On the 29th, he 'read some old Betty-letters from a year ago — not good for morale.' His copy of *Astounding Science Fiction* arrived on November 7th, with 'Ministry of Disturbance' in it and he found that it 'Looks good in print.'"[31]

Piper's back had started acting up again, and he told Ted Ranck that he wasn't going deer hunting that year, commenting, "It's getting to where I can't take it anymore." He stopped drinking, but that didn't help his back, and by the end of the month it was still bothering him. As suddenly as it began, the pain ceased early in December and he went to a meeting of the Mystery Writers of America in New York. He also learned that "Murder Frozen Over" was bounced by the Crime Club, and that didn't make him too happy.

Mike Knerr writes: "He went back to work, mostly manufacturing wastepaper, and had some domestic troubles with the local birds. 'The pair of pigeons still roosting over the back door, shitting all over everything. Wish I could harden my heart and murder both of them — instead, threw out some dry bread for them.'

"Don Coleman's mother, Freida called him and invited him to her wedding slated for December 27th, which probably brought back memories of his own marital problems."[32] Yes, and memories of friends lost, like Ferd and Fletcher Pratt.

Piper was finding it difficult to get a handle on *Little Fuzzy*. On December 15, he wrote: "Better to junk a week's work than spend months trying to sell an un-salable story, as with 'Murder Frozen Over.'" Even after he wrote it over, he didn't like it. A few days before Christmas he scribbled: "Don't like what I wrote during the last week; if anything, worse than what I scrapped." He put it aside to begin working on ideas for a 10,000 word mystery story.[33]

Knerr writes: "On Saturday, Don Coleman picked him up and took him to church to see Freida become a December bride to Jim Shannon. 'Freida and husband, Jim Shannon, off on honeymoon about 1600.' From then on parties were the order of the day touring the various clubs of the Williamsport area with Don and friends."[34]

December 24, Piper wrote: "Spent A.M. doodling and brain racking for ideas, and finally, while I was eating lunch, one emerged. Spent early A.M. developing it — insurance arson; man kills brother, who was responsible for fire in which a dozen factory workers die, because he feels he must be put to death for his crime but family must not be publicly disgraced." Another false start, but Piper kicked this idea around most of the day, then spent the evening reading "Murder at the Conference." Mike Knerr has this to say about "Murder at the Conference": "It suffers from same fault as all the other Jeff Rand mysteries, too many characters, too much bullshitting around."[35]

On Christmas Day, not being the slightest bit religious, he took in a movie, "and then found there wasn't a god damned restaurant open anywhere, so came home and heated a tin of clam chowder, and then worked more in the evening." As a kind of footnote, he added: "All in all, had a hell of a merry Christmas."[36]

After the Christmas let-down, Beam got back to work on the 27th, when he got four pages done on the new story and vowed that "as soon as I have it done in first draft, will go back to *Little Fuzzy*." The New Year came, and he spent the day "seeing in the New Year" with the Colemans.[37] Freida was settling into her new marriage and her children were about to fly off on their own over the next year or two, leaving Beam alone in Williamsport without his adopted family.

Don Coleman writes: "With me leaving town for a career in Cincinnati in 1957, I more or less lost contact as to the comings and goings of Beam. (I never knew he had fallen on the ice!) When Beam decided to come to Williamsport to live — and surely his closest friends were there — we in the family were ecstatic! It was truly wonderful. And then, eventually Diane and Sylvia would be leaving due to their marriages, and finally my mother remarried and left town ... and Beam. Now, he was alone, except for Ted Ranck. His ultimate fate was very sad and my mother always blamed herself.... She talked about the fact many times, how that things may have been different had she remained in Beam's Billtown."[38]

No one knows the future, and in retrospect it's hard to blame the Colemans for getting on with their lives; after all, H. Beam Piper showed himself to the world as this strong, hardy, self-reliant man who could damn well take care of himself. With his tailored suits and Victorian ways, he appeared to be a man of means, and not many outside the writing game know how poorly it pays — even its better journeymen. The only ones who make a killing selling books, other than publishers, are those few who occupy the top of the bestseller lists year after year. Beam, sadly, was not of their ilk.

CHAPTER 26

Fuzzy Problems

It was those damn Fuzzy books that killed him! They got his hopes up, then dashed them. Beam's plan was to write one book, or short story, in each century of his future history; not write three bloody Fuzzy novels, including one he never could sell.[1]

—Jerry Pournelle

By 1959 Piper was finding it increasingly more difficult to live on his sporadic writing income, but believed he had no other alternative—certainly not one that he would have chosen or tolerated. Piper was self-reliant to a fault and was not about to go into a new line of work. He was too old to work for a private patrol service, even had there been such in Williamsport, and his lack of educational background left him without the credentials to obtain a job more fitting to his talents. He had another ten years to go before he would have been eligible for Social Security benefits, even were he constitutionally able to accept "going on the dole," as he put it.

Mike Knerr writes:

The story, *Little Fuzzy*, wasn't going well, as usual, and he was manufacturing wastepaper at a steady clip. On the other hand, the nesting pigeons on the back porch were producing their own particular brand of "wastepaper" at about the same rate of speed. Finally, realizing that his waste could be burned, but that of the birds had to be scrubbed, Beam declared war. "...after lunch, up to Dicky Grugan's (a local hardware store) and bought four feet of 48" chicken netting and used it to block the entrance to back porch, then cleaned up the pigeon shit. Result, a pair of mighty disgusted pigeons."
And back to work.
On January 18th, the temperature dropped to minus three degrees and the story dropped with it. Beam scrapped everything as "utterly worthless" and started feeling "sick about the whole thing." The Betty memory was still working on him and a couple of days later he would write: "A hell of a bad day." During this period going to gun collector meetings gave him the diversion he needed and friends like Bill and Dick Houser, Lynn Henry, Cliff Breidinger and Louis Conrad were very important to him.
They, probably like everyone else, never knew it.[2]

Piper flew to New York on February 18 for a Hydra Club meeting at Basil Davenport's place, and when it was over he, Randall Garrett and Larry Shaw finished it off at a nearby pub. He talked to Ken White, heard nothing of interest, and headed back to Williamsport and to work. At home, as in Paris, the utilities were not working properly, and he had to call his landlord about the heat being off in the apartment. This sort of thing cropped up with curious regularity in the diaries.

Finally, he was making good progress on *Little Fuzzy*. On March 7, he got a call that a party was going on at the Colemans'. Freida was back from her honeymoon. It was undoubtedly just what he needed. "Got home sometime late, plastered. Just went to sleep. Maybe I'll get up early tomorrow and take a fresh start."[3]

By the end of March, his typewriter showed signs of heavy fatigue: "Getting a lot of double-strikes and jammed up words. Ought to be fixed, probably with a new one."[4] Financially, he was in another bind, with only a couple of hundred dollars to his name. As Knerr points out:

> Piper's income is almost laughable during this slump and only the most devout writing fanatic would have clung to the machine with such ardor. Beam clung to it for a lot of reasons—he had no trade, he loved writing and he was just too damn old to get another job. "What the hell," he once asked, "can a man my age do?"
>
> Beam made less than a thousand dollars in 1959 and, as a result, slipped even more deeply into the privacy of his own mind. He developed a much greater contempt for such things as Social Security, Income Tax and the welfare program. "I buy my Social Security in boxes of fifty [bullets jfc]," he once snapped.
>
> "Viva the new typewriter," he wrote on March 27th, and joyously hammered away at *Little Fuzzy*. On the last of the month he wrote: "*Little Fuzzy* <u>finished</u>." Then added, "Well, sort of." Finally, on the 4th of April he penned: "*Little Fuzzy* finished. (Honest to God)." He shipped it off to Ken White and girded his loins for the yearly battle with the IRS, or "the Federal shakedown" as he usually called it. "Managed to deduct last year's slender income down to where I only needed to pay $17.71 social security—a goddamned robbery." Slender is a Piper understatement, and he now had a mere $200.00 in the bank. At the time, working as a tech writer, I was making nearly three times that figure a month and I had trouble making ends meet.[5]

After finishing *Little Fuzzy*, Piper was at a loss for what to work on next. Mike Knerr writes: "He went back to trying to think of an idea for a detective story and, for some harebrained reason, shaved off his moustache the last of April. 'Don't know,' he admitted, 'whether I like me without it or not.' He finally decided he didn't and let it grow back. He was still having troubles with the pigeons; now they were invading his peanut parties for the squirrels in Brandon Park. His morale was sagging as low as his bank account and he wasn't happy about it."[6]

Astounding was Beam's primary market, as well as the best paying, and Ken White sent *Little Fuzzy* to John Campbell first. The rejection letter for *Little Fuzzy* from John W. Campbell dated May 13, 1959, did not help Beam's morale.

To a degree, Campbell was correct; there are a lot of viewpoint characters in *Little Fuzzy* and sometimes it's easy for even an astute reader to get lost. Part of this can be blamed on Piper's technique. As we've already mentioned, Piper — in the *Double-Bill Symposium* — offered this bit of advice on writing from a "viewpoint" character: "Name your viewpoint character in the first paragraph, if possible, and don't name him thereafter unless someone addresses him by name, or something like that."

Piper's reasoning is good: "You're giving his thoughts along with his experiences and actions. You don't think of yourself by name; not often, anyhow."[7] True, but fiction is not quite a mirror of life, as Campbell so astutely points out. Sometimes even the most observant readers need a few signposts.

The most confusing thing about the large number of viewpoint characters in *Little Fuzzy* is occasionally that it's hard to tell which character *is* the viewpoint character. This is a failure of technique, not Piper's concept. A few more carefully placed character names could have easily cleared up most of the confusion. It's something Piper does do in his later works, like *Space Viking* and *Lord Kalvan of Otherwhen*, where the use of unusual names, like Ptosphes and Harmakros, forces him to place more character name tags than usual.

After wasting a couple months on a dud title, "Pest Among Men," and a racketeering story that ended up in the incinerator — where all of Beam's duds ended up sooner or later — he began work on a new story in his Terro-Human Future History, "Hot Time on Kwannon," later published as "Oomphel in the Sky." On the Fourth of July he went to feed the squirrels at Brandon Park when he "stopped to light a colored-fire flare for some small boys; got home just in time to see fireworks on South Side from back porch."[8]

Piper's worsening financial condition was getting severe enough that he was beginning to sell off nine of his pistols to Robert Abels, a New York antique arms dealer. He preferred to sell them to out of town dealers so that the local collectors didn't know how desperate for cash he was getting. For Piper, this was going from bad to very bad. But *Little Fuzzy* was still bouncing all over New York—1959's major accomplishment book-wise—and his cupboard was bare.

Knerr writes: "On July 11, a three figure check ($400.00) arrived from Robert Abels and Beam breathed a sigh of relief. 'Up town to cash it and do some shopping. Had to make two trips. Got a bottle of rum; first for over a month, and vitimines [sic].' Bolstered by money, rum and vitamins he launched into the story with renewed vigor. A day or so later his vigor turned to vinegar. 'Will have to scrap everything done on story so far, start from scratch with everything new except the story-idea.'"[9]

In August, after several months of false starts and rewriting, he finished "Oomphel in the Sky" and went back to work on another one of his mystery stories that would go nowhere. Mike Knerr writes: "On Sunday, August 23rd, he wrote: 'Betty's birthday,' at the top of the page and sketched little red and blue flowers and ribbons around the name. To add to his dismal feelings, the weather clouded in on him with occasional rain. 'Dark and gloomy,' he wrote, as if it mirrored what he felt.

"Although he 'believed' he was getting somewhere with the story, it was heavy going interspersed with days of anger.... 'This was a bad-luck day,' he scrawled, on the 28th. 'Got a letter from Ken White — Gold Medal has bounced *Little Fuzzy*. Lost my Dunhill 4-color pen. The price of rum has gone up another .25 cents— Shit!' He seemed to add the 25-cent rise in the price of rum as the final capper to the whole day."[10]

Piper received a check for $513.00 from Ken on September 10, for "Oomphel in the Sky," which John W. Campbell had bought. The first thing he did was to go out and buy a new tailor-made suit for $310.00! Piper noted: "damned near enough money for a suit of armor."[11] After all the hard times of the past few months and with *Little Fuzzy* collecting rejections from New American Library, Lippencott, Ballantine, *Astounding Science Fiction*, and Gold Medal, it's hard to fathom his thinking. As Knerr writes: "Hardly the decision of a man who bitched about a quarter rise in the price of Myers Rum."[12]

On October 3, Piper received a letter from Ken White informing him that Avon had bounced *Little Fuzzy*, which through him into a tailspin. He writes: "Slept till 1000. Tried to get started on the story again. The damned thing is in a hopeless mess. Maybe something can be salvaged from it, but it looks, at present, as though I've had about four months work for nothing."[13] A few days later he pulled himself together, decided to do a complete rewrite and finished it in two weeks! Piper was averaging twenty pages of finished production per day, not counting scrapped pages.

As Knerr notes: "It was a bad decision and it took its toll on him physically and mentally."[14] Piper mailed off the new version to his agent on the 21st of October and noted: "The last two weeks on *Little Fuzzy* have taken quite a bit out of me and I can't seem to put it back again."[15] He went back to work on "Pest Among Men" until deciding, "Pest Among Men" is a sick story; can't do anything with it."[16] At the end of October, he dropped "Pest Among Men" again, and started thinking about a new science fiction story. Piper writes: "It looks as though I have a really viable story idea."[17] This was the birth of "When in the Course...," another story he was never able to sell.

He went to work on it and by November 2 was still struggling to get it started. Piper closed his bank account at the Chase Manhattan Bank by transferring his account to his Williamsport bank. "Now I have only $132.00, and this month's rent still unpaid."[18] His rent was only $40.00 a month, without utilities, except for gas.

Knerr writes:

On the 21st, both Beam and I (among others) received a call from Ray Young "who is organizing something called a writers forum, a meeting on 2 Dec. to which I am invited." Both of us were gun-shy about any such organization, but when we were invited we thought it over and decided to go. Beam, perhaps, out of loneliness for other scribes.

Ted Ranck again came around to invite him to go deer hunting in Tioga County and Beam said he would. "...wish now that I hadn't. Think I'll call him up and change that — tell him I can't go." Beam begged off the next day; with his eyes in the condition they were in, and with the various aches and pains he was having, it was ... a wise move. To sit at a desk about fifty-one weeks out of a year, then try to hunt rugged terrain for even a few days, would tax a much younger man than Beam.

On the evening of December 2nd, 1959, the area writers congregated at the Young residence on West Third Street. Mike Knerr tells us of his first meeting with H. Beam Piper: "At the meeting, I wasn't sure I liked Beam. I'd never met the man, nor had I read anything he'd written. Garbed in a black suit, vest and necktie, he looked like a character out of a Victorian novel. Ray told everyone to introduce themselves, and their line of writing to the group.

"I'm H. Beam Piper," Beam said, in turn, "and I write science fiction."

Someone asked, "Do you sell it?"

"Yes," Beam replied, no doubt holding himself in check among these dunderheads.

"May we touch your hem?" Kathryn Hoover asked.

"Hem touching," Beam said, with a twinkle in his eye, "will be at three P.M. Tomorrow."

I started to like him.[19]

Michael E. Knerr sometime in the early 1960s (courtesy Daniel Ward Knerr).

Piper had this to say about the meeting in his diary: "Had dinner at the Day & Night, and then to a meeting of something called the Creative Writers Forum, the moving spirit of which seems to be a young fellow named Ray Young. It was a rather enjoyable affair at that."[20] He was still having problems with "When in the Course..." and his finances. On December 5, he wrote: "The whole story simply fell to pieces on me, and I spent all day pawing around among them trying to put them into some kind of shape, and finally gave it up about 2200."[21] He stared to draw the story together, but by the 10th he was writing, "Story in a hell of a mess.... Will have to take a new start, change it completely."[22] Maybe it was the constant rejection of *Little Fuzzy*, but Piper didn't appear to be writing with his usual confidence. His diary entries were starting to echo those of 1955 and 1956, when he was almost completely stalled. He sold a .44 Colt Dragoon pistol to Dick Houser and wrote: "At least, I can pay my rent, for a month or so."[23]

On the 19th of December, he ripped "When in the Course..." apart again and started over. Piper was plagued with periodic losses of heat from the landlord's furnace, inconsiderate pigeons, the inability to get a story planned the way he wanted it — and now water dripping into the gunroom. He did receive a check from his agent for "The Answer," which had sold to *Fantastic Universe* months before. He was able to add $41.00 to his thinning bank account.

Beam ended 1959 working on a lecture for the Northern Tier Gun Collectors. On New Year's Eve, he fired "the eensy brass cannon" and read until 0300 A.M.

"Alone."[24]

CHAPTER 27

When in the Course...

Lunch at Heylmun's, got haircut, bought diary for next year, which I hope to live to complete. Also first bottle of rum since I can't remember when.[1]
— H. Beam Piper

"It was a confused several years for books during the early 1960s." Michael Knerr writes: "The ruling in March of 1960, by the US Court of Appeals that D.H. Lawrence's *Lady Chatterley's Lover* was not obscene was a major breakthrough. In and of itself, the ruling had little effect on general reading material, or science fiction, but it served to demonstrate that the times were on the verge of change — as were the reading tastes of the American people. It was a confused several years for books during the early '60s and it was hardly a time for a writer to make mistakes if he or she wanted to remain a selling (eating) professional. Yet, Piper still wanted to write mysteries that were more suited to the era of S.S. Van Dine (Philo Vance) and that crowd."[2]

Knerr continues "Beam and I became fairly close friends about this time but it was not until 1961, when I became a selling writer, that my opinions really meant much to him. This, of course, is understandable; at age fifty-six, and with dozens of published stories to his credit, his attitude was one of *the student doesn't tell the teacher how to write* — and he stuck to it.

"He lent me a carbon of 'Murder Frozen Over' and I read it. I'd read mysteries for years and was, by then, building quite a collection of Piper's science fiction. That was about the time that he was starting *Four-Day Planet*. 'Stick to science fiction,' I told him. In those days I had no idea why he was selling his guns (gun collectors do this all the time) and I had no idea how broke Beam was, nor how much in love he was with Betty. That information only surfaced after Ken White became my agent."[2]

After all the rewrites and complaining, "When in the Course" was finished on January 5, 1960, and mailed off to Ken the following day. On January 8, Piper was back to "doodling in evening; a lot of half-assed ideas, none of which go very far." He added, "The next one will be a detective story. I hope so, anyhow."[3] He was back to beating his brains out on "Pest Among Men" and was totally bogged down again. By the 26th, having torn up all sorts of beginnings, he started over. "This is the same damned thing I've done with every other story I've ever written, but I think in this case it's necessary. In order to get on with the story, I have to get the beginning established, or I'll go on planning and re-planning it and getting no further."[4]

On February 4, he wrote: "Letter from Ken White — Campbell has bounced 'When in the Course...,' and Dell is not going to publish *Little Fuzzy*. This is the worst of all."

This is John W. Campbell's rejection letter for "When in the Course...," sent to Kenneth White on January 20, 1960:

Dear Mr. White:

Piper has one, long-standing characteristic in his writing that causes trouble; he personalizes, identifies, <u>all</u> his characters equally. There are too many spear-carriers being treated as stars, which makes it hard for the reader to get the hang of the story. Real life may, indeed, be this way; but art is not the reproduction of life — that's photography of the snap-shot variety — instead it's an abstraction from and clarification of life.

That's one fault here. The second fault present is that the reader winds up with a vague feeling that nothing much happened. Agreed freely and fully that it's not true; a lot did happen. But the <u>*feeling*</u> can be there.

The problem is made as diffuse as the cast of characters. (That, too, is true of life ... but makes for ineffective art.)

If he had made The Problem the House of Styphon, then, at a particular period, under particular circumstances, the reader would sigh, feel "Ah! Now they've licked the problem," and be able to rest content.

As is ... where's the climax in this story?

Regards,
John W. Campbell, Jr.[6]

Ken White would continue to make the rounds, ever smaller as one pulp after another collapsed, with "When in the Course...," but it would fail to be published during Piper's lifetime. Fortunately, for posterity, it did turn up among the few surviving manuscripts and tear sheets of published stories when Ace Books took possession of Piper's literary estate. As editor of Piper's three short story collections, I was able to include it among the stories in *Federation*— the first ever collection of H. Beam Piper stories. Despite the story's flaws, it was quite a coup to be able to publish a *new* Piper short, made even more so by the fact that it was later recast into *Lord Kalvan of Otherwhen*.

Piper often reused the better elements of his unsold stories, and in this case he plucked-out the fictional kingdom of Hostigos out of "When in the Course...," transplanting it into the Paratime series as a small princedom in the Great Kingdom of Hos-Harphax on the Fourth Level, Europo-American, Aryan-Transpacific time-line.

As Campbell noted, there are several story problems with "When in the Course...": its meandering plotline, several subplots that for the most part go nowhere and a flat resolution that ends the story with a whimper. Yet, there are some good characters: Rylla, Ptosphes and Harmakros make their first appearance, and the gunpowder theocracy of Styphon's House (a capital idea) is introduced. It's actually fortunate that *Fantastic Universe, Amazing Stories* or some other 1960s salvage market didn't pick up the story, preventing Piper from recasting it into "Gunpowder God"— the first of the three Lord Kalvan novelettes.

Piper went back to being frustrated with the way "Pest Among Men" was going, and soon decided to take a break from it and write an article on the Battle of Cerignola. As Mike Knerr points out: "Unless he had planned to sell the article overseas, he would have done better to write about Appomattox or Gettysburg. A European battle fought in the sixteenth century wouldn't seem to draw much of an American audience — yet he launched into it and ... 'Up town to bank — am down to $20.00 now, worst ever — and got something for dinner.'"[7]

He spent a week writing the article; it's unfortunate there was no real market for it since he could bang them out so quickly. Writing and selling a nonfiction piece every few months would have solved most of his financial problems. Mike Knerr notes: "He mailed out the article, 'The Queen Comes Into Her Own,' on February 15th, and, it too, fell victim to editorial flack. He went back to working on 'Pest Among Men' and began considering the sale of some of his gun collection."[8]

Piper received a letter from Ken White on the 16th of March adding Putnam to "list of publishers who didn't want *Little Fuzzy*" On the 19th: "Horace Gold has bounced 'When in the Course...' as expected, with characteristic Goldian comments." Finally, on his birthday, "The whole story fell to pieces on me, and I spent most of the day among the wreckage, wondering how the hell I was ever going to get it put together again."[9]

Knerr writes:

> To those who are not familiar with writers and the world of writing, it should be pointed out that authors do not write on one line of subject matter necessarily. Bart Spicer, in the 1950s, wrote a lot of mysteries, but he also wrote historical novels. Francis Van Wyck Mason wrote historical novels, but he also wrote the Hugh North series of espionage—North, of course, being promoted in Army rank every other book. One familiar science fiction writer used to write "true confessions," and the list goes on. Writers, by the very nature of their profession, should not be pigeon-holed.
>
> On the other hand, if a writer yearns to write historical fiction, but knows that it won't sell at the moment, he either shifts to another subject that *will* sell—or he's a damned fool. Piper made a $675.00 advance on *Murder in the Gunroom* and never sold another mystery. While he insisted on writing material that wouldn't be published (when he could have been devoting his time to science fiction that would have sold), he was steadily going broke and constantly suffering from writer's block. After leaving Betty, in 1957, his earnings for the next two years totaled a mere $1,624.85, and prices were steadily going up. In 1960, his earnings were just $5.00 short of $1,400.00.[10]

While in general I agree with Mike Knerr's conclusion that Piper's writing efforts would have been better served on science fiction, writing science fiction didn't guarantee a sale either. In 1960, he was still getting rejection slips for both *Little Fuzzy* and "When in the Course...." In retrospect, we know that *Little Fuzzy* has become a minor classic in the science fiction field, while "When in the Course..." was unsalable. Still, had either sold, he might have focused more on science fiction. However, he was not writing to the tune of the time clock, but to his inner meter—which is why he stamped his unique personality all over his best works. What he learned writing unsuccessful stories like "Pest Among Men" and "When in the Course..." and articles such as "The Queen Comes Into Her Own" was transmuted into his other fiction works, such as *Lord Kalvan of Otherwhen*.

One of the unique aspects of H. Beam Piper's later writings is that they have a very "lived in" feeling; it's as if the author is a reporter from a different time or dimension—very believable. His knowledge of history and mankind gave them gravitas and verisimilitude. All Piper's rewriting and recasting of his stories gave them a solidity that few stories of that time had. Robert Heinlein during the 1940s and early 1950s wrote some good novels, but many of the early ones don't hold up today. (His juvenile efforts and later 1950s works like *Starship Troopers* being an exception.) Other than *Double Star, Citizen of the Galaxy* and *Beyond This Horizon* (which read like they could have been written by Piper), Heinlein's work of this period just doesn't have the "weight" of Piper's best novels.

I do not believe that it is coincidental that Piper wrote his best work after he married Betty in 1955. His characters became more "real" and multi-dimensional. Stories such as "Omnilingual" rank with the best science fiction tales of the era. His later novels had a believability and emotional depth that his earlier ones, like *Murder in the Gunroom, Full Cycle* and *Uller Uprising*, lacked.

Mike Knerr's own failed career as a novelist should have taught him that at the end of the day, success as a writer is not determined by how much money one makes, but by the quality of the work.

On April 8, Piper wrote: "Started planning on 'Pest.' Couldn't get anything done; seem to have completely lost contact with the story. Morale very low; money low, too." He was down to 41 cents in his pocket and $47.00 in the bank, and his income tax was due. "This is the worst yet, and no immediate prospects of more money." The following day, he wrote:

"found that I was only able to give a fraction of my mind to the story — money trouble too pressing and immediate. Ate up most of the food in the house today."[11]

Piper's finances were now in the worst state they had ever been in. On Monday April 11, things came to a head, and he wrote: "Up 0830, and tried to work on planning. Money trouble intruded to such an extent that I spent most of the time debating whether or not to shoot myself; proposition defeated by a very narrow vote, and may be brought before the house again if things don't get better. Am going to give 'Pest' a rest for a couple of days and try to cook up another short or novelette."[12]

Knerr explains:

> This was Piper's first decision to use a gun on himself, in the diaries, and it is significant in that he isn't really talking about money. He is talking about writing, and his tremendous problems in getting a story down on paper. It may have, at the time, seemed to him that money was the villain — yet he solved this whole "financial problem" over the coming weeks simply by selling a few guns.
> During April, Beam was biding his time in hopes that *Little Fuzzy* would sell, and he was keeping to a very rigid budget. He ate potato stew, made with Spam, and often dinner would be a can of soup, "...if a tin of soup may be so-called...." Or he would fry, "up an omelet using leftover potato stew as a base, and back to work afterward." On Sunday, April 24th, he treated himself to "...a nice dinner, smoked pork chops, mashed potatoes and peas, then out for a walk in the new long evening...."
> Dick Houser dropped in on the 15th: "Sold him the .44 Rogers and Spencer for $45.00, which will pay my rent next month and give me $5.00 to live on." Beam was sailing pretty well close-hauled, but he was certainly no stranger to that tack. Yet he still didn't stop writing detective stories. In fact, Beam was still working on "Pest Among Men" just before he died.[13]

It wasn't just the money problems or the frustration Piper experienced finishing his stories; it was the constantly draining, hard-scrabble existence that drove him to suicide. He would sell a story, then spin his wheels working on a new story that wouldn't quite jell, or finish another yarn, send it to his agent and have it rejected over and over again. There were no guarantees; he was only as good as his last sale.

Nor was Piper one to write to editorial order, or he would have been busy polishing off stories that John W. Campbell oftentimes handed him on a silver platter in his letters. Campbell respected Beam both as a writer and a working detective. Unfortunately, we will never know the tale Piper spun that turned his night watchman job into that of a detective, but I'm sure it must have been fascinating! Certainly, John W. Campbell bought it.

CHAPTER 28

Unexpected Help

Those guns were like his children, and he didn't like having to divorce them one at a time.[1]

— Don Coleman

H. Beam Piper was living very sparingly through April of 1960, hoping that *Little Fuzzy* would sell and take him out of the morass he was in. On May 1, still punching away at a first draft on "Pest Among Men," he wrote: "I piously hope, last attempt at first draft."[2] He went up to the Lycoming Historical Museum on May 1 to take out some of his pistols to sell — and found it locked up for the day. He went back home, disgusted. "Looks as though," he wrote, "I'll have to sell my Mantons." He didn't, as it turned out; according to Mike Knerr, the Joseph Manton dueling pistols remained with him.[3]

Mike Knerr writes: "Dick Houser again bailed him out of his financial troubles by buying quite a few guns from the collection for $278.00. It has been said that Beam had over a hundred pieces to his name, but that must have been many years before. Like any collector, he was wont to trade, or sell, to get a piece that he wanted, so a collection had a tendency to fluctuate considerably. The object of all this (barring a love for the items collected) was to buy cheap and sell dear, while still holding onto the best. Beam understood this. The swords and guns, other than the fact that he liked them, were money in the bank and he never hesitated to sell them."[4]

That Piper was in a "holding pattern" is obvious from his statement: "Bought a bottle of rum, which I must make last a long time." On May 7: "the story seems to be getting out of hand again." Also, "The brothers Houser in about 1500 and bought some more pistols."[5]

I believe that selling his pistols wholesale was beginning to stick in his craw. Piper had spent forty years building up his gun collection, and now he was having to sell it off in dribs and drabs just to pay rent and eat. As Don Coleman writes: "The thought of hocking a flint-lock Kentucky rifle in mint condition was for Piper like having a leg removed, or even his writing hand eliminated — for the sake of eating!"[6]

On May 7, Piper received a letter from Putnam Books from an editor named Bill McMorris, a friend of Kenneth White's, who wanted to discuss writing some science fiction juveniles. It was becoming obvious at last that "Pest Among Men" was not coming together: "Up 0830. Still trying to get story under way, and simply couldn't. The more I work at it, the worse it gets. I can't do a damned thing with it. Afraid it and the other story, 'Pest Among Men,' are both dead ducks, and I have wasted months on the latter and weeks on the short story."[7]

So Piper put away the mysteries and started working on jotting down ideas for a science fiction juvenile novel. He talked to his agent, Ken White, and decided on the 17th to go to New

161

York. Bill McMorris called him on the 19th and they made a luncheon appointment for May 27, 1960.

By way of research, Piper checked out two of Heinlein's juveniles, *Space Cadet* and *Tunnel in the Sky*, from the Brown Library. "Spent all evening reading *Tunnel in the Sky*, and was agreeably surprised at maturity of matter regarded as 'juvenile.' Finished it and to bed 0100."[8] By 1960 Heinlein was no longer writing juveniles, but writing adult novels to great acclaim.

Once again Piper started writing before he had the story plotted and worked out. On the 21st of May, he wrote: "Worked on story, started a rough first draft, without much idea of where it was going. Maybe this will work better than spending a couple of months making notes. Kept at it all morning."[9]

He picked up a plane ticket for New York on the 24th and went home to pack. He arrived in New York the following day to learn that Ken was still in Connecticut so, since this was his first visit to New York in some time, he took in the sights. "Great changes since last time, for worse." On the 26th he talked to Ken, had dinner at the Three Crowns and attended a Hydra Club meeting. He saw Hans Stefan Santesson (editor of *Fantastic Universe*), then had lunch and a long talk with McMorris, who presumably offered encouragement as Beam outlined the story he intended to write.[10]

In an October 4, 2005, e-mail, Bill McMorris writes: "In 1958–62 I was editor of children's books for G.P. Putnam's Sons and learned about the work of H. Beam Piper from his agent, Kenneth White. Ken arranged for me to have lunch with Piper.... As a result of the luncheon conversation — rather stiff, since both of us were reticent individuals — Piper agreed to do a book aimed at teenage readers."[11]

In a follow-up e-mail, Bill adds:

> The one time I met him for lunch, as I think I told you, our conversation was rather strained. I found his expression when he spoke a little disconcerting. He seemed to say everything with a fixed smile, whether we talked about Italian city states or science fiction. When I asked about the place where he lived, he said it was the YMCA (in Williamsport, Pa., I think) and without any preliminaries told me:
>
> "There is a gum ball machine in the lobby. Each day when I come home I stop and put in a coin. Sometimes a gum ball comes out and sometimes I get a little pretty."
>
> When I looked puzzled, he repeated, "A little pretty. A little dog or a little cat. I take them upstairs and put them on a shelf so they can play together."
>
> All this was delivered with the same soft tone of voice and fixed smile he had used throughout the meal. He looked at me expectantly. My mind finally wrapped around the fact that the "pretty" was a term my Arkansas grandmother often used to describe any attractive trinket. But what was I to do with this information? Laugh and possibly insult him? So I put on a grin that must have been similar to his own and simply nodded, hoping to project warm admiration for vending machine toy collectors everywhere.
>
> To this day I wonder if he was having some kind of joke on the callow editor or was he simply trying to relax the tension? If it was the latter, he picked the wrong, uptight bookboy.[12]

I suspect it was Piper taking advantage of a much younger editor, by pulling his leg, since he did *not* live at the YMCA at that time, but had his own apartment. Nor is there any evidence that he ever lived at the Williamsport YMCA. Admittedly, he did not *like* editors or think much of the breed and referred to them as the "lowest from of animal life in the universe."[13] The power they held over his words and fortune was too strong for his liking.

Piper had a very rough, gravelly voice so when uncomfortable, or talking with strangers, he spoke almost *sotto voce*. However, when comfortable, or with friends, he used his brusque voice to great effect, as evidenced in the September 14, 1950, tape recording of the "Unholy Trinity" sent to me by Don Coleman.

Beam did collect figurines, some he picked up during his walks, and referred to them as the "parade." In describing Piper's Williamsport writing room, Don Coleman writes: "A group of small ivory and ceramic figures occupied the area along the northern rim of the spacious desktop. These miniatures included elephants, cats, a Bengal tiger, a small 'little brown jug'— to which he affectionately referred to as the 'parade.' Whenever he would come to a break-ing point in typing, Beam would turn in his chair and face the animals, *talk* to them, place the 'jug's' handle over a pachyderm's tusk and rearrange their order within the 'parade.' After a short recess and a couple tastings from his rum highball, he would then light up his pipe, turn back to the typewriter and continue his thoughts."[14]

Upon his return to Williamsport, Piper ran into the same old wall: "Spent all day try-ing to organize story—couldn't seem to get anything done." This went on for the rest of the week and it wasn't until June 1 that he knocked out twenty-two pages of the first draft of *Four-Day Planet*. The next day he wrote: "This wasn't a very productive day, the day after a big day seldom is." He slowed the pace down and by June 10, he had ninety pages of a first draft.[15]

The same day a letter from his agent arrived, informing him that "Damon Knight, at Berkley Books, likes *Little Fuzzy*."[16] Damon was one of the foremost science fiction critics and writers of the 1950s and '60s and was working as an editorial associate at Berkley Books. This was a very good sign.

By June 24, Piper stopped writing because he was within twenty pages of the end. He wanted to start the final draft before continuing "so that I will have discrepancies cleared out." As Mike Knerr points out,

> The interesting thing to note here is that on *Four-Day Planet*, he didn't wallow through the baloney of a first-first draft, a first draft, a second-first draft ... *ad nauseum*. He had his usual troubles, tore up pages here and there and rewrote them, or bogged down for a day on plotting—but this one was a lot easier to write then, say, "When in the Course..."—and a damn sight better story.
>
> By July 17th, at 2330, *Four-Day Planet* was finished, all 224 pages of it. He had only used two drafts and he accomplished it with a minimum of wailing and gnashing of teeth. Not only that, but his writing was interrupted by writers' meetings, gun collectors' meetings and me dropping by every now and then to shoot the breeze.
>
> During this period of time Piper's morale is up, his mind is clear in what he wants to write and he doesn't mention problems of health. Although he doesn't say so in the diaries, he was probably run-ning pretty low on funds. All he states is that on the 19th he had planned to do some house cleaning and didn't get around to it. "Reaction to the pressure of getting *Four-Day Planet* finished, I suppose." He also "Began planning novelette, tentative title, 'Three Came to Asshur.'"[17]

With *Four-Day Planet* wrapped up, Piper's spirits were up. "Worked on planning all morning," he wrote on July 25. "Seem to be really getting something done on it." A dark note on the day was that "Berkley has bounced *Little Fuzzy*, in spite of Damon Knight's recom-mendation." He went back to working on "Three Came to Asshur," with the usual produc-tion of scrap paper, but minus a lot of his previous frustration.[18]

The contract for *Four-Day Planet* arrived on August 17, and Beam sold his 1836 U.S. pis-tol for $125.00.

Former Putnam's editor Bill McMorris notes:

> The story was lively and would appeal to boys, I felt, but some of the scenes were quite violent and I was afraid the library market—our principal source of sales—would pan it, so I asked the author to make a few revisions and tone it down a bit. Piper's response was, "You bought it, you do whatever you want with it."
>
> So I did some minor trimming of the most violent descriptions—probably a few dozen words— and the book was published with limited success. Not long after, Ken brought me *Little Fuzzy*. I

really liked the book, but it was too adult for the teenage market of those years and of no interest to the adult trade department at Putnam's. However, Janet Carse (*nee* Wood), wife of Bob Carse, one of the writers on our juvenile list, was newly employed as an editor at Avon and was looking for science fiction. With Ken White's permission, I sent *Little Fuzzy* to her, she loved it and got it published.[19]

Mike Knerr writes:

Sunday, August 21st, was a Williamsport Creative Writing Forum picnic at Anne Winter's house, north of Williamsport, and we all took turns plinking with Beam's .22 Smith and Wesson revolver. None of us would have qualified for the Marine Pistol Team and, unless it was an off day, Beam wasn't that good. When the party broke up, Bill Stroup took Beam home to meet his father, another pistol fan, and then to Richard Frank's house to see his science-fiction collection.

Richard Frank's entire book collection was fantastic. He had it, originally, in the house, but the weight of the books had begun to pull the floors away from the walls, so he moved it all down to his first floor garage and set it up like a real library. Most of us felt that if Richard didn't have a copy — it hadn't been printed.

On the 25th, Piper scrapped the whole damned story, "Three Came to Asshur." "Decided to get story back on track and only way to do it will be start from scratch. Begin anew, and I hope final, first draft." Ken also sent him his first check for *Four-Day Planet*, $900.00, which he banked. On August 30th, "Three Came to Asshur" died a sudden and violent death. Piper writes: "Up 0900 and started to work on story, and realized suddenly that the thing is no damned good and I have been wasting a month working on it."

On August 31st, just before leaving for the Pittsburgh Convention, Piper started to plan another juvenile "in case Putnam's finds *Four-Day Planet* a success and wants another." On September 2nd, he took a flight to the Iron City and, after checking into the hotel, took a walk to the Golden Triangle to see old Fort Pitt. He went up to the convention and spent the rest of the night drinking and talking. The next day, Saturday, "Ran into Fred Pohl, who says he has money for me. If so," Beam wrote dryly, "Age of Miracles still in operation."[20]

On the PittCon's last day, Piper wrote: "Had breakfast with a few of the fans and Randy Garrett and Clayton Rawson. Convention gradually burning out — auction, business meeting. Had a couple of drinks with Fred Pohl, Lester del Rey — who looks quite handsome with his grizzled Conquistador's beard — and their wives. They both know J-n McG-e, who is now at Red Bank, N.J."[21]

He was still angry with John McGuire and continued to use his initials in the diaries rather than spell out his name. He knew how to hold a grudge.

Piper left the next day and flew back to Williamsport where he picked up work again on a juvenile story for Putnam, trying to work up a good idea, more than anything. He could not, however, leave the Battle of Cerignola alone. His fascination with that conflict, and Gonsalo de Cordoba — the Great Captain — never seemed to leave him. His various entries, beginning on September 8, may shed some light on the progress (or lack of progress) of this unfinished novel.

"Worked A.M. on background for historical novel, probable title, *Only the Arquebus*, battle of Cerignola. Out P.M., did some shopping, got a haircut. Had dinner at Heylmun's, and home about 1930. Got Sabatini's *Life of Cesare Borgia* and, for the fourth time, Prescott's *Ferdinand & Isabella* out of the library. Spent most of the evening on them."[22]

On September 10, Piper wrote: "Worked for a while on background and planning. Trying to get a story, with love interest, to fit historical facts. Heavy going." Piper got everything he could from the book by Sabatini and shifted his attention to Prescott, but added wearily, "don't seem to have recovered from the PittCon yet."[23] As Knerr notes: "Small wonder: conventions of the science-fiction community seem to be marathons dedicated to see how long a person can stay on their feet and drink without collapsing."[24]

September 12, Piper wrote: "Worked on background A.M., got a volume of Guizot's

French History at library. Very little in it — Guizot was a patriotic Frenchman and the invasions of Italy by Charles VIII and Louis XII were not greatly to the credit of France. Worked all evening putting what I got from Sabatini together with Prescott. From now on it's going to be mostly Prescott. Still don't have an idea about fiction story."[25]

Meanwhile, Ken White was attempting to sell the serial rights to *Four-Day Planet* to *Astounding Science Fiction*. On September 12, in a letter to Ken, John W. Campbell wrote: "Putnam is right in buying this yarn by H. Beam Piper, *Four-Day Planet*, [it] makes an excellent book. But it doesn't make a good serial. And I suspect it's intended as a juvenile. Split into parts it would lose all sense of unity, I fear."[26]

Meanwhile, Piper spent most of the next two weeks in fruitless research and "doodling out notes" that didn't work into a story. On September 23, 1960: "I do have a lot of history, and have the geography of southern Italy in mind, but still no story."[27] As Knerr notes: "H. Beam Piper was not the kind of historian/writer who would tamper with the facts, even in a novel. Historical license was not a phrase he used at all. He was 'trying to work up an idea for a love-interest for story, or, rather, trying to invest the idea I have with some color of historical plausibility, and having heavy going at it.' When he turned in at midnight on October 2nd, he scribbled, 'I wish to Christ I could get something done.'"[28]

In a March 22, 1963, letter to Jerry Pournelle, Piper gave a plot summary of his historical novel, "Only the Arquebus":

> Having just finished a story in the VII Century A.E. [*Fuzzy Sapiens*], I have now dug out the historical novel on which I have been working intermittently, when I have not been pressed by necessity to get something quickly saleable done, for the last couple of years. This is early Sixteenth Century C.E. — 1502–1503, to be exact — and Ferdinand of Spain and Louis XII of France are fighting over the kingdom of Naples.
>
> This is strictly a zero-sum game; Ferdinand and Louis have made a treaty partitioning the Neapolitan Kingdom between them, and now each is trying to grab the whole thing and shove the other out completely. Ferdinand is a smart crook and Louis is a stupid one. Louis' commander, the Duc de Nemours, thinks war is a large-scale tournament, and its purpose is to enable gallant knights to perform deeds of valor and gain chivalrous renown; Ferdinand's commander, Gonzalo de Cordoba, thinks the purpose of war is the destruction of the enemy's armed force.
>
> In addition, the Spaniards have a new and terrible weapon, so dreadful as to make war unthinkable; it is called the arquebus. They have a lot of them, and the French haven't. Figure it out for yourself from there. The story will come to its final climax on the battlefield of Cerignola, where Nemours' knights and men-at-arms were shot to scrap-iron by Gonzalo's arquebusiers, a victory strikingly parallel to Andrew Jackson's at New Orleans.[29]

On October 5, Beam flew to New York for a Mystery Writers of America meeting, then talked to Ken, who told him that Putnam's wanted another juvenile. "The historical novel is going to be set aside for awhile," Piper wrote. "Think I can use the *Galaxy* story 'Graveyard of Dreams' as a starting point." He discussed it with McMorris over lunch, as well as the possibility of other stories in the future. Then hunted around town, without luck, for a copy of Heinlein's *Starship Troopers*. He returned to Williamsport on the 8th and found the new *Analog Science Fiction and Fact*, which used to be *Astounding Science Fiction*, in the mailbox. It contained "Oomphel in the Sky," as Piper put it: "finally published."[30]

He started working on his juvenile novel on the 9th: "spent all day working, which is to say, sitting at my desk smoking and drinking coffee and 'contemplating my navel' and doodling." The story began slowly and it wasn't until the 16th that he started to write on the typewriter; he wrote fourteen pages of first draft of what he was tentatively calling *Junkyard Planet*.[31] Nineteen-sixty may have been the most productive year of his career. True, he had more trouble getting *Junkyard Planet* written than he did with *Four-Day Planet*, but it was nothing compared to his usual symphony of agony.

Knerr writes: "On November 2nd, he stopped the first draft and began a synopsis of the book to send to Putnam; in this as well, he was frustrated: 'Story in a hell of a mess, don't know what to do with it.' By November 7th: 'Worked a little on planning, and finished the letters I had started to write, including the god damned questionnaire for Putnam. Up town, lunch at Heylmun's, and had myself photographed — Putnam wants some pictures of me.'"[32]

Former Putnam's editor Bill McMorris writes: "About *Junkyard Planet*: It was published by Putnam's after I left to go to W.W. Norton to start a juvenile division. My good friend Tom MacPherson replaced me (with my enthusiastic support) as editor of children's books at Putnam's. Tom, like so many others associated with Piper at that time, is no longer with us."[33]

By November 18, Piper had plotted out enough that he was already on the third chapter. "That leaves this god damned synopsis to tinker up, and then I can send it in and get started on first draft proper." He mailed the requested photos off to Putnam's and sent the synopsis on November 21. He then turned his attention to the main story and began serious writing on Thanksgiving Day.[34]

Knerr writes:

In the end, *Junkyard Planet* was easier to write than most of his stories, but it still gave him trouble. Piper never wrote anything as easily as *Four-Day Planet* and, oddly enough, it was one of his better novels. Beam was his own worst critic and, while a writer must be careful and critical of what he does, there are definite limits to how far he can go — especially when his bank account is below $100.00, as Beam's was on December 2nd, 1960.

Three days later a letter from Ken White, "McMorris liked the synopsis, is taking the story, contract will be drawn end of week, should have dough pre–Christmas." He didn't get it until the 31st. He did get the galley proofs for *Four-Day Planet* and corrected them while sweating over the new novel. He had, during the writing of this story, slipped back into his old pattern of writing a first-first draft, first-final draft, etc., and spent more time tying to figure out just where the hell the story was going.

His morale during December, seems high enough, although on the 13th, he wrote: "Up town after lunch to bank; so horrified at what I discovered my balance to be that I came directly home without getting my haircut as I had intended." He wasn't all that disturbed, however; after the evening's writers' meeting, he, Bill Stroup and I found a ridiculously noisy bar and dumped a few during our meeting-after-the-meeting, as usual.

The contract arrived by special delivery on the 17th, together with a bonus check of $85.00 for "Oomphel in the Sky." The contract advance on *Junkyard Planet* called for $450.00 on signing his name and another $450 on receipt of the manuscript. "Fired the *eensy* brass cannon and then felt too good to go back to work."[35]

On December 22, 1960, Bill Stoup — fellow member of the local writers' organization, called Piper with this news: "Lycoming Historical Museum was damaged, or destroyed? by fire this afternoon. The necessity which forced me to sell pistols this summer was a blessing in disguise — at least I still have some of my best left." Piper went to have Christmas dinner at the Lycoming Hotel and "then walked up town and looked at the museum. Except for broken windows all around, it seems not too badly damaged on the outside, but probably a wreck inside."[36]

According to Knerr, it was bad inside: "a considerable amount of displays were destroyed in the blaze.

"For the rest of the month, Piper slugged away at the story and when the check came for the advance on *Junkyard Planet*, it was New Year's Eve and he was unable to cash it. He celebrated the end of the year with Ted and Mary Ranck, and another couple, and fired the *eensy* brass cannon at midnight."[37]

CHAPTER 29

Little Fuzzy Finds a Home

Just loafed around — I never can get any work done the day the money comes.[1]
— H. Beam Piper

"Beam never made it home from the New Year's celebration at Ted Ranck's house," Mike Knerr writes; "sufficiently juiced ... he crashed there — waking up on the new dawn 'with a beastly hangover.' He went for a drive with Ted, who then brought him home, and for the first time there was no pork and sauerkraut for dinner. 'Was going to be energetic as hell and start the New Year off right. Didn't seem to make it. See what I can do tomorrow.'

"He worked hard on *Junkyard Planet* without all the usual fits and stops. For Beam, having the story planned out in advance gave the best results with less rewriting and fewer story breakdowns. Even he realized it, but unless prodded by an editor like McMorris of Putnam's Beam would not do the advance story planning required for him to complete the story — the worst part is that he *knew* he should do it, but still couldn't."[2]

In early January of 1961, Piper's ceiling began to leak and his typewriter began to fail. He put a pan under the leak but bought a new typewriter. "I think I shall have to fix it with a new one," he wrote.[3] Knerr notes: "He'd had this Smith Corona less than two years, but he'd given it a good workout!" Piper hauled it up to the store and swapped it on "a showy new model" of two-toned plastic and jet-age sleekness. "Writing with a new typewriter is a delight. I didn't realize how much work it was to punch the keys of the old one."[4]

January 20 was a "very bad day for morale" and he only did two pages, but his blue devils were allayed by attending a party for Freida Shannon (formerly Coleman), who was in town. "Home late, potted, went to bed at once." In the morning he learned that Avon had rejected *Little Fuzzy*. The "ceiling is still leaking," but he lived with it for two more weeks before calling the landlord and getting it fixed.[5]

Junkyard Planet was finished on February 26, with a minimum of fuss—for H. Beam Piper. The ceiling started leaking again, only now in the gunroom. He wrote: "stuck a pan under the leak, corrected the manuscript and mailed it off to Ken."[6]

On the 28th of February, Piper wrote: "Spent A.M. thinking about idea for a new story — I think I'll make it a Paratime story."[7] There's always been a question among Piper scholars as to why Piper stopped writing stories in his Paratime crosstime series; his last published Paratime story was "Time Crime," which appeared in the February and March 1955 issues of *Astounding*, a story of which he was quite proud. Some have hypothesized that he lost interest in Paratime, or changed his views on alternate probabilities— until, for lack of other ideas, he was forced to recast "When in the Course..." into "Gunpowder God." The diaries show that Piper hadn't forgotten the Paratime series, but just didn't have any story ideas that fit into the concept.

Piper spent the day occupied with the usual chores while his mind sifted through this new idea. By evening, he wrote this: "This is going to be a civilization in which the slaves run everything because the masters have delegated everything to them and allowed them to take over all problems of management."[8] What we see here is the germ of the idea for "A Slave Is a Slave," which ended up being put into the Terro-Human Future History instead of the Paratime series.

The new story idea didn't seem to be going anywhere and was shelved — for the time being — while Beam went through the usual Piper rigmarole for story generating, involving lots of *mea culpas* and angst. "Seem to be suffering from idea constipation. Still trying to get a story put together and getting nowhere on it. Running out of both food and money. Knocked off work about 2100, completely frustrated — story seems no good at all. Hope some kind of idea arrives; don't like to dump the whole thing."[9]

Knerr writes: "By March 4th, he was still struggling to get something worked into shape, but everything was a problem. He dug out his copy of Toynbee's *A Study of History*, searching for something to write about. Ken White wrote to him that McMorris had received *Junkyard Planet*. 'No idea,' he wrote, 'when they'll get around to mailing the check, or even if they will without wanting a lot of revisions.'"[10]

By end of March, "A Slave Is a Slave" had "gotten sick and died." However, he had a new idea: "think I have something for a short novelette — a race who feel rather than hear sounds; effect of new mechanical noises introduced by Terrans."[11]

April 10, 1961, was tax time, and Piper drew a dark cloud around the date, writing "Day of Disaster." He was still having trouble with the first-first draft of "Naudsonce." "Out P.M. to get my Income Tax fixed up — this time it cost me $40.00, counting Social Security, the latter a damned piece of extortion." Another roof leak the next day, "Snow on roof melting and leaking through badly into gunroom. At a little after 2200, a piece of ceiling plaster came down, about a square yard of it. Made some clearance of rubble, nothing else I could do, and then back to work on story planning. Whole gunroom in a hell of a mess." He called Wetzel and Rider, the landlord's agents, and they patched the leaks.[12]

By the end of April, Piper had thrown away all his previous work on "Naudsonce." "Read back on yesterday's work, very much dissatisfied. Out to get second sheet paper." He got home a little before noon, and after lunch began manufacturing wastepaper again, realizing that the story was both badly planned and badly written. "By late P.M. came to the conclusion that everything so far will have to be done over. Started on it after dinner, and kept at it till almost midnight, got 15 pages done."[13]

He kept doing his usual corrections, throwing away a dozen pages, then rewriting them. On May 2, he wrote: "Looked at the stuff I did today — terrible — will have to do it over."[14] Somehow he managed to finish another rewrite and still get it into the mail by May 4, 1961. At the same time, the cavalry arrived, in the form of a check from John W. Campbell for reprint rights to "Omnilingual" and a letter from his agent.

"Ken White says (cross fingers) that there may be a chance for a sale on *Little Fuzzy*," Piper wrote. "This has happened so many times before, though."[15] It appears Ken had a lot of faith in *Little Fuzzy*, since he had long since stopped trying to sell Piper's mystery novel and numerous mystery short stories. Ken's faith was well placed, considering the story has since become one of the most beloved tales in science fiction.

With "Naudsonce" off to his agent and money in the bank, Piper took it easy for a few days, working on story ideas and making notes for "Only the Arquebus." "Naudsonce" sold right away to *Analog* and Beam was paid $502.20 (less 10 percent) on May 23; he celebrated with dinner at the Lycoming Hotel. Afterwards, Piper went back to work on his historical novel. On May 31, he wrote: "The whole thing is a hopeless clutter of characters, historic events, fiction incidents, situations. Sometimes it looks as though I have too much story, and sometimes I don't have enough. Beginning to think that I should take a long rest from the Great Wars of Italy and do something else for a while. Detective story?"[16]

More typewriter trouble, this time with the new two-toned Smith Corona. "Trouble with typewriter — this machine is no damned good."[17] I had one of the early 1960s' two-toned Smith Coronas myself and it literally fell apart after a couple of years, and I wasn't typing half the wordage Piper was putting out.

On June 6, Piper took the train to New York for a Mystery Writers of America meeting. While in New York, he had lunch with Ken White and Bill McMorris of Putnam's. He wrote, "Nothing much came of it, but it lasted most all afternoon."[18] It's unfortunate that Beam hadn't worked up another juvenile for Putnam's in the weeks before the meeting; the two novels he wrote for Putnam's were among his best books and certainly went smoother than anything else he wrote during this period. He wrote the two of them in less time than it took him to write *Little Fuzzy*, which took years to find a publisher. It would have made more sense than working on another detective story which would never sell.

Writing a juvenile novel a year, like Heinlein did, would have been money in the bank and built up a core of young fans who might well have bought Piper's other novels. Heinlein worked that strategy to perfection and his juveniles were of the same caliber as Piper's.

Instead, Piper went to work on a mystery and after a week's work came up with "Juvenile Specialist," which he finished on July 12. It never sold. He was back to selling his pistols to Dick Houser for rent and food money. He put "Only the Arquebus" aside and tried his hand at another mystery, but the story idea was too complicated for a short and not weighty enough for a novel; after a week of frustration, it was abandoned and he went back to "A Slave Is a Slave" at the end of July.[19]

On July 3, he wrote: "Ernest Hemingway reported killed 'while cleaning a shotgun' — a suicide?"[20]

He spent the next month fighting with the first draft of "A Slave Is a Slave." But one thing about Piper: as much as he might fight a story out, once he had it firm in his mind and a complete first draft — he just ran with it. By the 18th of September he was well into the final draft, when interrupted by his agent. "He reports *Little Fuzzy* sold, after all these years to Avon. Will have to be some work done cutting it down at end, don't know what." At the bottom of his diary page he drew in red a fuzzy jumping up and down going, "Yeeeek!"[21]

"A Slave Is a Slave" was set aside while he worked on the *Little Fuzzy* revisions. "Called Janet, at Avon, in New York," he wrote on September 19: "She wants the last eighth or tenth of story compacted and a lot of the end-tying eliminated. Sat around for a while wondering what the hell to do next. Decided to use last half of version II and splice it to beginning of version I."[22]

Janet Wood had high hopes for *Little Fuzzy*, including Fuzzy dolls, a movie and all kinds of merchandising spin-offs. Therefore, it's not surprising that she was anticipating future Fuzzy novels and wanted the ending to *Little Fuzzy* to be open-ended. If the *Little Fuzzy* movie had been made and done right, it's quite possible there would have been some kind of Fuzzy mania. After all, this was the era of the hula-hoop, coonskin hats and Beatlemania. Piper, on the other hand, never thought in terms of series books; he had enough trouble finishing one novel without worrying about foreshadowing and setting up possible sequels. As desperate as he was in 1955 for salable story ideas, Piper never thought to do the sequel to "Time Crime," the ending of which is as open-ended as anything he ever wrote.

It was part of John W. Campbell's genius as an editor that he saw editing not as an end to his own writing career, but as a way to get an entire clan of writers writing *his* stories! Janet Wood saw the Fuzzy story as a great springboard for more tales, and history has proven her right. In fact, even before his death Piper was bedeviled by fans wanting more "of those damn Fuzzies!"—even when he couldn't find a publisher to buy them. An irony not completely lost on Piper himself.

Piper worked for a few days splicing the two versions of *Little Fuzzy* together, coming up with *Little Fuzzy* version III, which he then sent off to Ken. He took a holiday for a few days and then went back to work on "A Slave Is a Slave," the original title being, "A Slave Is a Slave Is a Slave."

Knerr writes: "Most of the young men in the Creative Writing Forum were gone; Williamsport is one of those rust belt towns where any youngster with grit and brains leaves as soon as possible. Piper had this to say: 'In evening, to meeting of Writing Forum at Cynthia Hoover's—now I am the only man among nine women.' At the bottom of the page he writes, 'Money dangerously low.'"[23]

The contract for *Little Fuzzy* arrived on September 26, but the money situation was getting serious again. When he completed "A Slave Is a Slave," Piper didn't have enough money to mail it to New York. He wrote, "If you can't eat, the next best thing is to sleep." Dinner was "some ice flavored with chili-sauce, and snippets of Vienna sausage. It was sort of good."[24]

Things got bad again in early October 1961, while Piper waited for his advance for *Little Fuzzy*. On the 2nd: "Up town, bled the bank account for another three dollars—now only two dollars left—and did some shopping." On Saturday, October 7, Piper wrote: "Got ready for a dash to the bank before noon to see if the check came—it did not. Have been trying to tell myself to stop worrying; nothing I can do about it. The situation is very bad, however. Only have 26 cents left, and all I had to eat today was six slices of bread and honey, and a little frozen pudding for breakfast. Don't know what the hell I'll do if the money doesn't come Monday."[25]

By Sunday Piper was down to his last couple of slices of bread and a pudding for breakfast. He had cut way back on his smoking, to a pipe full in the morning and one at night. "One left for breakfast tomorrow. Worked a couple of double-crostics; these are wonderful sanity savers—if I have any left to save.

"Monday—no check."[26]

Tuesday, October 10: "Up 0900. Today I was really expecting the check to come. It didn't. I keep telling myself it will surely come today; when it doesn't, I'm sure it will come tomorrow. After all, I did get the contract for it, didn't I? So I try to work, and I can't think of anything but what I'm going to eat when the check does come. And smoke fresh tobacco instead of crumbs salvaged from a bag of ashtray dumpings in the wastebasket. And I simply can't keep my mind on a lot of Spaniards in Italy in 1502. Beginning to feel weak and tired. No signs of hallucinations, yet. Shorter than usual of breath, heart acting up. Hope no permanent damage."[27]

The first question that comes to mind is: Why the hell didn't Piper sell another one of his guns? It's as if he's a kid playing with fire—daring fortune to pay up or burn him up!

The next day he bought another loaf of bread, which left him with 6 cents. As Mike Knerr puts it: "People 'in the arts' expect to run into problems with money and food—it comes with the territory. More than once I have listened to discussions about how rotten this country treats creative people, and it has a tendency to be amusing. We all knew, going in, that it would be rough, and Piper knew it as well. No one twisted his arm to make him what he was—nor any other writer for that matter. As Jack Woodford said: 'If it wasn't hard, any little mug could muscle in on the racket.'"[28]

On October 11, the check arrived; it was for $787.50. After eating and paying his bills, Piper went to his tailor shop to buy a new custom suit! The shop was closed: "Hope he hasn't gone out of business." No, he was sick, and Piper arranged for another custom suit to be made on October 13, "Gray tweed, this time."[30] It's hard to say whether this was the triumph of optimism over experience, or just Beam's way of poking fate in the eye with a sharp stick — if so, it usually came right back at him.

His month of near starvation forgotten, Beam decided he didn't like the gray tweed; instead he had a plain gray suit made that cost him $260.00.[30]

A few days later he put away the historical novel again and went to work planning *Space Viking*, deciding he had "a good story" in mind.[31] One has to wonder how much of this "historical science fiction novel" which was to take place in his own Future History was inspired, or even driven, by his work on "Only the Arquebus." For most writers, the old cliché— everything and anything is grist for the mill — is a truism, and it certainly was for Piper.

On October 31, he got the second check for *Little Fuzzy* (almost found money after two years of rejections) and he "just loafed around — I never can get any work done the day the money comes."[32]

Along with *Space Viking*, Piper had an idea for a story collection of his Terro-Human Future History stories. According to Mike Knerr: "It was for an anthology of his short stories, with interpolative sections in between explaining them. The stories he wanted to use were 'The Edge of the Knife,' 'Omnilingual,' 'Naudsonce,' 'Oomphel in the Sky,' 'Ministry of Disturbance' and 'The Keeper.' Piper wrote, 'Have doubts about it, both as to merit and salability.'[33] An anthology might have shed a lot more light on the scope of his 'history of the future' and how it had developed, but nothing ever came of it. It isn't known whether or not he ever broached the subject to a publisher, or even Ken White."

Interestingly enough, twenty-five years later I used almost the same lineup, with a few additions and deletions, for *Federation*: the first H. Beam Piper anthology featuring stories from the Terran Federation period of his Terro-Human Future History. Some of the other stories, "Ministry of Disturbance," "The Keeper" and "A Slave Is a Slave," appeared in a follow-up book about the later Galactic Civilization, titled *Empire*.

Piper flew to New York in early November to meet with Ken and John W. Campbell about "A Slave Is a Slave" and the revisions Campbell wanted him to make. Before leaving for the airport, he visited Janet Wood at Avon, who showed him the cover for *Little Fuzzy*. "The people at Avon are full of plans for pictorization [sic], Little Fuzzy dolls. My fingers determinedly crossed on all this."[34] Sadly, none of it worked out, but not before Janet asked Beam to do a sequel.

Back in Williamsport, Piper went to work on the Campbell-requested revisions for "A Slave Is a Slave": "Finally finished — I hope I've made the point, without over-making it, that the proletariat aren't good and virtuous, only stupid, weak and incompetent."[35] It went into the mail on the 13th and he went right back to work on *Space Viking*, one of his finest novels.

He took time out from planning the new novel to give a lecture on the Battle of Cerignola to John Hunsinger's students at Lycoming College. Ironically, the man who was thrown out of high school was asked to give a lecture on history at the local college. On December 6, he gave the talk and thought it was "a very poor performance, but the customers seemed to like it."[36] More Piper understatement.

"Letter from Bill Stroup," Piper wrote; "he wants to get Ken White as his agent. Not in favor of idea myself; don't think Ken White would want to handle him."[37] Bill Stroup was a member of the Creative Writing Forum, trying to break in to a writing career.

Piper spent the next couple of days working on *Space Viking*, "writing and tearing up beginnings." He also got the new *Analog*, which featured "Naudsonce." "Also review, brief but very favorable, by Schuyler Miller of *Four-Day Planet*. Started reading the latter over to see if it's really as good as Miller says—I think it is—and didn't get to bed till 0500, which really sets a record."[38]

He was down to writing the first chapter of *Space Viking* when he got a letter from Ken White telling him that he had the check for "A Slave Is a Slave." "He is also separated from his wife and in financial straits—wanted to borrow a hundred from me till the first of March. I agreed. Hope this doesn't turn out like Fred Pohl's divorce."[39] Fred, Piper's first agent, had gone through some tough times after breaking up with his first wife. He and Piper had a misunderstanding over some money and Piper, who wasn't one to forgive and forget, still nursed a grudge.

Piper received the check for "A Slave Is a Slave" on December 22, 1961. He was having problems with *Space Viking* so he put it aside and celebrated Christmas dinner with Ted and Mary Ranck and, of course, a good drunk.

On the 27th of December, Ted (one of the original "Unholy Trinity") picked him up and they went to the Colemans' house to celebrate Freida's third wedding anniversary. Piper had reached chapter two of *Space Viking* by New Year's Eve, and he knocked off writing "and made ready to greet the New Year—a better one than 1961, I hope not too optimistically—with three shots from the 'eensy' brass cannon."[40]

Chapter 30

Space Viking

As long as a book would write itself, I was a faithful and interested amanuensis and my industry did not flag; but the minute the book tried to shift to my head the labor of contriving its situations, inventing its adventures, and conducting its conversations I put it away and dropped it out of my mind. The reason was very simple ... my tank had run dry; the story ... could not be wrought out of nothing.

— Mark Twain

Piper started New Year's Day off writing and plotting *Space Viking* and later working double-crostics. "Had a couple of drinks at the Lycoming and home to a dinner of pork and sauerkraut, which I had been boiling all day."[1] The new novel was in the agonizing period, where he was writing mostly scrap paper, and he was still beating his brains to work out plot and character complications.

Piper flew to New York on January 18, 1962, to meet with Ken White and attend a Hydra Club meeting. Beam had reason to feel good about himself, money in the bank and a new novel, *Little Fuzzy*, coming out. Also, he was selling all his new short stories to John W. Campbell without having to shop them around in a drastically reduced market. There were now less than half a dozen science fiction magazines and most of the "pulp" writers were out of business.

Piper was not so fortunate with his mystery stories; he never sold another one, and from then on they play a less and less significant role in his life. On January 24, he learned that *Little Fuzzy* was on the stands. "Letter from Ray Young — he says *Little Fuzzy* out — why haven't I heard about this? — and he says he enjoyed it. Hope millions of others do."[2]

In early February, he was still working out the complications of *Space Viking*, including removing unnecessary characters "who didn't seem to be doing much for the story" and revising up to chapter five.[3] *Space Viking* is a complex work and has a number of time and location shifts to even complicate it further; it's not surprising that it was giving him considerable grief.

He received a letter from Ken White on Valentine's Day with some fan letters and a note to the effect that — no surprise here — Janet Wood, at Avon Books, wanted a Fuzzy sequel. For someone who wrote in two distinct "universes," it's odd that Beam didn't do more sequels; after all, his projected history of Pennsylvania was to be a trilogy. "Don't know what this could be, but can try," he wrote. He drew a red heart at the top of the diary page and filled it with, "Beam Still Loves Betty."[4]

On February 20, 1962, he wrote: "During lunch, became engrossed in the double-crostic I have been trying to construct for the past four or so years from a Machiavellian quotation, and have struggled with it all afternoon." Piper spent the evening at the Creative Writing Forum and when he returned home, he went back to work on the double-crostic: "Mercenary captains are either very capable men or not; if they are, you cannot rely upon them, for they will always aspire to their own greatness, either by oppressing you, their master, or be oppressing others against your intentions, but if the captain is not an able man he will generally ruin you.'" "Kept at it until wee small hours, and, by the Jesus! I got it finished!"[5]

Throughout February and March Piper was still having troubles working out the plot of *Space Viking*. On March 7, he wrote, "Worked all morning planning what I most devoutly hope is the final form of the story. Intended getting to work after dinner, but didn't. Just slumped and dozed and read. Felt like hell."[6]

Fan mail was trickling in from *Little Fuzzy*. On March 10, 1962: "A letter today, forwarded by Janet Wood, from a little girl in New Mexico, who wants me to send her a Fuzzy. Will have to write her — yes, Virginia, there are Fuzzies. Don't know exactly how." A welcome distraction from the typical plot morass a Piper story fell into before magically coming together in a rush of work. "Wrote a letter to the little girl — yes, there are Fuzzies, but we don't have any here."[7]

As Mike Knerr tells it: "The little girl's name was Margaret Ward, and she couldn't have picked a better time to write him. Beam was dragging himself through *Space Viking*, fighting to get the novel firm in his mind and even more firmly on paper. The letter made him laugh and melted his heart as well. It was the only piece of fan mail he ever framed. 'By Gawd,' he chuckled, when he told me about it, 'I wish to hell I *had* a Fuzzy to send her!'"[8]

Piper was still having trouble "getting narrative worked out, action sequence," but he was making progress. By April 1, he had 211 pages of the first draft: "Believe I will start final drafting tomorrow and do the last 50 or so pages of first draft when I get to it. May save me more work than it will make."[9] For the new few days he worked from 9:00 A.M. to after midnight and rarely left his typewriter. He managed to reach 77 pages in the final. Again, money was running out. "Things are back where they were last fall — the money is run out again. Things are worse than they were last fall; much worse. No money due me except $100.00 from Ken White."[10]

Income tax was higher; his writing income for the last year had been far over average. His income tax was $73.55: "Not as bad as I expected."[11]

On April 17, he reached page 185 and was getting close to his word budget. "Don't know what to do with story. Want to keep ending originally planned, but it will make story too long — want to work up some kind of a slam-bang ending in the 70-odd pages I have left, and can't think of one."[12]

On April 29, he wrote: "Worked on story all day — wasn't out at all. Finished to page 223 — too much wordage, and too much story left to tell. Don't know how I'm going to get it finished up in 50 more pages and that's the most I can allow myself."[13] Mike Knerr writes, "This is a rather puzzling entry and, naturally, Beam does not explain it. Apparently he set limits on himself, where wordage was concerned — unless this was something John Campbell had laid out. Most book publishers have a minimum word limit.... In 1962 that limit was 50,000 words, since then it has risen in direct proportion to the cover price."[14]

Piper's target market for all the science fiction he wrote was John W. Campbell's *Astounding/Analog* since he paid the highest rates and had the quickest pay-off time in the magazine business. Plus, he almost always got the Analytical Lab bonus from Campbell. To Piper, who was always broke, Campbell was the first and best market. In addition, the advances Piper was getting from Ace and Avon were far less than Campbell was paying. The best deal was to sell the first North American serial rights (for magazine publication) to *Analog* and then turn around and sell the paperback rights to Avon or even Ace Books, which was the primary salvage market and picked most of its inventory (especially for the Ace Doubles) from the magazines.

Of course, Campbell didn't like filling his monthly magazines with long novelettes, or worse a novel that would have to be serialized over several issues. He had to *really* like a yarn to serialize it; plus, he almost always had more novelettes on tap than he could use.

Somehow, some way, Piper managed to finish *Space Viking* by the 8th of May and was already thinking of the Fuzzy sequel on the 9th: "After dinner started re-reading *Little Fuzzy*. At it all evening till 0200, and off to bed. Feel just plain bushed after finishing *Space Viking*."[15]

Piper never planned on a *Little Fuzzy* sequel; in conversations with Jerry Pournelle he mentioned he thought it was one of his lesser works, probably due to its reliance on an overly cute alien critter.[16] To then have to go back and force out a sequel was painful. And it shows: "Spent A.M. doodling on story. Ideas don't seem to be arriving in any great numbers."[17] His wry wit was still intact, though.

On May 11, he wrote: "Money situation becoming very critical." This probably helped motivate him to work out the plot tangles for the *Little Fuzzy* sequel: for once, this novel had an eager editor waiting for it. He now had a title, *Fuzzy Sapiens*.[18]

Then some good news: "Campbell is taking *Space Viking* as a four-part serial, wants me to indicate installment breaks and write synopsis up for last three sections. Avon doesn't want it — Janet doesn't think it is in keeping with *Little Fuzzy*."[19] About that, Mike Knerr has this to say: "I invite anyone to try and figure *that* kind of logic out. *Space Viking*, in my not so humble opinion, stands as one of the best novels Beam ever wrote — and just what the hell did the book have to do with the Fuzzy thing? If Janet thought that Piper was just going to sit in Williamsport and crank out *Little Fuzzy* adventures just for Avon, she had another think coming.

"We laughed about it a lot, while Beam struggled to find a decent plot for the sequel. 'Hell, yes, we'll do "Little Fuzzy and the Jewels of Ophar"; "Little Fuzzy and the Golden Lion" and "Little Fuzzy at the Earth's Core." ... How's your drink? I'll get us a refill.'

"It was fun, but it never happened that way. The only way the Fuzzy series came about was through sheer struggle. Beam would have been the last person to admit it, but the Fuzzy books would eventually drive him up the wall."[20]

Piper's immediate financial problems were solved on May 25, when he received a $500 advance from Campbell for *Space Viking*. He went to work on the synopsis for John Campbell and sent it out on the 28th. The balance of $1,714 for *Space Viking* arrived on May 30, and Beam put $500 into a savings account in case money became scarce again.[21] He made more than three times the amount he got from Avon Books for the original novel, *Little Fuzzy*, and he was free to sell the *Space Viking* book rights to another publisher.

He was in high spirits and on June 5, wrote: "to Writers' Club meeting at Katherine Hoover's— I took three bottles of champagne, treat on *Little Fuzzy*, who promised drinks for the crowd when he got published." The following day *Analog* featured "a rave review of *Little Fuzzy*," and H. Beam Piper was as happy as he was ever going to be.[22]

In early June, *Space Viking* was rejected by New American Library, and on June 7, Piper decided to go to New York to talk to Ken and John W. Campbell about future stories after receiving this very generous letter from Campbell dated June 5, 1962:

Dear Mr. Piper:
I don't know what plans you have for a next story project, but the world-picture you've been building up in the Sword World stories, or Space Viking stories, or whatever you designate the series, offers some lovely possibilities.

Space Viking itself is, I think, one of the classics—a yarn that will be cited, years hence, as one of the science-fiction classics. It's got solid philosophy for the mature thinker, and bang-bang-chop-'em-up action for the space-pirate fans. As a truly good yarn should have!

One of the beauties of the set-up you've got is that it allows the exploration of cultures of almost all conceivable levels of complexity and technology. They can be examined either internally or externally—i.e., either by a native, or by a visitor.

Try this concept on for possibilities:

Mr. Campbell goes on for a page and a half sketching a possible Utopian culture and then challenges Beam to write him a yarn:

> If one of the old Federation techniques they've preserved was a genetic technique of the order of Heinlein's *Beyond This Horizon*, their Utopia would really be stable. The rulers would be just as much locked in the cultural system as the workers—as the queen is locked in the bee-culture. But they'd be good rulers—by imposed choice!
>
> What could—or should!—the Organization of Civilized Worlds do about such a planet? Why shouldn't a real, functioning Utopia be allowed to continue operations?
>
> Regards
> John W. Campbell[23]

Piper met with Campbell and Ken White in New York for lunch, but never pursued the Campbell story idea. While there, he talked with Janet Wood and showed her the *Analog* review of *Little Fuzzy*. At a Mystery Writers of America cocktail party he "met Cornell Woolrich; we continued drinking at a couple of bars afterward. Finally got back to the hotel around 0300."[24]

Back at the typewriter, Piper was finding the *Little Fuzzy* sequel tough going. "Still having trouble; can't get beyond the beginning." On July 1, he wrote, "Think I'm getting somewhere—dumping a lot of story complications that had been giving me trouble."[25] He didn't start on the first draft until July 6. "Will send in a few chapters and synopsis for an advance—swore I'd never do that again, but need money and so does Ken White."[26]

Knerr writes: "Besides Beam, Kenneth White's only other major client was James Blish and he was never prolific. Ken was still having financial difficulties due to his divorce. Beam, no matter how much he made, seemed unable to budget his finances. It just dribbled away within a few months."[27]

Piper continued work on *Fuzzy Sapiens* but had to curtail his working hours; he was having trouble working nights. "Didn't get back to work after dinner—why can't I work in the evenings anymore? Will have to get back to it."[28] He received a bonus check for $112.50 for "A Slave Is a Slave" along with a rejection of *Space Viking* from Monarch Books.[29]

He was having all the usual plotting and runaway character problems with *Fuzzy Sapiens* and it took him a month and a half—till August 15—to get the synopsis and the first few chapters done and mailed off to Janet Wood at Avon. He continued trying to plot out the story as he wrote it and was in a constant state of agitation. Knerr notes: "Beam would have rather cut his own throat then let any of us (the Creative Writing Forum) know that he was having so damned much trouble setting up a plot line."[30]

On August 29, Piper wrote: "Spent most of the day being frustrated. By evening I had given up hope of accomplishing anything." Ken wrote to tell him that *Little Fuzzy* had been sold to the Italian market for $270 and that Avon had approved the chapters and synopsis, with contract and advance to follow.[31]

On August 31, 1962, Piper flew to Chicago for ChiCon, the annual World Science Fiction Convention. "To hotel, and fell in at once with friends—partying started early P.M. and kept up all night literally. Got to bed about 0600."

The next day, "Up 1100. To Coffee Shop for breakfast, and then panel discussion, talks, auction sale. Masquerade party in evening and more parties—details rather vague—Jerry Pournelle and I singing? Lasted until 0600 again."

At the bottom of the page he put: "SECOND COMING OF CHRIST AT HAND—FRED POHL PAID ME—"[32]

On September 2, there was more partying. The next day, Piper wrote: "Managed to get in on tail end of lecture by Willy Ley and then a muster of the Hyborean Legion, and lecture by Jerry Pournelle on warfare 1962–2000 and political discussion which was adjourned from 1530 to 1730. Out for dinner, very tough shish kabobs. Partying resumed, first in my room and then in Robert Heinlein's. This time I fell out at 0400."[33]

After Piper's return to Williamsport, the eye problems started up again. "Bought a pair of eyeglasses at Woolworth's for a dollar and a half; amazed at the improvement in reading. They are reading glasses only—range up to '24'—but print looks clearer than I can remember it looking. Eyes don't get tired, either." Mike Knerr notes: "The Piper vanity, however, kept the glasses in secret. I never saw him wear them."[34]

On September 14, 1962, the contract for *Fuzzy Sapiens* arrived, and Piper signed it and sent it back. However, he was only on page 14 of the new book. He was still unable to work evenings, his most productive period of the day. He doesn't mention them at this point, but his backaches continued to plague him. They were at their worst at night, which was to be expected since Piper spent most of the day hunched over his typewriter. "Wish I could get back to work in evening—used to be able to work in evenings, that used to be my best time."[35]

Piper was throwing money away again, purchasing a new overcoat for $140. On October 1, the advance for *Fuzzy Sapiens* arrived: "Check from Ken White, advance of $875.00, less 10%, $787.50 arrived. Now I have to get the goddamned thing done." This Fuzzy novel was as slow going as the first one. He'd only reached page 58 by October 8. Not much enthusiasm for it, either. He was lucky to bang out five or six pages on a good day. He was outside a lot, reading or just loafing. The lack of progress and plot frustration—"Trouble seems to be, too much story; can't keep it simple"—kept him from enjoying his off hours. He was back to reading Prescott's three volume *Ferdinand and Isabella*, which wasn't helping the new book.[36]

On December 19, 1962, he wrote Jerry Pournelle: "I got home from the convention alive, sort of, and have been working on this infernal '*Little Fuzzy*' sequel ever since; wrote more or less completely, and scrapped at least three versions of it, and am now half done in final draft with what will be the final version. I had hoped to finish by the end of the year; now fear it will run me into the middle of January. There must be easier ways of making a living than this."[37] This lack of progress on *Fuzzy Sapiens* is confirmed by his diary entry of the 21st, "Worked on story—finished another short chapter XVI to page 150, nine pages. Had to transfer $200.00 from savings to checking account. Can't let this happen again till the former is filled in some more."[38]

Then it all went to hell again; on December 24 Piper scrapped everything he'd written. "This is a horrible thing to have happen at any time, let alone the day before Christmas."[39] He began at the beginning, trying to form coherent ideas that would work; he didn't have much luck. On December 31, he wrote, "Up 0930. Gunroom too cold to work in. I moved into dining room. A day of frustration—after almost eight months, I still have nothing that even looks like a story. This was one of my worst days.

"Up town 1700, dinner at Lycoming. Ted Ranck's in evening, 2000—to his place for New Year's Eve party; much to drink, a goodly crowd. Home at 0300, and to bed. Happy New Year!"[40]

CHAPTER 31

Sequelitis

Still groping — the more sequels you pile on, the harder they come, it seems.
Wonder how Earl Stanley Gardner does it.[1]

— H. Beam Piper

H. Beam Piper started the New Year of 1963 with a bang: "Up 1100. Had breakfast in dining room, but by noon the gunroom was inhabitable and moved into it. Working on an attempt to reconcile all the different Fuzzy stories I have put together in the last eight months and discarded. I don't like to mar this page with bragging or over-optimism, but this time it looks good. Mary Ranck called about 1430, inviting me to dinner — almost as big a crowd as last night, and sauerkraut was excellent. Didn't leave till 2011, and by the time I was home, felt too drowsy to do anything — read till about midnight, and to bed."[2]

This was another false start, and when the holidays were over he was back to fiddling "with story detail work, doodling and note scrawling."[3] On the 6th of January 1963, he tore up everything he'd done to date. As Mike Knerr writes, "The only thing that kept him banging away at this book and the one he would write in the future was the knowledge that Avon Books wanted them. He felt that this was more of a sure thing than the speculation he usually wrote under — and both he and Ken White needed the money. Ken, in addition to his domestic troubles, was having eye problems."[4]

Finally, on February 13, the paperback rights to *Space Viking* sold to Ace Books for a whopping $1,500 in two installments — it also came out as a novel, not one-half of an Ace Double, as his previous stories had been packaged. As Knerr writes: "This wasn't much money, considering the amount of work that had gone into the book, yet that was the going rate. One of the sad, but real truths of creative writing is that advances and royalties have never kept pace with inflation."[5]

Then, after all his struggles, *Fuzzy Sapiens* came together and he finished the novel on February 22, 1964. "Don't know what life without Fuzzies will be like, now, or what I will do next. Clean house, for one thing, I suppose." Exhausted from *Fuzzy Sapiens*, Piper went back to doodling notes on "Only the Arquebus": "Still trying to work up a fiction-story, with love interest, to match history."[6] He was still working out the mechanics of the story when the first Ace check for *Space Viking* arrived. For the time being, he was flush.

On March 22, 1963, Piper wrote: "Debby Crawford called me and wants me to help her in 'establishing a fictitious residence' in Pennsylvania. Divorce?" He had completely misunderstood the conversation. "I was April-Fooled today but good! The phone call, on the 22nd, wasn't from Debby, but from Betty — it didn't come from New York, but from France, and while I did hear something about 'fictitious residence' what it was about was that she is divorcing me. All this was explained in a letter from her today, with enclosures of some letters for me to sign, to be used as evidence.

"They were typed on French paper; I copied them on American paper and sent them off to her by airmail. Well I'd been expecting something like this, even if I had been trying to make myself believe we could get together again. Now I can stop kidding myself.

"Glad I didn't know it was Betty when I was talking to her—would have gotten emotional." At the top of the page he'd drawn a broken wedding band with a lightning streak through it and the words "All Fool's Day" beneath.[7]

As Mike Knerr notes: "The divorce wasn't over easily and it dragged on into 1964; and Beam didn't stop kidding himself at all. Like a drowning man clutching at a twig, he hung onto the idea that they would still get back together. He even sold a bunch of guns to have the money to meet her in New York while she was en route from California to Paris on February 16th, 1964. It was to be the last time they saw each other and the effect upon Beam was a great deal heavier than the diaries let on. His cast-iron refusal to compromise was beginning to have a tremendous effect on him and his career."[8]

"Just felt washed out today," Piper wrote on April 3, and comments on weariness begin to crop up more and more frequently—signs of a growing depression.[9] Four days later, he wrote, "Spent most of morning and early afternoon writing letters to Betty, tearing them up, and finally managed to get one written more or less to my satisfaction."[10] The separation was one thing, but divorce was something else—an end to all his fantasies about the two of them getting back together again. The divorce from Betty was sapping his strength and keeping him from his writing.

There was some good news, Ken White wrote: "The movie possibility for *Little Fuzzy* has become a reality—something simply called Moving Pictures Corporation [actually, the Motion Picture Company of America] is taking it, paying generously." He wasn't so pleased when he learned the same day that he was hit with an income tax payment of $344. His reaction: "Jesus!"[11]

Piper continued his fruitless doodling on "Only the Arquebus," getting nowhere fast. On the 17th of April, he flew to New York to sign contracts for the *Little Fuzzy* movie deal and attend a dinner of the Mystery Writers of America. "Saw Janet at Avon—everybody there delighted at movie of *Little Fuzzy*, and pleased with *Fuzzy Sapiens*." He and Ken had lunch at Jansson's, where they signed the contract.[12]

He was back in Williamsport on the 21st and writing another letter to Betty, which took several days. He tossed ideas around on "Only the Arquebus" until May 3, when he finally began a rough draft.

He was still waiting for the movie rights check, but it was slow in arriving. Instead he got a surprise, a check "for $226.41 from Mondadori in Milan for Italian rights on *Little Fuzzy*." The historical novel wasn't coming together, and he wrote, "worked on story, all morning on one page, must have done it over six times."[13]

All of June was wasted, flailing about with the historical novel, almost no real progress. On the 29th, Ken sent him the bonus check for *Space Viking* and the news that Avon wanted another Fuzzy book. He put away "Only the Arquebus" and began to work through ideas for another sequel—the working title was *Fuzzies and Other People*.[14]

Betty wrote again to tell him that the divorce had been postponed until October 4 and that they were still married. He was now mired in the new Fuzzy novel and totally frustrated. He received a letter from *This Week* magazine stating that they wanted 2,000-word mystery and suspense short stories. Piper went into his trunk and pulled out "Juvenile Specialist," "Precaution" and "Negative Pattern," and cut them down to the 2,000-word count and mailed them out on August 8. As Mike Knerr points out: "They never sold and five days were wasted."[15]

On July 15, Ken called to inform him that the rest of the Ace advance, $675, for *Space Viking* was in the mail, but the movie money was not forthcoming. "It seems MPC is undergoing re-organization ... going bust?" The final note was bad news indeed: "Janet Wood has been sacked at Avon — another of those publishing-house revolutions."[16] This was bad news, since Janet had been the in-house champion of *Little Fuzzy* and the sequels.

Bill McMorris writes: "About Janet Carse (Wood): I do not recall the circumstances surrounding Jan Carse's departure from Avon except that her husband, Robert Carse, was hugely annoyed about it. Bob was one of several Putnam authors who followed me to Norton from Putnam. He would mention from time to time developments with Fuzzy, i.e., possible movie interest, etc. I have the impression that Jan was eased out after changes in management at Avon, but I have no specifics."[17]

In a letter to Charlie and Marcia Brown, Piper wrote:

Dear Charlie and Marcia Almost:

In answer to your questions, which seem to be based on the situation as of our last meeting in Philly:

Space Viking is being book-published by Ace some time in August; a book all by itself, not an Ace Double-Barrel.

The sequel to *Little Fuzzy*, (*Fuzzy Sapiens*) will be published by Avon probably about the same time. I hope it is out by the time of the convention, which may stimulate sales.

For the last three months, I have been working on the historical novel, "Only the Arquebus." I have the story all plotted, and a good start made on the first draft. It is now shelved, however, since I have just had a letter from my agent telling me that Avon wants a sequel to the sequel to *Little Fuzzy*, and I want that finished and accepted as soon as possible, so the arquebus has been hung up temporarily. Inasmuch as this story is going to run to about 100–150,000 words, I never had any expectation of getting it all finished at one uninterrupted writing. If I have it finished in another two years, I will feel that I've done very well.

Little Fuzzy is also going to be a movie; I have already signed contracts on that. Beyond that, I don't know when or anything about it, except there is talk that it will be filmed in Europe, either Yugoslavia or Greece.

I am now in the process of being divorced, if my future–ex-wife can ever get her French lawyers to get all the red-tape untangled. I suspect that she just doesn't know who to bribe. We are writing to each other again, in a very cordial and friendly manner. She reports that our red dachshund, Verkan Vall, of whom she retained custody when we split up, was in a movie along with Bridgitte Bardo and Jean Gabin, a couple of years ago.

I seem to be getting to the bottom of the page. Well, best wishes, and am looking forward to seeing you both in Washington.

Beam[18]

Piper bought a big brass key from which to make an "eensy brass bombard" to go with the "eensy brass cannon." Then went back to work on the new Fuzzy novel, "getting nowhere at the speed of light."[19] He wrote a letter to the court at Nice, France, telling why he would not show up for Betty's divorce case on October 4. Then, he began to make preparations for the Washington, D.C., Labor Day science fiction World Convention where *Little Fuzzy* was a nominee for a Hugo Award for Best Novel.

He flew to Washington and spent most of his time talking and drinking with fellow science fiction professionals.

On April 26 of the previous year, Piper had noted: "Roan the auction man wanted to buy my sword cane. Turned him down, though I need money desperately — hunch?" Knerr writes: "Here again, is another Piperish entry. No real explanation, no reason — unless the reason was that Beam often carried the sword cane as a defense piece. It fit in very well with his manner of dress and no one ever knew that a twist of the gold handle could produce a yard of lethal steel. Needless to say, Beam seldom worried about the puny effect of a switch-blade knife."[20]

Jerry Pournelle explained why Piper would not part with the cane sword: "While at the '72 Discon, Beam and I were walking the streets of Washington D.C. late at night in search of a liquor store for some potables since the convention stocks were low in the Green Room. On one lonely stretch, we were approached by a young mugger, who demanded our wallets. When we refused, he sallied forth with his switchblade knife. Beam laughed and drew his sword out of the cane, raising it *en garde*, crying 'Aha!' The would-be-mugger fled as though he'd just seen a ghost."[21]

Piper truly enjoyed such exhibitions and, had the mugger not taken flight, was fully capable of running him through — and even finishing the job. It's hard to imagine him, regardless of his financial situation, ever selling the cane sword.

On August 31, he wrote, "Costume ball in evening, followed by party in Randy Garrett's room till 0500. Banquet and Hugo Award presentation was September 1st. Disappointed that *Little Fuzzy* didn't make it."[22] Having a Hugo Award, science fiction's equivalent to the Oscar, would have given Piper's career a big boost.

The next morning, "Met Fritz Leiber, Randy Garrett, Judy Merril at breakfast, and immediately became involved in a skit which was to be put on at end of convention. We put it on about 1530 — it was a 'catastrophy.' Afterward the convention started coming apart." He had to "chase like hell" to get his plane back to Williamsport the next day.

"Still groping, the more sequels you pile on, the harder they come, it seems.... At this all morning, and gave it up after lunch." It wasn't until September 14 that he appeared "to have 'groped' up something that looks like an idea." He continued with his usual stop and go production of wastepaper and over the next week wrote twelve pages. "Read in evening — seems I can't seem to force myself back to work in the evening."[23]

As Knerr notes: "D-day, as Beam called it, was October 4th: 'This is the day Betty's divorce action is supposed to come up in Nice.'"[24] Very little writing was done during and after the 4th. On October 7, he heard again from Betty: "Letter from Betty — the divorce went through, at 1117 Friday. Got nothing written, but think I have finally gotten something to use for a story."[25]

On October 21, he learned: "Letter from Betty — it seems we aren't divorced at all. All this business in court she reported in her last letter was just preliminary — there will have to be some delay before the actual decree is granted." On top of this he lost a five dollar bill: "a dreadful disaster now."[26]

Piper tore up what he'd written, discarded material and characters he no longer needed. "Down to where eating has become a problem," he wrote. Money was tight again and like a captain he battened down the hatches, laying in supplies for the coming storm — "coffee and tobacco enough to last awhile. Wrote a very strong letter to Ken White." Things were going from bad to worse. On November 12, he wrote, "Up 1000. Worked on final draft most of morning and early P.M., out for walk late P.M. First draft in unholy mess. Decided to do some final draft to pull it back into order — this is always an act of desperation."[27]

On November 14, Piper wrote: "Tried to get Ken White on the phone all evening without success. At least, phone rang so he still has one, and is presumably not dead."[28] Two days later he received the movie advance for *Little Fuzzy* and his financial problems were set aside — for a while. New dentures and the usual expenses, rent, utilities, food, rum; now, he was able to concentrate on writing *Fuzzies and Other People* again. He even brought the first part of the new novel to the Creative Writing Forum to get some feedback.

Knerr writes: "Probably everyone said it was great and, likely, so did I, although I don't remember that particular meeting. Piper didn't like it. He had this to say: 'Read some *Fuzzies and Other People*— dissatisfied with how it sounded. Think too much expository matter. Don't want to do all this over again, but think I ought to ... am convinced I'll have to go back and do over the first couple of chapters, too windy, too much straight exposition and recapitulation of previous stories.'"[29]

On November 22, Piper wrote: "Out late P.M. and had dinner at Rice's. Met an acquaintance who told me that President Kennedy had been shot and killed by an assassin in Dallas, Texas, today. Mike Knerr in this evening with some more news—the assassin probably uncaught, one suspect arrested. Shooting done with a rifle, telescoped-sighted Winchester 30–30? From a window, Kennedy and others with him in car shot, several killed."[30]

Knerr writes, "I went down to Beam's apartment with very little information, but he had learned that it had been a military rifle. I remember his statement to me that night. 'Now that,' he said flatly, 'is taking your politics too damned serious.'"[31]

On November 25, Piper left his apartment and "got lunch, and then up town. Found everything closed, banks, stores and all—mourning for President. Picked up a newspaper—it seems that Lee Oswald, the suspect the Dallas police were holding, was shot and killed by some local character while being transported from one jail to another. To keep him from talking?"[32]

The French dental plate, which had been giving him nothing but trouble since he'd had it made, needed replacing. With money in the bank, he decided to replace his false teeth and take a trip to New York for a Mystery Writers of America dinner on December 4.

Meanwhile, he was still slogging away on *Fuzzies and Other People*. Piper arrived in New York around noon and after checking into a hotel, took his French letters to the consulate, "where I found out little or nothing. Waiters at St. Denis more helpful. Appears I am not yet divorced. To MWA meeting. Naturally, much talk about the latest and greatest crime."[33]

He met with Ken White, but didn't find much to his liking. "This is one of the most pointless trips I have ever made to New York."[34]

Back in Williamsport at the typewriter, he found the going just as pointless: "Spent A.M. going over the story to date. Don't like it at all. Finally decided it is not good—scrapped it, started over, from the beginning, and worked on it all afternoon and evening. Got 15 pages in—my God, I hope—final, final draft, to end of Chapter II, by 2230, then read till 0200 and to bed. Back where I was a month ago!"[35]

On December 20, 1963, he wrote this short postcard to Charles and Marcia Brown: "I certainly will make the London trip in '65, if still alive and solvent then. I finally got the first advance on the picture rights for *Little Fuzzy*, six months after signing contract, due largely to persistence of Ken White. I'm afraid that is all, no mention of any production date. *Fuzzy Sapiens* won't be out until some time after the first of the year. Sorry I wasn't able to make it to the Philcon: were you there? Best wishes for a happy 1964."[36]

On the 24th of December, he found his dentures in equally bad shape. He could barely eat and had pain when holding his pipe—"intolerable!" He had the dentist grind them down and then grind them some more.[37]

Once again, Piper spent New Year's Eve with the Rancks and even fired the "eensy brass bombard" at midnight. He celebrated New Year's Day with his usual pork and sauerkraut dinner "slightly burned," but the pain from his dentures made it impossible for him to eat. "Made tapioca pudding, could eat that all right." Once again it was back to the dentist's to get them to fit right; along the way he discovered he was going broke again. "Drew some more money out of bank—account now below $100.00—what the hell did I spend it all for?"[38]

CHAPTER 32

Pigeon Pie

Worked all morning on first draft, pencil. Fried the pigeon for lunch in deep fat; delicious. Have moved the .22 Smith & Wesson to the kitchen in hopes of getting another one.[1]

— H. Beam Piper

The movie money held the wolf at bay into the new year, but not as long as he had hoped. New dentures and the usual expenses devoured it so that by the end of 1963, he was down to his last $100. *Fuzzies and Other People* was done and making its way to Avon, so his current insolvency appeared to be business as normal. But he needed cash desperately; Betty was coming to New York on February 13 and he wanted to be able to take her out to dinner.

During the first part of 1964 Piper was still hard at work on *Fuzzies and Other People* and by January 10, 1964, was up to page 135. The book was finally on track and he finished it and mailed it off to his agent on February 3. Once he smelled the end, he was off to the races.

Now he had a new project, "Worked in morning planning a new story, tentative title, 'Gunpowder God'— Paratime story about theocracy with corner on secret of making gunpowder." In part, the new story was based on the events and setting of "When in the Course...," the 1959 novelette he never could sell. "Will have to write this in three parts, 20–25,000 words apiece, since *Analog* is loaded with serials for the next three years."[2] He began with the usual doodling and planning, but mentioned that his morale was not very high.

On February 10, Piper was saved by the bell — again. "Started to write a letter and outline of my History of the Future for an English fan who wrote me c/o *Analog* three months ago. Was at it a little after noon when a miracle happened. Bill Houser put in an appearance, and I sold him five English pistols, the Nixon, the Field, the Collins d/b, the Collins pepperbox and the Manette, for $150.00 — this was a loss, but who expects full price from a dealer. At least, the pressure is off for a while. Up town P.M. to do some shopping, got in food for awhile, and got haircut."[3]

The next day he received a letter from Betty, announcing that she would be returning to France from California, on Sunday, February 16. He wrote, "I will go to New York to see her. Ken was enthusiastic about *Fuzzies and Other People*. Home 1700, read for awhile, worked on future history — I hope that blighter in Birmingham is duly appreciative."[4]

Piper was in New York at Idlewild Airport on February 16: "Betty got in 1715, right on schedule — the years show on her a bit. We had a few drinks, Daiquiris, and a delightful chat until her plane for France got in." He stayed in town for a while, then took a return bus to Williamsport and tried to sleep. "Awake all night, couldn't get to sleep at all. Arrived in Williamsport 0730, and home to bed immediately."[5]

Knerr notes: "The divorce, of course, went through, but Beam never seemed to give up hope. Although he was apt to make caustic remarks about their relationship, or to fluff off the whole thing light to anyone who might ask, inside he was neither bitter nor flippant about what had happened."[6]

Back home in Williamsport, Piper was having trouble concentrating. "Wasted the rest of the day doing nothing at all — reading, working double-crostics and otherwise avoiding work."[7] By the first week of March he was working on three drafts of "Gunpowder God," the first-first draft, the second-first draft and the first-final draft. On the 6th, he wrote, "A letter from Betty and one from Peter Weston in England thanking me for the future history letter. Started a letter to Betty; it bogged down and I gave it up."[8]

By the 13th, he was making progress, but having problems, "mostly because I'm getting too many things in for proper length of story." While things were improving on the writing end, they were not going so well on the financial end. "Food almost exhausted, money down to .93."[9] A call to Ken White on the 18th only gave him more bad news: Avon — now under a new regime — had decided not to accept *Fuzzies and Other People*. "Is now with Ace, but Satan only knows whether or when."[10] Not a surprise. The first thing the new editor had done was put the kibosh on *Fuzzy Sapiens*, giving it the ugliest, murkiest black-purple cover in paperback history — as if daring the fans to buy it. To add insult to injury — and guarantee that fans couldn't find it — they changed the title from *Fuzzy Sapiens* to *The Other Human Race*.

Typically, when a new editor comes into town, he or she scuttles all the major book prospects of his or her predecessor — after all, if they do sell well, it only vindicates the departed editor. In the industry these abandoned books are referred to as "orphans." If the new editor puts obstacles — read no publicity, few review copies, poor artwork — on their predecessor's works, well, of course, then they were bombs to begin with. Woe to the writer who gets caught in the crossfire, as Beam did with the Fuzzy sequels.

Avon never had much of a science fiction line, but a Hugo nomination for *Little Fuzzy* was big news, and they should have made a killing on the sequel. But in New York publishing, it's not *always* about the money. Ego is often the biggest coin of the realm. Writers are as disposable as cabs; there's always another one at the next corner.

Worse, for Piper, because Avon didn't want the third Fuzzy novel; as third book of a series, it was a dead-end book. Maybe if Piper could have gotten the rights reverted, he could have sold the whole Fuzzy shebang to Don Wollheim over at Ace. Wollheim, a long-time fan, knew the value of a good book, especially a good series. But, while Avon no longer wanted the Fuzzy books, the last thing they would do was revert them; after all, what if another house was able to sell the hell out of them? That would not look good to the parent company, and said editor might shortly find him- or herself in the unemployment line.

Piper was "beginning to be hungry" on his birthday, March 23. A few days later, he was working on the final draft of "Gunpowder God," but "only had some brown sugar to eat today."[11] He still had a little money in the bank and on Good Friday he went uptown to draw some money from his account. "Worked all morning, up town P.M. to get some money at the bank — banks all closed because some Jew was crucified 2000 years ago. Home, did some more work; up town about 1700; to buy a package of tobacco and a box of saltines."[12]

By March 30, Piper was down to $5.50 in his bank account and was working toward the finish of "Gunpowder God," the first Kalvan novelette, for *Analog*. He did finish it and mail it off to Ken White on April 2, and went right to work on "Kalvan Kingmaker," the next novelette in the series.

He mailed off "Gunpowder God" to Ken and began working on the next Kalvan novelette, "Kalvan Kingmaker." "Bought some tobacco — Prince Albert, my God! — and am now down to 12 cents!" A few days later he took his last two dollars out of the bank. By April 10, "Now have .25 cents, and that's all." He was living on cheese and crackers and chocolate. April 12, he wrote, "Spent the whole day alternately working and reading. Revising first draft, still in pencil, typewriter ribbon practically useless. Cooked a mess of tapioca, sugar and water, a sticky-sweet glue, which I was able to eat and that's all that can be said for it. Tobacco almost completely gone, by end of day had little less than two pipefuls left for tomorrow."[13]

Mike Knerr writes:

This sort of living, by now, was beginning to wear a little thin for Beam, and on several occasions he and I had discussed the idea of becoming "written out." It's a possibility that all writers have to consider, and it isn't an easy thing. At the age of twenty-eight, I *thought* about it but it was in the same abstract way that I thought about death.

"You think you'll ever get written out, Beam?" I asked one evening.

"Yes," he said flatly, without hesitating.

"What'll you do?"

He made his right hand into a "gun" with the index finger representing the barrel and stuck it in his mouth. He laughed.

"Jesus. That's messy."

The grin stayed on his face. "Someone else will have to clean up the mess."

He was right.

Beam was entering into one of the worst financial depressions of his writing career during the summer of 1964 and, I believe, a great deal of it had to do with his age, the situation with Betty and his declining ability at the typewriter. Through our various conversations, I'd always got the feeling that he *knew* that he couldn't produce forever, but I believe that he held out hopes of getting together a real best seller that would pull the "fat" of old age out of the fire.[14]

Piper sold a couple of pistols to his dentist, a fellow gun collector, and tried to finish "Kalvan Kingmaker." Then he got an estimated tax bill from the IRS. "Income Tax," he wrote, "amounts to $479.04 — couldn't pay it. Don't know what I'll do — that is putting it mildly."[15]

On April 20, "Worked all morning on first draft for 'Kalvan Kingmaker.' Letter from Ken White — tough shit all around — Ace, as well as Avon, has bounced *Fuzzies and Other People*, and John Campbell wants a rewrite done on 'Gunpowder God.'"[16]

Dear Ken:

We got troubles!

This is a lovely yarn; unlike many of Beam's Paratime series, he doesn't have too many individual characters named and described, until the reader tends to go slightly nuts trying to keep track of 'em.

But he does have too many words for us right now.

The situation is that we've got novels on hand and already scheduled through August 1965. Now when I run a novel installment, that takes about 25,000 words of the magazine; I can't run both a 25,000 word novel installment and a 25,000 word novelette; it wouldn't leave me enough room for the rest of the things I have to get in.

About 18,500 or so is the top length I can manage until sometime late in 1965.

He has a pair of characters in here who really aren't functional — the "blind" minstrel and the "stupid boy"; some wordage could be saved there — and Beam is still somewhat over par for the course on characters, even so.

Readers have objected to Beam's tendency to throw in detailed characterizations of dozens of individuals; the reader expects characterized personnel in a story to be important actors. Beam just enjoys describing personalities — which is fine, but gets readers lost.

If Beam can cut this to 18,500, I'll give him the full 4 cents bonus rate on acceptance.

Regards
John W. Campbell[17]

Piper rewrote it and sent it off in five days. Meanwhile, he was having the usual troubles with "Kalvan Kingmaker": "Worked all day on final draft, another re-do; this is getting tiresome, and, looking it over, I think it's going to have to be re-done again. Wasn't out at all, at it all day and typed 22 pages."[18] He found "Kalvan Kingmaker" was getting out of hand and decided to cut it into two stories to meet the word requirements at *Analog*. In the chopping, "Down Styphon!" became the second story in the proposed trio and he tried to sort them out.

On May 19, a letter from John W. Campbell and a check for a $684 advance for "Gunpowder God" arrived. He wrote: "Meant to get at it in evening, but simply surrendered to luxury of not having to give an immediate damn and got mildly potted. Letter from John W. Campbell accompanied check — he's enthusiastic about more stories of same sort. Will provide."[19]

> Dear Mr. Piper:
>
> Your yarn, as shortened, is fine; check on its way.
>
> Your suggestion for further yarns along the path you've sketched out is also fine. I'm definitely looking for stories with a bit more guts in them than the stuff that's standard American literature these days. The Apotheosis of the Common Jerk, or the Life of the Common Suburbanite, and his trials, tribulations, and insignificant temptations and naughtiness acutely disinterests me. Why authors think the frustrations and eroticisms of insignificant suburbanites are the most important materials possible for stories, I don't know.
>
> One thing I am very sure of; no story that's lived for more than a couple of centuries had a central character so vapidly incompetent as the standard "hero" of the standard modern American novel.
>
> Your Aryan-Transpacific paratime line allows for some grand yarns, with men who are damn well MEN, and women who aren't afraid to be different from men, and like it that way. It's a world where insurance hasn't been invented, and every individual is acutely and personally responsible for his own acts and behavior — which, as Bob Heinlein pointed out in "Beyond This Horizon" breeds a race having good manners, clear thinking, and fast reflexes!
>
> There's very little neurosis in such a culture. The neurotic gets himself killed off too quick to pass on his problem!
>
> ... But most particularly ... have fun! The general attitude of the conquerors of that cultural type was rather largely determined by an air of practical jokes, on a large scale, with murder, mayhem, and conquest as a sort of by-product.
>
> They had fun!
>
> Regards,
> John W. Campbell[20]

Mike Knerr brought Piper a copy of his latest Ace paperback version of *Junkyard Planet*— only Ace had re-titled it *Cosmic Computer*. He hadn't known it was even out. Piper worked hard on the new stories until the wee hours. "A little bat got in somehow; found him snoozing, upside down, at the top of the window frame in hall. With hall light on, he still thought it was still daylight — still there when I went to bed at 0130," he wrote. Knerr comments: "The bat left during the night; anyone else would have clobbered it, but if it would have hung around Piper would have fed it."[21]

Piper finished "Down Styphon!" on June 1, 1964, and went right to work on the third story, "Kalvan Kingmaker." He was hoping for a check, when instead he got a letter from Ken White: "Campbell wants rewrite on 'Down Styphon!,' long letter from Campbell enclosed." Piper was getting exasperated with all of Campbell's rewrites: "Hope this doesn't get to be a regular thing. Started re-writing; out 1900 to bank, now only have $8.00 in account."[22]

Piper managed to get "Down Styphon," the second re-titled Kalvan novelette, out the door, but all the rewrites from Campbell delayed the check. The money from "Gunpowder God" had gone quickly and by July he was again in bad shape, not only running low on food, but on writing supplies. On June 15, he wrote: "The check still not arrived; no money, practically no food." He was losing his focus on writing as his desperation grew. "Maybe I'm getting too hungry to work."[23]

On June 14, 1964, Beam wrote to Charlie and Marcia Brown:

Haven't seen a copy of what they call *The Other Human Race*, which I suppose is *Fuzzy Sapiens*. Thank you for letting me know. I don't suppose they've bothered to tell Ken White, either. I question if he'll be any more amused about this than I am.

I'm glad to hear that the paperback "Junkyard Planet" (*The Cosmic Computer*, for Christ's sake!) is selling well. I will probably be reaping the harvest in six months or so; they got the rights on it from Putnam's, and Putnam's will pay me. A paperback "Uller Uprising" I have been thinking about for some time; some day something will get done on it.

Paratime stories to date:

"Police Operation"	Astounding, July 1948
"Last Enemy"	Astounding, August 1950
"Temple Trouble"	Astounding, April 1951
"Time Crime"	Astounding, February and March 1955

Campbell has just bought another Paratime story, "Gunpowder God," and since then I have finished another which is still unreported, and am working on a third at present.

I haven't heard any more from the movie than Jim Blish has from his. Do we have an extradition treaty with Jamaica and the Bahamas? If not, that could be just the reason.

Best wishes, and try to get in touch with you — all the next time I get to NY.

Beam[24]

"Worked on first draft all day," Piper wrote on July 15: "using too many words to say the same thing too many times. Will have to get hold of this story and give it a good shaking." He added, "The check still un-arrived; no money, practically no food." As Knerr writes, "He was beginning to question the wisdom of paying his income tax so quickly and his 'desperation' about money grew over the ensuing days. By the 24th, he received a notice that the French Consulate in Philadelphia had something for him, which he suspected was the final divorce decree."[25]

By the 27th, things were starting to jell with "Kalvan Kingmaker": "All day on planning for the big battle scene, mostly trying to get the timing right. Tricky job, making everything fit. Shot one of the pigeons on the back porch with the .22 Smith & Wesson, now have to cut it up in salt water and put it in the refrigerator. I will never admit to anybody how many shots I needed at a range of ten feet to down it, but made a clean job, almost beheaded it. Writers' meeting tonight, didn't go. Could have gotten something to eat, but didn't want to have people asking, 'Why aren't you smoking?' No tobacco, no money to buy any. Worked for a while, read a little, now on *Drums Along the Mohawk*, to bed 2300. Tomorrow's menu, fried pigeon and the rest of that damned tapioca — gruel; after that —?"[26]

The next day: "Worked all morning on first draft, pencil. Fried the pigeon for lunch in deep fat; delicious. Have moved the .22 Smith & Wesson to the kitchen in hopes of getting another one. Wrote letter to Betty, up town late P.M. to mail it. Worked a little on first draft, typescript, in evening, read for a while, to bed 2300. I now have 15 cents. I have had 15 cents for a week, and I can't buy anything with it. There doesn't seem to be anything at all that can be bought for less than a quarter."[27]

On July 29: "Worked on first typescript, got another section done. Hastened to get dressed, in case check arrived today. It didn't, of course. Back to work, couldn't get started, spent all afternoon working a couple of double-acrostics. Out for walk about 1930. Found something I could buy for less than a quarter, a little bag of peanuts, half a wineglass full. Had them for dinner when I got back. They and a couple of spoonfuls of cinnamon flavored tapioca gruel were today's rations. I wish I hadn't been in such a damned rush to pay my income tax, back in June. That would have carried me for the rest of the year.[28]

"Worked on rereading, cutting down, on what I've done so far, till 0100, and to bed. Am beginning to feel a few hunger symptoms—weakness, dizziness, a general stomach-pit distress. Might be I could really starve to death, and don't seem to give a damn."[29]

Things were getting very bad, but at least he had the check for "Down Styphon!" coming. Part of the delay was that Ken White was very sick at this time; unfortunately, Ken kept that news from Piper.

On July 30, he wrote: "Working on cutting down and recasting what has already been done. Have to jettison a lot of nice bits—may be able to get them back in when I rewrite for book-form. Still nothing from Ken White. Wrote him a letter, par avion, to find out why."[30]

The next day: "Found heat on in gunroom. Typed another few pages of final first draft, worked on re-planning all morning and early P.M. Out for walk up town: got a small tin of chocolate syrup and used some to make chocolate tapioca pudding with milk, not the damned gruel I have been eating. Good. Surprising how a little food can help morale. Did some work in evening, read till past midnight, and to bed."[31]

"Kalvan Kingmaker," the third Kalvan novelette, was coming down the backstretch. On August 1, he wrote: "Worked all morning, early P.M., on planning-up to big battle; have to get my troop-strengths, movements and timing, order of battle; worked on this till mid-afternoon, then out for a walk up town, bought another small box of rice, cutting me down to 23 cents, plus a penny I found. Read in evening, to bed 2330."[32]

"Worked on pencil first draft in morning," he wrote on August 3. "No response to letter of Thursday to Ken White. Hungry; tobacco and coffee all but gone—only 25 cents. Worked most of afternoon, read in evening. To bed 2330."[33]

"The Money Came Today!!!" Beam wrote in large gold letters. He hurried to the bank and cashed the check for $513—banked most of it and did some grocery shopping. He spent the rest of the afternoon writing checks, catching up on rent, utilities and telephone bill. "Up town again 1800, did some more shopping, home 2000, after dinner at Rice's, spent evening reading, drinking highballs and nibbling."[34]

Knerr writes: "He ate more the next day, but for the first time noticed he wasn't bouncing back to form as quickly as before. After falling asleep in his chair, he wrote: 'Then felt too stupid to work, read a little, to bed at midnight. I suppose this is reaction to short rations of the last month; don't like it. Am weak, listless. Maybe if I get some food in me and put on some of the weight I lost; I'll be all right.'"[35]

Piper was spending some time on the third Kalvan novelette, but also a considerable amount of time helping the Lycoming County Historical Society set up some of their exhibits at their temporary museum on East Third Street. He was still on a shopping binge; only food this time. "Out shopping again in afternoon—the refrigerator is now positively congested in contrast to its emptiness last week and before."[36]

The constant struggle to write a salable story was getting old. For the first time in his life, Piper found himself just about completely alone: Freida Coleman had married and most of her children had left the nest, while Mike Knerr was newly married and working overtime as a reporter. Piper was weak and tired. At some point, during this period, he reached a decision: he would not allow himself to starve again—no matter what.

CHAPTER 33

Running Out of Steam

The word block suggests that you are constipated or stuck, when in truth you're empty. You feel the writing gods gave you just so many good days, maybe even enough of them to write one good book, and then part of another. But now you are having some days or weeks of emptiness, as if suddenly the writing gods are saying, "Enough! Don't bother me! I have given to you until it hurts! Please. I've got problems of my own."

— Anne Lamott

By August 4, the "Down Styphon!" money had come in and H. Beam Piper was hustling to get the new story out so that he would have some income to get him through the end of the year. *Fuzzies and Other People* was dead in the water, and the Piper story inventory was almost as bare as his kitchen cabinets the week before. With John Campbell overbooked with novels and novellas, Piper couldn't count on writing another novel, like *Space Viking*, to tide him over through the winter. His only ace in the hole was the money coming from Putnam with his share of the paperback rights to *Junkyard Planet*, probably less than $800. His plan was to sell all three Kalvan novelettes to Campbell and after they appeared in *Analog* sell the put-together novel to Ace Books.

On the 13th, Piper wrote: "Past the battle, now, and still have oodles of scenes, action, to get in."[1] In his spare time, he was helping friends set up their exhibits at the Lycoming County Historical Society temporary museum.

Mike Knerr writes: "His writing appears almost jaunty during these several days of working with friends at the museum, with no moaning at all about scrapping what he'd written. He was even working in the evening. His old friend Ted Ranck had been enlisted to help with the museum work, together with a Mr. and Mrs. Donald Carson, and there are happy notations in the diary about the men dropping by Beam's place, after work, for a couple of drinks. The story, although parts had to be re-done, was coming along at a fair rate of speed and he even found time to clean his own guns."[2]

There was another official looking letter from France on August 21, while Piper was cleaning the 9mm Mauser pistol. "Suspect that this is *It*." He went back to cleaning the Mauser and working on "Kalvan Kingmaker," which he was now calling "Hos-Hostigos."[3]

Piper was writing at a good clip, 10 to 15 pages a day, showing that when inspired he could still write the keys off a typewriter. He was going well until he was slapped with another tax bill: "Really got slapped with a sackful of shit today; seems I owe the city of Williamsport about $150.00 in taxes and tax penalties."[4]

He finished "Hos-Hostigos" and fired it off to Ken White on September 4. Enclosed was this letter to John W. Campbell:

Dear John:

Here's the third of the Kalvan stories. The original idea was that Kalvan should make his father-in-law, Prince Ptosphes, Great King; for reasons set forth in the body of the story, this didn't seem such a good idea, and Kalvan, as you will see, becomes Great King himself. Now, I am pretty much like Ike Asimov trying to figure out where to put the Second Foundation. Kalvan is Great King and Hos-Hostigos is really beginning to pick up Hos-power, but Styphon's House isn't down yet, let alone out, and the Great King of Hos-Harphax (down around Havre-de-Grace, Md.) isn't going to take this secession from his realm placidly. To carry the story on further, I'm going to have to do a lot of figuring. I still want to fight the battle of Breitenfeld at Gettysburg — Breitenfeld is an excellent battle for this cultural and technological level, and Gustavus Adolphus had about the same impact on the Austrian Empire and the Catholic Church as Kalvan is having on Hos-Harphax and Styphon's House.

The battle of Fyk, in this story, was actually fought, under the circumstances described, at Barnet, about twenty or thirty miles east of London, in 1471, between the Yorkist army under Edward IV and Richard, Duke of Gloucester, and the Lancastrain army under the Early of Warwick and the Earl of Somerset, and John Vere, Earl of Oxford, did the same thing to the Lancastrians that Balthames did to the Saksi. Even the incident of crawling forward and lying all night under the midrange trajectory of the guns is from Barnet.

This penicillin suggestion; this is the very last thing Kalvan would want to do. He doesn't want to shift Styphon's House into a new racket, he wants to smash it. As it stands, with a monopoly on gunpowder, they control the princes. But if he gets them working miraculous cures, he'd give them a popular following, which they now don't have.

I know you like victories by slick tricks, but slick tricks run out, sooner or later, and in any case they're good odds-cutters and that's all. The best answer to slick-trickery is always a fast punch in the nose. The Japanese tried that heroin trick in China, before the formal beginning of World War II, when Chiang Kai-Shek was in control. His answer to it was to kill all the heroin peddlers and all the heroin addicts, he could. Nothing like a hundred-odd grains of copper-jacketed lead injected at six or eight hundred fs at the base of the brain to cure anything. Of course, if Chiang had been a nice humanitarian type, it might have worked, but he wasn't.

So if Kalvan wants to destroy Styphon's House, and destruction is the only thing he can do about it, and wants to maintain his new Great Kingdom, he'll have to do it where it counts, on the battlefield. He can, and will, soften them up by all sorts of slick tricks; he can start them fighting among themselves — see what happened to Prince Gormoth, in this story — but when they're softened up enough, the troops will have to move in and finish it. As long as soldiers don't let statesmen, professional slick-tricksters, squander their victories at the peace conference, that settles it.

George Clemenceau made the remark that "War is too serious a business to trust to generals." Well, judging from the one he helped make at Versailles in 1919, peace is too serious a business to trust to statesmen.

Kalvan's big advantage, as will be noted, is that Styphon's hierarchy don't believe in Styphon themselves. Atheists make excellent clergymen in normal times, they never get scared by their own sermons. But offer them a chance to be martyrs and see what happens.

Yours cordially
Beam[5]

After mailing "Hos-Hostigos" and the cover letter to Ken White, Piper started work on an article on the use of firearms. "Spent morning and early afternoon working on the writers magazine article in pencil — getting it put into shape. Jan Robbins called on phone, told him about writers' meeting. About 1900, odd little incident —

"At my desk, heard hall door open stealthily. Thought it might be Jan slipping in prankishly; picked up a cutlass, also prankishly, and went down the hall. Instead, it was some perfect stranger, a young punk in dungarees, who was looking around in the hall. Surprised, scared when he saw cutlass, mumbled something about wanting to rent a room, and got out. Might have had some trouble with him, except for cutlass."[6]

Knerr writes: "That was the old H. Beam Piper and he appeared to be back to his true form, fooling around with guns from his collection or attempting to play a prank with a sword. His writing was picking up and he appeared fine.... He got 'Arms and the Writer' finished, mailed it out and launched into the novelized version of the three *Analog* stories."[7]

The book title was *Lord Kalvan of Otherwhen*, as Piper explains, "which is probably no worse than what Ace would call it, if they published it."[8] This puts to rest the stories that some anonymous Ace editor cut and pasted the three novelettes together, turning them into a novel. He started work on the novel on September 13, and by the 21st was already on page 155.

"On the following Sunday," Knerr writes, "he was 'within plain sight of the end (of *Lord Kalvan of Otherwhen*).' I dropped in on him, after phoning, to do an article on him and his collection for my newspaper. We photographed many of his pieces on the floor and I took a shot of Beam pulling the sword out of his cane. We talked awhile and I left: Piper went back to work, finally winding up his marathon writing stint on September 30th. I suspect there was more than a bit of desperation in his speedy novelization of the Kalvan novelettes. He needed to have some incoming money to take care of him through the winter."[9]

On October 3, Piper wrote, "Another do-nothing day; still fagged from getting *Kalvan* finished; ought to be snapping back, but seem to have little or no snap left in me. Fiddling with detective story I was working on four or five years ago—will probably waste months on it, get nothing out of it." He was also working on "The Tactical Seesaw" for a lecture he was giving at Lycoming College.[10]

On October 8, he wrote: "Wrote Ken White to prod him up; hope it gets results. Am beginning to distrust him."[11] What he didn't know was that Ken had died on October 2. Piper didn't learn about it until the 12th. "Still working on the lecture, am now up to the Thirty Years' War. Received a phone call from Ken White's wife with news of his death ten days ago. The manuscript of *Lord Kalvan of Otherwhen* is in her hands; doesn't know what's happened with 'Hos-Hostigos.' A hell of a situation! She gave me name and address of another agent, a friend of Ken's, Max Wilkinson. Will have to get in touch with him, see if he will represent me."[12]

The next day, Beam fired off a letter to John Campbell inquiring about "Hos-Hostigos":

Dear John:

I was informed yesterday of the death of my agent and good friend, Kenneth White, ten days ago. I had not heard from him for some time previous—I understand that he had been ill for several months—and do not even know if he received the manuscripts of the third Kalvan story or sent it on to you. This story is entitled "Hos-Hostigos.' I would much appreciate your letting me know whether you received it and if so what you've decided to do about it.

I have made arrangements by telephone with Mr. Max Wilkinson, of Littauer & Wilkinson, 500 Fifth Avenue, to represent me in the future. Agents are replaceable; friends aren't.

Nice cover for "Gunpowder God," but who told the artist that Pennsylvania State cops wear blue? They don't, they wear gray. And the red keystone doesn't belong, that's 28th Division, PNG. Otherwise splendid!

Yours truly
Beam[13]

Piper got a letter off to Wilkinson, his new agent, and went back to working out his upcoming lecture. On October 14, he got a letter: "Letter from an agent, Jay Garon, offering his services. A nice letter, shows that I am known and considered. Had to send regrets." Knerr notes: "It's strange that he didn't try to learn more about Mr. Garon, and put all his eggs in one basket—a basket he was taking on faith."[14]

Mike Knerr writes:

He wound up the lecture-reading time one and a half hours—and sagged again. "Not feeling well—cold and cough coming on." It was getting worse all day Saturday. I showed up in the afternoon and knocked on his door.

"Come in," Beam said, and lead me into the gunroom.

I asked what I usually asked: "What do you hear from Ken?"

He had just reached the corner of his desk, now in "winter position" facing west. He spun in surprise, his eyes wide. "Ken's dead," he said, after a second or two. "Didn't you know?"

It was my turn to be surprised. Finally I shook my head. "Nobody told me, Beam. What'll happen to our manuscripts?"

"Some chap named Max Wilkinson, a friend of Ken's, is sorting through things. I don't know how long that will take."

"You have his address?"

He gave it to me and we talked shop awhile. My decision was that I just wanted my manuscripts back, and I wasn't really interested in having another agent handling them. It had been fun, this writing venture, but I just had too much to do with the newspaper work to fool around with creative writing. I told that to Beam.

"You're quitting?" he asked. When I nodded, he said: "Well, you're young, Mike. What the hell can a man my age do?"

I didn't have an answer.[15]

Four days later, Piper wrote, "Home about 1830, and spent all night reading—fell asleep about 1930, woke, quite sleepless, at 2200, and read till 0600—'Murder Frozen Over'—the Jeff Rand story I never could sell. This is carrying it about as far as I ever have."[16]

He gave his lecture on the 19th to a gathering of the Phi Alpha Theta fraternity and returned home to work on story ideas. On October 21, he wrote, "Letter, very brief, from John Campbell—'Hos-Hostigos' bounced back to Ken White, with letter, so no money coming in."[17]

This is John W. Campbell's short note of October 19, 1964:

Dear Beam:

Your letter telling about Kenneth White's death came as a shock. I hadn't heard. "Hos-Hostigos" was returned to Kenneth on September 16th with a letter.

Regards,
John W. Campbell
Editor[18]

"Campbell probably wants rewrite. Nothing yet from Wilkinson—have I an agent, or haven't I? Morale badly down."[19] For a man who majored in understatement, Piper's last statement is a telling comment. The death of his friend and agent was a terrible blow; he had already run through several agents and didn't have a lot of faith in the breed. He couldn't reach his new agent and was feeling badly adrift. On the 26th of October, "Worked on story-planning till 1400—think something has finally arrived. Wrote to Wilkinson—is he or isn't he?—and to Campbell—what about 'Hos-Hostigos?'"[20] The next day his morale was sinking even lower. "Cough and cold persist; don't feel too good. Can't seem to get anything done."[21]

This is Piper's letter to John W. Campbell:

Dear John:

Your letter of the 19th arrived. As I think I told you in mine of the 13th, I had a telephone conversation with Mr. Max Wilkinson, of Littauer & Wilkinson, inquiring if he would be willing to take over as my agent. To this he agreed, but since then I haven't heard anything from him, although some report on the state of my affairs in Ken's hands at the time of his death seems rather overdue.

Now I don't know whether I have an agent or not, and until I hear something positive to that effect, I'll have to act on the assumption that I don't.

For one thing, I have not received the letter which you sent accompanying return of "Hos-Hostigos," and except for your brief note, know nothing about it. Apparently Ken was ill for some time before he died, and never got around to forwarding it on to me. I was delaying answer to yours of the 19th in hope that it would come in.

Do you want a revision of the story? If so, I would be deeply grateful if you would write me, giving me a resume of the letter which accompanied it back to Ken, and telling me what needs to be fixed up about it. If you would do so, I will get to work on it immediately.

I am, with best wishes and thanking you in advance.

Yours Cordially

H. Beam Piper[22]

This letter is as close to begging as Piper ever came, all but pleading for Campbell to send him a carbon of his revision letter. Sadly, Campbell never replied — or if he did, his letter is lost. There is no mention of a reply in Piper's diary.

This is what Campbell had to say about it all in the *Analog* letter column, Brass Tacks, almost six months later:

Dear Mr. Campbell:

Although you probably know this by now, I write this letter as a safety check.

Early this summer Ace Books published a novel, F-342, titled *Lord Kalvan of Otherwhen*. This novel was written by H. Beam Piper. The novelette "Down Styphon!" was the second of three parts of this novel. Therefore your claim that this was his last story was wrong. The completion of his novel will undoubtedly be welcome to the readers who didn't get the book.

I thought you only printed new material.

Scott Wyatt

This situation merits explanation.

The mixup occurred due to two closely timed deaths, with resultant confusions. *Analog* bought "Down Styphon!" — it was written for us, as a sequel to "Gunpowder God" — from H. Beam Piper, through Piper's agent, Ken White. Unfortunately, Ken White died suddenly, leaving all his affairs in a chaotic mess. (It was this, in part, that put Piper in such a financial jam, and caused the acute depression that led to his suicide.) No one seems to have known just what the status of affairs at Ken White's office was, and for months manuscripts, letters, checks and everything else were stalled on dead center.

Then Piper died.

Another "author's agent" took over responsibility for Piper's literary estate — but without adequate knowledge of the dilatation with respect to legal rights, et cetera, of many of Piper's stories.

Our agreement with Ken White was, as usual, that we would have first publication of "Down Styphon!" The new agency, because of the chaos White's sudden and completely unexpected death caused, didn't know that, and sold book rights to Ace Books.

Result: a complete confusion of rights and stories for which no one can be blamed.[23]

Obviously, John Campbell didn't have any idea just how desperate Piper's financial situation had gotten. Campbell, not known for his sensitivity, couldn't or didn't bother to read between the lines of Beam's letter and so Piper was left out on the ledge.

Piper was running out of money, his supposed new agent wasn't writing or returning phone calls, and then another disaster came on October 29, 1964: "Now the city income tax people are on me — I'm damned if I know how I'm going to make out. Letter from Wilkinson — he is acting for me, will go over Ken's files after the first, and he has sent *Lord Kalvan* to Ace."[24]

Knerr notes: "On the 30th he went to the bank and drew everything out but two dollars, did some shopping and returned to the gunroom for another writing session. There's no mention in the diary of what the new story was about or even a working title. He read his lecture to the Writers Forum on the 2nd of November."[25]

On Wednesday, November 4, 1964, Piper wrote: "Up 0930. Worked till mid-P.M. on planning. Out 1600 for a little, read in evening; to be 0030. Yesterday's election a bad — but not unexpected defeat; Goldwater carried Arizona and a few of the Deep South states; Johnson everything else, including Maine and Vermont. The only thing that will save this country now is an Act of God, and God doesn't exist."[26]

Knerr writes:

On Thursday, November 5th, Beam awoke at 9:00 A.M. and half an hour later it began to rain.

It was a Pennsylvania rain, a weeping, drizzling, persistent rain and, in retrospect, I can see him sitting at his desk looking at the beads and rivulets of water running down over the window pane. Frowning, the way he always frowned when he was deep in thought or perplexed by something. The red diary would be on the desk before him and he would have dropped the pencil. His eyes would be squinched into thin lines and his brows furled above them. He would be weighing the odds again, the way he always did.

Did he have an agent? Would Ace take *Lord Kalvan of Otherwhen*? Would "Hos-Hostigos" sell, or *Fuzzies and Other People*? Could he afford, with the little bit of money he had, to hold out until something finally came through? Could he go through another starvation period like the ones in the past? Was there any use to it all? He was sixty. Betty was gone. Ken was gone. He was tired, old and just a bit sick, and completely in the dark as to what had become of his work. The Nifflheim with it!

No matter how long he sat there weighing it all. An hour. Two. It all added up to more than he wanted to deal with. He cleared off the desk, wrote a little note and went into the bedroom for his .38 Colt Marshall and sat down again.[27]

He put up painters' drop-cloths in the gunroom, sat down in his office chair, brought out his pistol, stuck it into his mouth and fired.

CHAPTER 34

Let the Guns Bury Him

The only one that I thought might be all right was that walnut one. Gunstock wood.[1]

— Ted Ranck

Mike Knerr writes:

Rain.

It wept from a disgustingly gray sky, nearly the color of a lead bullet; it had been doing it for several days. At times, it poured and ripped what was left of the multi-colored autumn leaves from the trees, and sometimes it faded to a misty drizzle that seemed more to hang in the air than fall. The downed leaves had turned the mountain back of my house into a crazy-quilt pattern of reds and yellows.

I leaned against an upright on the porch, sucked on a quart of beer, and scowled at the sky. Sunday, November 8th, the one day I had off, and it was spitting rain. All week long, as a reporter for the *Shamokin Citizen*, I had written stories about traffic accidents, human interest junk, drew editorial cartoons and attended the various meetings of the school board, the fire department and the city council. I'd fought my way through the elections and we'd gotten the weekly newspaper put to bed until next week. On Saturday I'd covered a "milk bowl" football game, writing up the kids as though they were pros; they loved it, but their parents were always giving me a bad time because little "Johnny" hadn't been mentioned.

I'd earned a Sunday of tramping through the woods of Line Mountain, getting chortled at by irate squirrels, squeaked at by nearly invisible chipmunks and snorted at by curious does. I wanted to go check buck rubs and slashings; I wanted to see where the deer were moving, and where I'd be sitting on the opening day of buck season.

The last thing in the world I wanted was goddamn rain!

When the State Police officer cruiser slid down the mud of the dirt road, and stopped at the house, I had the sinking feeling that I would have to go to work again. A bad accident? A mine cave in? Nuts! Trooper Kraynak got out and ducked through the rain to the porch, his frayed D.I. hat covered with plastic against the water.

"Mike," he said. "Do you know an H. Beam Piper?"

"Sure. Why?"

"The Montoursville barracks called us," he went on. "Asked us to notify you because they can't locate any next of kin. He's dead."

I didn't say anything. I just stared at the rain, and at Kraynak. Beam had always said he would do it. He'd killed himself; I knew it. Somehow I knew it just as sure as I knew where the deer trails were in the woods.

"You all right?" Kraynak asked.

"How?" I asked, after nodding to his question.

"Suicide," Kraynak said gently. "He shot himself."

"Shit," I whispered.

"A neighbor got suspicious," Kraynak went on, "when they didn't see him around. Called the city

195

police. They went in and found him. The State Police are trying to locate any next of kin he might have had. You know any?"

I shook my head. "He mentioned once that he had some cousins scattered around, but I don't know any names. I guess I'll pack the car and go up. Hey, thanks, Kraynak."

"See you, Mike."

I watched him climb into the patrol car and drive down the road; then I went in and told my wife. We packed the kids in the car and started driving north through the lousy rain. We didn't talk much.

With the family tucked away at my parents' house, I climbed back in the car and drove downtown to the funeral home. It was dark by then, but the rain hadn't let up. It had fallen off to another fine drizzle and the streets were slick with it. The neon signs flashed against the wet asphalt and the traffic was only moderate. I parked the car, maybe a block from Beam's apartment, and went into the funeral home.

I hate those places. They smell of flowers and the lights are so dim you can't see anything and everyone talks in a hushed voice as if they figure they'll wake up the corpses. The carpet wouldn't make a noise if you were wearing lumberjack boots and when you go in, there isn't anyone there. Just the emptiness.

The emptiness and the damned low lights burning along the walls as if the place was a church. Finally a guy came out.

He was older, kind of wispy, dressed in a suit, with a smile that looked as though he'd pasted it on in the makeup room. He said, "Yes?"

"My name's Knerr," I told him, wondering why in the hell I was whispering. "I came to see about H. Beam Piper."

"Oh, yes. Mister Knerr. I'm glad you came. We couldn't locate any of Mister Piper's next of kin, and a Mrs. Hoover suggested we contact you."

"I guess we'll have to make arrangements, huh?"

"There's another gentleman here I'd like you to meet."

He led me somewhere and introduced me to Ted Ranck, a beefy pleasant man, with the stamp of the outdoors all over him. I liked him at once.

"We telephoned Mrs. Piper, in France," the undertaker was saying. "The will is in her name. We wanted to know about the arrangements, and Mister Piper's gun collection. She said to 'let the guns bury him.'"

Ted and I looked at each other.

"If you like," the man said. "you may pick out a casket. And don't worry about cost. The gun collection will pay for it."

Somewhere in this confused evening — I don't know if it was before or after I met Ted — the undertaker asked me if I wanted to see the body. I declined. I'd already seen too many dead men, and the last time I'd seen Beam he was on his feet. I didn't feel I wanted to see him with his arms folded across his chest and a lily in his fingers.

The undertaker led us to where the caskets were and told us to look around. We did. I think both Ted and I were a bit uneasy about it all, maybe me more than him.

We left the room and stood in the hall. Just kept trying to breathe with some kind of regularity.

"The only one," Ted said at length, "that I thought might be all right was that walnut one. Gunstock wood."

I glanced at him and he had a gentle smile on his face. Gunstock wood. Sure. "You're right, Ted. Hell, yes. Let's get it."

We got it. Ted and I — mostly Ted — made the arrangements to ditch Piper. When the funeral director asked about the minister, we both looked at each other, kind of grinned, and almost in unison said, "Nooo, I don't think Beam would like that at all." If anything could make H. Beam Piper walk out on his own funeral, it would be some preacher doing his thing at the side of the casket.

"Do either of you know about antique guns?" the director asked.

"Yeah," I said. "I do."

"Would you come by tomorrow and evaluate them?"

"Sure. I need the time off work anyhow."

He gave me a time, for the next day, when I could go down to the City Hall and evaluate the guns. I said goodbye to Ted, told him I'd like to see him again and climbed in the car to go back to my mother's house.

I never saw Ted Ranck again.

They kept the guns in the cells.

The cells at the City Hall were gray and they gave one the feeling that they were catacombs. The officer I talked to was nice and he informed me that there was one gun that they had thought was loaded. I told him that Beam's guns were all unloaded; except for the .38 he kept on his dresser — the one he had shot himself with.

"Well, we don't *know*," the officer said. "We don't know how to get it open."

He handed me the 9mm Mauser pistol and I opened it for him, bouncing the spring almost out of the magazine forward of the trigger guard. I slapped it back together and handed it back. "Unloaded."

They brought in a secretary with one of those shorthand typewriters to record the prices I mentioned. Then, as fast as they could, they handed me guns, swords and daggers — which I labeled prices onto. It was too fast. Only my knowledge of what Beam had told me, bailed me out of that mess. But I got it done and, in the end, I was only $12.00 off when they were sold. Beam was a good teacher.

The State Police managed to locate one of Beam's relations, Charles O. Piper. He was named executor of the estate. He asked me if I would help in assembling whatever literary material was available. This would be turned over to the attorney, William Askey. I agreed, and the following weekend we both went up and got the key from the City police. They had padlocked the door after they'd taken out Beam's body.

"Poor lonely old fellow," Charles said softly.

For a brief time, we simply wandered through the apartment, not knowing exactly where to start. It was a mess. There was scrap paper all over the place; there were files to go through and manuscripts to sort out. I guided Charles in the literary material, and he guided me in what should be classed as junk.

The desk was bare of anything but a large pool of dried blood where Beam had fallen forward. Behind the desk chair, the ceiling was a dark black hole with blood splatterings around it. I went out into the kitchen and stared out through the door at the pigeons on the roof of the garage in the alley. "Shit, Beam," I said helplessly, then went back to help Charles sort things out.

It took a lot of weekends.[2]

CHAPTER 35

The Funeral

Now his eyes were closed. Who can ever remember Beam Piper with his eyes shut?[1]

— Don Coleman

Don Coleman writes:

After police detectives had made their examination of the suicide area, the corpse of H. Beam Piper was removed and taken to Page Funeral Home.... Dick Allen, who was son-in-law to "old" Mr. Page himself, had known Beam through periodic writers' forums at the local library and had befriended the author over the past several years. The funeral home was only "a stone's throw" from the fatal scene. Allen found it quite tedious trying to reach Paris to inform Betty of the author's tragic demise, but after a multitude of calls he was able to get through.

Other than the police investigators and Page funeral agents, Diane and Sylvia Coleman were the last individuals to view and identify the remains of H. Beam Piper — whether this be privilege or just an unfortunate commitment — before the casket was sealed off forever. The body appeared "in perfect condition" after some patch-up work had been administered to the cranial section of the man who, just a few days ago, occupied a wealth of super-intellect. Now his eyes were closed. Who can remember Beam Piper with his eyes shut?

Although his closest friend "Fernando" had lain in this very building, while hundreds viewed a framed picture atop a closed coffin, his compadre Piper would move on without a public look-see....

About mid-morning, November 12th, a polished hearse pulled out of the Page Funeral Home garage with coffin and corpse loaded aboard. After the car had come around to the front of the establishment, Diane Coleman stepped aboard with raincoat and umbrella and seated herself between Dick Allen and an assistant for the one hundred mile journey back home to Altoona. Allen had asked Diane earlier to accompany them as "family representative" to which she gratefully accepted. In spite of "relatives" of some sort, Beam truly "had no one" from the family.

The weather was chilly and damp, but the confines of the magnificent limousine were quite comfortable. Diane found it obligatory to comply with the immediate reality of riding the "meat wagon"—a muddy term used by Beam, despite his otherwise elegant speech. Looking out over the hood of the vehicle, everything was absolutely normal to Diane, while twisting around to face the rear was cause for uneasiness ... just knowing Beam was "riding along behind." Actually, once the formally attired *crew* departed Williamsport for the mountains, the young lady shook off the queasiness displayed earlier at the mortuary.

According to Diane, "The first depressing part of the trip was the sight of bareness among the stately trees in the mountains and the lack of color along the highway. There were no wild flowers or mountain laurel now. It was like traveling through a black-and-white movie, except for the evident prominence of the majestic pine and spruce. It was almost as if these quiet valleys were aware — or more so, the furry inhabitants within — of this hunter's final fleeting presence."

Riding in this glistening black vehicle nearly one hundred miles with a dead man close behind was "an eerie experience" she noted. "What subject, outside of the obvious, could be talked about while riding so many miles to the cemetery, other than the significance of death...?"

Diane, of course, when asked about her association with Beam, proceeded at length to describe the happy and exhilarating times when he would visit, preceded by the lifelong camaraderie between her father and the writer. She would deny any friendship to be as close and enduring between two individuals—as the one that bound Piper and Coleman. Nostalgia continued until eventually, discourse became superfluous.

It had to be shut off. Diane could no longer be restrained, quickly forcing a breakaway from their morose conversation. She leaned over the assistant and opened the window and inhaled the cold invading air before looking at each of her *chaperones*.

"Hold it, guys!" she whooped. Shaking her head in partial disgust, she added, "Enough is enough. Let's stop puttin' on with the melancholy and change the jive. Just because you're undertakers and wearing those stiff suits doesn't mean you can't loosen up and make this trip a little more enjoyable."

Allen and fellow administrator were awed but smiled in exchange. These "guys" were trained to be polite and to express understanding, compassion and sympathy towards the bereaved. They could also find it within their honor as gentlemen to wait until some *idiot* such as Diane Coleman came forward and "broke the ice!"

Lightheartedness had to replace the somber surroundings of the morning, so Diane, with her nutty behavioral disposition — most surely acquired from the maternal branch of the Coleman clan, sprang out with one or two comical one-liners to kick off a fest of "Can you top this!" This provided the perfect opening for the morticians to come forth with jokes representative of their profession ... and there were many. It was amazing how suddenly the miles passed with this diversion into humor.

It was approaching noon but no one realized it except for the twitch in Diane's stomach. Outside the hearse was an on/off drizzle with prevailing cloud cover; the absence of the sun gave little indication of the time of day.

"Don't you boys ever eat?" inquired the brazen young miss, "or do we go without lunch? I'm hungry!"

Diane wondered immediately after her outburst whether she should have kept quiet or approached the question with discretion.

But Dick Allen responded with dispatch: "Of course we eat, and I'm hungry, too. The first chance we have, we'll pull over."

So Diane and her new friends pulled into a diner off the highway, ordering burgers, chips and milk shakes. Without the visible presence of the hearse parked in front of the entrance, the three customers could have been tagged as brokers or attorneys, insurance agents or realtors. But, no; they were a pair of morticians escorting a gal called *Di-Dee-Lou* — the latter being affectionately monikered by the prone cargo—just "dropping in for a little lunch."

The circumstances were both funny and sad; funny that Beam couldn't join the three, but would have to be content lying out there with a bottle of Myers's Rum nestled by his side; and sad that this party was en route to an Altoona cemetery with the body of H. Beam Piper — which, in just a short time, would be lowered into the depths of the earth — never to be seen again.

Upon entering Altoona, it was relatively easy for the gentlemen in the "stiff suits" to locate the Fairview Cemetery. The surroundings were dismal on this day as most graveyards tend to be and it was "hilly and hard to walk around." Stationed at the unpretentious gravesite were two gravediggers who had waited upon the arrival of the hearse, which they directed to park "close," before assisting with the coffin. There were also two "relatives of sorts" to witness the burial.

What a sad sight ... and feeling. There was no protective canopy roofing the gravesite. There was no clergyman present with the Holy Scriptures in hand. There was no handful of mournful friends standing about, clutching lace handkerchiefs and wiping away tears. There was no song of inspiration sung for the deceased nor the recitation of prayer. How totally incredible this somber scene. How utterly blasé the total affair.

Diane said a short prayer to herself for the soul of her (and our) good friend Beam Piper, while the gravediggers lowered the casket into the hole. They then took to shoveling mounds of wet dirt into the grave. And, as Dick Allen spoke a few parting words with the Piper kin, Diane turned away from the area. It was so hard for her to believe what was actually occurring, as she returned to the limousine feeling emptiness and frustration. Here was a man she had known her entire life, who after decades of his time, was read by science-fiction readers all over America, as well as Great Britain, Germany, Italy and France. It was hard for her to encompass what had so rapidly taken place — a scene so incredible, and "so crude and cruel." So very quickly was H. Beam Piper taken from this world.[2]

CHAPTER 36

The Last Good-Bye

He was an intellectual, and his butler-ish mannerisms were only more proof of his suave personality. He carried himself tall and straight and maintained a gentleman's gentleman elegance throughout his life. There just does not exist one of the same mold.[1]

—Don Coleman

We will never know exactly what it was that forced Piper's hand: illness, chronic pain and despondency; loneliness for Betty; the death of his agent and friend Ken White; or the difficulties of starting all over with a new agent who never answered his letters, when he felt "written out" and despaired of going through even one more cycle of starvation and salvation, when another check might or might not arrive just in time.

All of Beam's friends, such as Mike Knerr, Don Coleman and Jerry Pournelle, with whom I have talked and corresponded, bear a heavy weight of guilt for not having recognized Beam's desperation and loneliness—and for not having put out a helping hand.

Like Terry and John McGuire, Jr., Sylvia and Diane Coleman, Sally "The Big Noise" and Mike Knerr—Beam's "last kid"—and the rest of Beam's "kids" (some of whom I never uncovered), Don Coleman to this day feels a lot of guilt and anger over Beam's tragic suicide.

Don writes:

While writing "H. Beam Piper: The Early Letters," I was continually bringing up facts of Beam's existence to ... Becky, my wife. Periodically, during the early 1960s, we would drive back to Williamsport on vacation from Cincinnati (where I spent most of my business life) and invariably pass by Beam's third-floor apartment. I would calmly say to Becky, "That's Beam's place, up topside where the lights are on."

Now today, when I bring about this fact or that, I hear an outburst from across the room: "I am so very disappointed in you. Not one time did you give me the opportunity to meet Beam Piper. As many times as we passed that white building—not once. He and I could have really hauled it off with one another."

Beam never actually, through his entire life, showed any visible sign of complete despondency. I have never seen or heard of his openly revealing depression except for what he had written in "The Early Letters" of his time when, during the recession and pains of prohibition, a few bucks were needed here and there. Amid his closest friends, he made no hesitation in asking for financial aid. But wait ... this was pre-war (World War II) era. Now, in these final days, he was too proud to humble himself.

If only he would have broken that stubborn pride and come to his other beloved friend, Freida Coleman—there would have been no question as to the financial help and loving friendship given to the cause. Freida, with her meek and charitable mien, wrote recently: "...often thought if I had stayed in town, perhaps I could have helped him and avoided the tragedy." But between a new home in New England and eventual settlement in Florida ... the good lady was not available.[2]

In a time when close relatives and even the most celebrated lives are forgotten in a fortnight, Beam's "kids" have taken his tragedy to their old age—and in some cases to their death beds.

Mike Knerr wrote, in his August 26, 1982, letter to me: "I didn't know about a note, but then I was pretty broken up at the time—in fact, the reason his "lost" (*Fuzzies and Other People*) manuscript has been lost for so long is because I'm still pretty broken up about it. It didn't have to happen. Hell, I'd have supported him, had I known. Beam and Ray Bradbury taught me to write and that has to count for something."[3]

In a June 6, 2006, e-mail, Terry McGuire writes: "When the police called my father to tell him of Beam's suicide, my father was incredulous ... said it was not possible, and that someone must have murdered him. He insisted to the Police Chief that he read *Murder in the Gunroom*. To the end of his life, my father insisted there 'was no suicide.' He talked about conspiracy theory ... of course, the police ignored it as the ravings of another crazy SF writer."[4]

Marvin Katz, *Grit* reporter, wrote in Brass Tacks, in March 1965:

Dear Mr. Campbell:

I am a reporter for *Grit*, a weekly newspaper published at Williamsport and distributed in three editions throughout the area, state and nation. In the November 15th city edition, the full story of Mr. Piper's death appeared. I wrote the obituary....

Burial took place Thursday, November 12th, in Fairview Cemetery.... He had shot himself to death in his apartment at 330 East Third Street, Williamsport, sometime over the weekend.

Captain Lawrence P. Smeak, investigating officer for the Williamsport Police Department, said the author used a .38-caliber pistol which was part of a valuable collection of more than one hundred weapons which Mr. Piper owned.

... I met him once myself about a year ago. He was my first guest. My wife and I had just set up housekeeping when I learned that Forry Ackerman was about to make his much-publicized trip to east coast scifi-con. I invited Ackerman to stop at our house—meaning to get an interview with him. David Frank ... came along and brought Mike Knerr and Mr. Piper.

Well, the weather was bad and Ackerman never did show up, but we had an engaging hour or so gabbing. At first reticent, even shy, Mr. Piper warmed to the conversation quickly once he felt at ease. He proved a charming, gracious man, soft-spoken and witty, perceptive in his comments.

At one point he said he'd like to see a local science-fiction society formed, but that's as far as it went. In the months to come, my wife and I wanted to invite him to dinner but were frankly intimidated at the thought of disturbing him. An internationally famous writer, you know....

Now we realize we should have taken the initiative and asked him, but hindsight will always show the clear path that was formerly covered over. Personally, I suspect that loneliness may have been as important a factor in the final tragedy as any other consideration.

... The shock I felt when I first heard about the tragedy is gone. But although I met him only once, I doubt that I will ever lose the vivid recollection of his warm, gentle manner.

Perhaps the one consolation his fans can have is that he retained his full writing powers even to the end.

Marvin N. Katz[5]

Had H. Beam Piper's friends known of his desperate financial state and offered financial help, it is doubtful he would have accepted their charity. He was a proud and independent man—almost to a fault. If he had accepted, he would not have taken their charity for long, and—barring a bestseller—he would have gone broke again, and again. If, by some miracle, he could have held out to the late seventies when his work was once again in demand, he would never have gone hungry again. But that would have been a long fourteen years.

Meanwhile, going hat in hand to each of his dear friends—all of whom, sooner or later, would have gotten tired of bailing out their old friend—was not Piper's style. He knew human nature inside out. Go to the well once, and the well-keeper feels Christian charity. Go twice and he mumbles with forbearance. A third time and he curses your very existence.

Sure, Piper could have secretly continued to pawn off his gun collection, selling most of them in New York so that the local collectors wouldn't have learned how desperate he'd become. However, unbeknownst to Piper, science fiction was heading into stormy seas, as the New Wave broke over the field, bringing relevance, social reform, sexual freedom and speculative fiction to the forefront. Many of the field's old guard, such as Jack Williamson, Poul Anderson, and Randall Garrett, were dismissed as relics—dinosaurs—by the Young Turks led by Harlan Ellison, Judith Merril, Norman Spinrad and Michael Moorcock. Suddenly, adventure science fiction, of the sort Piper wrote, was considered passé and out of date.

In this piece written shortly before his death, Piper was eerily prescient, in this answer to the question in *The Double Bill Symposium*: "What do you consider the greatest weakness of Science Fiction today?"

> Not enough people read it, and there doesn't seem to be much of anything to do about it. I remember, years ago, Fletcher Pratt was bemoaning this situation and saying that we must enlarge our readership. I said then that it couldn't be done, and I still think so. It's like the attempt of Charles VII of France to create a French archery to compete with the English long bowman. He found he couldn't grab a lot of peasants out of the fields, give them bows, expect them to stand up to the English, who trained an archer by starting with his grandfather. We wouldn't have to go back quite that far to make science-fiction readers, but the type of inquisitive and speculative minds needed for the enjoyment of what we know as science fiction must be developed rather early, and our present school system seems to be doing little to help.
>
> When Charles VII found that he couldn't train French long bowman, he settled for training crossbowmen. They weren't as good on the battlefield, but they were the best he could do. What I'm afraid of is that the publishers who decide which stories will be bought and which bounced back will buy stuff suited to the mentality of a large mass readership, a readership that will accept as science fiction anything that casually mentions a spaceship or a World Government, without any confusing egghead stuff about what the planets the spaceship goes to are really like, or what a World Government would have to do.
>
> Then we'd be back where we started, only it wouldn't be nearly as much fun. Instead of Ol' Space Ranger doubling for Hopalong Cassidy and the cattle-rustlers all in the space-pirate business, we'd have psychological stories with robot psychologists, and Boy meets Girl — or maybe Boy meets Boy, to judge from some of the recent mainstream stuff— on a spaceship to Mars instead of a Caribbean cruise, and sagas of ad-agencies, in which thought transmitters take the place of TV.
>
> And the only real science-fiction writing left will be in the fanzines.
>
> I am almost sixty now. It gives me the most inexpressible pleasure to reflect that by the time this has happened, I shall be dead.[6]

He was sixty years old when he killed himself.

Of all the science fiction magazines, only John W. Campbell's *Analog Science Fiction and Fact*, even after Campbell's death in 1972, has kept afloat and healthy. While *Analog* was certainly H. Beam Piper's major market throughout his life, it was not always a safe harbor. The paperback explosion of the late 1970s, when Piper suddenly become a hot commodity, was still not in evidence in 1964. There were few publishing houses to support the many old timers who'd thrived during the pulp era.

However, Piper — in the last months of his life — appears to have made a huge tactical error. He sent his former agent's wife a copy of the manuscript of *Lord Kalvan of Otherwhen*, which then went into the hands of White's successor, Max Wilkinson. It appears that the new agent did not understand the relationship between H. Beam Piper and John W. Campbell; specifically, that the novel could not appear before all the contents were published in the magazine. The new agent sold the novelization to Ace Books before the second installment of the series was published in *Analog*.

Campbell blazed at this effrontery. He expressed some of his feelings in a letter to John D. Clark:

> That H. Beam Piper story business has caused one helluva mess. It goes this way: We bought the first and second Lord Kalvan stories from Piper, through his agent Ken White. "Hos-Hostigos," the third,

was submitted by Ken White, and I sent it back for some revision with an eight page letter of explanation.

Three months later, I heard from Piper that Ken White had died suddenly, leaving his affairs in such a mess that nobody had been informed and nobody knew what to do, and nobody had done anything for a couple of months. So Piper didn't know what I'd said about "Hos-Hostigos," and never got my letter. And I, by then, didn't remember the yarn exactly enough to be able to redo the letter without seeing the manuscript.

So Beam was broke, and apparently suddenly decided to go out sidewise ... suicidewise.

And he'd just contacted a new agent, and left his affairs in a mess, including neglecting to explain to the agent that *Analog* had bought some of his stories and not published them yet. So the agent, cleaning out his affairs, sold all the stuff [the Kalvan stories] to Ace. And the mess was thereby further glorified and transmigrated. Because Ace didn't own the right to properly copyright, and we couldn't properly copyright because Ace had improperly copyrighted and the legal situation is twice as complicated![7]

From the diaries, we know Piper's new agent Max Wilkinson never had any contact with him. We also know that after Piper's death — or possibly, even before — Wilkinson went ahead and sold the novel without providing for his client's best interests; that is, ensuring that Mr. Campbell's Kalvan novelette, specifically "Down Styphon!," appeared in *Analog* before the Ace Books edition was published.

It is possible this pre-publication fiasco would have been averted had Piper been alive. I did ask Don Wollheim, the Ace editor throughout the 1950s and 1960s, in person if he had known that "Down Styphon!" had not appeared in *Analog* when he published *Lord Kalvan of Otherwhen*; Don shrugged his shoulders and gave a sly smile. He and John Campbell were never friends, and I'm sure that Don enjoyed being able to stick one in Campbell's eye — not an easy thing to do under normal circumstances.

However, had *Lord Kalvan of Otherwhen* hit the book racks before "Down Styphon!" and "Hos-Hostigos" were published due to miscommunication between Piper and his new agent, all hell would have broken loose. He would not have sold another story to Campbell for the rest of his days. Campbell, like Piper, held a grudge like a bulldog. That being the case, Piper would have lost his major market, if not his only market. He certainly would not have fared well as the New Wave swept over the field.

The Piper revival of the late 1970s, in part, was a reaction to the New Wave; readers searching out classics from the Golden Age of SF, looking for good story telling, not flashy style and little substance. Within five years most of Piper's short stories and novels were republished by Ace Books, including a few newly "discovered" books, and he gained a new generation of fans.

Piper was above all a storyteller, a teller of tales that resonated with history and real life experience. He wrote words that still ring with truth and wisdom. During the Depression, he had worked as a railroad dick, rousting bums and giving nightstick justice to tramps and thieves in the Altoona car yards— some thirty years' worth. Then he married a wealthy socialite and was a gentleman around town in New York at its peak— "The Thin Man." He was an outdoorsman, hiker, gun aficionado. In his last years, he was a recluse working madly to get his fevered dreams down on paper. He knew love, he knew loss; he knew triumph, he knew despair. But most of all: he was the "Typewriter Killer"— H. Beam Piper.

Ventura II, a fanzine published shortly after Piper's death, included several appreciations of him, including this touching eulogy from science fiction author Jack Chalker, "The Lights Go Out":

H. Beam Piper (he never would tell anyone what the "H" stood for) was a talented and imaginative writer who endeared himself to the science-fiction world not just by his superb writings, but also by his sparkling wit and personality at various conventions and conferences. He was one of the special group you looked forward to meeting again and again, and who, you knew, would be the same cordial gentleman. No one was too big or too small, too famed or too unknown, that he could not talk with Beam as a friend. His pixie-like mannerisms and his twinkling eyes were always at the center of attention. Beam loved people, all kinds of people, and he was never happy unless there was a group nearby discussing history and antique weaponry, and he was often the life of any party.

He looked somewhat like the classic movie villain, with a thin moustache and a deep, piercing voice—but the twinkle in his eye betrayed his image, and this suited his impish sense of humor.

It was only in the past few years that he truly matured as a writer, and found his forte in the form of the novel, giving the SF world such masterpieces as *Space Viking* and the novel that truly won him universal acclaim and recognition by all, *Little Fuzzy*. His juvenile novels for Putnam's, *Four-Day Planet* and *Junkyard Planet*, showed him a master of all levels, perhaps the only man who could equal the gifts of Heinlein and Norton in writing juveniles that did not play down, and were often far superior to the bulk of adult fiction. Beam never wrote for adults or for juveniles—he wrote for everyone.

By 1964 it was very apparent that H. Beam Piper was one of the truly great SF authors, and from the time when he couldn't sell a novel to the magazine or hardback publishers (*Little Fuzzy* was universally rejected) he had, in a few short years, come up to where he would be ranked on the SF five foot shelf with every great writer in the business. In one sense he truly surpassed his contemporaries—his public knew and loved him personally as well.

In 1964 PhillyCon attendees were rather puzzled when Beam failed to appear for the festivities. He was so much a part of the East Coast's affairs that his very absence was almost physically noticeable. It was then that Sam Moskowitz told us that he had received word that on November 11th, 1964, just a few days before, Beam Piper had said his farewell to this world and gone on.

Beam's thoughts ran deep. He was a very complex man, a very unique and unfathomable man. Behind the villain's façade, beyond even the twinkling eyes and the pixie manner, there were things that showed in no external symptom, and like the ancient ones he studied and loved, he chose his own time and place of farewell, for reasons concealed from us all.

The news passed like a great snake through the Philadelphia audience. Few would or could believe he was gone. There are those of us who really can't believe it even now.

In a year that saw us lose many great men, for different causes—Hannes Bok, Cleve Cartmill, Mark Clifton, Aldous Huxley, T.H. White, C.S. Lewis, Norbert Weiner, and others—this loss was saddening indeed. To those that had the pleasure of knowing Beam himself, the loss is doubly felt.

H. Beam Piper (1904–1964) is gone—but his name will not be forgotten until men cease to imagine far places, new worlds out among the stars.[8]

Afterword

> There is no salvation for him who hath thus suffered from himself, unless it be
> speedy death.
>
> — Nietzsche

In "The Early Letters," Don Coleman writes: "Diane Coleman, the sole participant who represented the valley that Piper loved so dearly and who would witness his final act upon earth, sent off a letter to ex-spouse Betty ... reporting the concluding circumstances. A response from overseas arrived in late November:

> Piper
> Paris Palace
> Menton, Alpes Maritimes
> FRANCE
> 26 November 64

Dear Mrs. Coleman —

You were so very kind to send me such a good long letter and the clipping. He hoped his notice would be longer than Fletcher Pratt's — and it was. He would not have liked a minister or ceremony — I'm glad it was simple. One line in our French divorce pleased him very much — it was: "He always maintained his independence," he said he wanted that on his tombstone.

I know it will seem strange to you but I miss him terribly. I was so broken up when he left me in Paris and didn't accept it until the time had passed for the renewal of our passports. I knew he would never get a passport by himself. For five years I didn't know if he were alive or dead but since the beginning of the divorce, a year and ten months ago we have written regularly. We had almost nothing left except our interest in crossword puzzles and each lunch and dinner as I did my puzzle I would copy out the best words for him — now when I do my puzzles and find good words I hate to think that he can't share them.

I cannot believe that lack of money could have been the reason. He was always broke — and when he got a check — he blew it — and was broke again. There must have been something else. His last letter had been so cheerful, telling of a paperback coming out and three stories to put together. He was going to make a speech on Columbus Day — did he have a bad time at the speech? Or could he have been putting on one of his acts and pretending he was Ernest Hemingway or something? He would get awfully hurt or blue sometimes but his mind always turned around and he came out on top again. When I saw him at Idlewild in February he seemed healthier and steadier than when he was first with me.

Thank you so very much for your very kind letter — and for letting me talk to you now.

> Sincerely
> Betty

Please thank Mr. Allen who called me.[1]

Appendix A:
Piper Story Log

Michael E. Knerr sent me a photocopy of the Piper Story Log along with his introductory letter of August 14, 1982. He also references the Story Log several times in his unpublished manuscript, "Piper."

The Piper Story Log was later published in the March 1989 issue of the paperback collector's fanzine "Books Are Everything" in an article by Editor Elwanda Holland. In the introduction to "H. Beam Piper in Paperback," Holland explains how she obtained the Story Log: "A Friend was kind enough to lend me Piper's personal notebook, where he recorded his literary gains from his first professional sales to the last sale before his death. The friend wishes to remain anonymous because ... the notebook is not for sale at any price. I felt many of you would be interested in seeing them and to my knowledge, they have never been published before."

1946

9/25/46	*Time and Time Again* (mailed 6/22/46)	$147.50
	Astounding Science Fiction, pub. 3/47	

1947

7/11/47	*He Walked Around the Horses* (mailed 6/5/47)	
	Astounding Science Fiction	200.00

1948

1/16/48	*Police Operation* (mailed 1/2/48)	300.00
7/2/48	Anthology rights on *Time and Time Again*	37.80
	(*A Treasury of Science Fiction*, Crown Publishers)	337.80

1949

4/8/49	*The Mercenaries* (mailed 1/10/49)	200.00
	Astounding Science Fiction	

1950

4/8/50	*Last Enemy* (mailed 1/17/50)	500.00
	Astounding Science Fiction	
3/23/50	*John Mosby — Rebel Raider* (*True*)	1200.00
	Per Fred Pohl at 10% commission	-120.00
		1080.00	1080.00

5/16/50	*Operation RSVP* (*Amazing*)	200.00
	Per Pohl at 10%—	-20.00
		180.00	180.00

5/15/50	*Dearest* (*Weird Tales*)	70.00
	Per Pohl —	-7.00
		63.00	63.00

8/2/50	*Immunity* (*Future Stories*)	80.00
	Per Pohl —	-8.00
		72.00	72.00

10/19/50	*Dearest* (*Weird Tales*)	240.00
	Per Pohl —	-24.00
		216.00	216.00

1951

4/14/51	*Day of the Moron* (mailed 6/5/47) (*ASF*)	390.00
	Per Pohl —	-39.00
		351.00	351.00

6/6/51	Film rights on *Rebel Raider* (Disney Studios)	2000.00
	Per Pohl —	-200.00
		1800.00	1800.00

10/11/5	*Genesis* (*Future*)	80.00
	Per Pohl —	-8.00
		72.00	72.00

1952

5/21/52	Radio rights, *Time and Time Again*—	100.00
		-10.00
		90.00	90.00

8/12/52	Anthology rights, *Operation RSVP* and	
	He Walked Around the Horses—	50.00
		-5.00
		45.00	45.00
			135.00

10/17/52	Advance royalties, *Pistols for Everybody*	
	[working title]	
	Murder in the Gunroom, Knopf—	750.00
		-75.00
		675.00	675.00

| 10/37/52 | One-half share *Null* (*ABC, ASF* etc.) | 494.22 | 494.22 |
| | | | [*sic*] 1294.00 |

1953

2/26/53	On account, *Uller Uprising* (*Space*) —	300.00	300.00
	Advance, Twayne Pub.	+50.00	
		350.00	
		-35.00	
		315.00	315.00
6/10/53	Remaining due on *Uller Uprising*		405.00

1954

2/6/54	Royalties on *Last Enemy*		13.43
8/3/54	Royalties on *Last Enemy*		1.51
8/13/54	*Time Crime* — $1260 less 10%		1134.00
9/25/54	French rights, *Operation RSVP* — $50 less 10%		45.00

1955

| 7/18/55 | Bonus (1¢ per word) on first part of | | 189.00 |
| | *Time Crime* | 210.00 | |

1956

2/9/56	Anthology rights, *Police Operation*		45.00
2/25/56	Anthology rights, *Time and Time Again*		5.69
10/14/56	Anthology rights, *Time and Time Again*		.39
10/15/56	*Omnilingual* — $630 less 10%		567.00
12/20/56	*Lone Star Planet* half of solo price,		110.00
	shared with J.J. McG		
12/28/56	*The Knife Edge*		360.00

1957

2/9/57	Advance Royalties *Null* (*ABC*)		225.00
2/16/57	Bonus on *Omnilingual* (*ASF*)		81.00
3/23/57	*The Keeper* (*Venture*)		175.50
8/19/57	Advance royalties *Null* (*ABC*) —		225.00
	$250 less 10% to White		
9/2/57	*Graveyard of Dreams* (*Galaxy*)		189.00
10/25/57	Anthology (Faber), *He Walked Around the Horses* — $41.76 less 10%		37.56

1958

2/28/58	On Ace paperback publication of *Lone Star Planet* — $250 less 10% to K. White	225.00
7/8/58	*Ministry of Disturbance* — *Astounding*, $756.00 less 10%	680.40
7/14/58	On Ace paperback, *Lone Star Planet* — $250 less 10% K.W.	225.00

1959

4/23/59	*The Other Road* (*Fantastic Universe*)	(50.00) 45.00
9/10/59	*Oomphel in the Sky* (*Astounding*)	(570.00) 513.00
9/14/59	*He Walked Around the Horses* (English, Murray)	20.85
9/14/59	*He Walked Around the Horses* (Italian, Einaudi)	14.60
12/17/59	*The Answer* (*Fantastic Universe*)	45.00

1960

8/25/60	*Four Day Planet* (Putnam's)	900.00
12/17/60	Bonus on *Oomphel in the Sky*	85.00
12/31/60	Advance on *Junkyard Planet*	450.00

1961

3/14/61	Second advance on *Junkyard Planet*	450.00
5/3/61	Anthology rights on *Omnilingual*	112.00
5/23/61	*Mudstones* (*ASF*)	502.00
10/11/61	*Little Fuzzy* (first advance)	787.50
10/31/61	*Little Fuzzy* (second advance)	787.50
12/22/61	*A Slave Is a Slave* (*Analog*)	545.00

1962

5/15/62	Bonus on *Naudsonce*	83.30
5/25/62	Advance on *Space Viking*	800.00
5/31/62	Balance on *Space Viking*	1714.00
7/28/62	Bonus on *Slave*	112.50
9/1/62	Miscellaneous, incl. *The Return* from Pohl	258.37
10/1/62	Advance on *Fuzzy Sapiens*	787.50
11/16/62	Additional Royalties *Prologue to Analog* (*Omnilingual*)	45.00

1963

3/11/63	Advance from Ace on *Space Viking*	675.00
3/27/63	*Fuzzy Sapiens*, second installment	787.50
5/15/63	For Italian rights on *Little Fuzzy*	226.41
6/29/63	Bonus, *Space Viking*	303.50
8/19/63	Bal. due from Ace, *Space Viking*	675.00
11/16/63	Advance movie rights, *Little Fuzzy* (MPC)	900.00

1964

5/19/64	*Gunpowder God*	684.00
8/4/64	*Down Styphon!*	513.00

Appendix B:
The Future History

by H. Beam Piper

This short but concise piece by H. Beam Piper on his future history was written at the request of a young British fan, Peter Weston. The original letter has been lost, but the four-page piece on Piper's future history has survived; it originally appeared in Peter Weston's science fiction fanzine, in *Zenith* #4, May 1964 (Peter Weston, ed.), "Future History No. 1," by H. Beam Piper, pp. 11–14.

A Note on Atomic Era Dating

The Atomic Era is reckoned as beginning on the 2nd December 1942, Christian Era, with the first self-sustaining nuclear reactor, put into operation by Enrico Fermi at the University of Chicago. Unlike earlier dating-systems, it begins with a Year Zero, 12/2/'42 to 12/1/'43 CE. With allowances for December overlaps, 1943 CE is thus equal to Year Zero AE, and 1944 CE to 1 AE, and each century accordingly begins with the "double-zero" year, and wends with the ninety-nine year.

Dates AE and CE are converted by adding or subtracting 1943: thus 1964 CE is 21 AE, and 1066 CE is reckoned as 877 PreAtomic. Atomic Era dating did not become official until 2nd December, 2143, or 200 AE. The Gregorian calendar, with all defects, was adopted, merely setting back Jan. 1st to December 2nd. It took about fifty years for everybody to agree to it, and some fanatical religious sects opposed it to the end of the Terran Federation history.

First Century A.E.

World War II, 4 P.A.E. to 2 A.E. Nuclear energy, atomic bombs, V-2 rockets. Organization of UN., Korean War, A.E. 7–10. Artificial satellites, space-probes, etc. First landing on Luna, A.E. 27.

Collapse of UN owing to disputes as to national sovereignty over, and militarization of, Luna. World War III (Thirty Days War). Organization of First Terran Federation 32 A.E.

First landing on Mars. (Cyrano Expedition, Col. Hubert Penrose.) 53 A.E. (OMNILINGUAL: *Astounding SF*, February, 1957.)

Further explorations of Mars, Venus, Asteroid Belt and Moons of Jupiter. First Federation begins to crack under strains of colonial claims and counter-claims of member states.

Contragravity, direct conversion of nuclear energy to electric current, and collapsed matter for radiation shielding. Serious financial dislocations.

Second Century

World War IV. (First Interplanetary War.) A.E. 106–109; minor wars for ten years thereafter. Complete devastation of Northern Hemisphere of Terra. Second Federation organized by South Africa

212

and New Zealand, Brazil, the Argentine, etc. Wars of colonial pacification and consolidation; the new Terran Federation imposes System-wide pax.

Keene-Gonzales-Dillingham Theory of Non-Einsteinian Relativity, A.E. 172. Dillingham Hyperdrive developed, A.E. 183; First expedition to Alpha Centauri, 192 A.E.

Third Century, to Eighth Century

Atomic Era dating adopted, A.E. 200.
Period of exploration, colonization, and expansion.
FOUR DAY PLANET— Mid–IV Century (Putnam's; 1963)
ULLER UPRISING— 526 A.E. (in, *The Petrified Planet*, Twayne, 1953)
LITTLE FUZZY— 654 A.E. (Avon, 1962)
FUZZY SAPIENS—(Avon, 1964)
NAUDSONCE— Early VIIIth Century (*ASF* January 1962.)

Ninth Century

By this time, the Federation Government began to get into the hands of left-wing "Liberals," welfare-statists, planned-economy socialists, do-gooders, etc.

OOMPHEL IN THE SKY— 812 A.E. (*ASF* Nov 1960.)

Fox Travis on Kwannon as captain on staff of Maj. Gen. Maith.

Growing resentment to restrictions and controls, especially on newly-colonized planets. Formation of System States' Alliance to resist encroachments on colonists' rights by Federation Government.

Secession of System States Alliance from Federation, 839 AE. System States War, 842–854. Foxx Travis now General in command of Third Fleet-Army Force.

Complete defeat of Alliance; escape of Alliance Fleet from Abigor; they discover and colonize a planet outside Federation sphere of influence, which they name Excalibur, 855 A.E.

The Federation, already overstrained and top-heavy, begins to crack under strains of the System States War. Economic and political "time of trouble."

JUNKYARD PLANET— 894 A.E. (Putnam's, 1963)

...expanded from GRAVEYARD OF DREAMS (*Galaxy*, Feb. 1958)

Breakup of Federation continues at accelerating rate. Disintegration of TF Space Navy due to apathy and even hostility of "Liberal" government; resulting in spreading anarchy.

Tenth to Eighteenth Century

Terran Federation completely vanished by 1100 A.E. A few planets, Odin, Marduk, Baldur, Aton, Isis, etc., retain civilization, including hyper drive. The rest have sunk to low-order civilization in isolation or out-and-out savagery.

The Old Federation: Interplanetary and Interstellar Wars, Civil Wars, revolutions, anarchy. Rise of Neobarbarians.

The Sword-Worlds: Civilization established on Excalibur, colonization of other planets, Joyeuse, Durendal, Hautlclere, Flamberge, Gram, etc.

Development of loose feudalism from earlier and even looser town-meeting democracy. Technological advances, final stagnation.

About 1450 A.E., Sword World ships enter Old Federation space-volume, visit former Federation planets. Raiding expeditions set out, rise of the Space Vikings. By the beginning of the Seventeenth Century, Space Vikings have conquered Old Federation planets and established bases.

SPACE VIKING— Early XVIII Century (*ASF* Nov. 1962 — Feb. 1963)

Lucas Task organizes League of Civilized Worlds; work continued by the Bentriks, reigning house of Marduk.

By the time of the Nineteenth Century, the League has turned into the Galactic Empire. The Sword Worlds have declined to near-barbarism.

Twentieth Century AE Corresponds to the First Century Imperial

Period of Interstellar Wars. House of Bentrick firmly established by end of First Century; center of Empire transferred from Marduk to Odin by Stevan IV.

A SLAVE IS A SLAVE— Mid Third Century Imperial (*ASF* April 1962)

Empire completely consolidated by end of Fourth Century.

Period of cultural and political stasis and self-satisfaction.

MINISTRY OF DISTURBANCE— Twelfth Century Imperial (*ASF* Dec. 1958.)

Emperor Paul XXII and Prince Yorn Trevann undertake to arouse the Empire to new efforts.

Beyond this, with the exception of one story, THE KEEPER, about 30,000 years in the future, when the Fifth Empire was at the height of its power, and Terra was in the middle of another glacial age, I have not gone. THE KEEPER was published in the now defunct *Venture*.

Nothing else, with the possible exception of a novelette called THE EDGE OF THE KNIFE, *Amazing*, May 1957, belongs to the History of the Future. This was a story, time 1973 CE, about a history professor, who got his past and future confused, and had a lot of trouble as a result. It was written and published shortly before Sputnik I invalidated a lot of my near-future stuff, and made me swear off doing anything within a couple of centuries of now.

Appendix C:
The Terro-Human Future History

The following essay is an updated and expanded version of my introductions to the H. Beam Piper short story collections, *Federation* and *Empire*, published by Ace Books. Jerry Pournelle had several discussions with Piper regarding his Terro-Human Future History and I believe his lead-off comments highlight Piper's knowledge and understanding of history.

> There remain questions (about Piper's death). His extensive notes have never been found; yet I know that he kept a well-organized set of loose leaf notebooks with entries color-coded; a star map of Federation and Empire; a history of the System States War; and other materials including some of my own letters which answered historical questions he had posed. Somewhere out there is a gold mine.
>
> It isn't all lost. I have his letters; and some of his notes can be deduced from his writing. Beam firmly believed that history repeated itself; or at least that one can use real history to construct a future history. The casual reader will not easily deduce the historical models Beam employed. He was familiar with forgotten details: as an example, one of the battle scenes in Lord Kalvan of Otherwhen is drawn directly from the obscure Battle of Barnet in the Wars of the Roses. He knew the grand sweep of history, but he also knew the small tales; the intrigues and petty jealousies, heroism and cowardice, honor and betrayals.
>
> This, I think, is why his stories have such a ring of truth. They seem real because many were real. Such things as happen in Piper's statecraft have happened time and time again to real politicians.
>
> Jerry Pournelle
Federation

In my study of the life of H. Beam Piper, I ran head-on into a number of perplexing questions: Why, despite numerous reprintings have Piper's books been ignored by academic critics and scholars? How is it that the man who created one of science fictions most detailed and rigorous future histories received only the following note in Peter Nicholl's *The Science Fiction Encyclopedia*: "Many of his (Piper's) novels and stories ... are set in a common future history, but are insufficiently connected to be regarded as a coherent series"? And, why is Piper, who published most of his best fiction in Astounding/Analog and was rated third in Analytical Lab votes, seldom mentioned as one of the great Campbell writers?

The answers to these questions are bound within the Gordian knot of Piper's character, the low stature of science fiction and SF writers during the 1950s and 1960s, his premature death and the subsequent unavailability of most of his work until the late 1970s and early 1980s.

H. Beam Piper had a lifelong love affair with history. Off and on during the last few years of his life he was working on a major work, "Only the Arquebus," a historical novel about Gonzalo de C(rdoba and the Italian wars of the early sixteenth century. Jerry Pournelle still remembers many an evening spent with Piper in his hotel room discussing historical figures and events and how they might apply to the future. Piper had many keen insights into the past and often expressed a longing that he wished he'd been alive in the simpler days of the Christian Era, when Clausewitzian politics and nuclear wars were a faraway nightmare.

In several of his works Piper created characters who were historians or studied history as a hobby. In "The Edge of the Knife," a story about a college history professor who can sometimes see into the future, the professor says: "History follows certain patterns. I'm not a Toynbeean, but any historian can see that certain forces generally tend to produce similar effects." In *Space Viking*, Otto Harkaman, a Space Viking ship captain whose hobby is the study of history, says: "I study history. You know, it's odd; practically everything that happened on any of the inhabited planets had happened on Terra before the first spaceship." Vilfredo Pareto, a famous mid-twentieth century sociologist, said almost the same thing: almost every form of government or political-science possibility existed at one time or another among the Italian city-states of the Renaissance.

Piper also used historical events as plot models and for inspiration for his future history. In *Uller Uprising*, the first published work in Piper's Terro-Human Future History, he used the Sepoy Mutiny, a revolt in nineteenth century British-held India, when Bengalese soldiers were issued cartridges coated with what they "believed" to be the fat of cows (sacred to Hindus) and pigs (anathema to Muslims). This is confirmed by Piper in "The Edge of the Knife," an interesting story that fits sideways into his future history, where the history professor who sees into the future compares the planetary rebellion in Fourth Century A.E. (the Uller Uprising) to the Sepoy Mutiny. He also compares the early expansion of the Federation to the Spanish conquest of the New World.

Another historical analog used by Piper was the War in the Pacific during World War II. In *Cosmic Computer*, the planet Poictesme, the former headquarters of the Third Terran force during the System States War, has become in the post-war period a deserted backwater. Most of those remaining on Poictesme earn their living by salvaging and recycling old army vehicles and stores-a way of life that continued for some time on many of the Pacific atolls and islands after the war had ended. The survivors have created a belief system based on Merlin, the legendary super-computer that was reputed to have won the war for the Federation against the System States, which is reminiscent of the Cargo Cults much in vogue among the more isolated Pacific Islanders after the parachute drops of World War II.

Piper also paid great attention to historical detail, more so than any other previous SF writer since Olaf Stapeldon. In *Space Viking*, Piper gives the names of over fifty-five different planets and goes into historical, sociological and political detail on about twenty of them. This detail ranges from a short clause to pages of exposition concerning Federation history, past wars and historical figures, as well as comments on their political and sociological foibles.

Piper himself had a cyclical view of human history, one based on his study of history and influenced by Arnold Toynbee, the great English historian whose *A Study of History* had a great impact on the mid-twentieth century view of history. [For example, when Piper was working on story ideas for his short story "A Slave is A Slave," Mike Knerr wrote in his unpublished biography, "Piper": "Piper dug out his copy of Toynbee's *A Study of History*, searching for something to write about."]

Piper's Terro-Human Future History, which covers the fall of the Terran Federation, the Second Federation, the Sword Worlds, and at least four Galactic Empires, has much of the depth of Toynbee's study of human civilization. Furthermore, it can be demonstrated that Piper's civilizations pass through many of the same phases, the *universal state*, the *time of rebellion*, the *time of troubles* and the *interregnum*, that Toynbee used to describe past civilizations, such as the Greeks, Persians and Romans.

Where Piper and Toynbee diverge is on Tyonbee's insistence that "psychic forces" determine the course of history. In *A Study of History* Toynbee writes: "The Human protagonist in the divine drama not only serves God by enabling him to renew His creation, but also serves his fellow man by pointing the way for others to follow." Piper himself was a confirmed Agnostic. Although fascinated by parapsychology, and a believer in reincarnation, Piper was outwardly antagonistic toward organized religion, be it Buddhism or Christianity. There is no institution in Piper's work analogous to the early Roman Catholic Church, which Toynbee saw as the womb of western culture after the Fall of Rome.

Throughout Piper's future history, religion is played down or is the butt of satire, as in *Space Viking*, where he gives the following description of the pious Gilgameshers: "Their society seemed to be a loose theo-socialism, and their religion an absurd potpourri of most of the major monotheisms of the Federation period, plus doctrinal and ritualistic innovations of their own.

It is clear from Piper's conception of his own Terro-Human Future History that he believed that no human civilization would ever be more than a short stanza before the next verse of human history. Lucas Trask, the protagonist of *Space Viking*, sums up his and Piper's view of human history: "It may just be that there is something fundamentally unworkable about government itself. As long as

Homo Sapiens Terra is a wild animal, which he always has been and always will be until he evolves into something different in a million years or so, maybe a workable system of government is a political science impossibility..." To Piper this is a political reality which he accepts as neither good nor bad–just a law, like the Second Law of Thermodynamics.

Piper's Terro-Human Future History spans thousands of years through the First and Second Federation, the System States Alliance, the Interstellar Wars, the Neo-Barbarian Age, the Sword-World Invasions, the formation of the League of Civilized Worlds, the First, Second, Third and Fourth Galactic Empires, the first of which is described as containing 3,365 worlds, 1.5 trillion people and 15 intelligent races. Unfortunately, Piper's death prematurely ended his exploration into his History of the Future. Most of his stories and novels concern themselves with the Terran Federation.

The Federation included an area of over two hundred billion cubic light years and held over five million planets that could sustain life in a natural or artificial environment. Although internal evidence in the novels leaves us to suspect that only one thousand or so of these worlds were inhabited by man during the Federation period, there were still new worlds being colonized up until the time of the System States War in the ninth century A.E., before the Federation's decline and fall. The universal Lingua Terra of the Federation was an English-Spanish-Afrikanni-Portugese mixture of the old Terran (earth) tongues. Time is kept according to Galactic Standard, based on earth time in seconds, minutes and hours.

By the First Century, A.E., *Homo Sapiens* had become racially homogeneous. In *Four-Day Planet*, Piper states: "The amount of intermarriage that's gone on since the First Century, (had made) any resemblance between people's names and their appearance purely coincidental." Lingua Terra was also universal; by the Seventeenth Century, A.E. it was spoken, in one form or another, by every descendant of the race that had gone out from the Sol System in the Third Century." One could assume that by the time of *Space Viking* all racial differences had been lost, although there is some mention of new racial differentiation. On Agni, a hot-star planet, the inhabitants were said to be tough for Neo-Barbarians and to have very dark skin.

Where are the American-Sino-Soviet superpowers in Piper's Terro-Human Future History? And what has happened to the cultural domination of Europe and North America?

The answer to this question lies in Piper's earliest short stories and novelettes, many predating the creation of his Terro-Human Future History. Throughout his body of work, Piper shows a predilection for certain themes: nuclear war, the cyclical nature of civilization, the threat of barbarians from within society and from without, the citizen patriot, nuclear war, reincarnation, time travel, parapsychological phenomenon, etc. In many of his stories published in the 1940s and '50s the threat of a global nuclear holocaust is clearly on his mind–as it was on the mind of any sane person who lived in that era of nuclear brinkmanship.

Piper's first short story, "Time and Time Again," is where he first mentions a Third World War, one that takes place in 1975 (only one year prior to the date given to the "Third World War" in his History of the Future letter to Peter Weston). In "Flight From Tomorrow" (re-titled from "Immunity"), which was published in 1950, is the first story using Atomic Era (A.E.) dating and the first one to explore the rise and fall of civilization on earth. There are some glaring inconsistencies with later stories, which makes it impossible to place "Flight From Tomorrow" in the Terro-Human Future History, and the central idea that man could over time "adapt" to radioactivity is wrong, although that was not obvious at the time the story was written. It is certainly one of the more interesting stories in the Piper canon, and contains many of the ideas which we find in later Terro-Human Future Histories stories.

"Day of the Moron" could almost be called a part of the Terro-Human Future History; in this early story, Piper is clearly working out some of the background he later uses in his future history. However, there is no internal evidence that would make it a part of his Terro-Human Future History (nor does Piper place it there in his "letter").

It isn't until we get to *Uller Uprising* that we find the first story of the Terro-Human Future History. *Uller Uprising* has an interesting history of its own; it first appeared as one of three short novels in a Twayne Triplet (a series of three novels along a similar theme published in one large book by Twayne) in 1952. A shorter version, by some 20,000 words, was later published in 1953 in *Space Science Fiction*. It's very unusual for a book to be serialized after its initial book publication. All the stories in *The Petrified Planet* were based on a science essay by noted scientist Dr. John D. Clark, chief chemist at the Naval Air Rocket Test Station. The find of several so-called Piperisms, the curse Niflheim, for example, come right out of Clark's essay.

But while the *Uller Uprising* is a treasure trove of information on the Fourth Century, A.E., it doesn't tell us much about the early Terran Federation. Instead we have to go to "The Edge of the Knife" about the professor who *sees* into the future. The professor gets vision from the Third World War through the Third Imperium, storing his data in file folders, much as Piper was reputed to do. However, this story is most valuable for data on the early Federation:

> He sighed and sat down at Marjorie's typewriter and began transcribing his notes. Assassination of Khalid ib'n Hussein, the pro–Western leader of the newly formed Islamic Caliphate; period of anarchy in the Middle East; interfactional power-struggles; Turkish intervention. He wondered how long that would last; Khalid's son, Tallal ib'n Khalid, was at school in England when his father was-would be-killed. He would return, and eventually take his father's place, in time to bring the Caliphate into the Terran Federation when the general war came. There were some notes on that already; the war would result from an attempt by the Indian Communists to seize East Pakistan. The trouble was that he so seldom "remembered" an exact date.

Later in "The Edge of the Knife":

> There would be an Eastern (Axis) inspired uprising in Azerbaijan by the middle of next year; before autumn, the Indian Communists would make their fatal attempt to seize East Pakistan. The Thirty Days' War would be the immediate result. By that time, the Lunar base would be completed and ready; the enemy missiles would be supplied. Delivered without warning, it should have succeeded except that every rocket port had its secret duplicate and triplicate. That was Operation Triple Cross; no wonder Major Cutler had been so startled at the words, last evening. The enemy would be utterly overwhelmed under the rain of missiles from across space, but until the moon rockets began to fall, the United States would suffer grievously.

The end result, according to Piper, is World War III-the nightmare, in the 1950s and '60s, we all dreaded come to life. The new order is the Pan Federation, otherwise known as the First Federation, formed after the Thirty Days War. According to a security officer, who talks to our future visionary: "It's all pretty hush-hush, but this term Terran Federation (is) for a proposed organization to take the place of the U.N. if that organization breaks up...."

In "The Mercenaries," mention is made of the Islamic Kaliphate and a Fourth Komintern, which almost puts this story, which first appears in *Astounding* in 1949, into the Terro-Human Federation canon. Obviously, H. Beam Piper was already synthesizing his "view of the near future" as early as 1946 in "Time and Time Again" with the Hartley Presidency. I suspect, like Asimov and Heinlein, had he lived into the 1980s, Piper would have found a way to unite all his stories into one grand "universe."

There is no story covering the events on earth after the Thirty Days War, although in "The Return" there is a convincing portrait of earth devastated by a long-ago nuclear war. Nature has run riot and the human survivors are slowly beginning to rebuild civilization again. There are some interesting parallels and it could be argued that this story fits into the Terro-Human Future History several centuries after the System States War.

How did civilization repair itself after the Third World War? Certainly, by 54 A.E. (1996 A.D.) civilization had repaired itself enough to successfully mount a major archeological expedition to Mars, as described in "Omnilingual." (Like many visionary science-fiction writers of his time, Piper would have been aghast at how little the space program has come since Sputnik.) His own definition of Lingua Terra provides the loci of early Federation civilization, especially since most of the nations are in the Southern Hemisphere. We can safely assume that the English language influence comes from U.S. and British refugees from the Northern Hemisphere, as well as Australia. In *Four-Day* planet two major newspapers are mentioned, the *La Presna* from Buenos Aires and the *Melbourne Times*.

The government of the First Federation was based on the Corporate State-quite distinct from the Second Federation. By the time of the Second Federation, Piper compares the Federation government to that of Georgian England, a representative government with colonies and member states, rather than a strict monarchy. There are also charter companies (like the British East India Company) that discover and develop new planetary colonies, such as the Chartered Zarathustran Company which attempts to enslave the Fuzzies in *Little Fuzzy*.

Piper, in "The Edge of the Knife," compares Federation colonial expansion to: "And when Mars and Venus are colonized, there will be the same historic situations, at least in general shape, as arose when the European powers were colonizing the New Worlds, or for that matter, when the Greek city-states were throwing out colonies across the Aegean." Later he compares the early Federation with the Spanish Conquest, with events like the Uller Uprising and the Loki Enslavement. Many Federation planets have their own colonial governors who can only be overthrown by direct military intervention, and who are governed through and with the consent of a legislature.

Most of Piper's Terro-Human Federation stories, with the exception of "Graveyard of Dreams" and the novel it inspired, *Cosmic Computer*, involve the Federation's exploration and subjugation of new planets. *Cosmic Computer* takes place after the disastrous System States War (a thinly disguised version of our own Civil War), when the Federation has clearly entered its Toynbeean "time of troubles." In the follow-up novel, *Space Viking*, which takes place in the "interregnum," Piper writes that the System States War led to a period of instability and the eventual dissolution of the Second Federation. The Space Vikings, whose ancestors fled after the defeat of the System States Alliance, flee far beyond the boundaries of the Federation and create a dozen worlds named after famous swords.

The Terran Federation itself is well mapped out by *Four-Day Planet, Uller Uprising, Little Fuzzy, Fuzzy Sapiens, Cosmic Computer* and half a dozen short stories; however, only one novel, *Space Viking*, and three short stories exist to describe the next four to five thousand years. Furthermore, since *Space Viking* takes place several hundred years before the First Galactic Empire, there are some rather large holes indeed.

Eventually, the Interstellar Wars begin and the Second Federation is thrown into chaos, with only a few older worlds, like Marduk and Odin, retaining any vestiges of civilization and star faring space craft. In *Space Viking*, the descendents of the System States Alliance who fled from the Federation, return to prey on the worlds of the Old Federation which have over the centuries descended into barbarism.

It's only in the short story, "A Slave Is a Slave," that Piper explores the First Galactic Empire, during its expansion period, as it rediscovers the lost worlds of the former Federation. "A Slave Is a Slave" does illuminate some of the events after *Space Viking*, but leaves us with many questions more about where the Empire began and how it rose to power. *Ministry of Disturbance* takes place some eight hundred years later when the Empire is at peace and stagnating. This story sheds some light on a few of the previous Emperors, their reigns and the state of the once mighty Sword-Worlds, but again provides us with nothing concerning the genesis of the First Empire.

"The Keeper" is enigmatic at best, taking place in the Fifth Empire and reveals few clues regarding the fates of the previous four Empires and the current epoch. Terra, after several atomic wars, has fallen into barbarism and a new ice age. It has even been "lost" during the interregnums of several galactic empires. Terra is now only an outpost of the Fifth Galactic Empire, with only a nearby naval base for company. There are hints that civilization has spread far and wide throughout the galaxy, but certainly Earth is a backwater world.

Sadly, Piper's premature death deprived us of the full expanse of his History of the Future as well as some cracking-good yarns.

Appendix D:
Piper Weapons Inventory

This is H. Beam Piper's own inventory of his weapons collection on June 12, 1956, that he loaned for exhibition in the Thomas T. Taber Museum of the Lycoming County Historical Society, before he and his wife left for their extended stay in Paris, France.

H. Beam Piper
1314 Eight Street
Altoona, PA

12 June, 1956

Mr. Clement S. Coryell,
President Lycoming Country
Historical Society
1056 West Fourth Street
Williamsport, PA

Dear Mr. Coryell:

It is quite possible that I may have met you, through my friend the late Ferd W. Coleman, during one or another of my many visits to Williamsport during his life. If so, I regret that the occasion has quite slipped my memory. I was last in Williamsport in November of 1953, when I was helping Miss Bennet at the museum on Fourth Street in arranging the listing of firearms bequeathed by Mr. Coleman to the Historical Society, and, as I recall, I went that evening with Mrs. Coleman to a meeting of the Society. I go into all this by way of self-introduction, and to identify myself as a friend of the Lycoming County Historical Society.

I have very recently and very suddenly found myself obliged to go abroad indefinitely, and among the possessions which I cannot take with me is a collection of eighty-odd pistols, dating from the early Seventeenth to the early Twentieth Centuries. I cannot bring myself to sell them, and would much rather have them placed on exhibition where others could see them and enjoy them than boxed away in some storage-warehouse. When the idea of placing them on loan-exhibition occurred to me, the Lycoming County Historical Society's museum was my first thought.

A list of the collection is enclosed. If you would accept them as a loan, I will pay all packing and carriage charges to Williamsport, and if given enough time, will come to Williamsport and help list, card and arrange them, as I did with Ferd Coleman's things. I would estimate that they would require about a hundred square feet of case-space for proper display. I could have them shipped within a few days.

Moreover, I can assure you that any work you do on setting up the display will not be wasted on any over-night exhibition; the collection would remain in the Society's museum for a year at the very least, and quite possibly for a number of years. When I return from Europe, I expect to locate in New York, where the Constitutional "right of the people to keep and bear arms" is non-existent with respect to pistols, even antiques, and I may be staying there a while.

I would very much appreciate hearing whether the Historical Society will accept this loan or not as soon as possible. I certainly hope this decision can be made at executive level, without waiting for the next general business meeting, because I shall only be in Altoona until the end of next week, and it would be almost impossible for me to make shipping arrangements, at least prepaid shipping arrangements, after then. You cannot possibly regret more than I do this short notice; I am giving only the time I myself am give by the circumstances.

Very sincerely yours
H. Beam Piper

Wheellock

1. Flemish or French holster pistol, type used by Royalist cavalry in English Civil War, 1625–65.

Flintlock

2. French holster pistol, stocked in black horn, 1650–75.
3. Pair Italian holster pistols, 18½" over all. 1675–1774.
4. Spanish Miguelet-lock holster pistol, with belt-hook, 1675–1775.
5. Scottish all-steal Highlander, formerly in Royal Caledonian Museum, Glasgow, 1675–1700.
6. English screw-barrel greatcoat-pocket pistol, rifled; silver butt-cap hallmarked. 1728–29 (Probin).
7. French screw-barrel large pocket size, 1750–75.
8. Pair English holster pistols, brass barrels, 1745–75 (Whately).
9. French all-stell pocket-pistol, screw barrell [*sic*], 1750–75.
10. English military pistol, long type, half-ounce ball, 1750–1800.
11. English military pistol, short model, once ball; this specimen made for British East India Company 1810.
12. English small belt pistol, belt-hook (Lewis & Tomes), 1815–25.
13. English holster pistol 1775–1825 (Jones, Bristol).
14. English carriage pistol, 1775–1825 (Manning).
15. English holster or carriage pistol, 1800–10 (Bate).
16. English brass-barrel holster pistol, 1780–1815 (W. Ketland).
17. American brass-barrel pocket-pistol, 1770–1800.
18. American made double-barrel pistol, turnover barrels, probably made to match a double Kentucky rifle, 1770–1800.
19. American holster pistol, curly maple stock, probably Pennsylvania, date 1833.
20. U.S. Model 1836 Army pistol, dated 1837 (A. Waters).
21. Short English coachman's carbine, 1875–1900 (Wogden).

Percussion Pistols

22. U.S. Model of 1836, altered to percussion, dated 1838 (Waters).
23. U.S. Model of 1842, dated 1854 (Johnson).
24. English Dueling Pistol, 1820–25. (Wilkinson).
25. Pair English Dueling Pistols, 1845–60 (probably made for American trade) (Joseph Manton).
26. Pair English pocket or belt pistols, set-triggers for dueling use, made for American trade, 1835–60 (Chance & Son).
27. American pocket-pistol, sliver mounted, 1835–1860 (Tryon).
28. American pocket or belt pistol, said to be Philadelphia city police arm, 1835–50 (Tryon).
29. American pocket pistol, H. Deringer [*sic*]. Type and size used by J. Wilkes Booth.
30. English belt or carriage pistol, 1834–45 (Field).
31. English double-barrel pistol, 1840–60 (Collins).
32. English small belt pistol, 1840–55 (Nixon).
33. American underhammer pistol, 1850–70.
34. Kaan target or hunting pistol, curly maple stock, made from piece of rifle barrel. (Picked this one up in Williamsport, got it somewhere up around Hillsgrove) 1850–80.

35. American single-shot double-action, 1837 (Allen & Thurber).
36. American all-metal Fairbanks pistol, 1845–55.
37. American, small & cheap cast-iron pistol, type known as Yankee Fool-Killer, sold for about twenty-five cents, 1850–75.

Percussion Revolvers, Colt

38. Dragoon, First Model, 1848, .44, six shots.
39. Navy, 1851 Model, .36, six shots.
40. Navy, 1860 Model, .36, six shots.
41. Army, 1860 Model, .44, six shots.
42. Pocket, 1849 Model, .31, five shots.
43. Pocket, Model 1849, engraved, .31, five shots.
44. Pocket, Model 1849, Wells-Fargo type, .31, six shots.
45. Pocket, Model 1852, .36, five shots.
46. Police. 1860 Model, .36, five shots.

Percussion Revolvers, Other

47. Wesson & Leavitt (Mass. Arms Co.). This arm infringed the Colt patents; manufacture stopped. .31, five shots.

(All the following percussion revolvers were manufactured between 1856, when the Colt patents expired, and 1865.)

48. Ell's Double Action, .31, five shots
49. Cooper double-action, .31, five shots
50. Starr .44, six shots
51. Rogers & Spencer, .44, six shots.
52. Savage, .36, six shots
53. Beale's Navy, .44, six shots.
54. Freeman's, .44, six shots.
55. Massachusetts Arms & Co. Adams, .36, five shots.

Pistols, Metallic Cartridge

56. Hammond single shot, 44 RF
57. Remington double derringer, .41 RF
58. Sharps 4-shot, .22 short

Revolvers, Metallic Cartridge Colt

59. 1860 Army, altered to .44 CF. Six shots
60. Single Action Army, .45, six shots.
61. Double Action Army, .45, six shots.
62. "New Army" Model Commercial, .38 CF, six shots.
63. "New Army" Commercial, .32–20 WCF, six shots.
64. "Old Line" Pocket, .22 short, seven shots.
65. "New Line" Pocket, .22 short, seven shots.

Revolvers, Metallic Cartridge, Other

66. Remington .32 RF, altered from .31 percussion, five shots.
67. Smith & Wesson tip-up, .22 short, seven shots.
68. Smith & Wesson tip-up, .32 RF, five shots.

69. Smith & Wesson, first model single action, .32 CF, five shots.
70. Remington-Smoot, .30 RF, five shots.
71. Merwin & Hulbert, .32 CF, five shots.
72. New York Arms Co. "Columbian," .32 CF, five shots.
73. Kolb "Baby Hammerless," .22 short, six shot.
74. Webley Mark VI .455, six shots. (Not a Webley & Scott arm; probably made in Canada during World War II.)

A Number of Bullet Molds, Pistol Horns and Pistol Flasks

Dating on some of these arms, especially those of individual workmanship, will be less correct as to specific item than as to type. My arms-reference library has already been boxed up, and I'm a little vague on exact years for some of the makers. Substantially, however, the dates are accurate as to the time when arms of these types were made.

With the exception of #74, the .455 Webley, all of these types were used, even if not made, in America, and most of these types were used in the Colony or Commonwealth of Pennsylvania. With the exception of the venerable and still-popular Colt Single Action, none of the metallic cartridge models are in current production.

H. Beam Piper

Appendix E:
Piper Bibliography

A bibliography of original Piper works (novels, short fiction, and nonfiction) and reprintings by year of first publication as listed by David Johnson at Zarthani.net (www.zarthani.net) and reprinted by permission.

1927

A Catalogue of Early Pennsylvania and other Firearms and Edged Weapons at "Restless Oaks," McElhattan, Pa., Henry W. Shoemaker and H. Beam Piper, Altoona, PA: Times Tribune Co., 1927, 50 pages (nonfiction).

1947

"Time and Time Again," H. Beam Piper, *Astounding Science Fiction*, Vol. XXXIX, No. 2, April 1947 (December 1947 in Britain), pp. 27–43, short story with interior illustration by Vincent Napoli. Reprinted in (or adapted as):
    A Treasury of Science Fiction, Groff Conklin, ed., New York: Crown, 1948.
    Dimension X, Episode #39, NBC Radio, radio adaptation aired July 12, 1951, 30 minutes, script adapted by Ernest Kinoy, directed by Fred Way, with cast including David Anderson (young Allan) and Joseph Curtin (Allan's dad).
    Uberwindung Von Raum Und Zeit, Gotthard Gunther, ed., West Germany: Karl Rauch, 1952.
    X Minus One, Episode #33, NBC Radio, radio adaptation aired January 11, 1956, 30 minutes, script adapted by Ernest Kinoy, directed by Daniel Sutter, with cast including Jack Grimes (young Allan), Peter Fernandez, Joe DeSantas, Joseph Bell, Clark Gordon, Herm Dinken, Dick Hamilton, and James Ducas.
    The Worlds of H. Beam Piper, John F. Carr, ed., New York: Ace, 1983, pp. 9–28, with uncredited cover illustration.
    Isaac Asimov Presents the Great SF Stories: 9 (1947), Isaac Asimov and Martin H. Greenberg, eds., DAW, 1983.
    The Golden Years of Science Fiction: Fifth Series, Isaac Asimov and Martin H. Greenberg, eds., Bonanza, 1985.
    Crossroads of Destiny: Science Fiction Stories, P.D. Cacek(?), ed., Rockville, MD: Wildside Press, 2006.

1948

"He Walked Around the Horses," H. Beam Piper, *Astounding Science Fiction*, Vol. XLI, No. 2, April 1948 (December 1948 in Britain), pp. 53–70, novelette with interior illustration by Cartier. Reprinted in:
    World of Wonder, Fletcher Pratt, ed., New York: Twayne, 1951.
    Best SF 3, Edmund Crispin, ed., London: Faber and Faber, 1958.
    Aspects of Science Fiction, G. D. Doherty, ed., London: John Murray, 1959.

Science Fiction Through the Ages 2, I. O. Evans, ed., London: Panther, 1966.

A Science Fiction Argosy, Damon Knight, ed., New York: Simon and Schuster, 1972.

Isaac Asimov's Science Fiction Treasury, Isaac Asimov, Martin H. Greenberg and Joseph D. Olander, eds., Bonanza/Crown, 1980.

Space Mail, Isaac Asimov, Martin H. Greenberg and Joseph D. Olander, eds., Fawcett, 1980.

Paratime, John F. Carr, ed., New York: Ace, 1981, pp. 14–37, with cover illustration by Michael Whelan from "Police Operation."

The Golden Age of Science Fiction, Kingsley Amis, ed., Hutchinson, 1981.

Isaac Asimov Presents the Great SF Stories: 10 (1948), Isaac Asimov and Martin H. Greenberg, eds., DAW, 1983.

The Golden Years of Science Fiction: Fifth Series, Isaac Asimov and Martin H. Greenberg, eds., Bonanza, 1985.

Alternate Histories, Charles G. Waugh and Martin H. Greenberg, eds., Garland, 1986.

The Complete Paratime, Anonymous, ed., New York: Ace, 2001, with cover art by Dave Dorman.

Crossroads of Destiny: Science Fiction Stories, P.D. Cacek(?), ed., Rockville, MD: Wildside Press, 2006.

"Police Operation," H. Beam Piper, *Astounding Science Fiction*, Vol. XLI, No. 5, July 1948, pp. 8–35, novelette with interior illustration by Cartier. Reprinted in:

Space Police, Andre Norton, ed., Cleveland and New York: World, 1956.

The Best of Astounding, Anthony R. Lewis, ed., Baronet, 1978.

Paratime, John F. Carr, ed., New York: Ace, 1981, pp. 39–75, with cover illustration by Michael Whelan from "Police Operation."

Analog: The Best of Science Fiction, Anonymous, ed., and W. Galahad, 1985.

The Complete Paratime, Anonymous, ed., New York: Ace, 2001, with cover art by Dave Dorman.

Naudsonce and Other SF, Alan Rodgers, ed., Aegypan Press, 2006.

Five Sci-Fi Short Stories by H. Beam Piper, audiobook read by Mark Nelson, LibriVox, 2007.

1950

"The Mercenaries," H. Beam Piper, *Astounding Science Fiction*, Vol. XLV, No. 1, March 1950, pp. 57–77, novelette with interior illustration by Brush. Reprinted in:

The Worlds of H. Beam Piper, John F. Carr, ed., New York: Ace, 1983, pp. 29–55, with uncredited cover illustration.

Crossroads of Destiny: Science Fiction Stories, P.D. Cacek(?), ed., Rockville, MD: Wildside Press, 2006.

"Last Enemy," H. Beam Piper, *Astounding Science Fiction*, Vol. XLV, No. 6, August 1950 (February 1951 in Britain), pp. 5–60, novelette with cover and interior illustration by Walt Miller. Reprinted in:

The Astounding Science Fiction Anthology, John W. Campbell, Jr., ed., New York: Simon and Schuster, 1952.

The Second Astounding Science Fiction Anthology, John W. Campbell, Jr., ed., Four Square Books, 1965.

Paratime, John F. Carr, ed., New York: Ace, 1981, pp. 77–147, with cover illustration by Michael Whelan from "Police Operation."

Robert Adams' Book of Alternate Worlds, Robert Adams, Pamela Crippen Adams and Martin H. Greenberg, eds., New York: New American Library/Signet, 1987.

The Complete Paratime, Anonymous, ed., New York: Ace, 2001, with cover art by Dave Dorman.

Graveyard of Dreams: Science Fiction Stories, P.D. Cacek(?), ed., Rockville, MD: Wildside Press, 2006.

"Flight from Tomorrow," H. Beam Piper, *Future* combined with *Science Fiction Stories*, Vol. 1, No. 3, September/October 1950, pp. 36–49, novelette with interior illustration by Lawrence. Reprinted in:

The Worlds of H. Beam Piper, John F. Carr, ed., New York: Ace, 1983, pp. 111–134, with uncredited cover illustration.

Flight from Tomorrow: Science Fiction Stories, P.D. Cacek(?), ed., Rockville, MD: Wildside Press, 2006.

Flight from Tomorrow and Other SF, Alan Rodgers, ed., Aegypan Press, 2006.

Five Sci-Fi Short Stories by H. Beam Piper, audiobook read by Mark Nelson, LibriVox, 2007.

"Rebel Raider," H. Beam Piper, *True: The Men's Magazine*, December 1950, pp. 128–140, non-fiction article with interior illustration by Mario Cooper.

1951

"Operation R.S.V.P.," H. Beam Piper, *Amazing Stories*, Vol. 25, No. 1, January 1951, pp. 52–58, short story with interior illustration by Robert Jones. Reprinted in:

World of Wonder, Fletcher Pratt, ed., New York: Twayne, 1951
Amazing Stories: 40th Anniversary Issue, Vol. 40, No. 5, April 1966.
The Worlds of H. Beam Piper, John F. Carr, ed., New York: Ace, 1983, pp. 135–146, with uncredited cover illustration.
Amazing Science Fiction Stories: The Wild Years 1946–1955, Martin H. Greenberg, ed., Lake Geneva, WI: TSR, 1987.
Flight from Tomorrow: Science Fiction Stories, P.D. Cacek(?), ed., Rockville, MD: Wildside Press, 2006.
Graveyard of Dreams: Science Fiction Stories, P.D. Cacek(?), ed., Rockville, MD: Wildside Press, 2006.
Flight from Tomorrow and Other SF, Alan Rodgers, ed., Aegypan Press, 2006.
"Dearest," H. Beam Piper, *Weird Tales*, Vol. 43, No. 3, March 1951 (November 1951 in Britain), pp. 68–78, short story with interior illustration by Vincent Napoli. Reprinted in:
The Worlds of H. Beam Piper*, John F. Carr, ed., New York: Ace, 1983, pp. 57–75, with uncredited cover illustration.
"Temple Trouble," H. Beam Piper, *Astounding Science Fiction*, Vol. XLVII, No. 2, April 1951 (October 1951 in Britain), pp. 6–34, novelette with cover and interior illustrations by Rogers. Reprinted in:
Science Fiction Stories 5 (as "Machtkampf der Gotzen"), Walter Spiegl, ed. and transl., Frankfurt: Ullstein (#2804), 1970, pp. 7–41, ISBN 3-548-02804-7, DM2.80.
Paratime, John F. Carr, ed., New York: Ace, 1981, pp. 261–295, with cover illustration by Michael Whelan from "Police Operation."
The Complete Paratime, Anonymous, ed., New York: Ace, 2001, with cover art by Dave Dorman.
Five Sci-Fi Short Stories by H. Beam Piper, audiobook read by Mark Nelson, LibriVox, 2007.
"Day of the Moron," H. Beam Piper, *Astounding Science Fiction*, Vol. XLVIII, No. 1, September 1951 (March 1952 in Britain), pp. 7–34, novelette with cover and interior illustration by Rogers. Reprinted in:
The Worlds of H. Beam Piper, John F. Carr, ed., New York: Ace, 1983.
Naudsonce and Other SF, Alan Rodgers, ed., Aegypan Press, 2006.
"Genesis," H. Beam Piper, *Future* combined with *Science Fiction Stories*, Vol. 2, No. 3, September 1951, pp. 8–21, 37, novelette with interior illustration by Virgil Finlay. Reprinted in:
Shadow of Tomorrow, Frederik Pohl, ed., New York: Doubleday, 1953.
The Worlds of H. Beam Piper, John F. Carr, ed., New York: Ace, 1983, pp. 147–170, with uncredited cover illustration.
Isaac Asimov's Wonderful Worlds of Science Fiction # 6: Neanderthals, Isaac Asimov, Martin H. Greenberg and Charles G. Waugh, eds., New York: New American Library/Signet, 1987.
Flight from Tomorrow: Science Fiction Stories, P.D. Cacek(?), ed., Rockville, MD: Wildside Press, 2006.
Graveyard of Dreams: Science Fiction Stories, P.D. Cacek(?), ed., Rockville, MD: Wildside Press, 2006.
Flight from Tomorrow and Other SF, Alan Rodgers, ed., Aegypan Press, 2006.

1952

"Uller Uprising," H. Beam Piper, *The Petrified Planet: A Twayne Science-Fiction Triplet*, uncredited editor (Fletcher Pratt?), New York: Twayne, 1952 (hardcover), pp. 74–196, novelette. Reprinted in or reissued as:
"Uller Uprising, " *Space Science Fiction*, Vol. 1, No. 4, February 1953 (March 1953 in Britain), pp. 4–75, serial (part 1 of two parts) with interior illustration by Orban (serialization of 1952 novelette).
"Uller Uprising, " *Space Science Fiction*, Vol. 1, No. 5, March 1953 (April 1953 in Britain), pp. 120–156, serial (part 2 of two parts) with illustration by Orban (serialization of 1952 novelette).
Uller Uprising, New York: Ace, 1983, with cover illustration by Gino D'Achille, reissue including original introduction ("The Silicone World" and "The Flourine Planet") by Dr. John D. Clark. Reprinted from The Petrified Planet, pp. xi–xx.
Der Uller-Aufstand, H. Beam Piper (German translation by Dolf Strasser), Frankfurt: Ullstein, 1977 (#3306), with cover illustration by Paul Lehr.

1953

"Null-ABC," H. Beam Piper and John J. McGuire, *Astounding Science Fiction*, Vol. L, No. 6, February 1953 (July 1953 in Britain), pp. 12–54, serial (part 1 of two parts) with interior illustration by van Dongen, and
"Null-ABC," H. Beam Piper and John J. McGuire, *Astounding Science Fiction*, Vol. LI, No. 1, March 1953 (August 1953 in Britain), pp. 112–153, serial (part 2 of two parts) in with interior illustration by Pawelka. Reprinted in or reissued as:

Crisis in 2140, H. Beam Piper and John J. McGuire, New York: Ace, 1957 (D-227), with uncredited cover illustration ("double novel" reissue with *Gunner Cade*, Cyril Judd, alias for C.M. Kornbluth and Judith Merril).

Null-ABC, H. Beam Piper (and John J. McGuire, uncredited), German translation by Heinz Nagel, Frankfurt: Ullstein, 1972 (#2888), with cover illustration by Schoenherr.

Null-ABC, H. Beam Piper and John J. McGuire, Rockville, MD: Wildside Press, 2006.

Null-ABC, H. Beam Piper and John J. McGuire, Aegypan Press, 2006.

Murder in the Gunroom, H. Beam Piper, New York: Knopf, 1953, 243 pages, novel with dust jacket illustration by Georgianna Schiffmacher, hardcover, and reissued as:

Murder in the Gunroom, H. Beam Piper, Baltimore: Old Earth Books, 1993.

Murder in the Gunroom, H. Beam Piper, Aegypan Press, 2006.

1954

"The Return," H. Beam Piper and John J. McGuire, *Astounding Science Fiction*, Vol. LII, No. 5, January 1954 (June 1954 in Britain), pp. 70–95, novelette with interior illustration by Kelly Freas. Reprinted as:

The Science-Fictional Sherlock Holmes, Robert C. Peterson, ed., Denver: The Council of Four, 1960, pp. 105–137 (expanded version of 1954 novelette).

Empire, John F. Carr, ed., New York: Ace, 1981, pp. 183–214, with cover illustration by Michael Whelan.

Crossroads of Destiny: Science Fiction Stories, P.D. Cacek(?), ed., Rockville, MD: Wildside Press, 2006.

1955

"Time Crime," H. Beam Piper, *Astounding Science Fiction*, Vol. LIV, No. 6, February 1955, pp. 8–49, serial (part 1 of two parts) with interior illustration by Kelly Freas, and

"Time Crime," H. Beam Piper, *Astounding Science Fiction*, Vol. LV, No. 1, March 1955, pp. 85–131, serial (part 2 of two parts) with interior illustration by Kelly Freas. Reprinted in or reissued as:

Paratime, John F. Carr, ed., New York: Ace, 1981, pp. 149–259, with cover illustration by Michael Whelan from "Police Operation" (combination of 1955 serialization).

The Complete Paratime, Anonymous, ed., New York: Ace, 2001, with cover art by Dave Dorman (combination of 1955 serialization).

Time Crime, H. Beam Piper, Aegypan Press, 2006 (combination of 1955 serialization).

1957

"Omnilingual," H. Beam Piper, *Astounding Science Fiction*, Vol. LVIII, No. 6, February 1957 (June 1957 in Britain), pp. 8–46, novelette with cover and interior illustration by Kelly Freas. Reprinted in:

Prologue to Analog, John W. Campbell, Jr., ed., Garden City, NY: Doubleday, 1962.

Analog Anthology, John W. Campbell, Jr., ed., Dobson, 1965.

Great Science Fiction Stories About Mars, T. E. Dikty, ed., Fredrik Fell, 1966.

Apeman, Spaceman, Leon E. Stover and Harry Harrison, eds., Garden City, NY: Doubleday, 1968.

Mars, We Love You, Jane Hipolito and Willis E. McNelly, eds., Garden City, NY: Doubleday, 1971.

The Days After Tomorrow, Hans Stefan Santesson, ed., Little and Brown, 1971.

Where Do We Go from Here?, Isaac Asimov, ed., Garden City, NY: Doubleday, 1971.

Tomorrow, and Tomorrow, and Tomorrow..., Bonnie L. Heintz, Frank Herbert, Donald A. Joos and Jane Agorn McGee, eds., Holt, Rinehart and Winston, 1974.

Science Fiction Novellas, Harry Harrison and Willis E. McNelly, eds., New York: Charles Scribner's Sons, 1975.

Federation, John F. Carr, ed., New York: Ace, 1981, pp. 2–55, with cover illustration by Michael Whelan.

From Mind to Mind, Stanley Schmidt, ed., Davis, 1984.

Isaac Asimov Presents the Great SF Stories: 19 (1957), Isaac Asimov and Martin H. Greenberg, eds., New York: DAW Books, 1989

"Lone Star Planet," H. Beam Piper and John J. McGuire, *Fantastic Universe Science Fiction*, Vol. 7, No. 3, March 1957, pp. 4–66, novella with cover illustration by Virgil Finlay. Reprinted in or reissued as:

A Planet for Texans, H. Beam Piper and John J. McGuire, New York: Ace, 1958 (D-299), with uncredited cover illustration ("double novel" reissue, with *Star Born*, Andre Norton).

"Lone Star Planet" in *Four-Day Planet and Lone Star Planet*, H. Beam Piper, New York: Ace, 1979, pp. 219–340, with cover illustration by Michael Whelan.
    A Planet for Texans, P.D. Cacek(?), ed., Rockville, MD: Wildside Press, 2007.
"The Edge of the Knife," H. Beam Piper, *Amazing Stories*, Vol. 31, No. 5, May 1957, pp. 6–50, short story with uncredited interior illustration. Reprinted in:
    Empire, John F. Carr, ed., New York: Ace, 1981, pp. 13–59, with cover illustration by Michael Whelan.
    Flight from Tomorrow and Other SF, Alan Rodgers, ed., Aegypan Press, 2006.
"The Keeper," H. Beam Piper, *Venture Science Fiction*, Vol. 1, No. 4, July 1957, pp. 80–100, novelette with interior illustration by Cindy Smith. Reprinted in:
    Empire, John F. Carr, ed., New York: Ace, 1981, pp. 217–242, with cover illustration by Michael Whelan.

1958

"Graveyard of Dreams," H. Beam Piper, *Galaxy Science Fiction*, Vol. 15, No. 4, February 1958, pp. 122–144, novelette with interior illustration by Dillon. Reprinted in or reissued as:
    Junkyard Planet, H. Beam Piper, New York: G.P. Putnam's Sons, 1963, 224 pages, novel with dust jacket illustration by Herb Mott (expanded version of 1958 novelette).
    The Cosmic Computer, H. Beam Piper, New York: Ace, 1964 (F-274), with uncredited? cover illustration (reissue of *Junkyard Planet*).
    The Cosmic Computer, H. Beam Piper, New York: Berkley (Ace), 1963, with cover illustration by Michael Whelan.
    Der Verschollene Computer, H. Beam Piper (German translation by Dolf Strasser), Frankfurt: Ullstein (#3167), 1975, with cover illustration by Chet Morrow.
    Federation, John F. Carr, ed., New York: Ace, 1981, pp. 173–199, with cover illustration by Michael Whelan (reprint).
    Der kosmische Computer, H. Beam Piper (transl. Juergen Saupe), Pabel Terra TB (German), 1981, with uncredited cover illustration.
    Flight from Tomorrow: Science Fiction Stories, P.D. Cacek(?), ed., Rockville, MD: Wildside Press, 2006 (reprint).
    Graveyard of Dreams: Science Fiction Stories, P.D. Cacek(?), ed., Rockville, MD: Wildside Press, 2006 (reprint).
    Flight from Tomorrow and Other SF, Alan Rodgers, ed., Aegypan Press, 2006 (reprint).
    Five Sci-Fi Short Stories by H. Beam Piper, audiobook read by Mark Nelson, LibriVox, 2007 (reprint).
    The Cosmic Computer, H. Beam Piper, audiobook read by Mark Nelson, LibriVox, 2007.
"Ministry of Disturbance," H. Beam Piper, *Astounding Science Fiction*, Vol. LXII, No. 4, December 1958, pp. 8–46, novelette with interior illustration by von Dongen. Reprinted in:
    Seven Trips Through Time and Space, Groff Conklin, ed., Fawcett Gold Medal, 1968.
    Empire, John F. Carr, ed., New York: Ace, 1981, pp. 131–179, with cover illustration by Michael Whelan.
    Isaac Asimov's Wonderful Worlds of Science Fiction #1: Intergalactic Empires, Isaac Asimov, Martin H. Greenberg and Charles G. Waugh, eds., Signet, 1983.

1959

"Hunter Patrol," H. Beam Piper and John J. McGuire, *Amazing Science Fiction Stories*, Vol. 33, No. 5, May 1959, pp. 20–45, novelette. Reprinted in:
    The Worlds of H. Beam Piper, John F. Carr, ed., New York: Ace, 1983, pp. 77–109, with uncredited cover illustration
    Thrilling Science Fiction, Ultimate Publishing, June 1973, pp. 80–104, 115.
"Crossroads of Destiny," H. Beam Piper, *Fantastic Universe Science Fiction*, Vol. 11, No. 4, July 1959, pp. 4–13, short story. Reprinted in:
    The Worlds of H. Beam Piper, John F. Carr, ed., New York: Ace, 1983, pp. 185–197, with uncredited cover illustration.
    Crossroads of Destiny: Science Fiction Stories, P.D. Cacek(?), ed., Rockville, MD: Wildside Press, 2006.
"The Answer," H. Beam Piper, *Fantastic Universe Science Fiction*, Vol. 12, No. 2, December 1959, pp. 4–12, short story with uncredited interior illustration. Reprinted in:

The Worlds of H. Beam Piper, John F. Carr, ed., New York: Ace, 1983, pp. 171–183, with uncredited cover illustration.

Flight from Tomorrow: Science Fiction Stories, P.D. Cacek(?), ed., Rockville, MD: Wildside Press, 2006.

Graveyard of Dreams: Science Fiction Stories, P.D. Cacek(?), ed., Rockville, MD: Wildside Press, 2006.

Flight from Tomorrow and Other SF, Alan Rodgers, ed., Aegypan Press, 2006.

Five Sci-Fi Short Stories by H. Beam Piper, audiobook read by Mark Nelson, LibriVox, 2007 (reprint).

1960

"Oomphel in the Sky," H. Beam Piper, *Analog Science Fact — Science Fiction*, Vol. LXVI, No. 3, November 1960 (March 1961 in Britain), pp. 120–158, novelette with interior illustration by Bernklau. Reprinted in:
    Federation, John F. Carr, ed., New York: Ace, 1981, pp. 114–171, with cover illustration by Michael Whelan.

1961

Four-Day Planet, H. Beam Piper, New York: G.P. Putnam's Sons, 1961, 221 pages, novel with dust jacket illustration by Charles Geer, hardcover, and republished (reprinted) in:
    "Four-Day Planet," in *Four-Day Planet and Lone Star Planet*, H. Beam Piper, New York: Ace, 1979. pp. 1–216, with cover illustration by Michael Whelan.
    Die Vier-Tage-Welt, H. Beam Piper (transl. ???), Moewig Terra Astra (German), 1981, with cover illustration by Eddie Jones (reprint).
    Four-Day Planet, H. Beam Piper, Wildside Press, 2007 (reprint).
    Four-Day Planet, H. Beam Piper, Aegypan Press, 2007 (reprint).

1962

"Naudsonce," H. Beam Piper, *Analog Science Fact — Science Fiction*, Vol. LXVIII, No. 5, January 1962 (May 1962 in Britain), pp. 6–44, novelette with interior illustration by Morey. Reprinted in:
    Federation, John F. Carr, ed., New York: Ace, 1981, pp. 57–112, with cover illustration by Michael Whelan.
    Naudsonce and Other SF, Alan Rodgers, ed., Aegypan Press, 2006.

"A Slave is a Slave," H. Beam Piper, *Analog Science Fact — Science Fiction*, Vol. LXLX (sic), No. 2, April 1962, pp. 62–82, 113–142, short novel with interior illustration by John Schoenherr. Reprinted in:
    Empire, John F. Carr, ed., New York: Ace, 1981, pp. 63–127, with cover illustration by Michael Whelan.

Little Fuzzy, H. Beam Piper, New York: Avon, 1962 (F-118), 160 pages, with cover illustration by Victor Kalins. Reprinted in or reissued as:
    Encuentro en Zarathustra, H. Beam Piper, Bruguera, 1962? (Libro Amigo #472).
    Der kleine Fuzzy, H. Beam Piper (transl. Heinz Zwack), Moewig Terra Sonderband (German), 1964, with cover illustration by Karl Stephan.
    "Little Fuzzy," in *The Fuzzy Papers*, H. Beam Piper, Garden City, NY: Doubleday, 1977 (SFBC hardback).
    Little Fuzzy, H. Beam Piper, London: Futura Orbit, 1977, with uncredited cover illustration.
    Les hommes de poche, H. Beam Piper (transl. Jacqueline Huet), Paris: Librairie des Champs-Elysées, 1977 (Le Masque SF #64), with uncredited cover illustration.
    Der kleine Fuzzy, H. Beam Piper (transl. Heinz Peter Lehnert), Pabel Terra TB (German), 1979, with uncredited cover illustration.
    Fuzzy/Ruimteiking, H. Beam Piper, Netherlands: Centripress, 1979, with cover illustration by Michael Whelan (reprint).
    "Little Fuzzy," in *The Fuzzy Papers*, H. Beam Piper, New York: Ace, 1980, pp. 1–197, with cover illustration by Michael Whelan and interior illustration by Victoria Poyser.
    Little Fuzzy, H. Beam Piper, New York: Ace, 1962 (1981?), reissue with cover illustration by Michael Whelan.
    The Adventures of Little Fuzzy, H. Beam Piper with Benson Parker, New York: Platt and Munk, 1983, with cover illustration by Michael Whelan, children's adaptation.
    "Little Fuzzy," in *The Complete Fuzzy*, H. Beam Piper, New York: Ace, 1998.

Little Fuzzy, H. Beam Piper, Wildside Press, 2007.

Little Fuzzy, H. Beam Piper, Aegypan Press, 2007.

Space Viking, H. Beam Piper, Analog Science Fact — Science Fiction, Vol. LXX, No. 3, November 1962, pp. 6–52, novel serial (part 1 of four parts) with cover and interior illustration by John Schoenherr, and

Space Viking, H. Beam Piper, Analog Science Fact — Science Fiction, Vol. LXX, No. 4, December 1962, pp. 104–146, novel serial (part 2 of four parts) with interior illustration by John Schoenherr, and

1963

Space Viking, H. Beam Piper, Analog Science Fact — Science Fiction, Vol. LXX, No. 5, January 1963, pp. 111–55, novel serial (part 3 of four parts) with interior illustration by John Schoenherr, and

Space Viking, H. Beam Piper, Analog Science Fact — Science Fiction, Vol. LXX, No. 6, February 1963, pp. 120–162, novel serial (part 4 of four parts) with interior illustration by John Schoenherr. Reprinted in or reissued as:

> *Space Viking*, H. Beam Piper, New York: Ace, 1963 (F-225), with uncredited cover illustration (combination of 1962–63 serialization).
>
> *Vikingo espacial*, H. Beam Piper (transl. ???), Barcelona: Vertice, 1966 (Galaxia #48),
>
> *Space Viking*, H. Beam Piper, New York and London: Garland, 1975 (hardback).
>
> *Die Welten-Pluenderer*, H. Beam Piper (German translation by Dolf Strasser), Frankfurt: Ullstein (#3223), 1976, with cover illustration by Chet Morrow.
>
> *Space Viking*, H. Beam Piper, London: Sphere, 1978, with uncredited cover illustration.
>
> *Fuzzy/Ruimteiking*, H. Beam Piper, Netherlands: Centripress, 1979, with cover illustration by Michael Whelan (reprint).
>
> *Space Viking*, H. Beam Piper, New York: Ace, 1963 (1981?), with cover illustration by Michael Whelan.
>
> *Space Viking*, H. Beam Piper (transl. ???), Temps Futurs (France), 1982 (Space-fiction #3), with cover illustration by P. Adamov and F. Allot.

1964

The Other Human Race, H. Beam Piper, New York: Avon (G1220), 1964, 190 pages, with uncredited cover illustration, sequel to 1962 novel Little Fuzzy. Reprinted in or reissued as:

> *Wollie Sapiens*, H. Beam Piper, Netherlands: Scala, 1976, with cover illustration by Michael Whelan.
>
> "Fuzzy Sapiens," in *The Fuzzy Papers*, H. Beam Piper, Garden City, NY: Doubleday, 1977 (SFBC hardback).
>
> *Fuzzy Sapiens*, H. Beam Piper, London: Futura Orbit, 1977.
>
> *Tinounours sapiens*, H. Beam Piper (transl. Jacqueline Huet), Paris: Librairie des Champs-Elysées, 1978 (Le Masque SF #76), with cover illustration by Atelier P. Vercken.
>
> *Fuzzy sapiens*, H. Beam Piper (transl. Heinz Peter Lehnert), Pabel Terra TB (German), 1979, with uncredited cover illustration.
>
> "Fuzzy Sapiens," in *The Fuzzy Papers*, H. Beam Piper, New York: Ace, 1980, pp. 198–406, with cover illustration by Michael Whelan and interior illustration by Victoria Poyser.
>
> *Fuzzy Sapiens*, H. Beam Piper, New York: Ace, 1964 (1981?), reissue with cover illustration by Michael Whelan.
>
> "Fuzzy Sapiens," in *The Complete Fuzzy*, H. Beam Piper, New York: Ace, 1998.

"Future History No. 1," H. Beam Piper, *Zenith*, No. 4, May 1964 (fanzine, Peter Weston, ed.), pp. 11–14 (non-fiction article about the Future History).

"Gunpowder God," H. Beam Piper, *Analog Science Fiction — Science Fact*, Vol. LXXIV, No. 3, November 1964, pp. 17–36, novelet with cover and interior illustration by John Schoenherr. Reprinted in:

> *Created by Poul Anderson: Time Wars*, Martin H. Greenberg and Charles G. Waugh, eds., New York: Tor, 1986, pp. 27–74.

1965

"Down Styphon!," H. Beam Piper, *Analog Science Fiction — Science Fact*, Vol. LXXVI, No. 3, November 1965, pp. 10–46, novelette with cover and interior illustration by Kelly Freas, sequel to 1964 novelette "Gunpowder God." Reprinted in:

Robert Adams' Book of Soldiers, Robert Adams, Pamela Crippen Adams and Martin H. Greenberg, eds., New York: Signet, 1988, pp. 132–171

Lord Kalvan of Otherwhen, H. Beam Piper, New York: Ace, 1965 (F-342), 192 pages, with uncredited cover illustration (by Jerom Podwill?), expanded combination of 1964 novelette "Gunpowder God" and 1965 novelette "Down Styphon!," reprinted in or reissued as:

> *Lord Kalvan of Otherwhen*, H. Beam Piper, New York and London: Garland, 1975, hardcover.
> *Gunpowder God*, H. Beam Piper, London: Sphere, 1978, with uncredited cover illustration.
> *Lord Kalvan of Otherwhen*, H. Beam Piper, New York: Ace, 1965 (1981?), with Michael Whelan cover illustration.
> "Lord Kalvan of Otherwhen," in *The Complete Paratime*, Anonymous, ed., New York: Ace, 2001, with cover art by Dave Dorman.

1981

Fuzzy Bones, William Tuning, New York: Ace, 1981, with cover illustration by Michael Whelan (authorized sequel to 1964 novel *The Other Human Race*).

"When in the Course...," H. Beam Piper, in *Federation*, John F. Carr, ed., New York: Ace, 1981, pp. 201–284, novella, written c. 1960, with cover illustration by Michael Whelan, alternate version of the story 1964 story "Gunpowder God."

1982

First Cycle, H. Beam Piper with Michael Kurland, New York: Ace, 1982, 201 pages, with uncredited cover illustration by Barlowe.

Golden Dream: A Fuzzy Odyssey, Ardath Mayhar, New York: Ace, 1982, with cover illustration by Michael Whelan (authorized sequel to 1964 novel *The Other Human Race*).

1984

Fuzzies and Other People, H. Beam Piper, New York: Ace, 1984, 216 pages, with cover illustration by Michael Whelan, sequel to 1964 novel *The Other Human Race*. Reprinted in:

> *The Complete Fuzzy*, H. Beam Piper, New York: Ace, 1998.

1985

Great Kings' War, Roland Green and John F. Carr, New York: Ace, 1985, with cover illustration by Alan Gutierrez (authorized sequel to 1965 novel *Lord Kalvan of Otherwhen*), expanded and reissued as:

> *Great Kings' War*, John F. Carr and Roland Green, Boalsburg, PA: Pequod Press, 2006, with jacket illustration Alan Gutierrez.

1989

"Kalvan Kingmaker," Roland Green and John F. Carr, in *Alternatives*, Robert Adams and Pamela Crippen Adams, eds., New York: Baen, 1989, pp. 233–312, sequel to 1985 novel *Great Kings' War*, expanded and reissued as:

> *Kalvan Kingmaker*, John F. Carr with Roland Green, Pequod Press, 2000, with jacket illustration Alan Gutierrez.

"Siege at Tarr-Hostigos," Roland Green and John F. Carr, in *There Will Be War VIII: Armageddon*, Jerry Pournelle and John F. Carr, eds., New York: Tor, 1989, pp. 300–368, sequel to 1989 short story "Kalvan Kingmaker," expanded and reissued as:

> *Siege of Tarr-Hostigos*, John F. Carr, Pequod Press, 2003, with jacket illustration Alan Gutierrez.

Chapter Notes

Preface

1. Jerry Pournelle, Introduction: *Federation* (New York, NY: Ace Books, 1981), p. ix.
2. Marvin N. Katz, Brass Tacks, *Analog Science Fact — Science Fiction,* March 1965, pp. 92–93.
3. Jerry E. Pournelle, conversation with author regarding H. Beam Piper (Studio City, CA: May 25, 1972).
4. William H. Flayhart III, letter to author (Dover, DE: March 12, 2003), p. 1.
5. Michael E. Knerr, "Piper," unpublished manuscript in author's possession (Sausalito, CA: 1983) p. 2–3.
6. Fletcher Pratt, *World of Wonder* (New York city, N.Y.: Twayne Publishers, 1951) P. 22.
7. Knerr, "Piper," pp. 5–6.

Chapter 1

1. Anne McGuire, one-hour taped interview with author, Shrewsbury, NJ, June 9, 2001.
2. David Hines, e-mail to author, May 3, 2001.
3. Anne McGuire interview.
4. Don Coleman, "The Early Letters," unpublished collection of the H. Beam Piper–Ferd Coleman letters, in author's possession, dated 1991, pp. 272–273.
5. Michael E. Knerr, "Piper," unpublished manuscript in author's possession, dated 1983, pp. 2–3.
6. Jerry E. Pournelle, conversation with author, Studio City, CA, February 12, 1980.
7. Coleman, "The Early Letters," p. ii.
8. Hines e-mail, p. 1.
9. *Altoona Mirror,* Obituaries, September 10, 1902.
10. Hines e-mail, pp. 1–2.
11. Knerr, "Piper," pp. 13–15.
12. John J. McGuire, Jr., telephone interview with author, May 10, 2001.
13. Knerr, "Piper," p. 13.
14. Paul Schuchart, letter to author, April 19, 1981, p. 2.
15. Hines e-mail, p. 2.
16. *Altoona Mirror,* Obituaries, September 10, 1902.
17. Knerr, "Piper," p. 5.
18. J. Simpson Africa, *The History of Huntingdon and Blair County* (Philadelphia, PA: Louis H. Everts, 1883), pp. 210–211.
19. Starlight Web site, postscript to the biographical entry from *The History of Huntingdon and Blair County,* http://gwillick.tripod.com/bio/DrHBPiper.html, p. 2.
20. John H. Costello, "H. Beam Piper: An Infinity of Worlds: Part One," *Renaissance* 4.4 (Fall 1972): 2.
21. Pournelle, conversation with author.

22. Mike Knerr, telephone conversation with the author, September 26, 1982.
23. Knerr, "Piper," p. 14.
24. John H. Costello, "H. Beam Piper: An Infinity of Worlds: Part One," *Renaissance* 4.4 (Fall 1972): 2.
25. Paul Schuchart, letter to author, February 18, 1981, p. 2.
26. Hines e-mail, p. 2.

Chapter 2

1. Don Coleman, "The Early Letters," unpublished collection of the H. Beam Piper–Ferd Coleman letters, in author's possession, dated 1991, pp. viii–ix.
2. Terry McGuire, telephone interview with author, May 8, 2001.
3. Don Coleman, "The Early Letters," pp. 255–259.
4. Don Coleman, letter to author, November 19, 1991, p. 1.
5. Don Coleman, "The Early Letters," p. 5.
6. H. Beam Piper, *A Catalogue of Henry Wharton Shoemaker Weapons at Restless Oaks in McElhattan Pennsylvania* (Altoona, PA: Times Tribune Co.), p. ii.
7. Fred Ramsey, e-mail to "The Works of H. Beam Piper" Internet mailing list: piper-l@home.ease.lsoft.com, December 15, 2002.
8. Don Coleman, letter to author, October 19, 1991, pp. 1–2.
9. Don Coleman, "The Early Letters," pp. 4–5.

Chapter 3

1. Don Coleman, "The Early Letters," unpublished collection of the H. Beam Piper–Ferd Coleman letters, in author's possession, dated 1991, p. 165.
2. "Typewriter 'Killer,'" *Pennsy* 2.8 (Sept. 1953): 7.
3. Coleman, "The Early Letters," p. 3.
4. Wes Barris, Roster of Juniata Shops Built GG1s, Steamlocomotive.com.
5. Bill Bowers and Bill Mallardi, "The Double-Bill Symposium" (Akron, OH: 1969), p. 16.
6. "Typewriter 'Killer,'" p. 7.
7. H. Beam Piper, *Little Fuzzy* (New York: NY: Ace Books, 1984), p. 33.
8. Coleman, "The Early Letters," p. 8.
9. Coleman, "The Early Letters," p. 19.
10. Coleman, "The Early Letters," pp. 12–13.
11. Coleman, "The Early Letters," pp. 182–83.
12. Coleman, "The Early Letters," pp. 9–10.

13. Coleman, "The Early Letters," p. 15.
14. Coleman, "The Early Letters," p. 16.
15. Coleman, "The Early Letters," pp. 18–19.
16. Coleman, "The Early Letters," p. 37.
17. Coleman, "The Early Letters," p. 38.
18. Coleman, "The Early Letters," p. 49.
19. Coleman, "The Early Letters," pp. 50–51.
20. Coleman, "The Early Letters," p. 53.
21. Coleman, "The Early Letters," p. 54.
22. Coleman, "The Early Letters," p. 106.
23. Coleman, "The Early Letters," p. 153.
24. Coleman, "The Early Letters," p. 160.
25. Coleman, "The Early Letters," p. 161.
26. Coleman, "The Early Letters," p. 165.

Chapter 4

1. Don Coleman, "The Early Letters," unpublished collection of the H. Beam Piper–Ferd Coleman letters, in author's possession, dated 1991, p. 18.
2. Terry McGuire, telephone interview with author, May 10, 2001.
3. Coleman, "The Early Letters," p. 18.
4. Coleman, "The Early Letters," p. 46.
5. Coleman, "The Early Letters," p. 48.
6. Coleman, "The Early Letters," p. 48.
7. Coleman, "The Early Letters," pp. 51–52.
8. Coleman, "The Early Letters," p. 52.
9. Paul Schuchart, letter to author, April 19, 1981, p.1.
10. Coleman, "The Early Letters," pp. 67–68.
11. Coleman, "The Early Letters," p. 91.
12. Coleman, "The Early Letters," p. 106.
13. Coleman, "The Early Letters," p. 122.
14. Coleman, "The Early Letters," p. 138.
15. Coleman, "The Early Letters," p. 146.
16. Coleman, "The Early Letters," p. 185.
17. Coleman, "The Early Letters," p. 159.
18. Mike Knerr, telephone conversation with the author, September 26, 1982.
19. Coleman, "The Early Letters," pp. 246–248.
20. John J. McGuire, Jr., telephone interview with author, May 10, 2001.
21. H. Beam Piper, *Little Fuzzy* (New York, NY: Ace Books, 1984), pp. 27–28.

Chapter 5

1. Don Coleman, "The Early Letters," unpublished collection of the H. Beam Piper–Ferd Coleman letters, in author's possession, dated 1991, p. 14.
2. "Typewriter 'Killer,'" *Pennsy* 2.8 (Sept. 1953): 7.
3. Coleman, "The Early Letters," p. 89.
4. Coleman, "The Early Letters," p. 100.
5. Coleman, "The Early Letters," p. 24.
6. Coleman, "The Early Letters," p. 32.
7. Coleman, "The Early Letters," p. 35.
8. Coleman, "The Early Letters," pp. 35–36.
9. Coleman, "The Early Letters," p. 40.
10. Coleman, "The Early Letters," p. 41.
11. Coleman, "The Early Letters," p. 43.
12. Coleman, "The Early Letters," p. 116.
13. Coleman, "The Early Letters," p. 142.
14. Coleman, "The Early Letters," p. 148.
15. Coleman, "The Early Letters," pp. 166–167.
16. Coleman, "The Early Letters," pp. 1–2.
17. Coleman, "The Early Letters," pp. 18–19.

18. Coleman, "The Early Letters," pp. 42–43.
19. Coleman, "The Early Letters," p. 186.
20. Coleman, "The Early Letters," p. 141.
21. Paul Schuchart, letter to author, April 19, 1981, pp. 1–2.
22. Coleman, "The Early Letters," p. 143.
23. Coleman, "The Early Letters," p. 144.

Chapter 6

1. Don Coleman, "The Early Letters," unpublished collection of the H. Beam Piper–Ferd Coleman letters, in author's possession, dated 1991, pp. 144–145.
2. Coleman, "The Early Letters," pp. 100–101.
3. Coleman, "The Early Letters," pp. 6–7.
4. Coleman, "The Early Letters," pp. 8–9.
5. Coleman, "The Early Letters," p. 11.
6. Coleman, "The Early Letters," p. 12.
7. Coleman, "The Early Letters," p. 15.
8. Coleman, "The Early Letters," p. 117.
9. Coleman, "The Early Letters," pp. 144–145.
10. Coleman, "The Early Letters," p. 179.
11. Coleman, "The Early Letters," pp. 28–29.
12. Coleman, "The Early Letters," pp. 29–30.
13. Coleman, "The Early Letters," pp. 32–33.
14. Coleman, "The Early Letters," pp. 57–58.
15. Coleman, "The Early Letters," p. 59.
16. Coleman, "The Early Letters," p. 60.
17. Coleman, "The Early Letters," pp. 79–80.

Chapter 7

1. Don Coleman, "The Early Letters," unpublished collection of the H. Beam Piper–Ferd Coleman letters, in author's possession, dated 1991, p. 127.
2. Coleman, "The Early Letters," pp. 31–32.
3. Coleman, "The Early Letters," p. 33.
4. Coleman, "The Early Letters," p. 147.
5. Coleman, "The Early Letters," p. 164.
6. Coleman, "The Early Letters," pp. 39–40.
7. Coleman, "The Early Letters," p. 41.
8. Coleman, "The Early Letters," p. 41.
9. Coleman, "The Early Letters," p. 47.
10. Coleman, "The Early Letters," pp. 52–53.
11. Coleman, "The Early Letters," p. 91.
12. Coleman, "The Early Letters," p. 95.
13. Coleman, "The Early Letters," pp. 106–107.
14. Coleman, "The Early Letters," pp. 126–127.
15. Coleman, "The Early Letters," p. 129.
16. Coleman, "The Early Letters," pp. 130–131.
17. Coleman, "The Early Letters," p. 165.
18. Coleman, "The Early Letters," p. 167.
19. Coleman, "The Early Letters," p. 167.
20. Coleman, "The Early Letters," p. 178.

Chapter 8

1. Don Coleman, "The Early Letters," unpublished collection of the H. Beam Piper–Ferd Coleman letters, in author's possession, dated 1991, p. 42.
2. Michael E. Knerr, "Piper," unpublished manuscript in author's possession, dated 1983, pp. 16–17.
3. Don Coleman, letter to author, July 20, 2001, p. 2.
4. Coleman, "The Early Letters," pp. 23–24.
5. Coleman, "The Early Letters," p. 23.

6. Coleman, "The Early Letters," p. 34.
7. Coleman, "The Early Letters," p. 42.
8. Coleman, "The Early Letters," p. 44.
9. Coleman, "The Early Letters," p. 48.
10. Coleman, "The Early Letters," p. 49.
11. Coleman, "The Early Letters," p. 106.
12. Coleman, "The Early Letters," pp. 113–114.
13. Coleman, "The Early Letters," p. 118.
14. Coleman, "The Early Letters," p. 134.
15. Coleman, "The Early Letters," p. 170.
16. Coleman, "The Early Letters," p. 174.
17. Coleman, "The Early Letters," pp. 175–176.
18. Coleman, "The Early Letters," pp. 176–177.
19. Don Coleman, letter to the author, October 19, 2003, p. 2.
20. Coleman, letter to the author, p. 2.
21. Coleman, letter to author, p. 3.

Chapter 9

1. Don Coleman, "The Early Letters," unpublished collection of the H. Beam Piper–Ferd Coleman letters, in author's possession, dated 1991, p. 82.
2. Coleman, "The Early Letters," pp. 81–82.
3. Coleman, "The Early Letters," p. 82.
4. Coleman, "The Early Letters," pp. 87–88.
5. Coleman, "The Early Letters," p. 91.
6. Coleman, "The Early Letters," pp. 95–96.
7. Coleman, "The Early Letters," p. 98.
8. Coleman, "The Early Letters," p. 98.
9. Coleman, "The Early Letters," p. 99.
10. Coleman, "The Early Letters," p. 99.
11. Coleman, "The Early Letters," p. 102.
12. Coleman, "The Early Letters," p. 102.
13. Coleman, "The Early Letters," pp. 116–117.
14. Coleman, "The Early Letters," p. 120.
15. Coleman, "The Early Letters," p. 121.
16. Coleman, "The Early Letters," p. 126.
17. Coleman, "The Early Letters," p. 133.
18. Coleman, "The Early Letters," p. 134.
19. Coleman, "The Early Letters," p. 136.
20. Coleman, "The Early Letters," p. 137.

Chapter 10

1. Don Coleman, "The Early Letters," unpublished collection of the H. Beam Piper–Ferd Coleman letters, in author's possession, dated 1991, p. 165.
2. Coleman, "The Early Letters," p. 43.
3. Coleman, "The Early Letters," p. 47.
4. Coleman, "The Early Letters," p. 56.
5. Coleman, "The Early Letters," p. 57.
6. Coleman, "The Early Letters," p. 57.
7. Coleman, "The Early Letters," p. 49.
8. Coleman, "The Early Letters," pp. 59–60.
9. Coleman, "The Early Letters," pp. 60–63.
10. Coleman, "The Early Letters," p. 64.
11. Coleman, "The Early Letters," p. 72.
12. Coleman, "The Early Letters," p. 73.
13. Coleman, "The Early Letters," pp. 73–74.
14. Coleman, "The Early Letters," pp. 74–75.
15. Coleman, "The Early Letters," p. 83.
16. Coleman, "The Early Letters," p. 172.

Chapter 11

1. Don Coleman, "The Early Letters," unpublished collection of the H. Beam Piper–Ferd Coleman letters, in author's possession, dated 1991, p. 185.
2. Coleman, "The Early Letters," p. 149.
3. Coleman, "The Early Letters," pp. 150–151.
4. Coleman, "The Early Letters," p. 151.
5. Coleman, "The Early Letters," pp. 151–152.
6. Coleman, "The Early Letters," pp. 153–154.
7. Coleman, "The Early Letters," p. 154.
8. Coleman, "The Early Letters," p. 126.
9. Coleman, "The Early Letters," pp. 128–129.
10. Coleman, "The Early Letters," p. 130.
11. Coleman, "The Early Letters," pp. 163–164.
12. Coleman, "The Early Letters," p. 185.
13. Coleman, "The Early Letters," pp. 189–190.
14. Coleman, "The Early Letters," p. 189.
15. Coleman, "The Early Letters," p. 191.
16. Coleman, "The Early Letters," pp. 192–193.
17. Coleman, "The Early Letters," pp. 193–194.
18. Coleman, "The Early Letters," p. 192.
19. Coleman, "The Early Letters," pp. 162.
20. Coleman, "The Early Letters," p. ix.
21. Coleman, "The Early Letters," pp. ix–x.

Chapter 12

1. Don Coleman, "The Early Letters," unpublished collection of the H. Beam Piper–Ferd Coleman letters, in author's possession, dated 1991, p. 225.
2. Michael E. Knerr, "Piper," unpublished manuscript in author's possession, dated 1983, p. 17.
3. Fletcher Pratt, *World of Wonder* (New York City, NY: Twayne Publishers, 1951), p. 22.
4. L. Sprague de Camp, *Time and Chance: An Autobiography* (Hampton Falls, NH: Donald M. Grant, 1996), p. 215.
5. Coleman, "The Early Letters," p. 212.
6. Coleman, "The Early Letters," pp. 213–214.
7. Knerr, "Piper," p. 21.
8. Coleman, "The Early Letters," p. 214.
9. "Typewriter 'Killer,'" *Pennsy* 2.8 (Sept. 1953): 7.
10. Coleman, "The Early Letters," p. 215.
11. Coleman, "The Early Letters," pp. 225–226.
12. Coleman, "The Early Letters," p. 226.
13. Robert A. Heinlein, James Forrestal Memorial Lecture to the Brigade of Midshipmen at his alma mater, the U.S. Naval Academy at Annapolis, April 5, 1973.
14. Coleman, "The Early Letters," pp. 226–227.
15. "Typewriter 'Killer,'" p. 7.
16. Coleman, "The Early Letters," pp. 227–228.

Chapter 13

1. Don Coleman, "The Early Letters," unpublished collection of the H. Beam Piper–Ferd Coleman letters, in author's possession, dated 1991, p. 212.
2. Coleman, "The Early Letters," pp. 204–209.
3. Coleman, "The Early Letters," pp. 209–210.
4. Coleman, "The Early Letters," pp. 211–212.
5. Coleman, "The Early Letters," pp. 212–213.
6. Michael E. Knerr, "Piper," unpublished manuscript in author's possession, dated 1983, pp. 21–22.

Chapter 14

1. John W. Campbell, letter to H. Beam Piper, June 26, 1952.
2. Bill Bowers and Bill Mallardi, "The Double-Bill Symposium" (Akron, OH: 1969), p. 96.
3. H. Beam Piper, *Murder in the Gunroom* (New York, NY: Alfred A. Knopf, Inc., 1953), pp. 152–153.
4. Perry Chapdelaine, Sr., *The John W. Campbell Letters*, Vol. I (Franklin, TN: AC Projects, 1985), pp. 29–31.
5. H. Beam Piper, letter to John W. Campbell, June 18, 1951, p.1.
6. H. Beam Piper, letter to John W. Campbell (Altoona, PA: June 18, 1951) p. 1.
7. John W. Campbell, letter to Frederik Pohl, January 15, 1951, p. 1.
8. H. Beam Piper, letter to John W. Campbell, July 17, 1954, p. 1.
9. John W. Campbell, letter to H. Beam Piper, July 21, 1954, p. 1.
10. Michael E. Knerr, "Piper," unpublished manuscript in author's possession, dated 1983, p. 58.
11. Mike Ashley, *The Complete Index to Astounding/Analog* (Oak Forest, IL: Robert Weinberg Publications, 1981), p. 78.
12. John McGuire, Jr., telephone interview with author, May 10, 2001.
13. John H. Costello, "H. Beam Piper: An Infinity of Worlds: Part One," *Renaissance* 4.4 (Fall 1972): 1.
14. John W. Campbell, "Tribesman, Barbarian and Citizen," editorial, *Analog Science Fact — Science Fiction*, March 1965, p. 7.
15. H. Beam Piper, *Federation* (New York, NY: Ace Books, February 1981), p. 128.
16. Knerr, "Piper," p. 58.
17. John W. Campbell, letter to Kenneth S. White, Nov. 6, 1961, p. 1.
18. Knerr, "Piper," p. 165.
19. John W. Campbell, letter to H. Beam Piper, May 13, 1959, p. 1.

Chapter 15

1. John McGuire, Jr., telephone interview with author, May 10, 2001.
2. Terry McGuire, telephone interview with author, May 8, 2001.
3. John McGuire, Jr., telephone interview with author.
4. Terry McGuire, telephone interview with author.
5. John McGuire, Jr., telephone interview with author.
6. Terry McGuire, telephone interview with author.
7. Anne McGuire, one-hour taped interview with author, Shrewsbury, New Jersey, June 9, 2001.
8. John McGuire, Jr., telephone interview with author.
9. John McGuire, Jr., telephone interview with author.
10. Anne McGuire interview.
11. Anne McGuire interview.
12. Terry McGuire, telephone interview with author.
13. John McGuire, Jr., telephone interview with author.
14. John McGuire, Jr., telephone interview with author.
15. Terry McGuire, telephone interview with author.
16. Terry McGuire, telephone interview with author.

Chapter 16

1. Don Coleman, "The Early Letters," unpublished collection of the H. Beam Piper–Ferd Coleman letters, in author's possession, dated 1991, p. 173.

2. Michael E. Knerr, "Piper," unpublished manuscript in author's possession, dated 1983, pp. 23–24.
3. Knerr, "Piper," p. 30.
4. Coleman, "The Early Letters," p. 171.
5. Coleman, "The Early Letters," p. 173.
6. Coleman, "The Early Letters," p. 185.
7. Coleman, "The Early Letters," p. 195.
8. Coleman, "The Early Letters," p. 178.
9. Coleman, "The Early Letters," pp. 196–200.
10. Paul Schuchart, letter to author, February 18, 1981, p. 1.
11. Paul Schuchart, letter to author, April 19, 1981, p. 1.
12. Paul Schuchart, letter to author, April 19, 1981, p. 1.
13. Terry McGuire, e-mail to author, March 26, 2001.
14. Terry McGuire, telephone interview with author, May 8, 2001.
15. John McGuire, Jr., telephone interview with author, May 10, 2001.
16. Knerr, "Piper," p. 24.
17. John McGuire, Jr., telephone interview with author.

Chapter 17

1. Michael E. Knerr, "Piper," unpublished manuscript in author's possession, dated 1983, p. 26.
2. Council on International Education Exchange, Inc., http://www.answers.com/topic/council-on-international-educational-exchange-inc, Jan. 18, 2007.
3. L. Sprague de Camp, *Time and Chance: An Autobiography* (Hampton Falls, NH: Donald M. Grant, 1996), p. 215.
4. Knerr, "Piper," p. 28.
5. H. Beam Piper, letter to Alan Howard, Jan. 12, 1953, p. 1.
6. Michael E. Knerr, "Piper," p. 32.
7. H. Beam Piper, letter to Freida Coleman, September 4, 1955, p. 1.
8. H. Beam Piper, *Little Fuzzy* (New York, NY: Ace Books, 1984), p. 22.
9. Knerr, "Piper," p. 19.
10. Knerr, "Piper," pp. 19–20.
11. H. Beam Piper, diary entries for January 1, 1955, to August 27, 1955, from The H. Beam Piper Papers, Special Collections Library, The Pennsylvania State University Libraries, Altoona, PA.
12. Piper, diary entry for January 27, 1955.
13. Piper, diary entry for February 2, 1955.
14. Piper, diary entry for February 7, 1955.
15. Piper, diary entry for February 10, 1955.
16. Knerr, "Piper," pp. 32–33.
17. Knerr, "Piper," p. 33.
18. Piper, diary entry for February 19, 1955.
19. Knerr, "Piper," p. 32.
20. Piper, diary entry for February 23, 1955.
21. Piper, diary entry for February 24, 1955.
22. Piper, diary entry for February 28, 1955.
23. Piper, diary entry for March 3, 1955.
24. Piper, diary entry for March 4, 1955.
25. John McGuire, Jr., telephone interview by author, May 10, 2001.
26. Piper, diary entry for March 8, 1955.
27. Knerr, "Piper," p. 33.
28. Piper, diary entry for March 11, 1955.
29. Piper, diary entry for March 11, 1955.
30. Piper, diary entry for March 12, 1955.
31. Piper, diary entry for March 17, 1955.
32. Piper, diary entry for March 18, 1955.

33. Piper, diary entry for March 19, 1955.
34. Piper, diary entry for March 21, 1955.
35. Piper, diary entry for March 22, 1955.
36. Piper, diary entry for March 23, 1955.
37. Piper, diary entry for March 24, 1955.
38. Piper, diary entry for March 25, 1955.
39. Piper, diary entry for March 29, 1955.
40. Piper, diary entry for March 30, 1955.
41. Piper, diary entry for April 4, 1955.
42. Piper, diary entry for April 5, 1955.
43. Piper, diary entry for April 6, 1955.
44. Piper, diary entry for April 7, 1955.
45. Piper, diary entry for April 15, 1955.
46. Piper, diary entry for May 10, 1955.
47. Piper, diary entry for July 19, 1955.
48. Piper, diary entry for July 20, 1955.
49. Piper, diary entry July 29, 1955.
50. Piper, diary entry for August 1, 1955.
51. L. Sprague de Comp, *Time and Chance: An Autobiography*, (Hampton Falls, NH: Donald M. Grant, 1996), p. 168.
52. Piper, diary entry for August 2, 1955.

Chapter 18

1. H. Beam Piper, diary for January 1, 1955, through August 27, 1955, from The H. Beam Piper Papers, Special Collections Library, The Pennsylvania State University Libraries, Altoona, PA.
2. Rich Horton, alt.books.isaac-asimov.
3. John McGuire, Jr., telephone interview by author, May 10, 2001.
4. Piper, diary entry for January 8, 1955.
5. Piper, diary entry for January 12, 1955.
6. Piper, diary entry for January 16, 1955.
7. Piper, diary entry for January 26, 1955.
8. Piper, diary entry for January 27, 1955.
9. Piper, diary entry for February 1, 1955.
10. Piper, diary entry for February 2, 1955.
11. Piper, diary entry for February 4, 1955.
12. Piper, diary entry for February 10, 1955.
13. Piper, diary entry for February 15, 1955.
14. John McGuire, Jr., telephone interview by author.
15. H. Beam Piper, letter to Freida Coleman, September 4, 1955, p. 2.
16. Piper, diary entry for February 16, 1955.
17. Piper, diary entry for February 21, 1955.
18. Piper, diary entry for February 26, 1955.
19. Piper, diary entry for March 1, 1955.
20. Piper, diary entry for March 2, 1955.
21. Piper, diary entry for March 3, 1955.
22. Piper, diary entry for March 5, 1955.
23. Piper, diary entry for March 10, 1955.
24. Piper, diary entry for March 13, 1955.
25. Piper, diary entry for March 17, 1955.
26. Piper, diary entry for March 29, 1955.
27. Piper, diary entry for March 30, 1955.
28. Piper, diary entry for April 11, 1955.
29. Piper, diary entry for May 8, 1955.
30. Piper, diary entry for May 13, 1955.
31. John McGuire, Jr., telephone interview by author.
32. Piper, diary entry for May 14, 1955.
33. Piper, diary entry for May 15, 1955.
34. Piper, diary entry for May 16, 1955.
35. Terry McGuire, telephone interview with author, May 8, 2001.
36. John McGuire, Jr., telephone interview by author.
37. Piper, diary entry for June 3, 1955.
38. Anne McGuire, one-hour taped interview with author, Shrewsbury, New Jersey, June 9, 2001.
39. Piper, diary entry for June 22, 1955.
40. Piper, diary entry for June 8, 1955.
41. Piper, diary entry for June 22, 1955.
42. Piper, diary entry for July 30, 1955.
43. John McGuire, Jr., telephone interview by author.
44. Piper, diary entry for August 9, 1955.
45. Frederik Pohl, telephone conversation with author, June 14, 1979.

Chapter 19

1. Don Coleman, "The Early Letters," unpublished collection of the H. Beam Piper–Ferd Coleman letters, in author's possession, dated 1991, p. 279.
2. H. Beam Piper, diary for April 20, 1955, from The H. Beam Piper Papers, Special Collections Library, The Pennsylvania State University Libraries, Altoona, PA.
3. Piper, diary entry for April 21, 1955.
4. Piper, diary entry for April 25, 1955.
5. Piper, diary entry for May 4, 1955.
6. Piper, diary entry for May 5, 1955.
7. Piper, diary entry for May 7, 1955.
8. Piper, diary entry for May 7, 1955.
9. Piper, diary entry for May 18, 1955.
10. Piper, diary entry for May 18, 1955.
11. Piper, diary entry for May 25, 1955.
12. Piper, diary entry for May 26, 1955.
13. Piper, diary entry for May 27, 1955.
14. Piper, diary entry for May 30, 1955.
15. Piper, diary entry for June 2, 1955.
16. Piper, diary entry for June 9, 1955.
17. Piper, diary entry for June 14, 1955.
18. Piper, diary entry for July 5, 1955.
19. Piper, diary entry for July 6, 1955.
20. Piper, diary entry for July 15, 1955.
21. Piper, diary entry for July 11, 1955.
22. De Camp, *Time and Chance*, pp. 407–408.
23. Piper, diary entry for July 21, 1955.
24. Piper, diary entry for July 22, 1955.
25. Piper, diary entry for July 25, 1955.
26. Piper, diary entry for July 26, 1955.
27. Piper, diary entry for August 3, 1955.
28. Piper, diary entry for August 4, 1955.
29. Piper, diary entry for August 4, 1955.
30. Piper, diary entry for August 5, 1955.
31. Piper, diary entry for August 6, 1955.
32. Piper, diary entry for August 7, 1955.
33. Piper, diary entry for August 8, 1955.
34. Piper, diary entry for August 9, 1955.
35. Piper, diary entry for August 10, 1955.
36. Piper, diary entry for August 12, 1955.
37. Piper, diary entry for August 13, 1955.
38. Piper, diary entry for August 14, 1955.
39. Piper, diary entry for August 15, 1955.
40. Piper, diary entry for August 16, 1955.
41. Piper, diary entry for August 20, 1955.
42. Piper, diary entry for August 21, 1955.
43. Piper, diary entry for August 24, 1955.
44. Piper, diary entry for August 25, 1955.
45. Piper, diary entry for August 26, 1955.
46. Piper, diary entry for August 27, 1955.
47. Michael E. Knerr, "Piper," unpublished manuscript in author's possession, dated 1983, p. 38.
48. Knerr, "Piper," pp. 38–39.
49. Knerr, "Piper," p. 39.

50. Piper, letter to Freida Coleman, September 4, 1955, pp. 1–2.

51. Knerr, "Piper," pp. 39–41.

Chapter 20

1. Michael E. Knerr, "Piper," unpublished manuscript in author's possession, dated 1983, p. 23.

2. Knerr, "Piper," p. 45.

3. Knerr, "Piper," p. 45.

4. H. Beam Piper, letter to Lycoming Historical Society, June 12, 1956, pp. 1–2.

5. Knerr, "Piper," p. 46.

6. Knerr, "Piper," p. 46.

7. Knerr, "Piper," p. 46.

8. Knerr, "Piper," p. 47.

9. Knerr, "Piper," p. 40.

10. Knerr, "Piper," p. 48.

11. H. Beam Piper, letter to Peter Weston with 4-page attachment titled "The Future History by H. Beam Piper," February 16, 1964.

12. Knerr, "Piper," p. 47.

13. Knerr, "Piper," p. 48.

14. John F. Carr, *Federation* (New York, NY: Ace Books, February 1981), p. xii.

15. Knerr, "Piper," pp. 49–50.

16. Bill Bowers and Bill Mallardi, "The Double-Bill Symposium" (Akron, OH: 1969), pp. 68–69.

17. Knerr, "Piper," pp. 50–51.

18. Knerr, "Piper," p. 51.

19. Bill McMorris, e-mail to author, October 4, 2005.

20. Knerr, "Piper," pp. 43–45.

21. Knerr, "Piper," p. 52.

22. Knerr, "Piper," p. 52.

Chapter 21

1. Michael E. Knerr, "Piper," unpublished manuscript in author's possession, dated 1983, p. 60.

2. Knerr, "Piper," p. 52.

3. Knerr, "Piper," p. 52.

4. Knerr, "Piper," p. 52.

5. Knerr, "Piper," pp. 54–55.

6. Knerr, "Piper," pp. 55–56.

7. Knerr, "Piper," pp. 56–57.

8. Knerr, "Piper," p. 57.

9. Knerr, "Piper," pp. 57–58.

10. Knerr, "Piper," p. 58.

11. Knerr, "Piper," p. 59.

12. Knerr, "Piper," p. 59.

13. Knerr, "Piper," p. 59.

14. Knerr, "Piper," p. 61.

15. Knerr, "Piper," p. 61.

16. Knerr, "Piper," pp. 62–63.

17. Knerr, "Piper," p. 65.

18. Knerr, "Piper," p. 65.

19. Paul Schuchart, letter to author, February 18, 1981, p. 2.

Chapter 22

1. Michael E. Knerr, "Piper," unpublished manuscript in author's possession, dated 1983, p. 81.

2. Knerr, "Piper," p. 66.

3 Knerr, "Piper," pp. 66–67.

4. Knerr, "Piper," p. 67.

5. Knerr, "Piper," p. 68.

6. Knerr, "Piper," p. 68.

7. Knerr, "Piper," p. 67.

8. Knerr, "Piper," pp. 69–70.

9. Knerr, "Piper," p. 71.

10. Knerr, "Piper," p. 71.

11. Knerr, "Piper," pp. 71–72.

12. Knerr, "Piper," pp. 73–74.

13. Knerr, "Piper," p. 74.

14. H. Beam Piper, letter to Freida Coleman, May 13, 1957.

15. Knerr, "Piper," p. 72.

16. Knerr, "Piper," p. 72.

17. Knerr, "Piper," p. 74.

18. Knerr, "Piper," p. 74.

19. Knerr, "Piper," pp. 74–75.

20. Knerr, "Piper," p. 75.

21. Knerr, "Piper," pp. 77–78.

22. Knerr, "Piper," p. 78.

23. Knerr, "Piper," p. 32.

Chapter 23

1. Don Coleman, "The Early Letters," unpublished collection of the H. Beam Piper–Ferd Coleman letters, in author's possession, dated 1991, p. 251.

2. Michael E. Knerr, "Piper," unpublished manuscript in author's possession, dated 1983, p. 78.

3. H. Beam Piper, letter to Freida Coleman, September 19, 1957.

4. Knerr, "Piper," pp. 78–80.

5. Coleman, "The Early Letters," pp. 236–237.

6. Coleman, "The Early Letters," p. 237.

7. Knerr, "Piper," pp. 79–80.

8. Michael Wright, *Here Comes Sputnik,* August 30, 1997, http://www.batnet.com/mfwright/sputnik.html.

9. Coleman, "The Early Letters," pp. 251–253.

10. H. Beam Piper, letter to Peter Weston with 4-page attachment titled "The Future History by H. Beam Piper," February 16, 1964, p. 2.

11. Coleman, "The Early Letters," p. 253.

12. Knerr, "Piper," p. 31.

Chapter 24

1. Don Coleman, "The Early Letters," unpublished collection of the H. Beam Piper–Ferd Coleman letters, in author's possession, dated 1991, p. 231.

2. H. Beam Piper, letter to Freida Coleman, September 9, 1957.

3. Coleman, "The Early Letters," pp. 230–242.

Chapter 25

1. Michael E. Knerr, "Piper," unpublished manuscript in author's possession, dated 1983, p. 86.

2. Knerr, "Piper," pp. 80–81.

3. Knerr, "Piper," p. 81.

4. Knerr, "Piper," p. 82.

5. Knerr, "Piper," pp. 30–31.

6. Knerr, "Piper," p. 24.

7. Knerr, "Piper," p. 82.

8. Knerr, "Piper," p. 85.

9. Knerr, "Piper," p. 89.

10. Knerr, "Piper," p. 90.
11. Knerr, "Piper," p. 84.
12. Knerr, "Piper," p. 86.
13. Knerr, "Piper," p. 89.
14. Knerr, "Piper," p. 93.
15. Knerr, "Piper," p. 90.
16. Knerr, "Piper," pp. 90–92.
17. Knerr, "Piper," p. 92.
18. Knerr, "Piper," pp. 92–95.
19. Knerr, "Piper," p. 87.
20. Knerr, "Piper," p. 96.
21. Knerr, "Piper," p. 96.
22. Knerr, "Piper," pp. 96–97.
23. Knerr, "Piper," p. 97.
24. Knerr, "Piper," p. 97.
25. Knerr, "Piper," p. 98.
26. Knerr, "Piper," p. 97.
27. Knerr, "Piper," p. 98.
28. Knerr, "Piper," p. 98.
29. Knerr, "Piper," p. 98.
30. Knerr, "Piper," pp. 98–99.
31. Knerr, "Piper," p. 99.
32. Knerr, "Piper," p. 100.
33. Knerr, "Piper," p. 100.
34. Knerr, "Piper," p. 101.
35. Knerr, "Piper," p. 100.
36. Knerr, "Piper," pp. 100–101.
37. Knerr, "Piper," p. 101.
38. Don Coleman, letter to the author, July 20, 2001, p. 2.

Chapter 26

1. Jerry E. Pournelle, conversation with author, Studio City, CA, February 12, 1980.
2. Michael E. Knerr, "Piper," unpublished manuscript in author's possession, dated 1983, pp. 104–105.
3. Knerr, "Piper," p. 105.
4. Knerr, "Piper," p. 106.
5. Knerr, "Piper," pp. 107–108.
6. Knerr, "Piper," pp. 109–110.
7. Bill Bowers and Bill Mallardi, "The Double-Bill Symposium" (Akron, OH: 1969), p. 69.
8. Knerr, "Piper," p. 111.
9. Knerr, "Piper," p. 112.
10. Knerr, "Piper," p. 114.
11. Knerr, "Piper," p. 114.
12. Knerr, "Piper," p. 114.
13. Knerr, "Piper," p. 115.
14. Knerr, "Piper," p. 115.
15. Knerr, "Piper," p. 116.
16. Knerr, "Piper," p. 117.
17. Knerr, "Piper," p. 117.
18. Knerr, "Piper," p. 117.
19. Knerr, "Piper," pp. 118–119.
20. Knerr, "Piper," p. 119.
21. Knerr, "Piper," pp. 119–120.
22. Knerr, "Piper," p. 120.
23. Knerr, "Piper," p. 121.
24. Knerr, "Piper," p. 121.

Chapter 27

1. Michael E. Knerr, "Piper," unpublished manuscript in author's possession, dated 1983, p. 121.
2. Knerr, "Piper," p. 124.

3. Knerr, "Piper," p. 125.
4. Knerr, "Piper," p. 126.
5. Knerr, "Piper," p. 126.
6. John W. Campbell, letter to Kenneth S. White, January 20, 1960.
7. Knerr, "Piper," p. 127.
8. Knerr, "Piper," p. 127.
9. Knerr, "Piper," p. 127.
10. Knerr, "Piper," pp. 127–128.
11. Knerr, "Piper," p. 129.
12. Knerr, "Piper," p. 129.
13. Knerr, "Piper," pp. 129–130.

Chapter 28

1. Don Coleman, "The Early Letters," unpublished collection of the H. Beam Piper–Ferd Coleman letters, in author's possession, dated 1991, p. 271.
2. Michael E. Knerr, "Piper," unpublished manuscript in author's possession, dated 1983, p. 130.
3. Knerr, "Piper," p. 130.
4. Knerr, "Piper," pp. 130–131.
5. Knerr, "Piper," p. 131.
6. Coleman, "The Early Letters," p. 271.
7. Knerr, "Piper," p. 131.
8. Knerr, "Piper," p. 132.
9. Knerr, "Piper," p. 132.
10. Knerr, "Piper," p. 132.
11. Bill McMorris, e-mail to author, October 4, 2005.
12. Bill McMorris, e-mail to author, January 11, 2007.
13. Knerr, "Piper," p. 30.
14. Coleman, "The Early Letters," pp. 250–251.
15. Knerr, "Piper," p. 133.
16. Knerr, "Piper," p. 133.
17. Knerr, "Piper," pp. 133–134.
18. Knerr, "Piper," p. 134.
19. Bill McMorris, e-mail to author, October 4, 2005.
20. Knerr, "Piper," pp. 135–137.
21. Knerr, "Piper," p. 137.
22. Knerr, "Piper," p. 137.
23. Knerr, "Piper," pp. 137–138.
24. Knerr, "Piper," p. 138.
25. Knerr, "Piper," p. 138.
26. John W. Campbell, letter to Kenneth S. White, September 12, 1960.
27. Knerr, "Piper," pp. 138–139.
28. Knerr, "Piper," p. 139.
29. H. Beam Piper, letter to Jerry Pournelle, March 22, 1963.
30. Knerr, "Piper," pp. 139–140.
31. Knerr, "Piper," p. 140.
32. Knerr, "Piper," p. 140.
33. Bill McMorris, e-mail to author, October 4, 2005.
34. Knerr, "Piper," p. 141.
35. Knerr, "Piper," pp. 141–142.
36. Knerr, "Piper," pp. 142–143.
37. Knerr, "Piper," p. 143.

Chapter 29

1. Michael E. Knerr, "Piper," unpublished manuscript in author's possession, dated 1983, p. 164.
2. Knerr, "Piper," pp. 146–147.
3. Knerr, "Piper," p. 147.
4. Knerr, "Piper," p. 147.
5. Knerr, "Piper," pp. 147–148.

6. Knerr, "Piper," p. 148.
7. Knerr, "Piper," p. 148.
8. Knerr, "Piper," p. 148.
9. Knerr, "Piper," p. 149.
10. Knerr, "Piper," p. 149.
11. Knerr, "Piper," p. 150.
12. Knerr, "Piper," pp. 152–153.
13. Knerr, "Piper," p. 154.
14. Knerr, "Piper," p. 154.
15. Knerr, "Piper," p. 154.
16. Knerr, "Piper," p. 155.
17. Knerr, "Piper," p. 157.
18. Knerr, "Piper," p. 156.
19. Knerr, "Piper," p. 158.
20. Knerr, "Piper," p. 157.
21. Knerr, "Piper," pp. 159–160.
22. Knerr, "Piper," p. 160.
23. Knerr, "Piper," p. 160.
24. Knerr, "Piper," p. 161.
25. Knerr, "Piper," pp. 161–162.
26. Knerr, "Piper," p. 162.
27. Knerr, "Piper," p. 163.
28. Knerr, "Piper," p. 163.
29. Knerr, "Piper," p. 163.
30. Knerr, "Piper," p. 164.
31. Knerr, "Piper," p. 164.
32. Knerr, "Piper," p. 164.
33. Knerr, "Piper," p. 165.
34. Knerr, "Piper," p. 165.
35. Knerr, "Piper," pp. 165–166.
36. Knerr, "Piper," p. 166.
37. Knerr, "Piper," p. 166.
38. Knerr, "Piper," p. 166.
39. Knerr, "Piper," pp. 166–167.
40. Knerr, "Piper," p. 167.

Chapter 30

1. Michael E. Knerr, "Piper," unpublished manuscript in author's possession, dated 1983, p. 171.
2. Knerr, "Piper," p. 172.
3. Knerr, "Piper," p. 172.
4. Knerr, "Piper," p. 172.
5. Knerr, "Piper," p. 173.
6. Knerr, "Piper," p. 173.
7. Knerr, "Piper," p. 174.
8. Knerr, "Piper," p. 174.
9. Knerr, "Piper," p. 174.
10. Knerr, "Piper," p. 175.
11. Knerr, "Piper," p. 175.
12. Knerr, "Piper," p. 175.
13. Knerr, "Piper," p. 176.
14. Knerr, "Piper," p. 176.
15. Knerr, "Piper," p. 176.
16. Jerry E. Pournelle, conversation with author, Studio City, CA, February 12, 1980.
17. Knerr, "Piper," p. 176.
18. Knerr, "Piper," p. 176.
19. Knerr, "Piper," p. 177.
20. Knerr, "Piper," p. 177.
21. Knerr, "Piper," pp. 177–178.
22. Knerr, "Piper," p. 178.
23. John W. Campbell, letter to H. Beam Piper, June 5, 1962, pp. 1–2.
24. Knerr, "Piper," pp. 179.
25. Knerr, "Piper," pp. 179–180.
26. Knerr, "Piper," p. 180.
27. Knerr, "Piper," p. 180.
28. Knerr, "Piper," p. 180.
29. Knerr, "Piper," p. 183.
30. Knerr, "Piper," pp. 183–184.
31. Knerr, "Piper," p. 184.
32. Knerr, "Piper," p. 184.
33. Knerr, "Piper," p. 184.
34. Knerr, "Piper," p. 185.
35. Knerr, "Piper," p. 185.
36. Knerr, "Piper," pp. 185–186.
37. H. Beam Piper, letter to Jerry Pournelle, December 19, 1962.
38. Knerr, "Piper," p. 187.
39. Knerr, "Piper," pp. 187.
40. Knerr, "Piper," p. 188.

Chapter 31

1. Michael E. Knerr, "Piper," unpublished manuscript in author's possession, dated 1983, p. 189.
2. Knerr, "Piper," p. 190.
3. Knerr, "Piper," p. 192.
4. Knerr, "Piper," p. 192.
5. Knerr, "Piper," p. 193.
6. Knerr, "Piper," p. 194.
7. Knerr, "Piper," pp. 194–195.
8. Knerr, "Piper," p. 195.
9. Knerr, "Piper," p. 195.
10. Knerr, "Piper," p. 195.
11. Knerr, "Piper," p. 196.
12. Knerr, "Piper," p. 196.
13. Knerr, "Piper," pp. 196–197.
14. Knerr, "Piper," p. 198.
15. Knerr, "Piper," p. 199.
16. Knerr, "Piper," p. 198.
17. Bill McMorris, e-mail to author, October 4, 2005.
18. H. Beam Piper, letter to Charles and Marcia Brown, July 2, 1963.
19. Knerr, "Piper," p. 200.
20. Knerr, "Piper," p. 175.
21. Jerry E. Pournelle, conversation with author, Studio City, CA, February 12, 1980.
22. Knerr, "Piper," p. 200.
23. Knerr, "Piper," pp. 200–201.
24. Knerr, "Piper," p. 202.
25. Knerr, "Piper," p. 202.
26. Knerr, "Piper," p. 203.
27. Knerr, "Piper," pp. 203–204.
28. Knerr, "Piper," p. 204.
29. Knerr, "Piper," p. 205.
30. Knerr, "Piper," p. 205.
31. Knerr, "Piper," pp. 205–206.
32. Knerr, "Piper," p. 206.
33. Knerr, "Piper," pp. 206–207.
34. Knerr, "Piper," p. 207.
35. Knerr, "Piper," p. 207.
36. H. Beam Piper, postcard to Charles and Marcia Brown, December 20, 1963.
37. Knerr, "Piper," p. 207.
38. Knerr, "Piper," p. 211.

Chapter 32

1. Michael E. Knerr, "Piper," unpublished manuscript in author's possession, dated 1983, p. 220.
2. Knerr, "Piper," p. 212.
3. Knerr, "Piper," p. 212.

4. Knerr, "Piper," p. 213.
5. Knerr, "Piper," p. 213.
6. Knerr, "Piper," p. 213.
7. Knerr, "Piper," p. 213.
8. Knerr, "Piper," p. 214.
9. Knerr, "Piper," p. 214.
10. Knerr, "Piper," p. 215.
11. Knerr, "Piper," p. 214.
12. Knerr, "Piper," p. 214.
13. Knerr, "Piper," p. 215.
14. Knerr, "Piper," p. 216.
15. Knerr, "Piper," p. 217.
16. Knerr, "Piper," p. 218.
17. John W. Campbell, letter to Kenneth S. White, April 15, 1964.
18. Knerr, "Piper," p. 218.
19. Knerr, "Piper," p. 218.
20. John W. Campbell, letter to H. Beam Piper, May 19, 1964.
21. Knerr, "Piper," p. 219.
22. Knerr, "Piper," p. 219.
23. Knerr, "Piper," p. 219.
24. H. Beam Piper, letter to Charles and Marcia Brown, June 14, 1964.
25. Knerr, "Piper," p. 220.
26. Knerr, "Piper," pp. 220–221.
27. Knerr, "Piper," p. 221.
28. Knerr, "Piper," p. 221.
29. Knerr, "Piper," pp. 221–222.
30. Knerr, "Piper," p. 222.
31. Knerr, "Piper," p. 222.
32. Knerr, "Piper," p. 222.
33. Knerr, "Piper," p. 223.
34. Knerr, "Piper," p. 223.
35. Knerr, "Piper," p. 223.
36. Knerr, "Piper," pp. 223–224.

Chapter 33

1. Michael E. Knerr, "Piper," unpublished manuscript in author's possession, dated 1983, p. 224.
2. Knerr, "Piper," p. 224.
3. Knerr, "Piper," p. 224.
4. Knerr, "Piper," p. 225.
5. H. Beam Piper, letter to John W. Campbell, September 5, 1964.
6. Knerr, "Piper," p. 225.
7. Knerr, "Piper," p. 225.
8. Knerr, "Piper," pp. 225–226.
9. Knerr, "Piper," p. 226.
10. Knerr, "Piper," p. 226.
11. Knerr, "Piper," p. 226.
12. Knerr, "Piper," pp. 226–227.
13. H. Beam Piper, letter to John W. Campbell, October 13, 1964.
14. Knerr, "Piper," p. 227.

15. Knerr, "Piper," pp. 227–228.
16. Knerr, "Piper," p. 228.
17. Knerr, "Piper," p. 228.
18. John W. Campbell, letter to H. Beam Piper, October 19, 1964.
19. Knerr, "Piper," p. 228.
20. Knerr, "Piper," p. 228.
21. Knerr, "Piper," p. 228.
22. H. Beam Piper, letter to John W. Campbell, October 26, 1964.
23. John W. Campbell, Brass Tacks, *Analog Science Fact — Science Fiction*, January 1966, p. 153.
24. Knerr, "Piper," p. 229.
25. Knerr, "Piper," p. 229.
26. Knerr, "Piper," p. 229.
27. Knerr, "Piper," pp. 229–230.

Chapter 34

1. Michael E. Knerr, "Piper," unpublished manuscript in author's possession, dated 1983, p. v.
2. Knerr, "Piper," pp. i–vii.

Chapter 35

1. Don Coleman, "The Early Letters," unpublished collection of the H. Beam Piper–Ferd Coleman letters, in author's possession, dated 1991, p. 283.
2. Coleman, "The Early Letters," pp. 282–289.

Chapter 36

1. Don Coleman, "The Early Letters," unpublished collection of the H. Beam Piper–Ferd Coleman letters, in author's possession, dated 1983, p. 296.
2. Coleman, "The Early Letters," pp. 290–291.
3. Michael E. Knerr, letter to author, August 26, 1982.
4. Terry McGuire, e-mail to author, June 6, 2006.
5. Marvin N. Katz, Brass Tacks, *Analog Science Fact — Science Fiction*, March 1965, pp. 92–93.
6. Bill Bowers and Bill Mallardi, "The Double-Bill Symposium" (Akron, OH: 1969), p. 106.
7. John W. Campbell, letter to John D. Clark, November 18, 1965, p. 1.
8. Jack L. Chalker, "The Lights Go Out," in *Ventura II* (Norfolk, VA: 1965), pp. 27–28.

Afterword

1. Don Coleman, "The Early Letters," unpublished collection of the H. Beam Piper–Ferd Coleman letters, in author's possession, dated 1983, pp. 293–294.

Bibliography

Africa, J. Simpson. *The History of Huntingdon and Blair County.* Philadelphia, PA: Louis H. Everts, 1883.

Altoona Mirror. Obituaries. September 10, 1902.

Ashley, Mike. *The Complete Index to Astounding/ Analog.* Oak Forest, IL: Robert Weinberg Publications, 1981.

Barris, Wess. Roster of Juniata Shops Built GG1s. Steamlocomotive.com.

Bowers, Bill, and Bill Mallardi. "The Double-Bill Symposium." Akron, OH: 1969.

Campbell, John W. Brass Tacks. *Analog Science Fact — Science Fiction,* January 1966, p. 153.

_____. Letter to Fred Pohl. January 15, 1951.

_____. Letter to H. Beam Piper. June 26, 1952.

_____. Letter to H. Beam Piper. July 21, 1954.

_____. Letter to H. Beam Piper. May 13, 1959.

_____. Letter to H. Beam Piper. June 5, 1962.

_____. Letter to H. Beam Piper. May 19, 1964.

_____. Letter to H. Beam Piper. October 19, 1964.

_____. Letter to John D. Clark. November 18, 1965.

_____. Letter to Kenneth S. White. January 20, 1960.

_____. Letter to Kenneth S. White. September 12, 1960.

_____. Letter to Kenneth S. White. November 6, 1961.

_____. Letter to Kenneth S. White. April 15, 1964.

_____. "Tribesman, Barbarian and Citizen." Editorial. *Analog Science Fact — Science Fiction,* May 1961.

Carr, John F. Introduction to *Federation.* New York, NY: Ace Books, February 1981.

_____. "The Last Cavalier: H. Beam Piper." *Analog Science Fact — Science Fiction,* January 1988, pp. 161–174.

Chalker, Jack L. "The Lights Go Out." In *Ventura II.* Norfolk, VA: 1965, pp. 27–28.

Chapdelaine, Perry, Sr. *The John W. Campbell Letters.* Vol. I. Franklin, TN: AC Projects: 1985.

Coleman, Don. "The Early Letters." Unpublished collection of the H. Beam Piper–Ferd Coleman letters. In the author's possession. Dated 1991.

Costello, John H. "H. Beam Piper: An Infinity of Worlds: Part One." *Renaissance* 4.4 (Fall 1972).

Council on International Education Exchange, Inc. http://www.answers.com/topic/council-on-international-educational-exchange-inc. Jan. 18, 2007.

De Camp, L. Sprague. *Time and Chance: An Autobiography.* Hampton Falls, NH: Donald M. Grant, 1996.

Heinlein, Robert A. James Forrestal Memorial Lecture to the Brigade of Midshipmen at his alma mater, the U.S. Naval Academy at Annapolis. April 5, 1973.

Holland, Elwanda. "H. Beam Piper in Paperback (1957–1965)." *Books Are Everything!* Vol. 2, no. 2. Whole Number 8. Richmond, KY: March 1989.

Horton, Rich. alt.books.isaac-asimov.

Katz, Marvin N. Brass Tacks. *Analog Science Fact — Science Fiction,* March 1965, pp. 92–93.

Knerr, Michael E. "Piper." Unpublished manuscript in the author's possession. Dated 1983.

Piper, H. Beam. *A Catalogue of Henry Wharton Shoemaker Weapons at Restless Oaks in McElhattan Pennsylvania.* Altoona, PA: Times Tribune Co.

Piper, H. Beam. Diary entries for January 1, 1955, to August 27, 1955, The H. Beam Piper Papers, Special Collections Library, The Pennsylvania State University Libraries, Altoona, PA.

_____. *Federation.* New York, NY: Ace Books, 1981.

_____. *Empire.* New York, NY: Ace Books, 1981.

_____. Letter to Alan Howard. Altoona, PA: Jan. 12, 1953.

_____. Letter to Charles and Marcia Brown. July 2, 1963.

_____. Letter to Charles and Marcia Brown. June 14, 1964.

_____. Letter to Freida Coleman. September 4, 1955.

_____. Letter to Freida Coleman. May 17, 1957.

_____. Letter to Jerry Pournelle. December 19, 1962.

_____. Letter to Jerry Pournelle. March 22, 1963.

_____. Letter to John W. Campbell. June 18, 1951.

_____. Letter to John W. Campbell. July 17, 1954.

_____. Letter to John W. Campbell. September 5, 1964.

_____. Letter to John W. Campbell. October 13, 1964.

_____. Letter to John W. Campbell. October 26, 1964.

_____. Letter to Lycoming Historical Society. June 12, 1956.

_____. Letter to Peter Weston with 4-page attachment titled "The Future History by H. Beam Piper." February 16, 1964.

_____. *Little Fuzzy.* New York: NY: Ace Books, 1984.

_____. *Murder in the Gunroom.* New York, NY: Alfred A. Knopf, Inc., 1953.

_____. Postcard to Charles and Marcia Brown. December 20, 1963.

Pratt, Fletcher. *World of Wonder,* New York City, NY: Twayne Publishers, 1951.

Ramsey, Fred. E-mail to "The Works of H. Beam Piper" mailing list: piper-l@home.ease.lsoft.com. December 15, 2002.

Starlight. Postscript to the biographical entry from *The History of Huntingdon and Blair County.* http://gwillick.tripod.com/bio/DrHBPiper.html.

"Typewriter 'Killer.'" *Pennsy* 2.8 (Sept. 1953): 7.

Weston, Peter. "Future History No. 1," H. Beam Piper. *Zenith* 4 (May 1964).

Wright, Michael. *Here Comes Sputnik.* August 30, 1997. http://www.batnet.com/mfwright/sputnik.html.

Index